Biotechnology:

The University–Industrial

Complex

Biotechnology:

The University–Industrial

Complex

Martin Kenney

Yale University Press
New Haven and London

Designed by Susan P. Fillion
and set in Helvetica display and Times Roman
text type by Rainsford Type, Ridgefield, Conn.
Printed in the United States of America by
Vail-Ballou Press, Binghamton, N.Y.

Library of Congress Cataloging-in-Publication Data
Kenney, Martin.
  Biotechnology : the university–industrial complex

  Bibliography: p.
  Includes index.
  1. Biotechnology.   2. Biotechnology industries.
I. Title.
TP248.2.K46 1986   338.4'7660'6   86-1694
ISBN 0-300-03392-3 (alk. paper)

*The paper in this book meets the guidelines for
permanence and durability of the Committee on
Production Guidelines for Book Longevity of
the Council on Library Resources.*

10 9 8 7 6 5 4 3 2 1

For Shoko

Contents

Tables

Figures

Acknowledgments

Т his book grew out of my curiosity about the impact of the new biotechnologies on agriculture. As I delved deeper into the subject, I was compelled to examine the logic of the development of the entire biotechnology industry. Thus, the book is the result of that logic of research that seems to guide the researcher down unanticipated paths.

I want to thank Frederick Buttel of Cornell University for providing the intellectual space and constant support for my research. Ronald King and Porus Opadwala, both of Cornell University, were always helpful and willing to comment upon my work. Thanks go to Jack Kloppenburg, Jr., of the University of Wisconsin–Madison. Our many discussions of the biotechnology industry were invaluable in clarifying my ideas and in prompting my writing. I would also like to thank Michael Domach of Carnegie-Mellon University for his helpful insights into the way universities and industry interact. Finally, I thank the Department of Rural Sociology at Cornell University for its support of my somewhat unconventional topic.

I will always deeply appreciate the comments I received on the manuscript from a number of readers. First and foremost, I thank Charles Weiner of MIT for his constant and unstinting help, which ranged from permitting me to use his voluminous files to a very valuable reading of the manuscript. His help was vital. Sheldon Krimsky of Tufts University has also been of tremendous assistance both in commenting on my manuscript and in helping me with my research. Further, his early encouragement of my research on the biotechnology industry was vital. Finally, I would like to thank Peter Katzenstein of Cornell University for his comments and advice. However, it goes without saying that I am solely responsible for any errors or opinions that remain.

Thanks go to Robert Ubell for always being available for valuable counsel. Thanks also go to my secretary at Ohio State University, Carol Stull, who was cheerful and ever helpful in completing the book. I also thank Marian Neal Ash and Lawrence Kenney of Yale University Press for their help in making the book a readable document.

I would like also to thank my parents for their support. Nicos Mouratides of San Diego State University introduced me to sociology and the sociological imagination, and I shall always be grateful for his constant encouragement. Most of all, I want to thank Shoko Tanaka.

Biotechnology:

The University–Industrial

Complex

Introduction

It's not something that doesn't have a future, if we only give the bacteria a chance. . . . I am constantly amazed at what these little creatures can do. They're the greatest nonunionized force in the country.   *(Howard E. Worne, president of Worne Biotechnology)*

The history of the use of biological systems for the fulfillment of human needs can be traced back as far as 6000 B.C., when the Sumerians and Babylonians fermented a kind of beer. Biotechnology at its simplest can consist of such a familiar activity as this or as selecting seeds from better plants. The use of biological processes in production has experienced many changes over the centuries but has always, until recently, involved naturally occurring organisms whose internal metabolism was not understood.

In the late 1700s and early 1800s agriculture began to develop a more sophisticated technical base, with breeding programs, crop rotation, and the beginnings of mechanization. Applied biology played an important role in the advance of the science of biology in the nineteenth century. For example, Louis Pasteur, while studying fermentation as a researcher for the French wine industry, disproved the theory of spontaneous gen-

1

eration and demonstrated that "microbes" were responsible for fermentation.

A central influence on biology in the twentieth century has been the application to biology of new information and knowledge from the physical sciences. The key discovery on the road to the creation of biotechnology occurred in 1953, when James Watson and Francis Crick correctly theorized the structure and operation of the DNA molecule. This fundamental discovery led to increased research and understanding of the biochemical processes involved in the production and reproduction of life.

The fact that DNA separates and replicates when a cell divides makes it possible to generate large numbers of exact copies, or clones, of any cell. In bacteria with doubling times of twenty to forty minutes, huge quantities of clones can be rapidly grown, and each cloned bacterium will produce the substances for which its DNA is coded. These bacteria can then be harvested and the desired chemical extracted. Or, alternatively, selection and engineering can produce microorganisms that will secrete the desired substance into a fermentation medium. The new biotechnologies make living cells into tiny factories for the production of items satisfying human needs. In appendix 1 I describe at greater length the technical background of the DNA discovery and other developments in modern biotechnology.

The myriad definitions of biotechnology indicate the difficulty of explicitly delineating its boundaries. The Office of Technology Assessment defines it as "the collection of industrial processes that involve the use of biological systems" (1981:viii), but this definition is so broad that it includes the traditional technologies of brewing and pickling. In 1982 the Organization for Economic Cooperation and Development (OECD) issued a report on biotechnology in which it was defined as "the application of scientific and engineering principles to the processing of materials by biological agents to provide goods and services" (Bull et al. 1982:21). This definition too includes the traditional technologies of plant breeding and fermentation.

In this book, I use a narrower definition, restricting the word *biotechnology* to the new biological techniques that found commercial applications during the 1970s and 1980s. To simplify matters further, I use the term *recombinant DNA* only to refer to a specific process. I do not generally use the term *genetic engineering* because it is vague, preferring instead to subsume it under biotechnology.

The growth of the biotechnology industry has come at a propitious time. The economic stagnation of the last ten years has coincided remarkably well with the prediction of theorists who see long waves in economic history. Periods of economic crisis induce businesses to economize in traditional production practices as well as to search for new technologies and processes. As Schumpeter (1964) so vividly demonstrated, in stagnation periods entrepreneurs with new ideas come forward to lead capitalism into technologies that form the basis of new industries. Mandel (1978) and Mensch (1979) associate a group of core technologies with each upward phase of the waves. So, for example, the long upward movement in the world economy from 1896 to 1914 was led by innovations such as the electric motor and the internal combustion engine. Both provided tremendous potential for lowering the costs of production, and the electric motor provided the decentralized power source required to organize the assembly line. The next expansionary wave dated from 1945 to 1970, and the important technologies in this period included petrochemicals (synthetic fibers, plastics, and other polymers) and electronics. If the long-wave theory is correct, a new set of technologies is now appearing to lead the next recovery.

These technologies or productive forces cannot have such tremendous impact without severely affecting the social relations of a society. In periods of crisis not only are new technologies adopted, but old institutions are transformed or entirely swept away. Concomitantly, regions develop unevenly—former centers of economic activity decay as others rise. For example, the 1930s marked the demise of New England and New York as industrial centers and with them went their craft unions. In the postwar period technology assisted in making the automobile, suburbia, plastic, and television hallmarks of American society. These were all facets of the American "miracle," which was based on the concept of mass consumption/mass production pioneered by Henry Ford. Today, with the decline of the Rust Belt we see the weakening of the CIO industry unions—precisely the ones created to cope with change in the 1930s. The new centers of growth are New England and the Sun Belt.

The American growth model based on mass production is now in crisis for a number of reasons, including the fact that the assembly-line production model has run its course; the breaking down of tasks no longer can provide the constant increases in efficiency necessary to permit rising real wages and profits. Industries such as petrochemicals and pharmaceuticals are experiencing reduced discovery rates, that is, an increasing number of compounds scanned with fewer commercial successes. On the consumption side, cost increases are skyrocketing in the very areas that mass production does not address, such as medicine and other services.

It has been predicted that a new economic regime based upon the information technologies will emerge. This regime will provide new methods for organizing production by centralizing decision-making at corporate headquarters while decentralizing the work sites. The factory of the future will be characterized by a constant flow of information and feedback as production is undertaken by robots and computer-integrated manufacturing systems. Increasingly, production will be rigorously controlled and at the same time multivalent; different products will be producible in the same factory. Simple reprogramming will be all that is required—production lines need not be dedicated to one particular process.

Biotechnology is an information-intensive technology and will very easily fit into a restructured economy based on information. Indeed biotechnology will provide one of the new economy's crucial underpinnings. Biotechnology could be a significant factor in increasing real living standards by lowering production costs in the following industries: food processing, agriculture, pharmaceuticals, forestry, chemicals, waste disposal, and energy. With the exception of agriculture and forestry, these are the very industries that experienced dramatic price increases in the 1970s. Biotechnology will be able to bring less developed countries (LDCs) more explicitly into the global economy by increasing the sales of agricultural seeds, fertilizers, and crop protection chemicals to them and by increasing agricultural productivity, so that they can sell more in the world market. Neither computers nor the new communication technologies can so fundamentally affect LDCs; only biotechnology can provide needed inputs to areas of the globe that are yet without television or even electricity. The need for medicine and food is acute and constant.

Biotechnology, genetic engineering, and recombinant DNA—each of these terms, imprecise though it may be, refers to an entire package of production techniques that will have a profound impact on the world economy. Every production process that uses carbon-based materials will be affected by biotechnology.

The attraction of industry to biotechnology was slow initially but rapidly increased as the potential financial gains became clear. The biotechnology industry's ability to attract capital (by 1984 over $3 billion) has benefited greatly from the networks already in place for financing computer startups and, in a more general sense, from the general disinvestment in basic industries that has freed money for high tech investments. In this way venture capital, by selecting new areas for investment, is the cutting edge of the restructuring of the U.S. economy.

The creation of new social relationships to accommodate biotechnology has been rapid. The most striking institution to come out of this transformation is the startup company formed by entrepreneurs and university professors and funded by venture capital. The pervasive role of professors in managing and directing the startups is unique in the annals of business history. In a survey of only 20 percent of the total number of biotechnology companies, Krimsky (1984:15) identified 345 academic scientists involved in publicly held companies. Biotechnology, a science that is capable of being commercialized, has been totally dependent on university research. In no other fledgling industry have university scientists played such an all-encompassing role.

Other sciences—organic chemistry, electrical engineering, computer science, and physics—have undergone a transformation from a science to a

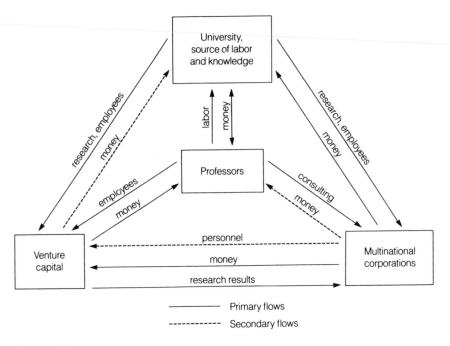

Source: Author

Figure Introduction.1. Schematic of Biotechnology University–Industry Relationships

technology, with some scientists leaving academe to start companies. But none of these earlier technologies was developed entirely in academia. The computer industry, for example, attracted developers who were not university professors or Ph.D.'s—Steven Jobs of Apple Computer, Edson D. deCastro of Data General, and Mitchell Kapor of Lotus Development Corporation. Furthermore, professors left universities to launch computer firms; they generally did not remain in the university, nor was it common for administrators to attempt to use professors' work in private industry as a source of university income.

Since biotechnology was born in the laboratories of American research universities, I begin with the university as an institution and its relationships with industry (see fig. 1). There have been many types of university–industry linkages, but I focus on the new relationships, the most striking of which is the multimillion-dollar, multiyear contract between a single university and a single company. University biology departments have been disrupted as great numbers of biologists have become entrepreneurs or at least deeply involved in commercial affairs. The shortage of labor for the biotechnology industry is being overcome by enlarged graduate programs, which increasingly are tracking students toward companies. Undergraduates and two-year college students are being trained for routine work, though many time-consuming tasks such as gene sequencing are being automated. Traditional relationships among professors, among department members, and between faculty and students have been affected. External changes in sources of funding and professorial income have changed the university's internal environment. I try in the book to provide an understanding of the strategies and motives of the people involved and to evaluate the benefits and losses for the universities themselves.

I then turn to the industry and examine the two types of commercial organizations involved—startup companies and large multinational chemical and pharmaceutical corporations. The success of the startup company is predicated upon its ability to grow from inception to profitability rapidly and efficiently. The growth process is fraught with complications, and the corporate leadership must develop an effective corporate strategy to lead the company to success. One crucial element is the provision of an environment for the important research personnel that encourages product development; at the same time information must flow well inside the company for management purposes, while a veil of secrecy is maintained vis-à-vis the outside world.

Because biotechnology is likely to have its greatest impact on agriculture, I examine this aspect of the birth of the new industry in some detail. I argue that biotechnology will transform agricultural production and the institutions traditionally associated with it, such as the land grant universities and the seed industry.

Finally, I discuss briefly the larger arena of global competition in biotechnology and speculate on the implications of the industry's structure for the success of various nations in this last important technology of the twentieth century. And I pose questions that my study raises about the institutional patterns being set by the development of the biotechnology industry.

The biotechnology industry was launched in the glare of camera lights and has continued to attract public attention. The publicity given to the commercialization of biology has been attributed to a variety of factors, including the increased numbers of science writers, greater distrust of science, and the increasingly cynical attitudes of society toward scientists. However, even with all the attention lavished on the new industry, this book is the first serious analysis focusing on the actual mechanisms of its development. I focus not on individuals but rather on institutions and individuals within institutions as they pursue their goals. The book chronicles the shattering of the ideology of pure science under the impact of economics. The creation of the biotechnology industry is the history of dedicated, intelligent, and usually rational scientists creating and being swept into the whirlwind of a social transformation. Scientists, university administrators, entrepreneurs, and business executives—all act in a world that is only partially of their own making.

1. DNA

The stunning revelation by a group of researchers from the University of California, San Francisco (UCSF) and Stanford that DNA could be cut, recombined, and inserted into a foreign bacteria that would then express the new gene opened a new era for biology. The practical applications of this technical feat were recognized at first only as a new tool for research. But within three years the commercial potential had become clear to entrepreneurs. The rise of the National Institutes of Health (NIH) as a funding agent plays a crucial role in the emergence and triumph of molecular biology; subunits of NIH such as the National Cancer Institute and its viral oncology unit are especially important. Molecular biology's unique world view would in the late 1970s adapt easily to the profit motive. It is necessary therefore to summarize briefly the history of molecular biology: its sponsors, environment, and research agenda.

From Biochemistry to Molecular Biology

The core discipline for the biotechnology industry is molecular biology, although microbiology, biochemistry, immunology, virology, and cell biology are also important. The cluster of techniques and practices represented by these fields was first explored and developed in research universities throughout the world. But the scientific study of the chemistry of living organisms was not original or novel to the discipline of molecular biology, for already in the mid-1800s German physiological chemists were actively applying chemical techniques to biological research. Biochemistry was very successful at Cambridge University and in the United States became a service discipline within medical schools.

Intense pressure in the period from 1900 to 1930 forced a restructuring of medicine into the "scientific" medicine epitomized by the "modern" physician (Flexner 1910; E. Brown 1979). The techniques used in biochemistry—imported from chemistry, a "hard" science—were precisely what was required to give a more scientific aura to the medical profession. Thus, biochemistry secured a patron, but simultaneously the patron influenced the research agenda: in American and many European universities, the biochemists' professional role was teaching medical students and training medical graduates in clinical investigation. Biochemists depended on clinicians for financial and political support, and clinicians depended on them for training and new diagnostic techniques. This symbiotic relationship shaped most biochemists' careers (Kohler 1982:7) and in fact limited the types of questions that biochemists asked. "Basic" research was not emphasized. A typical activity of biochemists was vitamin research, which was "extremely popular, in large part owing to its practical and economic value for medicine, agriculture, and industry" (Kohler 1975:303). In adopting the "applied" ethos of the medical schools biochemists resembled agricultural scientists of today in their limited, applied emphasis.

The handicap of the applied perspective is illustrated by the fact that important discoveries such as George Beadle and Edward Tatum's one-gene—one-enzyme concept, Jacques Monod and Francois Jacob's operon and central dogma of gene expression, Linus Pauling's alpha helix, and Watson and Crick's double helix "were all the work of biologists, chemists, and physicists, who made it clear that they regarded biochemists as plodders" (Kohler 1982:325). Biochemistry, trapped in its institutional context, was overshadowed in scientific achievement by the new field of molecular biology. Though successful in the United States by the middle of the 1930s, biochemistry was facing institutional competitors that were infringing upon its academic turf. The competitors were asking new, more general, and abstract questions regarding the nature of life.

The newest and most successful of biochemistry's competitors was to be molecular biology, whose origin can be traced to Warren Weaver's "support for the application of new physical and chemical techniques to biology in the 1930s" (Kohler 1976:279). Weaver, a mathematical physicist at the University of Wisconsin, became the director of the Rockefeller Foundation's biology program. His vision of the biological research agenda was one of "exact, analytic, vigorously formulated, reductive experimentation based on the methods of physics and chemistry" (Yoxen 1981:89). Research generally was to be funded not by institutional grants, that is, disbursement or grants-in-aid to institutions, or small grants to individuals, but rather by "project-grants" of medium size (Kohler 1976:297).[1] The project-grant was usually three years in duration and selective in that the recipients exclusively were top scientists. Further, the foundation extended institutional grants to only a few institutions, and these were envisioned as examples for other institutions to emulate. The creation of "centers of excellence" was a permanent objective of the Rockefeller Foundation.

Weaver's new funding style helped to create molecular biology and pioneered a pattern of "management of science" that was unique in noncorporate institutions (Kohler 1976; Yoxen 1981). Kohler (1976:304) summarizes the effects of Weaver's focus on biochemistry (in the form of molecular biology) for research investment:

Because Weaver's conception of the scope and direction of academic disciplines was much broader than those of the scientists whom he supported, his policy resulted in real changes of direction within certain disciplines, biochemistry in particular . . . . Weaver thought that the most promising work in "biochemistry" was being done by outsiders to the discipline, and he acted accordingly. As a result a new generation of biochemists emerged in the late 1930s, many from the Rockefeller Foundation programme; they knew how to use isotopes and the ultracentrifuge, and they combined a knowledge of organic chemistry with a sensitivity to physiological processes.

The success of Weaver's agenda became clear in the post–World War II period, when molecular biology made numerous important scientific advances. Weaver's unwavering financial support of scientists using new, sophisticated techniques provided the technical base upon which the "new" biology was built. The "marketplace of science" ensured that other scientists would be required to follow suit. The project-grant funding pattern provided seed money to set up molecular biology as a field of study; it soon expanded, finding a niche in many elite universities such as Harvard,

1. The new project-grant system of philanthropy did elicit opposition, even from certain old guard trustees within the Rockefeller Foundation, such as Simon Flexner. The crux of the objections was that the project-grant system, by directing research in certain directions, would cast the foundation in the role of planning research, thereby interfering with scientific individualism (Kohler 1976:297–98).

MIT, Stanford, and Caltech (Weaver 1970:581–82). In light of the remarkable research successes of the new biology the choice for biochemists
was to either respond to the agenda set forth or be condemned to under-
funding and the loss of position and prestige. By the 1970s increasing
numbers of biochemists had shifted their research agenda to the so-called
basic questions that molecular biology had raised—questions of the production and reproduction of life—and, increasingly, away from characterization of metabolic pathways and other traditional subjects of biochemistry
(Kohler 1981:333; Kohler 1975:315; Judson 1979:220).

Weaver's role as a representative of the Rockefeller Foundation was
vital, because his channeling of funding both set the agenda and provided
physicists and chemists with the resources with which to undertake biological research. Project-grants provided the funds necessary to purchase
equipment and build up a research team. Concomitant with the application
of these new tools to biological research was the physical requirement that
scientific laboratory staffs be expanded. This expansion led to a division
of labor and increased specialization. The head of a laboratory was a
scientist-entrepreneur whose primary task was to ensure that funds would
continue to be secured. The scientist-entrepreneur would shift his research
into areas that appeared to be "hot" in funding, drawing upon the ideas
of successive waves of graduate and postdoctoral students. Scientists, apparently "free" to choose their areas of research, were being managed and
channeled through the funding mechanism.

Molecular biology's unique emphasis was to reduce "life" to an assem-
blage of molecules. More precisely, alternative visions of biology such as
those of taxonomy, nonmolecular developmental biology, and population
biology were in a relatively weak position. The molecules to be examined
were not simple water and carbon dioxide molecules but rather the larger
molecules constituted of hundreds and even thousand of atoms, that is,
the macromolecules. In biochemistry the bulk of experiments examined
the more numerous and immediately useful proteins. On the other hand,
molecular biology was bequeathed the agenda of discovering the "secret
of life" (which was defined as the ability of a group of molecules making
up a cell to self-replicate). This agenda required the tools that the Rockefeller Foundation was prepared to provide. Some have gone so far as to
argue that in the pre–World War II period molecular biology was a set of
tools searching for a subject (Yoxen 1981). But the tools implied a reductionistic answer. And despite its success, molecular biology continues to
be attacked as a science that reduces life to the mere actions of molecules
and denies the emergent properties of life processes that separate the
animate from the inanimate (Lewontin 1974; 1983).

The ideological importance of the scientific success of molecular biology
should not be underestimated. For example, it has given rise to sociobiology

and pseudoscientific books such as *The Selfish Gene* (Dawkins 1978). Peculiarly, a number of the principal founders and forefathers of molecular biology, such as J. D. Bernal, Linus Pauling, Salvador Luria, Herman Muller, and Jacques Monod, were political radicals and expected their radical conceptions of biology would debunk traditional science (Yoxen 1981:74). Yet the ultimate outcome of their research would in the late 1970s provide a technological support for economic growth. What in the 1930s, 1940s, 1950s, and 1960s appeared as a radical new biology and "pure" basic research, in the 1970s and 1980s was transformed into a basis for commerce.

The War Years

The U.S. scientific establishment was mobilized during World War II under the leadership of Vannevar Bush and James Conant. The Office of Scientific Research and Development (OSRD) was created to advise the military regarding possible applications of science, the most well known of which is the Manhattan Project. The biological and medical sciences formed the Committee on Medical Research (CMR), which allocated money to medical topics that would aid the war effort. Though the physicists received the bulk of military-related government expenditures, the CMR spent $25 million, of which nearly $6 million went for malarial research (Yoxen 1981:92). A notable number of medical successes emerged from the war effort, including the development of penicillin, the sulfonamides, gamma globulin, renal steroids, and cortisone (Strickland 1972:17). The achievements of applied medical research highlighted the value and potential of biological science and provided a powerful argument for postwar funding.

The rapidity with which medical advances were made during World War II impressed Congress. For example, blood plasma, which had received $14,000 in research funds from the Rockefeller Foundation in 1938, was brought into production during the war by the federal government at a cost of over $500,000 (Strickland 1972:17). In contracting with private companies to produce blood plasma, the government simultaneously created a new commodity. The medical achievements, combined with the Selective Service report that "approximately one-third of the men examined for induction into the military were physically or mentally unfit" (Strickland 1972:19), helped to convince the federal government to undertake a more active role in funding health-related research. It appeared to be self-evident that increased research would lead to better health. In any case, research was the path of least political resistance for upgrading medical health.

During World War II the structure and institutions pioneered by private funding agencies in the 1930s were consolidated and brought under the aegis of federal funding. The relationships between science and the government became much closer during the war. Government involvement in funding research through the OSRD and CMR was the opening wedge for a new patronage of the sciences. However, despite the utility and success of the wartime government/university scientist partnership, it was not clear that after the war the relationship would endure. The war years had created a new awareness of the potential benefits of medical research, but no agency was positioned to become the champion of federally funded medical research.

Postwar Medical Research Policy

The forces that had stymied national science policies before the war regained strength with the ending of the national emergency. The goal of scientist-administrators such as Vannevar Bush was to form a "national science agency" whose task it would be to fund all types of research. The aim of Bush, James Conant, and others was to create a National Science Foundation (NSF) that was immune from "politics." Conant and Bush planned to channel all federal funding for the sciences through NSF. Science was to become a self-governing community funded by Congress but not answerable in terms of its research agenda.

President Truman's program for conversion to peacetime singled out medicine and public health as areas of research to be supported as a matter of public policy (Strickland 1972:22). In the two years immediately preceding the war (fiscal 1940 and 1941), NIH's budget had been about $700,000, with less than a third of that awarded in extramural research grants. By contrast, private foundations in 1940 gave $4.7 million for medical research (Strickland 1972:27). With the exception of a small cancer research program, the federal medical effort was confined to animal diseases and carried out by the Department of Agriculture (USDA). The immediate postwar period was characterized by intense lobbying by three groups: scientist-administrators for an NSF to conduct basic biological research, the NIH for acquiring the leading role in medical sciences, and interest groups such as the American Cancer Society for an autonomous entity to conduct a "war on cancer" (Strickland 1972: chaps. 2–3).

The threat that the proposed NSF might capture medical research galvanized NIH to seek the transfer of military and CMR wartime medical contracts to its jurisdiction. A [successful] campaign to secure control of these contracts provided NIH with a $4 million extramural grant budget in 1947 and a bureaucratic claim to precedence. Further, on Capitol Hill congressmen quickly perceived the political advantage of promoting medical research and the "war" on disease, especially cancer. Politicians learned that voting for increased health appropriations would never lose them votes.

The question was not whether to spend on health but rather how to determine the appropriate expenditure targets. The National Health Program of 1949 proposed not only increased research but also compulsory national health insurance, hospital construction funds, and federal aid for medical education. In bitter political battles the American Medical Association (AMA) resisted all government intervention in medicine, but it eventually yielded on research (Strickland 1972:38). The virulence of the AMA's opposition to government intervention guaranteed that in the next forty years the bulk of the federal public health effort would go into research and facility construction (Starr 1982:289; Stark 1982:75). In the process, medical research programs also became conduits for federal aid to medical education and university hospital construction through provision of overhead, construction of teaching and research facilities, etc. The importance of top researcher-entrepreneurs was reinforced because they became not only the justification for allocating other funds to the medical school but also persuasive salesmen of the importance of research.

A bill founding the NSF and also allocating research monies to it was passed into law in 1950. Strickland (1972:86) describes the policy that evolved:

> National medical research policy, as it gradually evolved in the postwar years, included the following elements accepted by the executive, Congress, the bureaucracy, and specialized interest groups: the federal government would support both basic and targeted research; it would support both through the National Institutes of Health, though NIH's main concern was to be the conquest of specific diseases; it would also support targeted research through agencies having missions inviting special attention to particular problems; and it would provide for the support of basic, nontargeted biological and biomedical research through the National Science Foundation.

It was now national policy to conduct medical research to "improve" the health of the American people. Within this context of increasing funding, molecular biology would be very effective in enlarging its disciplinary scope.

As figure 1.1 indicates, there were nearly constant research funding increases in current dollars for NIH. NIH funding reached the $1 billion mark in 1967. In this atmosphere of growth every discipline was able to expand, and the overhead from government contracts became an increasingly large source of revenue for medical school and university administrations (Hierich 1979). In this environment the remarkable success of molecular biology, as measured by the prizes it was awarded and the

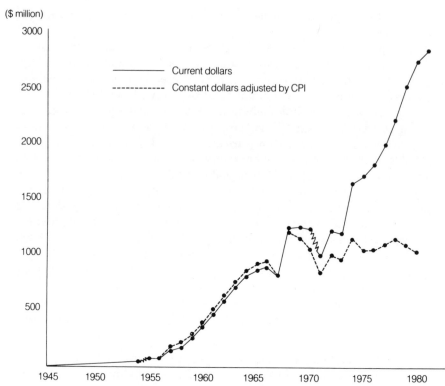

($ million)

Source: National Institutes of Health, *Extramural Trends*, various years

Figure 1.1. National Institutes of Health Extramural Funding Trends, 1945–1980

recognition afforded to molecular biologists, increased its ability to garner larger amounts of research funds. In addition, molecular biologists started to claim that because of developments in the understanding of DNA, they could discover the cause of cancer and provide a cure for it. An example of the acceptance of these claims is the spectacular growth of the NIH Viral Oncology Program in the 1970s (table 1.1). The assertion was well received in political and business circles because it focused on the molecular level rather than on an examination of the release of carcinogens into the workplace and the environment. In fact, the funding decreases in the 1980–83 period occurred because of a shift in NIH research priorities to examination of environmental causes of cancer. As in earlier matters regarding the proper role of the federal government, the path of least re-

Table 1.1. The Funding History of the NIH Viral Oncology Program

Year	Amount ($ million)
1965	10.0
1966	18.6
1967	19.1
1968	19.5
1969	19.2
1970	21.2
1971	36.1
1972	48.2
1973	64.5
1974	81.6
1975	86.5
1976	101.6
1977	100.2
1978	106.7
1979	110.5
1980	106.3
1981	94.6
1982	87.5
1983	86.4
1984	93.3
1985	106.7

Sources: Adapted from Krimsky 1982:59; NIH 1985

sistance was favored. The search for a cancer cure was a justification for much of the NIH-funded molecular biological research.[2]

In the postwar science bureaucracies such as the NIH and NSF, funds were allocated to investigators on a competitive basis. The majority of the grant proposals were evaluated through the peer review process, a system that encouraged the most successful professors to recruit more graduate students and postdoctoral researchers to work on their projects, thereby expanding their empires (Stockton 1980:62). For these scientist-entrepreneurs to continue to receive funding they found it necessary to direct their research toward topics currently in vogue. Scientific achievement was judged on the basis of grants, prizes (Nobel, Lasker, Merck, Novo), and publications. Having a large research staff made it possible to produce more results and secure greater recognition. The key was to ensure that grant money continued to flow into the laboratory. A professor could no

2. Whether cancer is an environmental disease—that is, contracted from pollutants—or caused by a pathogen or genetic abnormality is still unsettled. In molecular biology the causes of disease are sought at the genetic level. Thus the social relationships that produce carcinogens and create a polluted environment are not the subject of debate and research. This leads to a depoliticization of the etiology of the disease.

longer remain alone and aloof in his laboratory because large sums of capital for equipment purchases were required to remain in competition. The intensity of the competition is described by James Watson (1968) in his book *The Double Helix* (see also Latour and Woolgar 1979).

Warren Weaver's accomplishments had many results, but perhaps the most significant was the creation of a framework in which scientists would need to compete for grants. Before World War II, NIH conducted its research intramurally, but in the postwar period it became the most important extramural medical research funding agency. The competitive grants program ensured that the best-equipped laboratories would garner the bulk of the grant monies. In the period from 1972 to 1981, the top twenty institutions never received less than 51 percent of total extramural grants (NIH 1981:90). Concentration has remained relatively constant, even after a major effort in the 1970s to decentralize grant giving. Competition for monies on the basis of a peer review system pressures researchers to produce relatively quickly (within three years), and longerterm projects are subject to the vagaries of politics. The grant application process can also be time-consuming, using as much as 30 percent of a researcher's time.

NIH and NSF funding allowed the development of an enormous medical research base in the United States and made possible the construction of numerous laboratories and even entire research complexes. The grants process allowed the building of research empires and created powerful barons such as Sidney Farber of Sidney Farber Cancer Institute fame. Yet the inherent competitiveness of the system was checked by the requirement that results be publicized so as to justify refunding of grants. The peer review system guaranteed that information flowed within the academic community.

DNA as a Program—After the Double Helix

In the early twentieth century some biologists theorized that living organisms are based upon inanimate molecules and postulated that one could understand an organism by its molecular constituents (Yoxen 1981:70–75). As Brenner (1974:785) explains it, "Molecular biology is nothing more than the search for explanations of the behavior of living things in terms of the molecules that compose it." There was considerable argument in the nineteenth and early twentieth centuries as to whether proteins or nucleic acids were the molecules that carried the genetic information. But the work done by Griffiths and Avery in the 1940s demonstrated the centrality of DNA in heredity (Portugal and Cohen 1977). The criteria that biologists felt were essential for the molecule governing heredity were that it must be easily reproducible and yet complicated enough to contain all of the required genetic information.

The triumph of molecular biology and the signal that it had arrived as a discipline was the theorization by Watson and Crick of the double helical structure of DNA in 1953. This discovery, though serendipitous in its particular timing, did not appear in a vacuum; it was a synthesis of information gathered by a number of other researchers (Portugal and Cohen 1977:263).[3] P. B. Medawar (1968:3), recipient of the Nobel Prize for Medicine in 1960, commenting on the Watson–Crick model, said: "If Watson and Crick had not made it, someone else would certainly have done it— almost certainly Linus Pauling, and almost certainly very soon. It would have been the same discovery, too; nothing else would take its place."

Francis Crick (1974:768) agreed with Medawar, writing in *Nature*, "I doubt whether the discovery of the structure could have been delayed for more than two or three years." The immediate acceptance of the Watson–Crick model was in marked contrast to that of some past scientific discoveries which have had long delays before being assimilated. For example, Mendel's discovery of the basic laws of genetics was unappreciated for nearly forty years.

The actual race to discover DNA's structure has been described by a number of authors (Watson 1968; Olby 1974; Portugal and Cohen 1977; Judson 1979). James Watson in *The Double Helix* provides a vivid portrayal of the extremely intense competitive race to be the first to accurately theorize the DNA structure. Watson feels that competition in science is fundamental. Judson (1979:194) quotes him as saying, "I probably understated it [competition]. It is *the dominant motive* [Judson's emphasis] in science. It starts at the beginning: if you publish first, you become professor first; your future depends on some indication that you can do something by yourself. It's that simple. Competitiveness is very, very dominant."

The invidiousness of this rivalry is evidenced by Watson's "pleasure that Pauling would not get the chance to see any X-ray pictures at King's College London" (Judson 1979:130). Linus Pauling was denied a passport to travel to England in 1952 by the U.S. State Department because he was accused of being a communist—another scientific casualty of the McCarthy era. The competition is based not merely on the desire for prizes but also on guaranteeing academic survival, that is, the continuing ability to secure grants through the peer review process.

However, Francis Crick argues that competition was not so dominant in the DNA work and that awards such as the Nobel Prize were not even discussed. Crick's view is to some degree borne out by the fact that the

---

3. In molecular biology there are repeated cases of bitter competition between two or more research groups with each releasing results nearly simultaneously.

X-ray photographs made by the competing group headed by Wilkins at King's College were quickly passed on to Watson and Crick. In this period molecular biology still had a relatively free flow of information. Pauling felt that the Wilkins-Franklin X-rays provided the advantage that brought success to Watson and Crick (Judson 1979:91). Such exchanges of information in molecular biology are based on scientific tradition and are reinforced by the scientific journals' requirement that described materials in an article must be made available to other researchers upon request. The materials and information were freely circulated for the use of other researchers.

Watson and Crick's discovery of the structure of DNA was a watershed for biology in that it provided a clear demonstration of the power of the reductionistic model. Max Delbrück, the noted physicist turned biologist and nominal head of the "phage" group, upon becoming aware of the double helix model, was overjoyed that DNA was not a "stupid" molecule. He was reacting to an earlier tetranucleotide hypothesis that DNA was a molecule made up of equal numbers of the four bases in a predetermined repetitive sequence (Portugal and Cohen 1977: chap. 4). Delbrück was happy that the Watson and Crick DNA model contained the possibility of sufficient variation so as to potentially contain the diverse material of inheritance. The double helix DNA model was chemically and structurally simple, but the possible variations in the order of base pairs are huge.

The double helix model quickly led to questions regarding the actual sequences of the code and how information is transmitted to the cell. The early 1950s were a period of intense interest in computer programming and cybernetics, and these intellectual models were adopted to provide a heuristic for "decoding" DNA (Judson 1979). The great French Nobel Laureate François Jacob, who entitled the first chapter of his book *The Logic of Life* "The Programme," conceived of the control of living processes in this way: "The particles move from end to end of the messenger nucleic acid, like the reading head of a tape-recorder passing over the tape" (Jacob 1982:276). Jacob (1982:1) writes:

Heredity is described today in terms of information, messages, and code. The reproduction of an organism has become that of its constituent molecules. This is not because each chemical species has the ability to produce copies of itself, but because the structure of macromolecules is determined down to the last detail by sequences of four chemical radicals contained in the genetic heritage. What are transmitted from generation to generation are the "instructions" specifying the molecular structures: the architectural plans of the future organism.

DNA is the information source for the operation of the cell.

The analogy that Jacques Monod (quoted in Judson 1979:211–12) uses for the cell reiterates the point:

The cell is *entirely* cybernetic feedback system. The regulation is entirely due to a certain kind of circuitry like an advanced electronic circuit. But it is a chemical circuitry—and yet it transcends chemistry. It is indirect. It enables the cell to gain a degree of liberty from the extreme stringencies of direct chemical interactions. And it works virtually without any expenditure of energy. For example, a relay system that operates a modern industrial chemical factory is something that consumes almost no energy at all as compared to the flux of energy that goes through the main chemical transformations that the factory carries out. You have an exact logical equivalence between these two—*the factory and the cell* [my emphasis].

Monod's analogy exhibits remarkable prescience, for within ten years of his making this statement bacteria would be producing insulin in a factory.

Sydney Brenner, a noted molecular biologist, is quoted as saying, "Molecular biology has been terribly mechanism oriented" (Judson 1979:219). The success of molecular biology in applying the concepts of cybernetics and assembly line production as an analogy for understanding life processes has been staggering. The essence of the molecular biological model of life is stated by Brenner: "If you say to me, here is a hand, here is an eye, how do you make a hand or an eye, then I must say it is necessary to know the program; to know it in machine language which is molecular language; to know it so that one could tell a computer to generate a set of procedures for growing a hand, or an eye" (quoted in Judson 1979:22). In *Scientific American*, David Hopwood (1981:91), the John Innes Professor of Genetics at East Anglia, wrote, "A microorganism is a finely tuned integrated machine that has evolved to serve its own purposes: survival and reproduction."

If life can be characterized as a computer program, then understanding of the programming language made reprogramming a possibility. The reductionism inherent in molecular biology in its "basic" science days had by the mid–1970s become increasingly practical. Sydney Brenner laments: "Nobody publishes theory in biology—with few exceptions. Instead they get out the structure of still another protein. I'm not saying it's mindless. But the mind only acts on the day-to-day" (quoted in Judson 1979:218). In a sense, the mechanistic model has returned to haunt biology because it has led to the creation of mechanism-oriented scientists. As with Henry Ford's assembly line, once the idea was demonstrated as practical for one product, it remained only for the engineers to apply it to other products and optimize various operations of the line.

Doubtless forty years ago Weaver and the Rockefeller Foundation had no idea where the research they funded would lead. They believed this research would lead to better health—that is, that basic knowledge of the cell could lead to medical breakthroughs. However, they could not have foreseen the tremendous productive potential that molecular biology would unlock.

Molecular Biology—A Tool-Oriented Science

The history of molecular biology has been one of developing new tools for research. In fact, as with other human production, new tools set new agendas. In the early days the tools were simply imported from physics and chemistry (Yoxen 1981; Kohler 1976). But in the 1960s biologists developed their own new tools, which were not merely mechanical gadgets or radioisotopes, but rather enzymes and various biochemical preparations for use in manipulating the materials that make up living organisms. For example, polynucleotide phosphorylase, which is the enzyme responsible for transcription of RNA from DNA, was used by Khorana and Nirenberg to puzzle out the genetic code, and then knowledge of the genetic code became a tool for further experiments. In similar fashion, phages and pieces of DNA called plasmids became tools for scientists.

In retrospect, the ability of scientists to apply the mechanistic model to life processes is a considerable feat. The emphasis on not merely characterizing or taxonomizing a biological process, but on being able to truly manipulate it created an activist knowledge that would eventually be amenable to industrial use. The development of molecular biology was realized in a continuous and intricate web of experiments and progress. The theory always posed the question, How does this biological process work? The crux of the explanation was always the rigorous characterization—in physical terms—of life processes.

The discovery of DNA had set off a wave of research aimed at understanding the mechanism by which DNA transferred its encoded information from the nucleus to the cell and the deciphering of the code implied in the structure of the DNA molecule. Throughout the 1950s increasing numbers of biochemists began to take up molecular genetics, and the research effort expanded. Further, departments of immunology, virology, and microbiology were colonized by proponents of molecular explanations. However, other academic departments such as botany, neurology, and developmental biology remained relatively unaffected, and the research practices in the land-grant university system—such as those in plant breeding, agronomy, and the other applied biology departments—were in this period unaffected by the new knowledge created in molecular biology.

These discoveries provided the base from which the ability to recombine and reinsert the DNA into a cell would come. The theory that Watson and Crick had propounded in 1953 was amply proven in the 1960s. The pragmatic approach to science ensured that the types of problems chosen for study were those of making a process or procedure work. The discoveries of the 1960s regarding researchers' ability to cut, splice, and construct DNA sequences in vitro would in the 1970s lead to attempts to reintroduce the DNA into living organisms.

The Recombinant DNA Debate[4]

By 1971 it had become clear to molecular biologists that a virus could be used to reinsert DNA into bacteria, and with this development a debate began in scientific circles regarding the safety of transferring genetic materials from one organism to another (Krimsky 1982a: chap. 3). Because the virus technique was laborious and difficult to perform, only a few labs could use it, and the urgency of the safety debate did not seem overwhelming. But in 1973 a major breakthrough occurred in the laboratories of Stanley Cohen (Stanford) and Herbert Boyer (UCSF) when they succeeded in moving genes between a number of organisms. The importance of this method is that, unlike the virus technique, the use of plasmids "was so simple that high-school pupils could easily learn it" (Lear 1978:66).[5] This invention led to the important Cohen-Boyer gene splicing patents (see appendix 2) and was the single pivotal event in the transformation of the "basic" science of molecular biology into an industry.

Among biologists a discussion began in the early 1970s regarding the health dangers inherent in bacteria and viruses containing recombinant DNA. After some debate Paul Berg and ten other leading molecular biologists not only called for a temporary moratorium on certain types of experiments, but also recommended that NIH form an advisory committee to evaluate the hazards associated with rDNA. Further, they convened an international meeting of scientists in 1975 to review scientific progress in rDNA (Berg et al. 1974:303). This meeting, the Asilomar Conference, brought together 140 prominent biologists "for the purpose of assessing the risks of the new technology and establishing the conditions under which research could or should proceed" (Krimsky 1982a:99). The conference agenda was structured by the conference organizers, all top molecular geneticists, to preclude debate on social or ethical issues—only "biohaz-

4. This discussion is not intended to examine the rDNA debate exhaustively or analytically. The subject has received much attention from a number of different perspectives (Lear 1978; Watson and Tooze 1981; Krimsky 1982; Jackson and Stich 1979). In this work the bitter debate regarding rDNA is the "prehistory" of the events to be examined. Curiously, less than ten years after the debate began it has disappeared almost without trace.
5. A clear exaggeration, but the discovery of how to use plasmids did simplify DNA recombination.

ards" were to be considered.[6] The conference was originally meant to be limited to scientists, but after some controversy the press was allowed to attend. The outcome of Asilomar was a report delivered to the National Academy of Sciences and an article published in *Science* that reiterated that certain experiments should be deferred until further information was available. Asilomar served to create a working consensus among the majority of the scientists directly involved with genetic engineering regarding acceptable experiments, but it also increased public awareness of the scientific advances being made in molecular biology and raised fears of epidemics caused by escaped organisms.

One day after the 1975 Asilomar Conference the NIH Recombinant DNA Advisory Committee (RAC) met for the first time (Krimsky 1982a:350), but not until sixteen months later did it issue its guideline recommendations. This lack of progress infuriated scientists because some of their experiments remained in voluntary suspension. The drafting process had been arduous, and the guidelines went through many revisions as scientists haggled over exact wordings (Wade 1975). An early draft of the guidelines was revised in stricter form because it did not meet the requirements of many middle-of-the-road scientists (Krimsky 1985).

Already in 1975 Senator Kennedy's Subcommittee on Health had held a session on genetic engineering that raised questions regarding the proper role of government in overseeing potentially dangerous research (Krimsky 1982b:165). By the end of 1975 the rDNA debate had left the confines of the scientific community and had become a topic discussed in newspapers such as the *New York Times, Boston Globe*, and *Washington Post*. A new phase in the rDNA debate began in 1976 as the internal debate within the scientific community became politicized and was discussed in a number of public forums.

The most dramatic public debate occurred in 1976, when the Cambridge, Massachusetts City Council called upon Harvard University to justify its decision to construct a P-3 genetic engineering containment facility (P-3 designates a containment level considered to be moderate and includes special engineering features such as airlocks). After a bitter debate the city council asked Harvard and MIT to desist from carrying out P-3 experiments until a civilian review board could draw up recommendations for the city council. In January 1977 the city council voted to allow P-3 experiments subject to certain restrictions in addition to those required by the NIH guidelines, which had been issued nearly simultaneously with the initiation of the Cambridge council hearings. The Cambridge hearings and the accompanying ordinance actions transmitted a shocking message to scientists:

6. This is certainly understandable in the sense that they did not believe themselves trained or competent in these concerns. Further, to predict the social outcomes of rDNA then was totally impossible, given the state of the knowledge about what it could do.

local jurisdictions could regulate laboratory research on the basis of the overall health and safety of the community (Krimsky 1982a). Other state and local governments throughout the United States established committees to oversee university rDNA research in their jurisdictions (Wade 1977a:558–59). This increased activity brought fears among scientists of a chaotic set of laws differing from one local jurisdiction to another. The lack of national legal uniformity implied that researchers at some universities would have a comparative advantage over others, that is, strict regulations would be more costly to comply with and might slow down research progress—an important consideration in the bitter competition for grants. The tenor of the rDNA debate had taken an ominous turn from scientists' expectations at the time they raised the topic of biohazards.

The NIH guidelines released in 1976 were exactly that—guidelines. They were mandatory only for recipients of federal funding and exercised no control over research undertaken or funded by industry. In response to this and other concerns, Senator Kennedy's Subcommittee on Health held its first *Oversight Hearing on Implementation of NIH Guidelines Governing Recombinant DNA Research*. These hearings determined that regulatory legislation was necessary to extend mandatory safety procedures to all genetic engineering research (U.S. Congress 1976). At this stage other interested parties joined the debate—most notably the Pharmaceutical Manufacturers Association and environmental groups such as the Environmental Defense Fund and Friends of the Earth (U.S. Congress 1976:III; Norman 1976:89).[7]

The issuance of guidelines—the goal scientists had sought—rather than end debate served only to further publicize the "dangers" of rDNA. In 1977 both Senator Kennedy and Representative Rogers wrote legislation (S1217 and HR7897) that would make the guidelines mandatory and would appoint advisory groups including nonscientists to be selected from the general public. The public debate led scientists in paroxysms of hyperbole to charge Senator Kennedy with "Lysenkoism" (Wade 1977b). At the beginning of 1977 it appeared likely that federal regulatory legislation would be passed, but by the end of 1977 no bill had been acted upon. In 1977 biologists had not united against legally binding regulations providing the law also contained a federal preemption of the local standards being put into effect by cities and states around the United States (Dickson 1978:664); by 1978 biologists had united to resist legal control. However, 1977 and 1978 were the high-water mark of the rDNA debate, and the final decision in the Congress was to do nothing. In the actual event a

---

7. The other important but then largely unnoticed event was the formation of the first rDNA-based venture capital company, Genentech. Stanley Cohen had joined the scientific advisory board of Cetus in 1975.

number of factors combined to ensure that no bill passed, including intense lobbying not only by scientists but also by university administrators organized in a group calling itself Friends of DNA, the increasing promise of valuable products being developed from rDNA, and the fact that no hazards had yet materialized.

This period also saw a new element added to the rDNA debate—the possibility that tremendous profits might be reaped by using these new research techniques. In the race to produce human hormones in bacteria, NIH rules were broken by researchers who inserted a rat insulin gene into a bacteria (Wade 1977c). At UCSF these commercial developments created internal departmental stresses. UCSF microbiologist David Martin, commenting on the growing controversy regarding scientists' ability to make commercial products by genetic engineering, said, "Capitalism sticking its nose into the lab has tainted interpersonal relations—there are a number of people who feel rather strongly that there should be no commercialization of human insulin" (Wade 1977c:1342).[8] By 1978 the debate over regulation had become increasingly bitter as environmental groups and public interest activists fought to tighten control over rDNA research and scientists and increasingly industry resisted these demands.

The first major revisions of the guidelines were announced in December 1978 as it became clear that many of the restrictions were unnecessarily harsh. These downgraded safety requirements on many experiments and formalized the modification procedures for the guidelines. A voluntary registration system for industry and nonNIH-funded rDNA work was established. Other important revisions increased the RAC membership "from sixteen to twenty-five with approximately one-third public members" and established Institutional Biosafety Committees at each institution to ensure that the guidelines were being enforced; the latter were required to have "two members and not less than 20 percent of the membership" unaffiliated with the institution (Krimsky 1983:10). These provisions regarding public participation were the fruits of the intensive lobbying by environmental activists and public interest groups.

In response to the subsiding of public concern and interest, the guidelines were relaxed twice in 1980 and again in 1981 and 1983 (Krimsky 1983:10). The most important aspect of these revisions was the exemption of other host-vector systems that were of scientific or industrial interest. The guidelines were also revised to allow for secret sessions by RAC to protect proprietary information presented by corporate laboratories. The other major change came in 1981 when the distinction between large-scale and small-scale experiments was dropped, completely satisfying a request by Eli Lilly (Krimsky 1983:11).

8. David Martin, criticizing capitalism in 1977, would five years later be appointed Genentech's vice-president of research (*Chemical Week* 1982d:16).

From 1978 on the guidelines came under attack from numerous scientists. Most scientists—many of whom had now become employees of companies or were on retainer—wanted to dispense with the guidelines entirely (Germann 1981). However, due to the threat of local governments' introducing or threatening to introduce local regulations, it was decided to retain a semblance of regulation (Sun 1982). In reality the 1983 revision made nearly all conceivable rDNA experiments exempt from the guidelines.

By 1979 a new group of players had entered the regulation game—the giant pharmaceutical and chemical companies. The obvious fact that biotechnology would become an important industrial technique led Congress to new worries. In 1980 the Senate held hearings regarding the role of government in facilitating the establishment of a biotechnology industry (U.S. Congress 1980). It is quite remarkable how quickly doubts regarding safety receded once it appeared that profits could be made from this new technology. The simultaneous growth of small biotechnology startups financed by venture capital and the increased interest of multinational corporations created a backdrop of intense entrepreneurial activity for the congressional hearings and NIH guideline revision meetings. Even as deliberation regarding control, safety, and ethics was in progress, the business world was exploding with activity.

As a legacy of the rDNA debates, a number of ordinances in cities and towns exist across the country, the RAC and the Institutional Biosafety Committees continue to guarantee some type of oversight in rDNA experiments, and there is an increased public awareness of the importance of science (Krimsky, Baeck, and Bolduc 1982). Yet perhaps the most interesting outcome of the debate is that it had so little impact. Genetic engineering, a scientific research tool, has become an industrial tool in less than ten years, the first five years of which were marked by intense debate. Charles Weiner (1982) has observed that the rDNA debate called attention to the potential that genetic engineering had—in the process convincing a few venture capitalists that products with commercial value could come from these scientific techniques. The remainder of the book examines the relationships that grew out of this debate that raged in the 1970s.

2. The University

and the Corporation

In the long run, the establishment of ties between academic institutions and industrial corporations, large and small, may turn out to be one of the most important "scientific" developments of the 1980s *(Culliton 1981:1196)*.

The knowledge engendered by science is a social product because of its historical roots, its public resources, and "because it has become an indispensable part of our common culture." We have a right to control science not because of its failure but because of its success *(Willard Gaylin quoted and paraphrased in Krimsky 1982:168)*.

The stagnant economy that has prevailed since the late 1970s has increasingly been reflected in university budgets. Nearly all of the costs of staff, equipment, and physical plant have outpaced inflation, contributing to a squeeze on university finances. Fears regarding decreases in federal funding for biomedical research have not been entirely warranted, though the rate of increase in biomedical research funding has slowed substantially. Reagan's victory in November 1979 distinctly changed the U.S. political climate in two ways: first, scientists and university administrators feared (unnecessarily, as it turned out) that Reagan would drastically cut budgets for all scientific research.[1] Second, Reagan changed the climate regarding the

1. Nixon was the last president who wanted to cut science and research budgets and was unsuccessful, especially in the biomedical area (Strickland 1972:230).

acceptability of industrial participation in public activities. The new ideology was that any activity that could be privatized should be. The federal bureaucracy—the vital provider of monies—would object little to corporate funding and control of university research. With this in mind, we may examine new policies of the federal government that are assisting in the creation of new university–corporate relationships.

The breakdown of the postwar growth model is reflected in the slowdown of productivity growth. State managers and corporate executives agree with the proposition that "Everybody in the economy stands to gain, directly or indirectly, from higher productivity; or to lose from lower productivity. There is a lot of misinformation about that. Some people think it all goes to profits, and some think it goes to labor. Everybody gets a share" (Fabricant 1978:495). Fabricant argues for an identity of interests between labor and business; that is, if all groups cooperate to expand the economic pie, he says, everyone can have a larger slice. To counteract their falling profit rates manufacturers needed to develop technologies that lower production costs. In the United States over the last forty years universities have been an important source of new technologies (for example, lasers, computers, robots, and many other products were born in university laboratories). In the emerging field of biotechnology the lack of corporate expertise led to unique new arrangements between industry and corporations at institutional levels that are affecting a number of the university's traditional values and norms.

Universities serve American society, and by implication industry, through the performance of the following three functions:

1. Universities provide trained labor power.

2. Universities perform research, the results of which cannot immediately be transformed into profitable activities; that is, universities create social knowledge.

3. Universities produce much of the ideology that legitimates the U.S. economic and social system, for example, through the social sciences.

Each of these functions contributes to the reproduction of the social system as a whole, and the first two are crucial for continued profitable production. Research is vital because its success provides the basis for increasing the productivity of workers and the profits of private firms.

The universities have long provided trained labor power, the costs of which training have been met, in large part, through tuitions and state subsidies. The provision of trained workers at little or no cost to corporations represents a socialization of one of the major costs of reproducing the entire economic system. The increasing technological complexity of advanced societies continually requires longer training periods at ever higher cost. Corporations are reluctant to bear this expense and, in fact, due to the profit imperative, will not do so voluntarily.[2]

E. E. David, Jr. (1982:44), the president of Exxon Research and Development Corporation, which expends nearly $500 million per annum, maintains that the most important role of the university is to provide "a steady supply of well-educated graduates." Peat, Marwick, Mitchell and Company (PMM) (1981:8), in a report written for Cornell's Corporate Liaison Committee, put the matter even more strongly: "In our interviews [with key corporate executives] the reply [to the question of what companies need most from universities] was the provision of an adequate supply of technically and scientifically trained graduates. In a word, *manpower*" [emphasis in original]. Workers are of immediate importance to companies because they are the living labor required every day to ensure not only that the companies remain profitable, but also that the presently standing factories, offices, and research laboratories are staffed. University training is even more vital in a milieu of international economic competition, in which a less skilled labor force can translate into a deteriorating competitive position. The relative total technical capacity of a country's workers has become pivotal for production systems that are based on the production and application of information or knowledge.

The second great task of the university is to perform research that has no immediate application to production. E. E. David, Jr. (1982:44) notes that after the training of workers, the most important role of universities is to perform basic science and provide "scientists able to offer fresh insights." A number of corporations make grants to universities for basic research. On the other hand, the PMM survey (1981:9) emphasized that "Industry R and D executives respect the capability of the leading universities in basic research but with few exceptions they do not feel obliged to underwrite it." Indeed, the individual manager responding to his fiduciary responsibility to stockholders is not in a position to expend resources that will not return a profit. The university, on the other hand, is not fettered by the need for financial return and can, in the words of Ralph Hardy (1982), ex-Du Pont vice-president for biological research, perform "scouting on the frontiers of knowledge." Corporations have no intention of paying for the "scouts" until a potential El Dorado has been discovered.

Universities also provide ideological justifications for U.S. society. The use of professors to sanctify various corporate and governmental actions is well known. Albert Meyerhoff (1982a:A11), the senior defense attorney

---

2. This is a case of the "prisoners' dilemma." If one company contributes enormous resources to support and maintain a university, other companies will receive the benefits of that funding. Therefore, the first company cannot afford to contribute too much. The traditional solution to the dilemma of how to secure financial support for public goods has been to levy taxes, but with the current profit squeeze companies resist this solution.

for the Natural Resources Defense Council, in criticizing a high-level conference of university administrators and corporate executives, argued, "If the universities become the captives of chemical companies and high technology firms, public trust in academia will rapidly disappear. The loss of trust may be the biggest price paid by universities in exchange for a few pieces of gold." Strikingly, a statement issued by university administrators, university scientists, and industry personnel attending the conference in 1982 at Pajaro Dunes, California, to discuss the relationships between university and industry agreed with critic Meyerhoff by stating that the "independence and integrity of the university and its faculty," even though "faced with unprecedented financial pressure," was a sacred trust. Further, "the universities are a repository of public trust" that must be preserved (Pajaro Dunes Biotechnology Statement 1982:8). There can be no doubt that the ideological image of the university as an institution not explicitly concerned with private profit and as an unbiased arbiter of political struggles is an important support for the U.S. social system as a whole.

The current changes in the relationship between universities and industry are undermining the universities' traditional roles in a number of ways. One reason the commercialization of biotechnology is such an interesting phenomenon is the possibility that biotechnology is the cutting edge for the creation of new social relationships, though it is still unclear what the final stable configuration of these social relationships will be. Nevertheless, changes in the university are proceeding extremely rapidly and could quite possibly disrupt the entire reproduction function of the university. This and the following two chapters examine the various patterns of university–industry relationships at an institutional level, especially those relationships that are of particular importance in biotechnology. However, examination of the most pervasive arrangement—that between individual professors and companies—is deferred to chapter 5.

University–Corporate Relations

Simply using a university lab to put profits into private pockets is "wrong, destructive, and divisive. . . . What's a university want to be? If they have to save themselves by being an arm of industry maybe they're not worth saving" *(Jeffrey Miller, an American geneticist at the University of Geneva, paraphrased and quoted in J. Fox 1981a:43).*

Universities have obviously felt a civic responsibility to answer appeals to think about collaborative efforts to increase productivity. Such concern is not entirely selfless, since higher education has a vital stake in the long-term strength of our economy. . . . More important still, faculty members and administrators are hard-pressed financially and perceive opportunities to benefit

financially from efforts to improve their relations with
industries   *(Derek Bok, president of Harvard
University 1981:25).*

Jeffrey Miller and Derek Bok, members of the academic community,
typify the ongoing debate in American universities regarding the proper
role of the university in society. A focal point for this discussion is the
relationships being entered into between universities (or certain faculty
within universities) and the biotechnology industry. The debate is not new
and has occurred frequently. For example, in 1923 Dean Barus of Brown
worried that "industrial support of academic research might have a negative
influence on the educational role of universities" (Weiner 1982:127). Kenneth Pitzer (1955:792), then professor of chemistry at the University of
California, Berkeley (UCB), echoed somewhat similar thoughts in an article in *Science*:

> Some industrial funds have been supporting research in a manner that
> has been very effective. On the other hand, some industrially sponsored
> research in universities should probably not have been put in a university
> at all. I do not mean that industrial activities in this area are better or
> worse than those of government; I mean simply that the best of the
> industrially sponsored activities are excellent and should serve as models
> for further expansion.

These early discussions regarding the proper role of the university vis-
à-vis corporations centered on organic or synthetic chemistry. In one sense,
biotechnology is merely a continuation of this debate in the field of biology.
Strictly speaking, the current debates regarding biotechnology can be considered as another chapter in the continuing expansion of understanding
of the natural world that opens new realms to exploitation by profit-making
entities. Yet there are new features to the university–industry bonds being
forged (Weiner 1982:131), and these will be examined in the next chapters.

The postwar science funding boom created a new patron for the sciences
in the form of the federal government. Federal funding was largely allocated through the peer review process, which had the effect of making
scientists dependent on fellow scientists for evaluation of their work and
for continued funding. The role of the state as a funder of basic (non-
commodity-oriented) research fostered a powerful ideology—one of scientists working for the public good to improve the health status of Americans. According to this ideology, industry's motives—especially that of
profitability—were suspect, and the applied science orientation of industry
was considered to be scientifically uninspiring to scientists.

Xerox's vice-president of research, George Pake (1980:44), has re-
marked that the postwar funding pattern "featured one notable difference
compared to the pre-war period: relatively plentiful Federal funds for sup-

port of basic and even some applied university research seemed to have the effect of weakening the occasional pre-war ties between industry and university, particularly in industrial support of academic research." Prager and Omenn (1980:379) accordingly observe that "there has been a marked decline in linkages between academia and industry."

In the late 1970s the issue of innovation (in the Schumpeterian sense) increasingly became a topic of interest, and universities were perceived to be a key source of innovations. For example, the preface of an Organization for Economic Cooperation and Development (OECD) (1980:6) report bluntly declared, "The issue that confronts us is the necessity to establish new relationships between the scientific–technological–industrial community, government officials and the general public." Writing in *Science*, Denis Prager, at that time the senior policy analyst at the Office of Science and Technology Policy (OSTP), and Gilbert Omenn, then associate director for human resources at OSTP (1980:379), theorized—on the basis of scant evidence—that the decline in postwar university–corporate linkages may be a contributing factor to the erosion of the innovation process in the United States.[3] In nearly every current statement on the present economic malaise, the university is looked upon as the source of new technologies which are to spark sustained long-term recovery. University-developed technical fixes are touted as central in overcoming economic stagnation.

The impetus for closer university–industry relations comes not merely from universities and corporations, but also from the government. Over the past decade the U.S. federal government has launched repeated initiatives to strengthen university–corporate linkages. Specific programs have included the loosening of rules regarding disposition of patents acquired during the course of federally funded research; the passage of the 1980 Tax Reform Act, which provided tax write-offs for industry-funded university research and development; and "seed" money financing of research consortia consisting of a university and several corporations.[4] Prager and

---

3. The need OECD saw for having the general public involved was discarded in the United States, where the general public's relation to science need only be to pay the bills.

4. The 1980 Tax Reform Act provides that 65 percent of the corporate research and development expenditure increases in universities after July 1, 1981, could be used to calculate a tax credit. So if company A contracted for $1 million of research to university B, then company A would receive a credit of 25 percent of $650,000, or $162,500. This is in addition to the normal tax deduction, which at the corporate tax rate of 46 percent is $460,000. Also, the timing is important because of the use of base years, etc.; so it is in the interest of the funding company to start low and increase funding. Finally, the donation of research equipment receives favorable treatment. Instead of receiving merely the cost of equipment as a deduction, the company receives the average of the cost and sales price, with the provision that this average cannot be greater than double the cost price. These tax breaks clearly provide important fiscal reasons for corporations to purchase university research (Feinschreiber 1981).

Omenn (1980:384) argue in *Science* that "the federal government can play a facilitating role in fostering university–industry cooperation primarily by providing incentives and removing disincentives to such interaction." The increased strength of the "university–corporate partnership" has been lauded by William Raub, former associate director of NIH. Raub (1981:80), testifying in a recent hearing, said, "Mr. Chairman, I am pleased to say that I believe the NIH–university–industry relationship is sound and gives promise of growing stronger in the years ahead." William Carey, in his role of executive officer of the American Association for the Advancement of Science (AAAS), supporting government efforts to bring together industry and the university, wrote:

> Industry, in my experience, makes considerable use of university scientists, and it is a very good thing. At a time when industrial productivity and lagging innovation mark so much of the U.S. national economy, access to both basic science and potential applications serves not only corporate goals but social purposes   (Carey 1980:5–6).

Carey's assumptions are that technology will improve the U.S. economy and that corporate goals and social purposes can be equated.

The Types of University–Industry Relationships

Of the two major categories of university–industry relationships, the first consists of those relationships based on individual faculty members selling their labor power as consultants to or acting as proprietors in companies. The second level consists of relationships of an institutional nature— arranged either through departments or the central administration—which are more formalized. The explosive growth of interest in biotechnology is creating new types of interactions. The large sums of capital being invested and the urgency of the research effort are catalyzing new efforts to speed the "transfer of technology" from the university to industry.

At the macro level, connections between universities and corporations are constant due to the fact that they are both important social institutions. For example, the commodities used by the university, ranging from sophisticated laboratory instruments to toilet paper, are provided by industry. In simple physical terms, the university is dependent upon commodities which are produced in the larger economy. The money to purchase these commodities must be extracted from the economy through taxes, tuitions, contributions, or sales of services. The contributions must come either from individuals or from corporations. The university, being part of society, is subject to the strains and stresses of the current economic conditions and in response is seeking nontraditional funding sources.

Before I examine the actual types of university–corporate relationships, it is important to emphasize that university research is largely supported

Table 2.1. Research and Development Expenditures at Universities and Colleges by Sources of Funds FY 1983 (All Institutions)

Source	Expenditures ($ million)	Percentage
Federal government	5,387	63.6
State and local governments	653	7.7
Industry	457	5.4
Institutional funds	1,347	15.9
All other sources	630	7.4
Total	8,473*	100.0

Source: National Science Foundation, 1985b
* Error due to rounding

by federal government funds (table 2.1). In fiscal year 1979, 64.0 percent of university research and development monies came from the federal government, and another 7.7 percent originated from state and local governments. Corporate contributions were the smallest source. Simultaneously, as table 2.2 indicates, universities perform approximately half of all the basic research in the United States, nearly double its share in 1953. Industry provides less than 20 percent of the funds used for basic research in the university sector. The meagerness of corporate contributions is documented in table 2.3. Industry's share of basic research expenditures has declined by nearly 50 percent from 1953 to 1981. The all-pervasive federal research monies are the baseline of support for university research and will continue to be of primary importance regardless of the changes in corporate contributions. The American research system has been and is, quite simply, based on federal (that is, public) funding.

Table 2.4, which lists the various types of university–corporate relationships, demonstrates that the closeness of the ties between the two institutions increases from top to bottom. The starred types of arrangements are especially important in biotechnology. Long-term contracts, with one exception, are exclusively in the area of biotechnology. Each type of

Table 2.2. Basic Research Performance by Sector, 1953 to 1984 (percentages)

Year	Total	Federal government	Industry	Universities	FFRDCs*	Other nonprofit institutions
1953	100.0	22.9	34.2	25.0	7.5	10.4
1960	100.0	13.4	31.4	36.2	8.1	10.9
1970	100.0	15.4	17.4	51.1	7.7	8.7
1980	100.0	14.6	16.4	49.8	9.7	9.5
1984	100.0	15.5	19.4	48.5	8.3	8.3

Sources: National Science Foundation 1984:33; National Science Foundation 1985a
* Federally Funded Research and Development Centers

Table 2.3. Sources of Funds for Basic Research by Sector, 1953 to 1984 (percentages)

Year	Total	Federal government	Industry	Universities	FFRDC s	Other nonprofit institutions
1953	100.0	56.9	34.7	2.3	0.0	6.1
1960	100.0	59.7	28.6	6.0	0.0	5.7
1970	100.0	69.8	15.0	10.0	0.0	5.2
1980*	100.0	68.7	15.6	10.0	0.0	5.6
1984*	100.0	66.5	18.5	10.1	0.0	4.8

Sources: National Science Foundation 1984:33; National Science Foundation 1985a
* rounding error

Table 2.4. Existing Types of University–Industry Relations

Between individual professors and corporations:

Faculty consulting and research

Between universities and corporations:

Corporate contributions

a. undirected
b. fellowships
*c. directed

Industrial procurement of services

a. education and training
*b. contract research
*c. patents

Industrial affiliates such as MIT and Stanford School of Medicine

Cooperative research

a. NSF-funded industry–university research centers such as MIT's Polymer Processing Laboratory

Privately funded research centers

*a. Multicorporate, such as Engenics, Cornell Biotechnology Institute
*b. Single funder, such as MIT's Whitehead Institute

*Long-term contracts such as Monsanto–Harvard, MIT–Exxon, and Hoechst–MGH

*University-controlled companies to exploit research

*Private companies that secure patent rights for resale, such as Research Corporation and UGEN

Source: Author
* Important types of arrangements in the biotechnology industry.

relationship has a different history and in some cases is in existence only at a select few universities.

Corporate Contributions

The most prevalent and least objectionable relationship between universities and industry is the undirected contribution. This can be used by the university as it sees fit. However, in fiscal year 1979–80, corporate grant-giving to universities totaled only about $300 million, less than grants by foundations, alumni, or nonalumni individuals (Council for Financial Aid to Education 1981:3). The statistics regarding these grants are not disaggregated according to criteria such as directed versus undirected or basic versus applied. Undirected grants from corporations in all likelihood account for no more than 5 percent of the revenue of major private universities. PMM (1981:15) has calculated that all corporate gifts and grants to major private universities provide only 12 percent of their revenues and less than 3.1 percent of the public universities' revenue. Further, it is unlikely that unrestricted grant income will grow significantly (and it might even decrease) as companies discover that they can purchase something from the university with their grant money.

Fellowships and directed grants are especially prevalent in engineering and the physical sciences and are growing in the biological sciences. Directed contributions either target a substantive research area or leave it to the department's discretion to allocate the funds. Other funds are donated directly to a professor's laboratory. In many cases, the particular professors are doing research either of general or of specific interest to the company. A contribution of as little as $5,000 or as much as $200,000 may secure access to the professor and his students. An example of how such a relationship is initiated is given by Eric Walker, the vice-president for science and technology at Alcoa, and Robert Hampel, director of technical development at Alcoa:

The device used [to induce university professors to talk with the Alcoa representative] is to send a young industry researcher to visit the university which is doing the best work in his field, then provide him with a check, in Alcoa's case for $5,000, which the young industry representative can leave with the professor to help support a graduate student or to provide general support for the work, but to leave it only if he thinks the work being done is good and useful. Since most professors hope the industry representatives will visit again next year with similar results, there is a real incentive to communicate and to establish a lasting relationship   (Walker and Hampel 1974:27).

The relationship between the professor and the industrial donor most resembles a patron–client relationship and has been and is the norm in fields such as engineering.

James Bonner, a plant molecular biologist at Caltech and founder of the agricultural biotechnology company Phytogen, has described the role of the professor most aptly: "Each academic scientist is today an entrepreneur, employing a larger or smaller corps of colleagues supported by the funds which the scientist can charm out of federal and private sources, funds in the form of grants and contracts, all obtained by virtue of his scientific standing and his gift of grantsmanship" (Bonner 1981:28). Bonner's professor is an academic entrepreneur; not only the professor himself, but his entire laboratory is dependent on his grant-securing abilities. The number of corporate contracts with professors is large. For example, Allied Corporation claims to have twenty-eight grants at major universities, and Allied is by no means the largest corporate funder (*Journal of Commerce* 1982:22B).

The directed, or targeted, grant is now prevalent in the majority of university molecular biology and biochemistry laboratories. These relatively small grants do not provide the funding corporation with any unique claim on the results of the university research. They do, however, provide a "window on the technology." Also, the "personal" relationship with the professor may provide the company with the inside track on hiring graduate students. For example, in some fields of engineering a student's thesis advisor may attempt to compel a student to accept employment with a certain company. This so-called channeling can include the professor's blocking of job offers from other companies. A thesis advisor can apply intense pressure on his student to secure the desired result (Interview 1981). The directed grant to a professor is not without strings, invisible though they may be. More important, it is an inducement to develop a closer relationship, one in which money is given to further industry's goals.

Industrial Procurement of Services

In many cases industry desires more specific items or services such as advanced training and education or contract research. Continuing education and/or training in certain advanced techniques can lead industry to send employees to take courses at a university. In an ambitious scheme, Stanford University offers degree programs by television for electrical engineers in Silicon Valley—tuition is double that for a regular Stanford student (Rosenberg 1982:56). Biotechnology corporations are also dispatching employees to universities but usually in conjunction with a larger contract or arrangement. Continuing education is not yet of importance to the biotechnology industry because of the field's novelty.

Universities have always performed contract research. This is especially true of both medical schools and land grant universities, which have been more than willing to conduct experiments on the efficacy and safety of new chemicals and other proprietary items. The same is true in biotechnology;

for example, the W. R. Grace Company contracted with researchers at the Illinois Institute of Technology to "develop economic methods for converting inorganic sulphate to sulphur using bacteria" (*Biotechnology Bulletin Report* 1983:3). The success of this research would solve an important waste problem for the company and leave a marketable product, sulphur. Grace has also contracted with the University of Georgia to research desulphurization of high-sulphur fuels through the use of bacteria (*Biotechnology Bulletin Report* 1983:3). Contract research is common throughout academe and has become prevalent in biotechnology. Biologists and students commonly assume that nearly every molecular biologist has a corporation supporting his laboratory. This type of support is usually arranged through a university-created administrative unit that oversees outside research funding and yields overhead to the university.

Universities have traditionally supplied not only highly trained professional labor power with graduate degrees but also less thoroughly trained technicians. A number of institutions (colleges) are starting programs to produce labor specifically trained to be technicians in biotechnology laboratories (Adelman 1982b, 1983b; Amatniek 1983). Educational institutions such as the University of Maryland, Baltimore County; East Carolina University; the State University of New York, Plattsburg and Fredonia; and Cedar Crest College are developing programs to meet a perceived need for technicians.

Genex Corporation believes that these technicians will be very useful and has already committed to hire a specified number of technicians in a summer training program. However, there remains debate within the industry as to whether technicians with bachelor's degrees are really needed or qualified. An unnamed "industry source" is quoted in *Bio/Technology* as saying, "Understanding the fundamentals of biochemistry is the most important thing. The techniques evolve very rapidly. . . . You'll never be able to step out of these places into a job unless you're coming out of a place with a research background" (Amatniek 1983:468). This unnamed source assumes that every such worker is going to become a researcher, but already the high skill levels of genetic engineering are being broken down and replaced by the less skilled personnel. Certain tasks such as DNA sequencing are being routinized and will be performed either by low-paid technicians or by sequencing machines (Gebhart 1983; Hunkapiller et al. 1983). The highly paid, equity-owning researchers of venture capital firms cannot afford to waste their time on routinizable tasks.

The above-mentioned institutions are responding to the perceived need for technicians in the traditional manner of the American educational system. For the preparation of this type of labor power universities are, in some cases, receiving corporate support in the form of research materials. For example, the University of Maryland, Baltimore County, has received research materials from Becton Dickinson, Genex, Martin Marietta, and

Amersham Chemicals, among other companies (Amatniek 1983:467). In general, the jobs these technicians are preparing for have usually been filled by those trained in biological sciences in research universities. Whether the new cadre, trained as technicians, will displace the bachelors and masters of science graduates is unclear.

Industrial Affiliates

Industrial affiliate programs, a number of which have been initiated at universities across the country, provide preferential access by corporations to participating faculty members. The more notable programs include the MIT Industrial Liaison Program and the Stanford University School of Medicine affiliate program (Gurin and Pfund 1980:546–47). The MIT program has been very successful, annually drawing an aggregate over $4.8 million in membership fees from 280 corporations. Companies enrolled as affiliates usually receive directories of current research, paper reprints, and help in arranging visits, and they are invited to attend seminars and symposia specially prepared for them (PMM 1981:42). Affiliate programs represent a relatively noncontroversial strategy for raising funds and have been adopted by many universities and administrative subunits. For example, a discussion memorandum prepared by A. Kossiakoff (1981:5), the chief scientist at Johns Hopkins' Applied Physics Laboratory, and circulated to administrators states, "A university-wide association on the MIT model is not attractive for Johns Hopkins because of the University's high degree of diversity. However within particular fields in which Hopkins is preeminent, the University may well find association with a group of companies to be useful." The industrial affiliates program, though successful in certain cases, is a model that in most cases provides little leverage for corporations.

In 1981 PMM (1981:41), summarizing the reactions of corporate executives to the proliferation of affiliate programs, wrote:

> The rapid increase in these programs has provoked an adverse reaction in some major companies; we heard a number of complaints in the course of our interviews. One complaint is that at some universities a major corporate donor may be denied access to a particular department unless an additional contribution is made to that department's affiliates program; another is that the services offered are not significant; a third is that there are simply too many. One large company that now belongs to 15 such programs is systematically turning down all further requests.

The industrial affiliate model has been successful in garnering limited amounts of support, but it is not a rapidly expanding type of relationship. It is doubtful that affiliate programs will have an important effect on either internal or external university relations. Affiliate programs normally do not provide what a company wants most—a distinct advantage over its competitors.

Federally Funded Cooperative Research Centers

The objective of a federally funded cooperative research program is to create centers to conduct research with the financial support of a number of companies. Since 1973 the NSF has been funding centers in which a university and a number of corporations cooperate on research topics of interest. The NSF support for these centers usually lasts five years, at the end of which period the center is expected to be self-supporting (Senich 1982:142). NSF measures the relative success of the centers by their viability after federal support terminates, that is, do they remain at an equivalent rate of funding on the basis of corporate contributions? The most successful center is the MIT Polymer Processing Laboratory. Each of twelve companies involved contributes between $20,000 and $80,000 annually, depending on its plastics output, does joint research, and is allowed an early opportunity to commercialize results (Pake 1981:46). Other research consortia include the Cornell Submicron Facility, the University of Delaware Catalysis Center, and the North Carolina Furniture Institute; these still require federal funding and some may never become self-sufficient (NSF 1982). In fact, the Furniture Institute is now defunct. These centers provide not only research access, but also venues in which corporate scientists can share information with other corporate scientists without being subject to antitrust laws (Noble and Pfund 1980:250).

In 1982 the first applications were received to initiate NSF-funded cooperative research centers for biotechnology. A consortium of Duke University and the University of North Carolina and a number of companies will soon receive funding from NSF to study monoclonal lymphocytes (Schwarzkopf 1984). This grant is part of North Carolina's effort to establish an important biotechnology business based on research and development conducted at three universities: Duke, the University of North Carolina, and North Carolina State University (Cooper 1982). The University of Wisconsin-Madison received a $55,000 planning grant to explore the possibility of creating a hybridoma research center (Schwarzkopf 1984). Other NSF-funded feasibility analyses are being conducted by a consortium made up of Purdue and North Carolina State University to investigate plant molecular biology; the University of Texas Health Center to study molecular targeting; and the University of Minnesota in the area of bioprocessing (Schwarzkopf 1984).

Though federally funded research centers will continue to be formed, interest in this particular form of cooperation is limited for a number of reasons. One is that the federal bureaucracy moves relatively slowly, and since biotechnology places a premium on rapid movement many universities are not willing to wait for NSF action. However, the most debilitating handicap is that companies involved in these consortia are direct competitors, and therefore the center provides little competitive leverage for the participating companies. For this reason the amount of funding any company is willing to commit to such a venture is small. From the corporate perspective it is strategically more sensible to fund research that will provide exclusive rights or some other competitive advantage.

Research Centers and Consortia
Funded Privately or by Universities

Many universities have eschewed NSF funding and have either used their own funds or succeeded in securing industrial, foundation, or state government funds to create research centers or institutions. Prominent examples in biotechnology include the Cornell Biotechnology Institute and the University of Michigan Center for Molecular Genetics. A somewhat different arrangement has been developed between UCB and Stanford, whereby a private company, Engenics, is connected to the universities through the Center for Biological Research (see table 2.5 for a partial listing of centers that are either established or in the process of being established).

Still another example is the $10 million national competition among universities sponsored by Sohio to create "centers of scientific excellence." Originally, Sohio advertised for eight areas of special interest, two of which were related to biotechnology—separation science and agriscience and technology. In response to the first "help wanted" advertisement that Sohio placed in *Science* (Sohio 1983a), over one thousand university proposals were received (Frutchy 1983), and the competition was expanded to twelve areas (see figure 2.1). Sohio's objective in sponsoring this competition was "to encourage high quality, innovative, university-based research, *in partnership with industry*" [emphasis added]. The partnership Sohio envisions is a unilateral arrangement with the university. The actual relationship will comprise a center in the sense that the university will centralize faculty from different departments to form a research team for Sohio.

The concept of the biotechnology center or institute is one that has attracted universities that do not have first-rank molecular biology departments. The center has thus been a response to weakness and to the fear that corporate largesse in biotechnology will soon end. The strategy calls for the university to draw together researchers from various departments, thereby providing a larger base of good researchers and hopefully creating synergies. The creation of centers was also prompted by the fear that the most talented and mobile researchers might leave the university if they are not provided with a more favorable working environment and accessible funding. This problem occurred at Cornell when Gerald Fink

ANNOUNCING
AN EXPANDED COMPETITION

- Due to an overwhelming response, Sohio has extended the deadline for entering its $10 million national competition among colleges and universities in support of <u>Centers for Scientific Excellence</u>. All entries are due by <u>April 1.</u>

- Sohio has also expanded the scope of the competition to include more research categories as listed below.

Sohio recognizes the crucial need to strengthen research in scientific areas of critical importance to its future and the nation's long term economic productivity. The objective of this competition is to encourage high quality, innovative, university-based research, in partnership with industry.

Winners of the competition will be eligible for up to $2,500,000 over a five-year period, depending upon the type and extent of research undertaken. Research proposals will be judged by a panel of Sohio scientists and representatives from the academic/scientific community. The initial requirement for entry shall be a five page prospectus of proposed research in one of the following fields:

Surface Science
(including electrochemistry, colloid science, surface corrosion, and heterogeneous catalysis).

Separation Science
(including membrane technology, selective adsorbents).

Control Theory & System
(including information processing, data base engineering; sensing).

Agri-science & Technology
(including plant genetics, cellular and molecular biology, chemical regulators, biomass conversion).

Metal Extraction Science & Technology
(including leaching, insitu extraction, solvent extraction and ion exchange, electrometallurgy and high temperature processes).

Structural Engineering, Arctic Engineering, Offshore Platform Design, & Geotechnical
(including properties and behavior of steel and concrete structures in sea ice and deep ocean waters, seafloor geotechnical properties and sea ice movement and physical properties of ice).

Petroleum Reservoir Science & Technology
(including enhanced oil recovery processes, rock/fluid interactions, fluid mechanics and reservoir modelling.)

Geophysical & Geologic Science
(including geochemistry, paleontology, palynology, three component seismology, monitoring of EOR using surface seismic, and artificial intelligence used for exploration interpretation).

Mining Technology
(including slope stability, rock mechanics, blasting, mine planning, reserve modelling, robotics and mine ventilation).

Photoconversion Science & Technology
(including photovoltaics, photochemistry, laser induced chemistry or catalysis).

Synthetic Fuels
(including syngas production and conversion, coal chemistry, shale retorting, and oil upgrading).

Materials Science
(including polymers, ceramics, composites, amorphous materials).

For additional information, contact Ms. Jennifer Frutchy at (216) 575-8479 or write: Director, Corporate Contributions, The Standard Oil Company (Ohio), The Midland Building, 840-T, Cleveland, Ohio 44115.

 The Standard Oil Company (Ohio)

Source: Sohio 1983b

Figure 2.1. Sohio Advertisement

43

Table 2.5. Major Biotechnology Centers or Programs at Universities*

University	Date established	Funding ($ million)	Sources of funds	Building	Colleges involved	Special comments
Univ. California, Berkeley, and Stanford (through Engenics)	1981	10.0	Bendix General Foods Koppers Mead Noranda Mines Elf Aquitaine	No	Engineering, medical school	A research consortium funded by companies
Univ. California, Berkeley Plant Gene Expression Laboratory	1984	8.0	USDA, private, university	Yes	Agriculture, engineering	Plant gene expression
Cornell University Biotechnology Institute	1983	7.5	General Foods Union Carbide Eastman Kodak State government University	Planned	All colleges	State of New York has provided $2 million in funding and an additional $18 million is pending
Univ. of Illinois Center in Crop Molecular Genetics	1983	2.0	Sohio Co.	No	Agriculture	Funded solely by Sohio
Biotechnology Center	1984	None yet	None yet	No	All colleges	The center will be organized as industrial associate program
Univ. of Michigan Center for Molecular Genetics	1982	8.0	Howard Hughes Medical Institute Salsbury Laboratory	Yes	Medical	
Michigan State Univ. Biotechnology Center	1983	6.0	State legislature Kellogg Foundation	Planned	All colleges	Connected with private company, Neogen

New Mexico State Center for Semi-Arid Plant Biotechnology	1984	State legislature	7.0	Planned	Agriculture	Only area of research is desert plants
Rutgers Univ.	1985	Bond issue	34.0	Yes	Agriculture, medical school	One center for agriculture and one for medicine

Sources: Interviews and articles
* This table is not exhaustive; many other centers have been formed and many others are still in the planning stage.

left to join the Whitehead Institute (WI), which is affiliated with MIT, and continue his consulting for Collaborative Research, a biotechnology company based in Waltham, Massachusetts. Michigan lost an important senior researcher, David Jackson, to Genex. Similar fears plague many schools as the bidding wars among universities and university and industry for first-rate biologists continue. A University of Michigan report found that

> molecular biologists have suffered from low visibility on campus. This has made it difficult to recruit quality researchers. "The University currently remains in danger of losing its best researchers in recombinant DNA and hybridoma-based investigation," the report said. The Center [for Molecular Genetics] is committed to reversing that trend   (Adelman 1983a:11).

A similar situation can be assumed to exist at many universities, and their response has been to secure funding for a biotechnology center.

Like other second-tier molecular biology schools, Cornell had to strengthen its biotechnology program out of fear of being left behind. The best professors are being lured from the second-rank schools to those centered in Boston and San Francisco. For example, WI will open thirteen faculty positions for senior researchers in the next ten years, and Massachusetts General Hospital (MGH), with $70 million it has received from Hoechst, will be hiring molecular geneticists. Only through securing significant funds and creating a more congenial atmosphere—especially providing opportunities for interdisciplinary research—can universities such as Michigan and Cornell compete (Jaschik and Kuntz 1982:9). Robert Barker (1982:2–3), former director of Cornell's Division of Biological Sciences, expressed the gravity of the situation by saying, "We must move in this direction [toward the institute] whether or not industries collaborate."

The idea of developing a biotechnology institute at Cornell was first broached in plant sciences in 1981 because of their lack of success in securing corporate funds. The vice-president of research at that time, Donald Cook, later gathered approximately thirty-five faculty members and drew up the center's plan. During 1981 Cornell's Corporate Liaison Committee also received a contractor's report from PMM outlining possible mechanisms to secure increased corporate funding. In 1982 Professor Walter Lynn, the director of Cornell's Science, Technology and Society Program, received a university grant to examine the feasibility of a center. The Faculty Council of Representatives approved the concept of a biotechnology institute consisting of five companies that would contribute $8 million each over five years (Cornell University Faculty Council 1982). The center was to bring together more than four hundred scientists and faculty members (*Cornell Chronicle* 1983:1) (This number should be viewed skeptically, as far fewer will actually be involved.)

At the Cornell Faculty Council of Representatives meetings, there was limited debate with a professor from the Business School, Alan McAdams, who argued that if only five companies were allowed to join it would appear as though Cornell was merely working for them. McAdams argued further that on one level the research is supposed to be freely available and open to all, but on another level the university is saying that it is available only to the member companies. Vice-President Cook retorted that "open to all" meant that everyone could read the results in scientific journals (Cornell University Faculty Council 1982).

Nonetheless, the faculty council voted in favor of the "blue sky" proposal, which intimated that up to $40 million in corporate funding over five years would be coming to Cornell. The corporate sponsors of the research were going to be given the following in return: royalty-free, nonexclusive licenses for any products developed, Cornell's willingness to accept corporate scientists, and an inside track on Cornell postdoctoral and graduate students. The institute's executive board was to consist of fourteen members: one each from the proposed five companies, eight from the university, and the director, who was to be appointed by the Cornell Board of Trustees (Cornell University 1982:4–5). This venture into corporate biotechnology was accompanied by much less debate than at most universities, a fact due in part to excellent timing by the administration in its scheduling of the faculty council meeting the week before final exams and in part to general apathy at Cornell.

By September 30, 1982, Cornell's initial estimate of five companies at $8 million each over five years had dwindled to four companies providing a total $26.6 million over the five years (Kuntz and Jaschik 1982:8). Cornell's search for possible corporate partners was predicated upon securing one company from five different industrial areas: chemicals, pharmaceuticals, food processing, agriculture, and chemical processing. Robert Barker had said, "We wouldn't take seven. . . . there are several possible sets of five" (Kilian 1983:16). Also, Barker's estimates of total contributions had shrunk to five corporations investing $1 million per year for five years (Kilian 1983:1). In the end three corporations, Eastman Kodak, General Foods, and Union Carbide, pledged $2.5 million each, spread over six years (Strom 1983:3).[5] Corning Glass had been announced as a member of the institute (Jaschik 1983:1), but it pulled out at the last moment. In fact, the largest investments in the institute are coming from the New York state government, which will invest a total of $20 million, and Cornell University, which will contribute $10 million (Snyder 1985). None of these

5. The companies now investing in biotechnology are well known for their role in petrochemical pollution. For example, Union Carbide, a biotechnology investor, received wide notoriety for the Bhopal, India, poison gas leak disaster that claimed 2,000 lives.

companies, with the exception of Corning, are known for capabilities in genetic engineering. The center is less a research alliance or cooperative effort than a one-way teaching effort.

The center, or institute, idea is receiving favor in a number of scientific areas. In Cornell's case it has been emphasized repeatedly that the research concerned is expected to be basic (Barker 1983; Blodgett 1983). However, even though the research is to be open and basic, a sticking point in negotiations was the question of patent exclusivity (Blodgett 1983). The companies finally did agree on royalty-free licenses (Snyder 1985). Another important question is whether the bulk of the eligible professors will participate, as many are already tied up with other companies through various research contracts, consultancies, and equity positions. Will it be more lucrative for them to join the biotechnology institute? This is as yet an unanswered question. One strategy for circumventing any given professor's many commercial commitments is to provide funds for that person to do research in areas in which he or she has not worked previously (Blodgett 1983). Of course, the efficiency of these highly specialized researchers in doing research outside their specialties may be limited.

If Michigan and Cornell are creating packages to lure industry, the reverse is true at UCB and Stanford. Engenics has been established by a number of venture capitalists to commercialize the bioprocessing work of professors at UCB and Stanford. Engenics has six corporate sponsors, each of which contributes $1.7 million and in return receives a total of 35 percent of the shares in the new company. A further 35 percent of the shares were given to the founders and key professionals at Engenics, including Professors Channing Robertson of chemical engineering at Stanford and Harvey Blanch of chemical engineering at UCB (*San Francisco Examiner* 1982:C1). The remaining 30 percent were donated to the Center for Biotechnology Research (*Chemical Week* 1982b:23). The center immediately received $2.4 million to support projects in laboratories in the departments of chemical engineering at Stanford (Channing Robertson), medical microbiology at Stanford (Abdul Matin), and chemical engineering at Berkeley (Harvey Blanch). In return, the investing companies are entitled to licenses to exploit any patents resulting from the research.

The center is the unique feature in this arrangement, in part because its only relation to Engenics, a for-profit corporation, is that it is a stockholder. All patents are held by the universities, and licenses will be granted to Engenics and the participating corporations at commercial rates. Additionally, the center's governing board of trustees will have no affiliation with Engenics or with the six participating companies (Pramik 1982:22). Professor Robertson, a consultant for and prime mover behind the company, has said, "A great deal of care has been taken to maintain this separation [between the center and Engenics] not only to protect the intellectual sanctity of the situation but to ensure that the Center can operate free from external pressures" (Pramik 1982:22). The nonprofit center is committed to reinvesting any dividends or capital gains into more biotechnological research.

Donald Kennedy, the president of Stanford University, echoed a familiar refrain of university administrators regarding the novelty of the "experiment" in new relations when he said, "I believe that this novel approach [Engenics] to the funding of research and technology can set a pattern for long-term support for university research which can contribute significantly to meeting future needs" (*San Francisco Examiner* 1981:C1). The UCB chancellor, Michael Heyman, also expressed his approval: "We enthusiastically endorse this promising experiment in a new form of university–industry relationships. We will follow this exciting development closely to assure that it brings the greatest advantage both to the universities and to the supporting companies" (*San Francisco Examiner* 1981:C1). Whether or not this model will prove to be generalizable remains to be seen, but, like the Cornell Biotechnology Institute, Engenics brings together a group of noncompeting companies that are relatively weak in biotechnology (interestingly, General Foods has joined both the Engenics and Cornell experiments). None of the companies makes a large investment, yet each gets the benefit of a substantial aggregate investment.

That the participating companies are not direct competitors makes cooperation more feasible. However, an important obstacle to the creation of more of these consortia within the top universities is the limited number of professors who have not already established relationships with various companies. The welter of existing contracts between departments and companies further limits the possibilities for creation of centers and institutes, since these existing contracts may preclude equal access to research results by companies participating in the biotechnology institute. On the other hand, it is definitely true that the center concept is sweeping American universities as state after state develops plans to spur economic development on the basis of the expertise residing in its universities. University administrators see this "economic development" fad as a method for boosting their flagging cash inflows.

Single Funder Institutes

The creation of health research institutes by single funders has a long tradition. The two most noteworthy examples are the Rockefeller Institute for Medical Research, founded in 1901, and the Carnegie Institution of Washington, founded in 1907. In recent years enormous sums of private monies have been funneled into biomedical research, especially through charities such as the American Cancer Society. Further, private philanthropists have contributed significant funds in the attempt to "cure" cancer. For example, the Howard Hughes Medical Institute, which supports research at medical centers at more than fifteen universities, contributed $8 million to build a molecular genetics research unit at the University of Michigan (*Chemical and Engineering News* 1984:21). In 1985 the Hughes Medical Institute sold its shares in Hughes Aircraft to General Motors for a figure in excess of $5 billion, thereby becoming the largest foundation in the world. Another example is the Interferon Foundation, founded in 1977 by two Texas oilmen, Leon Davis and Roy Huffington. By 1982 the foundation had solicited $9 million, the bulk of which was donated by the oil industry (Adelman 1982a:18).

The most important biological research institute created in the last fifty years is the recently formed Whitehead Institute (WI). The WI grant is worthy of further examination for two reasons. First, the WI grant is the largest gift that has been made for medical research since the Carnegie and Rockefeller grants. Second, a number of the important issues regarding university–corporate relationships—such as outside influence on the research agenda and on professorial appointments, access to research resources, and the ownership of patents—were raised in faculty debates. MIT has considerably closer relations with industry than most universities. For example, MIT's Advanced Engineering Design course produces items for industrial clients (Di Iorio 1981:3), and the Sloan Automotive Laboratory was formed by an industrial consortium of five companies (*Tech Talk* 1982b:1,7). The importance of the proposed WI was that it brought into stark relief the boundaries of what could and could not be purchased from MIT. Other examples of MIT's close liaison with industry include large contracts between MIT and Exxon, between MIT and W. R. Grace, and contracts between a microelectronics industry consortium and the department of electrical engineering.

The decision of the MIT Corporation to accept the Whitehead offer was the result of prolonged negotiation among a number of parties. The dramatis personae were multimillionaire Edwin Whitehead, the founder of Technicon Corporation, a supplier of precision instruments to clinical laboratories;[6] David Baltimore, Nobel Laureate, an American Cancer Society Professor of Microbiology, director of the MIT Center for Cancer Research, a founder and large stockholder in Collaborative Research, a then member of the Recombinant DNA Advisory Committee, and soon to be director of WI; and the MIT administration, especially President Gray and Provost Low. The other participants in this debate were a number of faculty members who believed that the affiliation would be contrary to the interests of the university. This group included a very conservative member of the biology department (Sheldon Penman) and the most liberal member (Jonathan King) (Hanson 1983:25).

6. In May 1980 Technicon was sold to Revlon for $400 million, making Whitehead the largest shareholder in Revlon (Norman 1981a:416). Revlon is also making investments in biotechnology.

Whitehead had been approaching universities regarding the founding of an institute since 1973, and in 1974 had begun negotiations with Duke University. The negotiations were aborted after three years because Whitehead apparently demanded too much control over the workings of the proposed research facility (Knox and Cook 1981:14) and because the constant fluctuation in the price of his Technicon stock shares made their value difficult to assess, thereby introducing an element of uncertainty into any gift (Norman 1981a:417). The turning point of Whitehead's search came when he made the acquaintance of David Baltimore through the president of Rockefeller University, Nobel Laureate Joshua Lederberg, a Whitehead consultant. Baltimore advised Whitehead regarding the structure of the proposed institute, especially emphasizing that "it should be affiliated with a major university" (Norman 1981a:417); he probably recommended MIT. Negotiations with MIT began in 1980, and the proposal was announced in spring 1981. On July 6, 1981, a letter generally describing the proposed MIT affiliation with WI was sent to the faculty to be discussed at a series of faculty meetings in September (Norman 1981b).[7] The important provisions of the proposal as submitted to the faculty are summarized in table 2.6.

The WI affiliation proposal unleashed debate that centered on the provisions permitting WI to appoint professors who would become full members of the biology department. In a letter signed by thirty-three faculty members and circulated in November to the entire faculty, Professors Buchanan of biology and French of physics wrote:

WI faculty would eventually constitute one-third of the membership of the Biology Department. Appointment to the WI would, in all likelihood, be initiated through its director. The Biology faculty as a whole would have the power to approve or disapprove individual appointments, but would have no control over the fact that a large number of faculty positions would be specifically committed to WI   (Buchanan and French 1981:1–2).

Thus, Whitehead essentially bought the right to appoint faculty. The important precedent set was not the creation of an institute, but rather the fact that nondepartmental bodies were permitted to choose faculty members subject to the approval of the biology department.

In effect, up to twenty members of the MIT biology department will be hired employees of the WI. The response to this objection has been the argument that WI would choose only the best scientists available, so the department would not be packed with incompetents (Dummer 1981). How-

7. MIT regulations do not require faculty approval, but President Gray and Provost Low were said to be reluctant to send the agreement to the MIT Corporation for approval without faculty assent.

Table 2.6. Summary of MIT–Whitehead Institute Affiliation Agreement

---

— MIT will receive $7.5 million endowment to support teaching and research in departments with joint professors. Whitehead will finance building and equipping a 130,000-square-foot research facility and will provide $5 million annually until 2003 and a bequest of $100 million upon his death.

— The board of directors includes three members designated by MIT; Whitehead's three children; three additional members chosen with the concurrence of both MIT and the institute and the director (Baltimore); and John Sawhill, former president of NYU; Herman Sokol, president of Bristol-Myers, Co.; Dr. Leonard Skeggs, a professor of biochemistry at Case Western Reserve University; and Dr. Lewis Thomas, chancellor of the Memorial Sloan-Kettering Cancer Research Center.

— The institute will have up to twenty joint faculty positions shared with MIT departments. These professors will have teaching responsibilities commensurate with current faculty and the institute will pay joint faculty salaries.

— The institute will own all inventions and other intellectual property created by personnel it funds. The institute's patent policies will be reasonably comparable with those of MIT.

— The affiliation agreement initially operates for ten years and renews automatically for five-year periods unless the other party is notified. If MIT terminates the agreement, it is responsible for salaries of all professors with joint appointments.

— An affiliation coordination agreement is created to mediate disputes.

— The institute has access to all MIT facilities normally available to MIT faculty and staff.

Sources: Hanson 1983; Noble 1983

ever, the "professional competence" of the scientists was not the concern of WI opponents; the major point of contention was rather the process of choosing new faculty, that is, will it be a collegial choice or an appointment from outside (French 1981:3)?

The fact that WI, and especially its director, David Baltimore, would have the right to choose faculty appointments was thought to be tantamount to setting the research agenda. Buchanan and French (1981:2) believe that "the unequal method of appointing new faculty could lead to a distortion in both the teaching and research programs of the Biology Department." Professor Malcolm Gefter, executive officer of the MIT biology department, in a letter circulated to all faculty members the day before the faculty vote on the WI affiliation proposal, argued:

The issue before us is whether or not we as a "university," an academic community, can afford to embrace the kind of support for the biological sciences proposed by Mr. Whitehead. . . . The selection of faculty members based upon their area of research only is not in the spirit of living in the university community. . . . our department participates in granting an MIT appointment to WI faculty, we expose ourselves to the requirement of supporting these faculty members that were never chosen by us with regard to the totality of their contributions to the academic community or for their overall "value" to the biology department. This is clearly spelled out in the agreement   (Gefter 1981:1–2).

Gefter makes two points: first, if MIT should decide to disaffiliate from WI in the future, the department will be forced to support the WI appointees. Second, and most important, the department would be packed with professors whose research agendas were chosen on the basis of their usefulness to WI's agenda and not to biology as a discipline. Despite the objections of some faculty members the WI affiliation proposal passed overwhelmingly with only an added proviso expressing concern over certain aspects of the affiliation (MIT Faculty Minutes 1982).[8]
    For the MIT administration WI appeared to be a simple way of quickly expanding the biology program. David Baltimore is quoted as saying, "It [WI] is a chance for MIT to grow at a time when federal financing for education is decreasing" (Cooper 1981:1). The enticement was increased funding and strength in a growing field of industrial interest. The threat was Baltimore's indication that he would leave if the institute did not go forward (Penman 1982; Noble 1982:144). MIT had to take him seriously because already in 1981 a number of top researchers had made career moves. For example, Howard Goodman had left UCSF for MGH and Philip Leder had left the National Cancer Institute for Harvard Medical School (HMS). One of the reasons Goodman departed was a $70 million grant he received from Hoechst Chemical to build his own genetics department. (This will be discussed in greater depth in the section on long-term contracts.) Nevertheless, it seems certain that the administration would have accepted WI without such threats.
    The WI is an opportunity for Baltimore to create his own research operation. Not surprisingly Baltimore had been accused of having ulterior motives that relate to his holdings in Collaborative Research, but he answers the accusation thus: "Before the public disclosure of my holdings, I had discussed any possible conflicts of interest with officials at MIT and with the Whitehead Institute Board, and had been advised that they saw no conflict. I must, however, make every effort to avoid any suggestion of conflict of interest and have pledged myself to do so" (Baltimore 1982:13). The first MIT–WI appointment was Gerald Fink, formerly of Cornell University and a consultant for Collaborative Research (Collaborative Research 1982:11). Though it is not true that all WI professors work for Collaborative, the reasons for appointments to WI will continue to be questionable. Baltimore is not, as portrayed in *Science*, a "man in the middle of the commotion" at MIT (Norman 1981a:417) but rather a prime creator of the commotion.
    MIT Provost Francis Low (*Tech Talk* 1981:1), in a letter to the faculty

8. The final WI affiliation agreement was never circulated to the faculty (Weiner 1984).

urging approval of WI, wrote: "I believe the arrangement that is being evolved between MIT and the Whitehead Institute is unique among universities in the United States. Our colleagues elsewhere will doubtless watch our experience with interest. I am pleased that we are taking a leading role in exploring this new kind of relationship intended to strengthen our effectiveness in teaching and research." Provost Low was correct in observing that WI was a new type of relationship, but its reproducibility is questionable, as few universities would be offered such a high price to buy faculty positions and few would be willing to sell so much.

Hanna Gray, president of the University of Chicago, opposed the MIT _WI affiliation, saying,

> It could compromise the traditional process of making faculty appointments within a university. . . . I am fundamentally very conservative about involvement of universities and corporations. I am very wary. One ought to bend over backward not to allow things to happen which, however well protected or well intentioned they may appear to be, nonetheless could lead away from some of the essential things universities have to guarantee   (Noble 1982:147).

The MIT–WI affiliation agreement in all likelihood is not precedent-setting, though certain of the provisions are unique. The affiliation opens questions regarding the rules under which the university operates. These new arrangements—or, as the administrators euphemistically term them, "experiments"—are also demonstrating that the formerly sacrosanct rights of faculty, such as the ability to hire their colleagues, are open to change. At MIT one traditional prerogative was eroded; at Cornell industry scientists joined academic departments. The university was adjusting to a new and closer relationship with sponsors and attempting to secure financial benefits from its new partner.

3. Long-Term

Research Contracts

Success will depend, in the end, on whether [the company] bought the right researchers, whether they can produce marketable products or techniques (*a Hoechst executive quoted by Sanger 1982:A18*).

The most striking arrangement in biotechnology is the large, long-term, one university/one corporation contract. As can be seen in table 3.1, these contracts have in three years resulted in more than $140 million being funneled to thirteen universities, medical schools, and independent research laboratories. An examination of all the major contracts reveals that only one was negotiated in a nonbiotechnology field—the one between Exxon and MIT for combustion engineering (though more recently Sohio has provided $2 million grants in nonbiology fields). However, industry is making major new penetrations in the computer industry.[1] The leadership of Harvard and MIT in signing these contracts has been crucial in legitimizing large university–industry contracts. But the assiduous work done by NSF, AAAS, and

---

1. IBM's gifts and major discounts to universities for personal computers and larger machines is a major effort to make students IBM-compatible.

Table 3.1. Summary of Large University–Industry Research Grants in Chronological Order*

Year	University	Company	Amount ($ million)	Duration (years)	Investigator	Area of research
1974	Harvard Medical School	Monsanto	23.5	12	M. Folkman B. Vallee	Cancer tumors
1980	MIT	Exxon	8.0	10	J. Longwell P. Sarofim	Combustion
1981	Massachusetts General Hospital	Hoechst	70.0	10	H. Goodman	Genetics
1981	Harvard Medical School	Du Pont	6.0	5	P. Leder	Genetics
1981	UC Davis	Allied	2.5	3	R. Valentine	Nitrogen fixation
1981	Scripps Clinic & Research Foundation	Johnson & Johnson	30.0	—	—	Synthetic vaccines
1981	Washington Univ.	Mallinkrodt	3.8	5	J. Davie	Hybridomas
1981	Yale	Celanese	1.1	3	N. Ornston	Enzymes
1982	Johns Hopkins	Johnson & Johnson	1.0	—	—	Biology
1982	Rockefeller Univ.	Monsanto	4.0	5	N. Chua	Photosynthesis
1982	Washington Univ.	Monsanto	23.5	5	—	Biomedical
1982	MIT	W. R. Grace	8.0	5	P. Thilly	Amino acids
1982	Yale	Bristol-Myers	3.0	5	—	Anticancer drugs
1982	Cold Spring Harbor	Exxon	7.5	5	—	Molecular genetics
1983	Rochester	Kodak	0.45	—	—	DNA
1983	Medical Univ. South Carolina	Chugai	0.5	3	A. Strelkauskas	Monoclonal antibodies
1983	Univ. of Illinois	Sohio	2.0	5	—	Plant molecular genetics
1983	Columbia	Bristol-Myers	2.3	6	A. Efstratiadis	Gene structure

All years a number of large grants by Agrigenetics to various researchers at a number of universities

Source: Author's compilation
* I have made an attempt to be exhaustive, but because of the secretive nature of many universities these data are tentative and incomplete

corporate science organizations to legitimate new relationships should not be underestimated. With the exception of the University of California, Davis (UCD), and the recent contract between Sohio and the University of Illinois, all of the major corporate grants have gone to private universities and research institutes. It is doubtful that this can be ascribed merely to the superior research facilities and faculty members at the private schools. It is probably due at least partially to the closer ties that private universities have with wealthy individuals through their trustees and corporation members. Conversely, the public nature of state-supported institutions makes them somewhat more accountable and therefore less easily purchased (see, for example, California Rural Legal Assistance 1981).

In the earlier cases the corporation directed the grant to specific investigators (see table 3.1), but in some of the later grants internal review boards consisting of university members and corporate employees were organized to select the projects to be funded. The university administration serves as an intermediary and legitimater of the relationships. For the professors these arrangements are an opportunity to increase their research budgets and be relieved of the constant insecurity that is associated with peer review and grantsmanship. The security provides them the opportunity to concentrate on research. Finally, the monies facilitate the building of greater empires and, of course, the winning of prestigious prizes.

The funding corporation purchases the research skills not only of the principal investigator but of the entire laboratory, thus securing access to captive labor power as well as research results. These workers (postdoctoral researchers) are in a weak position, untenured and badly paid, and therefore are easily channeled into a particular company. This practice assumes added importance as increasing numbers of the large petrochemical companies assemble internal biotechnology research staffs. Recruitment is not simply a process of placing an advertisement in *Science*; the best students are invariably hired through "old boy" networks. The professors (as thesis chairmen) are crucial links in this process. Furthermore, if a company is strongly connected with an important professor it may learn through him of the activities of other scientists and, by implication, of the activities of their industrial sponsors.

The frenzy of investment in the 1981–82 period was motivated partly by the feeling among corporate executives that since their competitors had invested they should also. The contract that Du Pont signed with HMS for $6 million in 1981 appears to have been a riposte to Monsanto's contract of 1974 and to Hoechst's contract of earlier that year (see table 3.1). Obviously, in each agreement there are unique factors, but just as obviously there is a pattern to these agreements.

Harvard Medical School and Monsanto

The 1974 HMS–Monsanto agreement, the outcome of prolonged negotiation, was described in *Science* as "an agreement that is unprecedented in the annals of academic business affairs" (Culliton 1977:759). The size of the grant ($23 million) and its duration (twelve years) make it an unusual investment for a corporation more accustomed to short-term, focused research. According to Monte Throdahl, then group vice-president for technology at Monsanto,

> when the company thought about establishing a major biological research branch of its own, it discovered that biochemistry is the province of the universities, and not many biochemists were interested in coming to industry. We realized we couldn't build a biology department by hiring people away from the medical schools, so we thought about collaboration   (Culliton 1977:760).

Simultaneously, Derek Bok, the president of Harvard University, was advocating increased cooperation between the university and industry, and this agreement translated that advocacy into reality.

This first large grant went largely unnoticed until the *Boston Globe* published a report on the arrangement in 1976. Only two researchers, M. Judah Folkman and Bert Vallee, both HMS professors, receive funds from this contract. Vallee had been a Monsanto consultant for years and was one of the professors in the 1970s with whom the company discussed its increasing interest in biology (Culliton 1977:760). The primary objective of the funded research is to discover a theorized substance, a tumor angiogenesis factor, which it was believed controlled the provision of blood to growing cancers.

The contract provided $200,000 per year for each professor's laboratory, a $12 million endowment to be used to support persons affiliated with the Folkman–Vallee research, and money for equipping one floor of a new HMS building and construction of industrial facilities to supply biological research materials (Culliton 1977:763). In return, Monsanto was given the right to secure an exclusive worldwide license for all inventions or discoveries made in connection with the project agreement (Harvard University 1976:9). The university did retain the right to require Monsanto to license any inventions to others if it does not proceed to commercialization in a "stated period of time," which remains secret (Harvard University 1976:10).

This pioneering agreement transformed a number of previously standard practices. First, it led to a reevaluation of Harvard's policy that no therapeutic or health agents could be patented except for dedication to the public (Culliton 1977:761). The reception of a large corporate endowment was sufficient to change this policy, and a new patent policy document was issued on November 3, 1975 (Harvard University 1975). The new policy provided more flexibility in the granting of licenses in exchange for remuneration.

Second, the Monsanto funds were not allocated through the peer review process. In Culliton's (1977:761) words, "The time-honored system of peer review on which researchers rely so mightily was not called into play," although it may be questioned whether professors actually care if the peer review process, with its endless forms and proposals, is abandoned. The Monsanto grant did not prevent Folkman from receiving NIH funds of $135,000 in 1977, $144,000 in 1978, and $155,000 in 1979 to continue his tumor angiogenesis factor studies (Culliton 1977:761). The advantages cited by professors of industrial funding are its long-term character based on short proposals and rapid decisions. Corporate executives can ill afford to spend excessive time on relatively unimportant matters, and neither can prominent professors.

Many observers have been concerned about the possibility that corporate funding of research may lead to control of the research agenda. Monte Throdahl, the Monsanto vice-president who conducted negotiations in 1974, is quoted in the *Harvard Crimson* as saying, "We don't want to direct their [Folkman and Vallee] research. . . . We're not competent to judge—we were very impressed by the work going on there, and we decided to give them the grant" (Slack 1981:3). Joyce Brinton, then assistant to the dean for finance and business at HMS, "flatly denies that the corporate money in any way interferes with the researchers or the University as a whole. 'The research is very clearly under the direction of the researchers. Harvard is very jealous of its academic freedom. This is something that the University regards as sacred' " (Slack 1981:3). The concern about corporate control of the research agenda has largely replaced the concern regarding the peer review system. Critics who are worried about outside influence on the research agenda focus on the individual and his project—not recognizing that the act of funding itself creates the agenda. One need not ask or force an investigator to do specific research—one need only fund the proper scientist to do what he wants to do. This method of managing science was pioneered by the Rockefeller Foundation, as we saw in chapter 1.

The Harvard–Monsanto agreement was the first of a new type of corporate–university relation in which large sums were directed to specific researchers who continued their work while remaining at the university. After ten years of research tumor angiogenesis factor was finally isolated, and the gene coding for its production was cloned (Marx 1985:161); additionally, a researcher in Folkman's laboratory discovered a bone powder that the firm Collagen (of which Monsanto owns 30 percent) will commercialize (Slack 1981:3). The bone powder is a prime example of the emergent characteristics of research serendipity—a quality that the university environment seems particularly suited to nurturing. These serendipitous outcomes are the discoveries that industry is seeking. Monsanto needs Folkman and Vallee's expertise (and that of the workers in their laboratories): they are purchasing their imaginations. Monsanto does not want these professors to do what the corporation wants but rather to show the corporation what is possible. So Monsanto agrees with its critics; Monsanto does not seek to influence the research process, but rather to benefit from its results. Similarly, publications are delayed only if there is a market reason; otherwise it is important to Monsanto to keep these researchers in the information flow of the university by permitting them to publish and to garner academic recognition. Monsanto understands this.

For five years the Harvard–Monsanto agreement stood alone, unimitated. But during that time an entirely new industry, genetic engineering, was in the process of forming. The 1974–75 economic crisis during which the Harvard–Monsanto agreement was signed was rather mild. In the next economic crisis the social and political environment and emphasis on innovation and privatization were more pronounced, and more corporations scrambled to tap the scientific capabilities of the university. The HMS-Monsanto agreement, an oddity when it was entered into, was in fact a harbinger.

MIT and Exxon

In 1980 MIT and Exxon signed a ten-year, approximately $8 million research agreement to study combustion engineering. The research agreement was proposed by an Exxon vice-president of corporate research to Malcolm Weiss, deputy director of the MIT Energy Laboratory and former Exxon employee. Additionally, of the principal investigators, John Longwell was also a former Exxon employee (MIT News Office 1980:2). Under the terms of this agreement Exxon chooses the projects it wishes to fund from proposals submitted by faculty. The execution of the agreement is managed by a committee of two MIT professors, Longwell and Adel Sarofim, and two Exxon representatives (Pake 1981:47). MIT included in the agreement a stipulation that 20 percent of the research funds were to be allocated at the sole discretion of Longwell and Sarofim for combustion engineering research (Pake 1977:47; MIT n.d.:2).

The matter of publications is important because U.S. law allows patenting of inventions for only one year after first publication, and in many European countries mere publication invalidates all patent rights (appendix 2). This problem and the fact that publications are the "currency" of academia create a tension between the urge to be the first to publish and the need to delay for patent filing. The MIT–Exxon agreement provides for a ninety-day delay for patent filing, and there are clauses that control the presentation of findings at professional meetings (MIT n.d.:3). This agreement, like the earlier Harvard– Monsanto one, recognizes that the research process is near enough to applications and commodification to warrant the negotiation of favorable patent positions. Companies fund universities to enhance their competitive position, and this requires a re-channeling of information flow into the commercial patenting process. The MIT agreement expressly envisions the participation of a "large group of students [and] post-doctoral fellows" (Pake 1981:47). As in the earlier agreement not only the principal investigators but also their entire research groups are involved. MIT is providing access to the groups it is charged with educating, and the professors have very direct interests in promoting certain research topics. The effects of this shaping of the educational agenda are unclear. Is a student who is completely integrated into one narrow field (partially chosen by private sources) prepared for a future in which science and technology will experience continual revolutions?

Massachusetts General Hospital (MGH) and Hoechst, A.G.

The two earlier large, long-term contracts (Harvard Medical School–Monsanto and MIT–Exxon) were not in genetic engineering, but they proved to be models for university–corporate relations. The first major biotechnology contract was signed between MGH, the primary teaching and research hospital for the HMS, and Hoechst of Germany, one of the world's largest chemical companies, on May 20, 1981. The grant disbursements will total approximately $70 million over ten years. The size of the agreement and the fact that one month later HMS accepted $6 million from Du Pont indicate the acceptability of these arrangements. Hoechst's contract was awarded to secure the services of a single person—Howard Goodman and his laboratory.

Goodman's potential for producing commercial products was proven. In 1977, while at UCSF, "Goodman, collaborating with William Rutter, was the first to announce the cloning of insulin genes" (Culliton 1982b:1200). Subsequently, he cloned growth hormone and Australia antigen, a surface protein of the hepatitis B virus (Culliton 1982b:1200). Howard Goodman's research successes were precisely in the areas where products were closest to being produced commercially. For example, Eli Lilly commenced sales of bacterially produced human insulin—the first product of genetic engineering—in October 1982 (Patterson 1983:50). Test kits using monoclonal antibodies that key on a hepatitis B surface antigen are also already being marketed (*Wall Street Journal* 1983c:17), and growth hormones for humans, cows, swine, and chickens are close to marketability (Chase 1983:14). Howard Goodman has a particular ability to choose experiments that will have commercial applications, and a professor with this skill is valuable to any company. Obviously Hoechst will not want to pressure him to change his research agenda.

Goodman's insulin work in 1977 "brought the attention of Hoechst scientists, with whom he began to consult" (Culliton 1982b:1200). In 1980 Goodman approached Hoechst to fund a molecular biology center at UCSF. However, the large UCSF bureaucracy was slow and unwieldy, and so when MGH offered Goodman a position he accepted—and with Goodman came Hoechst (Culliton 1982b:1200). Goodman's move and Baltimore's threatened move from MIT if the WI was not approved indicate the power of research entrepreneurs. University administrators are faced with a dilemma: if they object to a potential arrangement, the professor may simply move to another university; if they accept it they resemble a minister who is merely asked to bless a marriage in return for a certain fee.

Ronald Lamont-Havers, MGH director of research (1981:90), describes the situation in which researchers and administrators find themselves:

> I can assure you, sir, that in institutions such as our own where scientists are all on soft money, they have to raise their own money. The jeopardy their careers and the people who work for them is in at the present time with regard to Federal funding (this includes the jobs of administrators) has put a great deal of strain on them. And so therefore they were as anxious [sic]. Thus a [sic] matter of fact, the pressure for us to get involved with industry came out of our scientific community not out of the administration.

The long-term agreement protects the research entrepreneur from the constant worries regarding funding and makes longer-term projects possible without the constant fear of funding loss. Under the current uncertain conditions regarding federal funding, Hoechst's offer would have been irresistible for most researchers and institutions.

The MGH–Hoechst arrangement is the only contract that has been released to the public. The contract disclosure came about under threat of subpoena by the congressional Committee on Science and Technology, which was worried by the fact that a German company was purchasing exclusive access to taxpayer-funded research. Congressman Gore, a central figure in recent hearings regarding the commercialization of biotechnology, expressed the committee's concern succinctly while questioning an MGH representative: "Now, isn't it a little unfair to the American taxpayers after this 20-year investment that's ongoing at the rate of $25 to $26 million a year, to give the cream of the results to a foreign company that gets exclusive rights" (U.S. Congress 1981:91). The fact that Hoechst was not a U.S. company made the proposal to subpoena the contract acceptable.

The MGH–Hoechst agreement commits the company to spend $3.6 million in 1982 and 1983 for research and $6 million per year in 1984–90 for research, or a total of $49.2 million. Additionally, Hoechst pledged $15 million "toward the construction of about 4 floors in the planned new Wellman Research Building at MGH" (Knox 1981:22). The contract stip-

Table 3.2. Benefits to Hoechst of the MGH–Hoechst Agreement

— Hoechst has the right of first refusal for funding all projects in the department.

— All scientists will be regular members of the MGH staff and nominated for faculty membership at Harvard Medical School.

— Scientists will devote their time primarily to research.

— Scientists can consult only for nonprofit organizations and only insofar as consulting does not interfere with Hoechst-sponsored research.

— All consulting with other companies must be cleared by Hoechst.

— The department will once a year hold a two- or three-day symposium for Hoechst employees.

— Hoechst has the right to have four of its scientists in the department at any one time.

— Any collaboration outside the department must guarantee Hoechst at least a nonexclusive license.

— All manuscripts must be submitted to Hoechst thirty days before submission to a journal.

— Hoechst receives exclusive licenses for all commercially exploitable discoveries.

— In 1990 the agreement is renewable for further five-year increments.

— Goodman must report research progress to Hoechst representatives at least three times a year.

— Hoechst will have access to the postdoctoral and graduate researchers in Goodman's laboratory and in the hospital in general.

Source: Massachusetts General Hospital 1981

ulates that all equipment and furniture be purchased with grant monies (Culliton 1982b:1202). The contract is written to minimize the objections that Congressman Gore and others raised concerning the commingling of federal and private funds (Lamont-Havers 1981). In fact a General Accounting Office (1982) team found no commingling of funds. Hoechst has created a department at MGH that is financially independent of MGH and also of the controls that are linked to federal grant monies.

Hoechst has purchased more than a "window on the technology." The benefits to the company are listed in table 3.2. Hoechst has acquired not only the rights to discoveries but also permission to have up to four company scientists in the department at any one time. During the course of the agreement Hoechst will be able to build a cadre of researchers trained in a first-rate laboratory in state-of-the-art genetic engineering techniques. However, there is a danger that university researchers will become more employee-like. Burke Zimmerman, ex-assistant to the president of Cetus, has charged with some hyperbole that "essentially, everyone in that lab is an indentured servant to Hoechst" (quoted in Sanger 1982:A18).

From MGH Hoechst purchased more than merely exclusive licenses. The newly formed department's scientists are required to devote the preponderance of their time to research—that is, Hoechst's research. Also,

Hoechst's scientists will be allowed access to all research as if the MGH scientists were workers and the Hoechst personnel were management.

The power that this agreement gives Hoechst is most evident in the case of Dr. Brian Seed, a newly appointed department member who has a consulting relationship with Genetics Institute, a Boston-based biotechnology company. MGH has retained a law firm to negotiate a relationship with Genetics Institute that protects Hoechst's investment. The MGH lawyers are demanding that Seed be allowed to pass any information he acquires working for Genetics Institute to Hoechst, in exchange for his passing information gathered in the department the other way (Budiansky 1982b:383). Will this information be "passed" to the public? This incident demonstrates that despite the repeated assurances that the MGH–Hoechst linkage would not restrict information flow (Lamont-Havers 1981:92), information flow has been restricted (*Harvard Gazette* 1981a:1).

Whether the agreement "represents a new model for a cooperative venture between private industry and a nonprofit institution," as Charles Sanders, the then general director of MGH (now executive vice-president for Squibb and Co.), was paraphrased by the *Harvard Gazette* (1981a:1) as saying, remains an open question. The restrictions that accompany the agreement in some ways reduce the department to an appendage of Hoechst's research. For the MNCs the key is to ensure exclusive access to the creative workers in the university. Hoechst wrote an elaborate contract to ensure its total control of the department's funding and exclusive access to the information produced. This contract ensures that only Hoechst will secure these scientists' products.

Harvard Medical School and Du Pont

One month after the MGH–Hoechst agreement was reached, HMS signed a $6 million, five-year contract with Du Pont to fund the formation of a genetics department. In this case Harvard had lured a top NIH molecular biologist, Philip Leder, and Du Pont provided him with a grant. Under the terms of the agreement, Du Pont will receive an exclusive, worldwide license to products or patents resulting from the research. Leder is expected to continue his research on the "mechanism by which genes direct the assembly of two essential types of protein: globin, the protein in hemoglobin . . . and [the proteins that make] antibodies" (*Harvard Gazette* 1981b:1). Under this arrangement it is again doubtful that the research will be compromised. Leder's work is already in commercially very lucrative areas: antibodies and protein synthesis (Barrett 1981:6), both of which are areas in which Du Pont has had great interest. The point of view of most of the people involved in these arrangements is best expressed by Joshua Lederberg, Nobel Laureate in biology and president of Rockefeller University, who has said regarding a large Monsanto–Rockefeller University contract that there are no conflicts because the research is funded "where the sponsor's goals converge with the university's independent priorities" (*GEN* 1982c:29). Du Pont knew the research agenda and chose to support it. Another argument regarding control of the research agenda is the fact that these scientists are specialists; they cannot simply change research to areas that hold more interest for a company. The funding is extended because of their expertise at what they are doing. Regardless, few company scientists are competent to direct scientists such as Leder or Goodman.

With these three contracts the Massachusetts pole of the biotechnology industry set a pattern of the university selling its expertise to large MNCs. On the West Coast these university contracts are not prevalent, and the method of commercialization has been for professors to start firms in partnership with venture capital. A number of professors from East Coast universities have formed companies—for example, David Baltimore (MIT), Walter Gilbert (Harvard), Mark Ptashne (Harvard), and Philip Sharp (MIT). The large contracts have been very important to the large corporations because of their inability to convince top researchers to join their companies (A. Brown 1982:11; Harsanyi 1981:117). Harvard's example of signing three large contracts quickly spread to other universities on the East Coast and to Washington University in St. Louis.

University of California, Davis, and Allied Corporation

The UCD–Allied contract was the only important long-term contract promulgated on the West Coast except for the Scripps Clinic–Johnson and Johnson agreement and the Scripps Clinic–Pittsburgh Plate Glass Co. (PPG) contract. The turmoil that accompanied the UCD contract makes it highly unlikely that the UC system will negotiate another. The contract particulars were that it was to run for five years, provide a total of $2.5 million, making it "aproximately equal to the average annual receipt of all other private gifts and grants made in support of U.C. agricultural research" (Meyerhoff et al. 1981:2). The research areas were improving plant productivity and plant energy and nutrient use efficiency (Hess 1982:65). The principal investigator was Ray Valentine, a UCD professor of biochemisty and member of the experiment station staff. The research project for biological nitrogen fixation had been funded for five years at $3.9 million by NSF, but by 1980 "it was clear that support for research in this area by the foundation was being cut back" (Hess 1982:69). Valentine established contact with Allied, and after negotiations with UCD signed a contract in June 1981, giving Allied an exclusive, royalty-bearing license to any patents and publication delays of up to thirty days (Hess 1982:65), provisions that are standard in most contracts that have been signed.

This apparently standard contract was upset by a number of factors internal and external to the university. UCD has been under attack for many years for conducting research for agribusiness rather than for small farmers, farmworkers, and consumers (Friedland and Barton 1976; California Rural Legal Assistance [CRLA] 1981). The political pressure on UCD was intense because its engineers have been instrumental in developing labor-displacing machines while receiving funding from growers' groups (Friedland and Barton 1976). This climate of controversy at UCD has created an awareness of "conflicts of interest" and the dangers of corporate control of research.

Shortly after securing the Allied Corporation grant for UCD, Ray Valentine founded and became vice-president of a small agricultural biotechnology firm, Calgene. Then, one week after UCD secured the Allied Corporation grant, Allied purchased 20 percent of Calgene's stock for $2 million.[2] In an action independent of the Valentine–UCD contract, CRLA had filed a comment before the California Fair Political Practices Commission asking that California's employee disclosure laws be applied to university professors. The Calgene affair became a salient example of what the CRLA considered a conflict of interest. At this point a public relations debacle was looming, so Charles Hess, the dean of Agriculture and Environmental Sciences, had to act. As Hess describes his actions,

> I offered Professor Valentine three options. One, was to disassociate himself from Calgene. Two, was not to be on the Allied contract. And three, was to not be a member of the Agricultural Experiment Station, and become a regular 9-month faculty member. . . . Ray chose not to be on the contract. I notified Allied that we would not be able to do research under Ray's portion of the contract. That was a million dollar decision essentially—of the $2.5 million contract, $1 million would have supported Ray's research   (Hess 1982:66).

Valentine also resigned as Calgene's vice-president and became a director at Calgene.

Along with Valentine's apparent conflict of interest came repeated charges that Valentine was exploiting students (Manning 1981; Boly 1982b). So serious were the accusations that the graduate advisor for microbiology, JaRue Manning (1981), advised that "Professor Valentine not be allowed to accept any graduate students in the Graduate Group in Microbiology." Another professor, Emanuel Epstein, in a memorandum to Dean Hess (Meyerhoff 1982b:56–57) lamented that already at UCD there was a restriction of information flow. UCD was unique in the seriousness of campus debate that followed and the fact that there was sig-

---

2. In February 1984 Allied canceled its research contract with Calgene and began the process of liquidating its equity interest in Calgene (*Journal of Commerce* 1984:22B).

Table 3.3. Various Provisions of the Washington University–Monsanto Agreement

---

— The agreement provides WU with $23.5 million over five years.

— The agreement is at the institutional level, that is, not on the basis of individual investigators.

— All funding will be approved by an internal peer review system consisting of four Monsanto employees and four WU School of Medicine faculty.

— In the third year of agreement and every two years thereafter an outside peer review team will evaluate the scientific merit of the funded research.

— 30 percent of the funds are allocated to basic research, 70 percent to more "applied" research; all product development will be done by Monsanto.

— Monsanto scientists and technicians will "spend time in University laboratories" learning new techniques and collecting information (Kipnis 1982:18).

— All patents vest in WU with exclusive rights to Monsanto.

— Thirty-day delay of publications for patent purposes.

— The program director must be approved by the company—if he is not acceptable Monsanto can immediately suspend all funds, and if an acceptable director is not found in six months then the contract is considered breached (Kipnis 1982; Schneiderman 1982).

— WU researchers have access to Monsanto's tissue culture facilities.

Sources: Various publications

nificant success in ameliorating some of the abuses. CRLA's success in its petition to require fuller disclosure of faculty financial positions has ensured greater awareness of nonacademic influences on university research at UCD.

Washington University and Monsanto

If we wanted to build up our research staff in-house we would have to hire people that would lead us to concepts superior to our competitors. Washington U.'s medical school is an intellectual resource we couldn't hire. It is almost impossible to recruit senior faculty members   *(Dr. Thomas Lewis, the Monsanto director of corporate research, quoted in A. Brown 1982:11).*

In the HMS–Monsanto and MIT–Exxon agreements rights to the research of individual investigators were purchased, and in the MGH–Hoechst and HMS–Du Pont agreements rights to the research of new departments were purchased. The WU–Monsanto contract provided for access to the entire School of Medicine. Important aspects of the contract are summarized in table 3.3. The large size of the contract ($23.5 million) and its comparatively short duration (five years) are noteworthy. Though definitions such as "basic" and "applied" are tenuous, this agreement is aimed toward commodity development. The product development aspect of this agreement is repeatedly emphasized in testimony by David Kipnis, Busch Professor and chairman of the internal medicine department at WU: "This agreement combines these [Monsanto's and WU's] joint resources at an institutional level and should facilitate not only the acquisition of new fundamental knowledge but *also its useful application for the public benefit*" [emphasis added] (Kipnis 1982:16). Later in the same testimony the point is reiterated: "70 per cent [of Monsanto funding] will go toward support of 'specialty' projects for which there is significant public need [a market] and *potential commercial* utility in terms of technology and/or products" [emphasis added] (Kipnis 1982:18).

Monsanto's senior vice-president for research and development, Howard Schneiderman (1982:21), speaking at the same hearings, was even more forthright: "Through this collaboration we expect to discover novel products which address major human diseases and health conditions for which there is presently no cure and no adequate therapy. We view this aim as both socially responsible and commercially attractive." Later in the same testimony Schneiderman (1982:21) said, "Monsanto's association with Washington University . . . is a plan to enhance Monsanto's and America's technological competitiveness in world markets by tapping into the spectacular research skills of one of our great academic institutions." As the principals in this agreement have testified, the agreement is much more explicitly focused on product creation than are other agreements.

The WU–Monsanto agreement resembles the Hoechst agreement in many ways. First, it allows only Monsanto employees access to the university laboratories. It is fully expected that they will be intimately acquainted with ongoing research, thus having tremendous opportunities for the appropriation of graduate and postdoctoral students' ideas. This is vitally important because those ideas are the very same ones upon which an aspiring scholar would build a career. Similarly, all patents will be held by WU, but Monsanto will have an exclusive license—a publicly created research base is functioning as a support for corporate profitability.

The mechanism for selecting the research to be funded is a scientific advisory board consisting of department chairmen from the four participating departments and four top Monsanto science administrators. These eight board members review projects submitted in response to a request for proposals and decide which should receive funding. To ensure that this review process has maintained adequately high standards, in the third year of the agreement an outside panel is to be brought in to judge the adequacy of the research effort. An important concern of Monsanto is that as the WU scientists become insulated from the stimulus of the competitive grants system, there will be a lagging in the commercialization race—especially because competitors will be able to purchase access to research and services from professors at other universities and WU professors will be somewhat insulated from competition. The review panel is an insurance for Monsanto that it is continuing to receive state-of-the-art research.

As with MGH–Hoechst, the individual faculty members who apply for Monsanto research monies "must reveal to the university advisory committee all kinds of relationships, including research and consultantships, to assure that conflict is avoided" (Kipnis 1982:35). This contract guarantees to Monsanto that any professors working for it will have allegiance to Monsanto. It is forthrightly announced that "any financial gain to be derived from this collaborative effort will accrue not to individual investigators, but rather to the institution, to the cognizant department in the Medical School and to the specific laboratory responsible for the creative effort" (Kipnis 1982:18–19). This was perhaps the strongest response to that date from university administrators moving to control their faculty, that is, the labor power in genetic engineering. The reasons for their success in this effort include the dearth of venture capital in the St. Louis area and a strong lead from senior faculty members.

Recognition of WU's success in attracting corporate research funding is demonstrated by the fact that at the Pajaro Dunes Conference, organized by Stanford, the University of California, Caltech, MIT, and Harvard, WU was the only other university invited to send a representative. In addition to the Monsanto contract, WU has received $3.8 million from the Mallinkrodt Co. to conduct hybridoma and monoclonal antibody research. Mallinkrodt will have an option to secure a royalty-bearing, exclusive license for any products discovered. WU has thus successfully tapped the financial resources of these two St. Louis–based companies, Mallinkrodt and Monsanto.

Massachusetts Institute of Technology and W. R. Grace

The MIT–Grace contract is significant because it indicates the spread of these relationships from departments of molecular biology and medical schools to other departments such as food science and chemical engineering. Grace, which already was funding three projects in food sciences at MIT, made a corporate decision to become more involved in biotechnology. In pursuit of this goal Grace increased the scope of funding at MIT. The agreement provides between $6 and $8.5 million over five years to fund research "in such general areas as biological removal of toxic organic compounds from streams and soil, selective synthesis of specific peptides from individual amino acids, amino acid separation, and transamination of alpha keto acids to amino acids" (*Tech Talk* 1982c:4). As part of the agreement MIT can spend 20 percent of the grant at its sole discretion for microbiological research.

A committee of four company representatives and four MIT representatives solicits proposals campus-wide and decides upon their relative merits—much as in the WU–Monsanto agreement. There will be short prepublication delays to examine the manuscripts for patentable ideas. All patents vest in MIT, but Grace has as a minimum a royalty-free license and possibly an exclusive license (*Tech Talk* 1982c:4). However, Grace scientists do not have the right to work in university laboratories, and their control over the professors' other activities is limited. The Grace agreement is not exceptional except in that it targets the less glamorous areas of biotechnological research.

The Other Agreements

Table 3.1 demonstrates that in dollar terms 1980 was the most significant year for large agreements, with a total of $103.4 million being allocated to various universities and research institutions for biotechnological research. Omitted from the tables are the many smaller grants professors have received and the $120 million WI, which affiliated with MIT in 1981 (the money was not given to MIT). In 1982 $47 million were granted, but in 1983 only about $5 million has been reported (though the Sohio grants have added $2 million to biotechnology and another $8 million in other areas). The main reason for the slowdown is that many professors and institutions are already inextricably linked with a company. Only one large contract was signed in 1983, that between Columbia University and Bristol-Myers.

The other contracts involved less important universities that could not demand as large sums of money. Robert Rosenzweig (1982:107), then Stanford's vice-president for public affairs, in congressional testimony, stated,

> The general feeling among university people with regard to forming more arrangements with industry, and you asked specifically about the attitudes at Stanford. In both cases I think reality has begun to assert itself. . . . Very few people think that the very large highly publicized contracts are likely to be duplicated very widely or become any thing like the norm.

The period of most intense action appears to be over. However, as the 1985 Scripps Clinic and Research Foundation–PPG contract indicates, wherever opportunities arise long-term contracts will be signed.[3]

3. However, in January 1985 PPG Industries, Inc. (formerly Pittsburgh Plate Glass) announced that it had signed a $120 million, fifteen-year contract with Scripps Clinic and Research Foundation to do basic biotechnology research on pesticides. As part of this contract PPG will relocate its current biotechnology researchers from the Mellon Institute to Scripps Clinic in San Diego. Scripps will also hire approximately one hundred scientists and technicians. This effort is larger than any agricultural biotechnology effort in the U.S. agricultural universities (Scarr 1985:A1).

The only $5 million plus contracts not discussed here are the one between Scripps Clinic and Research Foundation and Johnson and Johnson for approximately $30 million to study artificial vaccines and the one between Exxon and Cold Spring Harbor Laboratory for $7.5 million. The Exxon–Cold Spring Harbor contract allows up to six Exxon scientists to be in residence at the laboratory at one time. The departments to receive the funding in the Scripps–Johnson and Johnson agreement are those of cellular and developmental immunology, immunopathology, and molecular immunology (Prescott 1981:8). The announcement of the agreement sparked a controversy as to whether Scripps researchers had abused scientific etiquette by not freely reciprocating in the exchange of information regarding a process for synthetic vaccine production. In this case the UCSD/Salk group published first, but the Scripps group was the first to file a patent application. The role of Johnson and Johnson in this situation is unclear, though they could materially benefit from this turn of events (Wade 1981).

Few unusual provisions occur in the remainder of the contracts, and exclusive licenses and publication delays of thirty to sixty days are the norm. Chugai Pharmaceutical's funding of A. Strelkauskas at the Medical University of South Carolina was one of the first large agreements between a Japanese company and an American university, although other Japanese companies have invested in research contracts with professors in American universities (*Chemical Week* 1983b:39). The few contracts that have been in effect seem to have operated with almost no disagreement between the parties, and in the case of the HMS–Monsanto arrangement two potential products have been discovered.

The institutional nature of each agreement raises questions regarding the benefit that accrues to the university from its linkage to the corporation. In most agreements, the university is unable to extract the normal overhead which is routine in smaller grants or government funding. For example, in the HMS–Monsanto agreement the school received an endowment of $12 million, the income of which is to be used for the duration of the agreement to fund work in Volkman's and Vallee's laboratories. This endowment at the end of the grant reverts to HMS's sole use (Culliton 1977:763), yet for twelve years Monsanto can use its proceeds. This amount is significantly less than that which accrues from the normal overhead charged on most university contracts with governmental agencies.

In the MGH–Hoechst agreement the company will contribute $15 million to the construction of a new medical building (Knox 1981:22), but in the other contracts there is no mention of overhead contributions—the overhead which permits facilities such as libraries, gymnasiums, and grounds, to name but a few, to be maintained. To meet operating costs the university administrations must turn to alumni, tuitions, and government grants. As Kahne (1982:70) has remarked, "More sophisticated funders of engineering research at universities (not the U.S. Government) are now specifying how funds are to be allocated, to avoid siphoning off by other parts of the university." The "sophisticated" investor, with the acquiescence of the administration, buys only what is economically valuable. These grants encourage the hypertrophy of one segment of the university while the other segments are allowed to atrophy. The long-term effects on the atmosphere of the university and quite possibly the creativity engendered in that atmosphere are unknown. The question of renewal is important because the universities have expanded to accommodate new researchers and enlarged laboratories. A decision by a company to terminate the contract would necessitate a radical shrinkage in the university's scientific labor force. This reality puts the company in an excellent bargaining position when the contract expires.

In most agreements administrators, though faced with a fait accompli, enjoy certain benefits. The relationships operate through controllable channels, and the patents generated could provide future royalties. Corporate funds allow larger research staffs, which can apply for more federal funding and thereby generate greater overhead. Also, many grants provide monies for graduate students—that is, tuition and money for computers and electron microscope time—and pay for maintenance. In each of these grants the equipment purchased for the laboratory reverts to the university (or researcher, depending upon the grant) when the project ends. Thus the administrators, though perhaps with misgivings, can anticipate financial benefits accruing from these arrangements.

The signing of these large, long-term contracts adds a new dimension to university–industry connections. There are reasons to wonder whether it is proper for the university to, in effect, lease laboratories and departments to industry. In none of the arrangements is a public interest in the evolution of this powerful new technology addressed. Both administrators and corporation executives assume that the traditional prerogatives and customs of the university, some of which date from the Middle Ages, can be sold to the highest bidder. Whether these long-term contracts will benefit the university and ultimately society cannot be answered.

4. Chaos and

Opportunity–The

Universities Respond

[We] are now seeing an entirely new pattern of affiliation among university researchers, universities, and high-technology industry. It takes a variety of forms: large grants from single firms to university laboratories, with commitments to exclusive licensing; an array of equity consulting agreements between individual faculty members and firms; still stronger linkages between faculty members and firms that involve the migration of entire programs of research into the proprietary sector, often with a level of supervision by the faculty member that approaches live management; active programs of technology licensing on the part of universities; and others *(Pajaro Dunes Biotechnology Conference prospectus 1981:3).*

The suddenness with which biotechnology became big business caught university administrators unawares, and relationships of many sorts blossomed between university and industry. Some institutions used traditional patent marketing entities such as the Research Corporation or new entities such as University Genetics to keep their interactions with industry indirect. And in fact Stanford University attempted to launch a patent pooling arrangement to decrease the costs to each university of having its own licensing operation and to facilitate corporate licensing. However, attempts at bringing order to the chaos of university marketing were doomed from the beginning.

Harvard made the ultimate bid to take advantage of the opportunities in biotechnology by attempting to launch its own genetic engineering start-up corporation. However, a storm of criticism convinced Harvard to back down, and the consensus was that the first-rank universities would not become directly involved in corporate ventures. This did not prevent second- or third-tier universities such as Michigan State from launching a for-profit company, but for most universities direct university participation in private industry was beyond the pale of acceptability.

Administrators attempted to get a handle on the wide variety of university–industry relations by convening the Pajaro Dunes Biotechnology Conference, but the conference ended with a statement of generalities on the values the university must protect. In the decentralized, competitive, U.S. university environment each university wants to retain maximum flexibility to solicit funds; general principles mean little. Given these conditions the process of industry purchasing university knowledge and expertise will not only go on unabated and uncontrolled, but will probably spread to other parts of the university.

Patent Marketing Entities, Profit and Nonprofit

Entities that secure and license patents for universities include the Research Corporation, University Patents, and the Wisconsin Alumni Research Foundation (WARF). These act as a buffer between the university and the corporation seeking to license a university invention. In many universities the cost of a patent office with its ancillary staff is not warranted because of the limited number of inventions. In these cases entities such as Research Corporation and University Patents can be useful, and both have become involved in licensing genetically engineered organisms and other biotechnology patents.

The Research Corporation has been in existence since 1912 as a nonprofit private foundation, both receiving and licensing inventions and disbursing grants with its "profits." In return for receiving the inventions an agreed-upon percentage of royalties received is returned by the Research Corporation to the university and the inventors (Research Corporation 1981:29). The corporation is already administering Roy Curtiss's invention of a weakened *E. coli* bacterium, an adapter molecule that is used for splicing DNA strands, and a number of other biotechnological inventions (Research Corporation 1981:25–26). Over the years the corporation has funded numerous biologists who have been important in the growth of biotechnology, including James Watson, Francis Crick, Marshall Nirenberg, Max Delbrück, and Severo Ochoa (*Foundation News* 1980:25).

University Patents was founded in 1974 and now holds exclusive license to inventions from ten major universities such as the universities of Chicago and Pennsylvania (*GEN* 1981a:9). Like the Research Corporation, University Patents returns royalties to the inventor and to the university. In 1982, University Patents spun off University Genetics (UGEN) as a profit-making subsidiary to concentrate on biotechnology. UGEN not only solicits finished inventions, but also provides funding. The awards are designed "to bring a project from the research stage to one where it is close to development for public utilization. This means that funding for one year only is available from UGEN. In certain special cases a second or more years of funding may be available from UGEN's industrial affiliate" (University Genetics n.d.:1). The role of UGEN is to find inventions in universities and then secure an industrial sponsor.

The request for proposals that UGEN circulated to universities stated that the evaluation of proposals was to be based not only on scientific merit. "In addition, the proposal [would] be evaluated by market analysts and investment counselors concerning the potential licensing of the technology" (University Genetics n.d.:3). The "Budget and Information Guidelines" describe very succinctly the academic price UGEN extracts: "Unless otherwise permitted by UGEN, the investigators will send to UGEN a synopsis of material to be presented orally at least one month prior to proposed lecture date, and publishable material at least three months prior to proposed publication, so that any novel material may be considered for protection" (University Genetics 1981:2). In cases in which a university accepts money from UGEN, it will be under strict constraints regarding communication with the scientific community.

WARF is a nonprofit foundation chartered in 1925 for the sole purpose of providing monies to the University of Wisconsin (Fred 1973). An important aspect of WARF's mission has been to act as the patent licensing arm of the university. WARF not only licenses certain biotechnology patents, but also has made a $3 million investment in Cetus Madison, a Cetus subsidiary headed by a University of Wisconsin professor, Winston Brill (Pramik 1983c:20).[1] In another arrangement WARF has sold an exclusive license to Advanced Genetic Sciences (1983:18) to commercialize an ice nucleation bacterium. The WARF model has received some attention as a possible mechanism for licensing biotechnology patents while separating the university from the day-to-day administration of the patents (Omenn 1981). But the model has not been adopted at many institutions and remains somewhat of an anomaly.

A proposal advanced by Stanford and UC was to form a University Licensing Pool for Biotechnology (ULAB) so as to pool the bulk of current university biotechnology patents and create a "one-stop shop." It was hoped that this would simplify the patent negotiations for companies that wished to secure a number of licenses. ULAB was envisioned as making the market for university patents more orderly (M. Edwards 1983) and thus helping to solve an important problem that Peter Farley of Cetus had mentioned as early as 1980 in congressional hearings (Farley 1980:26). The bulk of the funds collected by ULAB were to be returned to contributing

1. Cetus Corporation sold 51 percent of its interest in Cetus Madison for more than $60 million to W. R. Grace and Company (*Chemical Week* 1984).

universities (Pramik 1983d). Both Stanford and UC felt that some semblance of order would be beneficial to the chaotic marketing of university patents. Whether this had any relationship to the Pajaro Dunes Conference the year before can only be speculated.[2]

The research for the ULAB proposal was funded by Monsanto, Research Corporation, Abbott Laboratories, Eli Lilly, Schering-Plough, SmithKline Beckman, and Hoffmann-La Roche. Industry increasingly worries that the large number of patents being filed on the basis of university research could stifle corporate operations. Hugh d'Andrade, senior vice-president for Schering-Plough, is paraphrased in *Science* as saying, "Industry . . . is currently faced with two choices in the licensing of patents—negotiate individually with universities or we use the technique anyway, which constitutes infringement. Neither is acceptable. The pool proposal 'has its problems, but it's better than the two alternatives' " (Sun 1983a:1303). In a situation reminiscent of the patent controversies that engulfed the electric motor industry in its formative years in the 1890s, defensive patenting may result in a proliferation of patent infringement and litigation. Yet within two months of ULAB's introduction the proposal was already dead. According to Roger Ditzel (1983) of the UC patent office, industry's interest in the proposal was minimal, and the entire idea was shelved.

ULAB's advantages were that it would reduce the transaction costs of negotiating with many different universities that hold biotechnology patents. By being a central source of patented techniques, ULAB would promote prompt knowledge of the newest techniques. Finally, by returning funds to be spent on university research, ULAB would provide aid to educate future corporate employees and to produce more inventions. For universities ULAB could shift the emphasis from exclusive to nonexclusive licenses, thereby trying to shift corporate competition from research to scale-up and production. The editor of *Bio/Technology*, Christopher Edwards (1983), believes the ULAB proposal would have been of most value to institutions that do good scientific work but do not have good licensing administration, and that therefore ULAB would have been less useful for first-tier universities such as Stanford and Harvard. The point that Edwards misses is that ULAB is an effort to promote biotechnology as an industry by facilitating its growth and easing the current interuniversity competition.

Objections to the proposal were on two levels. First, the granting of nonexclusive licenses is likely to yield lower amounts of revenue for the university (C. Edwards 1983:217). The revenues returned would be further decreased by the share for ULAB's administrative overhead. Second, by

---

2. This speculation was denied by Stanford's Neil Reimers (1983). The concept of ULAB had also been mentioned even earlier by UC–Stanford patent attorney Bertram Rowland (1982).

committing universities to nonexclusive licenses, ULAB would remove the impetus to seek large, long-term corporate grants. For corporations the single most important disadvantage was that ULAB would prevent any company from deriving the benefits of exclusive licenses. The critical advantage of a patented technique, exclusivity, is lost, and with it the potential for reaping monopoly rents or large licensing royalties. The emphasis on proprietary molecules, etc., by American corporations indicates that they are interested in receiving monopoly returns and not in competing in the sphere of production.

The advantage to universities of patent licensing arrangements is eliminated by the need to hire an in-house patent staff. Much of Research Corporation's earnings are reinvested in noncommercial research, whereas UGEN is constituted to make a profit. It might be expected that other companies resembling UGEN will be formed to exploit various university inventions, and they could serve a useful function in providing a buffer between universities and corporations. But it seems unlikely that their importance will grow substantially because the major research universities are shifting to in-house patent administration. In all probability, WARF, ULAB, UGEN, and the Research Corporation will not have an important effect on the industry, and these models will not become generalized. On the other hand, it does seem possible that certain rules regarding licensing will become standardized, though the exact mechanism for creating such a consensus does not currently exist.

University-Sponsored Corporations

The most obvious method universities may employ to profit from research performed in their laboratories and also to retain professors is to form university–professor joint ventures. The attractions of forming a separate company are obvious—the university could profit from its professors' inventiveness, while the professors could be given an equity interest and consulting contracts—while remaining a professor. The potentially large profits from biotechnology startup companies have tempted more than one university administrator. The most important and sustained consideration of a university's active participation in a biotechnology firm occurred in 1980 at Harvard. In this particular case, Harvard considered launching a company in partnership with senior researcher Mark Ptashne.

University ownership of companies whose principals are professors had already been attempted by MIT in the mid 1970s. Among the reasons for the MIT program's failure and termination was the relatively limited leverage MIT received for the effort—without further investment capital, gains promised to be small. Also the appearance of conflicts of interest posed serious problems. Paul Gray (1981:53), the president of MIT, described a possible scenario if a university is a major backer of a startup company: "Typically you have a faculty member who is also involved as an equity holder, perhaps as a consultant, and a faculty member who is continuing, as well, to work on this project in his laboratory, must operate often with continued sponsorship from the same Federal agency." MIT discontinued its development corporation not only for ideological reasons, but also because it would have required increased investment.

Harvard's attempt to secure income from professorial research was intimately linked with the 1975 change in Harvard's patent policies that was motivated in part by the 1974 Monsanto–HMS agreement.[3] By 1977 Harvard had created a patent office whose mission was to increase faculty awareness of the importance of patenting (Atkinson 1982). Steve Atkinson, the patent officer at Harvard University, met with Mark Ptashne, who had developed new methods of engineering bacteria to express proteins, but found it difficult to convince Ptashne to patent his invention (Hilts 1982a:178–179) because Ptashne was interested in "pure" science, not in profitability. His attitude was at least partially a reaction to Walter Gilbert's forming of Biogen; Ptashne did not approve of Gilbert's activities. Nonetheless, Ptashne finally reluctantly filed for a patent. Ptashne's patent (assigned to Harvard) did not immediately attract corporate interest, but in April 1979 General Electric's venture capital subsidiary offered $500,000 for patent rights. But even as the GE offer was being made, a scheme to secure greater profits was being developed. Harvard would start a company in partnership with a number of venture capitalists to exploit Ptashne's work (VerMeulen 1982:48). The plan was that Harvard would supply the patents, professors, and facilities, and venture capitalists would supply money and marketing know-how (Solbrig 1982:4).

In June and July 1980 the administration began to sample the mood of the university regarding a joint venture. In private meetings the faculty was largely against the formation of a company, but the administration, eyeing the possibility of large capital gains, forged ahead. The crucial moment occurred when the administration circulated to all faculty members a discussion memorandum written by Daniel Steiner (1980), the general counsel to the university, entitled "Technology Transfer at Harvard University." The memorandum, though detailing the pros and cons of a possible joint venture, was essentially an endorsement. (The points raised in the memorandum are summarized in table 4.1.) Interestingly, what has been characterized as a debate was in reality more of a storm of protest from nearly every quarter (students, faculty, alumni, the press, and the society at large). The protests brought about the rapid demise of the plan.

What were the larger issues that were brought to the fore in this incident? Essentially, Harvard was broaching the question of whether a university

3. The best discussion of the internal conflicts at Harvard University regarding the proposal to start a Harvard biotechnology company is Snider (1981).

Table 4.1. Summary of "Technology Transfer at Harvard University"

Positive aspects of university–industry involvement

— University technology might help to revitalize the U.S. economy.

— The income generated could help support research which may come under increasing financial pressure due to possible federal cutbacks.

— Harvard faculty are entering into commercial arrangements and the university may be able to assist them.

— The licensing of patents and ownership of equity in new companies might secure substantial financial return.

— Harvard's participation in companies could be used to ensure that professors do not become too deeply involved in commercial activities.

— Harvard's involvement in the company could be used to discourage undue secrecy and outside control over the research agenda and to prevent the total separation of professors from the university.

Negative aspects of university involvement

— The potential of inequality of faculty access to university assistance.

— Official university involvement might encourage researchers to divert time and energy from academic pursuits.

— Even the appearance of conflicts of interests would harm the university and its image.

— Conflicts could arise regarding the allocation of space and resources due to the perception that commercially successful professors were favored.

— The improper use of Harvard's name could cause problems.

— A variety of ethical and public interest questions might arise.

Source: Steiner 1980

should embark upon profit-making ventures. The university has had a number of roles in society, but until the Harvard proposal universities had not considered commercial operations (with the exception of cases such as the MIT Development Corporation). Because of Harvard's role in setting examples (for example, the long-term university corporate contracts), the possibility of precipitating a chain reaction of university-sponsored corporations posed the definite possibility of universities beginning to compete directly with industry.

The *New York Times* (1980a) carried an article on October 27, 1980, discussing the formation of a Harvard-owned company. Derek Bok's picture was on the front page, and a picture of Walter Gilbert, a professor at Harvard and a principal in Biogen, was on the continuing page. This and other publicity convinced Harvard that the launching of a company was unwise. Though privately the decision not to proceed had been made on November 1, 1980, it was not released until November 17, 1980 (VerMeulen 1982). In the intervening days numerous editorials and articles appeared in the national press castigating Harvard's proposal to create a company. This is typified in the editorial that appeared in the *New York Times* (1980b:34) on November 13 entitled "Profit—and Losses—at Harvard." The editorial questioned the wisdom of Harvard (read any university) accepting an equity position in a startup company:

> But consider the risks [of forming a corporation] as well. Where would the search for commercial success end? Why shouldn't a university's law school establish a prosperous law firm, the business school a consulting company, the engineering school a construction company? Universities that seek a legitimate return from the ideas and inventions of their faculties must be careful not to lose their academic souls.

The *New York Times* was simply observing that the university's role is not to engage in commerce. Even the private universities that have steadily tried to reorganize on a more "businesslike" plane will receive tremendous resistance from other sectors of society if they attempt to become profit-making entities.

DeWitt Stetten, Jr. (1981:64), a Harvard graduate, ex-chairman of the NIH Recombinant DNA Advisory Committee and deputy director of science at NIH, commented in a speech at the Battelle International Conference on Genetic Engineering:

> On the occasion of my 50th commencement anniversary at Harvard, I did as most of my classmates did, I made a gift. I have since written to the president of Harvard telling him while I was happy and proud to be able to have made a gift to the Harvard Corporation, I would have been far less happy and far less proud to have made a gift to the Harvard For Profit Business Syndicate. In fact, I doubt that I would have made a gift at all.

In Stetten's opinion the proposed company would change his relationship to the university. When the outcry over the possibility of Harvard becoming involved in a profit-making enterprise began to affect alumni the plan was a clear liability. No startup company could begin to provide the sums that are donated to Harvard by its alumni.

Concerns regarding the role of the university as an institution also surfaced. Otto Solbrig (1982:7–8), a Harvard professor of biology, expressed the possibility of a changed relationship in a presentation at the AAAS meetings thus:

> The last area of concern is the one that worries me most. It has to do with the position of the University as an institution in the society. We all recognize that the University is not as detached and impartial as we would like it to be, or as some purists would prefer it to be. . . . we all become dependent on the sources of funding, and funding agencies can exert a variety of pressures to influence our behavior. Nevertheless, we

should strive to maintain certain values, and in my opinion, there are some that should not be compromised. A very fundamental value is the freedom to speak to the issues that are of concern to society as impartial experts. Nuclear energy, genetic engineering, pollution control, and behavior modification are some of the fields that concern and frighten society, and which we have to address as experts with technical knowledge. I fear that the credibility of the University could be seriously hurt if we were to be seen not as impartial experts, but as interested parties likely to benefit financially from the exploitation of new technologies.

Solbrig indicates that the role of the university is more important than merely conducting research. The very fact that the university is not profit-making means that it has a special role. The university can provide a "disinterested" party whose "experts" are able to mediate some social struggles such as in the area of pollution. This role as mediator is clearly threatened by the commercialization of academic science and cannot be lightly cast aside by overly rapacious administrators.

With the exception of a few critics (Noble 1982; Lewontin in Campbell 1980:3; Cavalieri 1981), most observers have accepted the need for closer university–corporate relations. But most commentators and participants have agreed that the university must not take part in profit making directly. For example, David Baltimore, MIT biology professor and principal in Collaborative Research, is quoted (in Hirshson 1980:19) as saying, " 'I'm very gratified he [Bok] made the decision [not to become involved in a company]. I think it's the right course. . . . the universities have to separate their investment policies from their academic policies.' " But David Baltimore finds little objection to professors founding companies or to a university accepting a large sum of money to create an institute that would not follow normal university protocol—as occurred barely six months later in the case of the MIT –WI affiliation.

Harvard's proposal to participate in effect in a company utilizing the skills and research of its own faculty members tested the structural limits of the transformation the university is undergoing. The entrepreneurial possibilities in biotechnology were tempting. University administrators envisioned a significant flow of discretionary cash generated by their own corporations. Walter Gilbert had demonstrated the possible profits that had escaped the administration, and a repetition of that occurrence was exactly what administrators wished to either prevent or cash in on. Ultimately administrators were unable to achieve either goal.

In 1981 President Bok in the *President's Report* to the Harvard Board of Overseers concluded that the proper role of the university in technology transfer should be:

Consulting arrangements, industry-associate programs, patent-licensing, research agreements with individual firms or groups of companies—all of these afford useful opportunities to stimulate technological innovation. . . . The same cannot be said of efforts to join the university with its professors to launch new entrepreneurial ventures. In such enterprises the risks are much harder to control, and there are few benefits to society or the academy that cannot be achieved in other ways. Instead of helping its professors to launch new companies, therefore, the university would do better to seize the initiative by asking the faculty to consider this new phenomenon in order to fashion appropriate safeguards that will maintain its academic standards and preserve its intellectual values" (Bok 1981:35).

Thus, President Bok saw little merit in the Harvard business plan, although Daniel Steiner only six months earlier had been quoted as saying that there were "no overwhelming obstacles to the plan being approved by Dr. Bok" (Dickson 1980b:769). The underlying motivation for Harvard's consideration of the scheme to cash in on biotechnology remained. Bok (1981:35) declared that the relations between professors and companies had to be examined closely to ensure that the professors discharge their university duties. Walter Gilbert, who would eventually be forced to leave Harvard, summed up Harvard's motives thus: "Actually the university has only one motive: remuneration" (Aisenberg 1982:16).

Harvard's debate seemed to succeed in convincing most other universities that the university corporation was not the best method of securing a greater share of the value of research conducted in their laboratories. In the Pajaro Dunes Conference, affirmed but unsigned by the presidents of MIT, Harvard, Caltech, Stanford, and the UC system, it was resolved that "it is not advisable for universities to make . . . investments [in companies in which their own faculty are principals] unless they are convinced that there are sufficient safeguards to avoid adverse effects" (*Tech Talk* 1982a:8). The Stanford University Committee on Research (1981:20) was even more explicit, stating, "In general, Stanford should not accept equity in companies as part of licensing agreements which arise from commercialization of University research results if any current faculty member participates in that company as either a significant stockholder or line manager. Nor should Stanford invest University capital in such ventures."

The result of the debate conducted at Harvard was that most universities would continue to invest their monies conservatively—much like a pension fund. The proposed Harvard company was renamed the Genetics Institute and was formed by Ptashne, a business partner, and the three venture capital companies—VenRock, Greylock, and J. H. Whitney—which earlier had been negotiating with Harvard. Ptashne has been said to be "somewhat bitter about the whole affair, even though he now stands to become very rich" (VerMeulen 1982:55). Importantly, this case illustrates that the social forces at work were able to shape the conditions in such a manner as to give Ptashne little choice but to join a commercial firm. The university was prepared to sell his skills if he did not.

Harvard chose not to invest in a company composed of its faculty members. For very different reasons in 1981 Michigan State University (MSU) founded a private, for-profit company, Neogen, to finance MSU biotechnology research, and the MSU Foundation allocated $50,000 for the startup (Pinkelman 1982:12). The other Neogen investors "included a major retirement fund, a venture fund specializing in agriculture and energy development, a bank holding company, and Michigan's largest venture capital firm" (Neogen n.d.). The MSU Foundation owns 30 percent of Neogen and derives profits from this equity position (Michigan State University 1983:2). Neogen provides grants to MSU professors for research the company believes it can develop and commercialize.

John Cantlon, MSU vice-president for research and graduate studies, has argued that Neogen was needed because

> The Lansing area needs a biotechnology company that will help the state strengthen and diversify its economy and also help MSU retain key faculty being courted by out-of-state firms. . . . Neogen might not have been necessary . . . if there had already been viable biotechnology companies in East Lansing. But since there weren't, we needed to create one   (quoted in Downs 1983:2).

MSU, facing the dilemma of losing faculty members to the startups, chose to resolve this difficulty by creating its own startup. As part of this general shift at MSU, conflict of interest rules were changed to allow professors to acquire equity positions in Neogen and allow faculty to act as consultants to Neogen (*MSU News-Bulletin* 1982).

The Michigan auditor-general detailed three ways in which participating faculty could benefit from Neogen:

1. Increased funding of research projects in their particular areas of expertise.

2. Increased likelihood of personal financial reward through sharing in patent royalty revenue from their sponsored research. Faculty would receive 15% of all royalty revenue or could exchange this for an equity position in the private research corporation.

3. The ability to provide lucrative consulting services to the research corporation as the corporation commercially develops the discoveries (Pinkelman 1982:14).

Whether these incentives will be enough to induce professors to stay at MSU remains an open question.

However, the Michigan auditor-general also criticized Neogen because of "potential conflicts of interest for personnel of the research corporation, the foundation, and MSU. There are interlocking personnel and finances of the three organizations and, therefore, the Auditor-General concluded that transactions among the organizations are at less than 'arm's length' " (Pinkelman 1982:14). Conflict of interest has been the only criticism of the arrangement.

MSU, a public university, decided to form Neogen two years after Harvard decided not to invest in a company containing its own faculty. The reasons for Harvard's refusal to found a company appear not to have bothered the MSU administration at all. This may be partially explained by the fact that Harvard's location near a number of biotechnology startups provides ample opportunity for professors to secure extramural financial rewards. The founding of Neogen was a novel and perhaps unique measure by a land-grant university (LGU) to cope with the serious depletion of their molecular biologists.

Pajaro Dunes—An Attempt to Develop a Consensus

I was very pleased that in recent conversations with you and Derek Bok, Murph Goldberger, and Paul Gray, there was unanimous interest in having a conference on commercialization and basic research. I would like to propose that we shoot for a date in March, 1982, at a venue somewhere near here. I recognize that this presses us all with regard to timing and scheduling. I also, however, have the sense that this problem [unrestrained industry–corporate interactions] is getting larger faster than we are coping with it, so I think some haste is desirable   *(Donald Kennedy, president of Stanford to David Saxon, president of the University of California System 1981c:1).*

More significant than the comparatively narrow makeup of the Pajaro Dunes Conference was the paucity of its results. The document produced by the conferees consisted only of the vaguest of guidelines. Moreover, it failed to address the vital issues surrounding conflicts of interests or the use of exclusive patents provided to business entities contributing to university research projects   *(Meyerhoff 1982b:59).*

The near frenzied excitement in 1981 about investment in biotechnology—a number of big contracts were signed and more were being negotiated, Genentech had made a spectacular initial stock offering, and numerous biotechnology companies had started up with their university-affiliated scientists—created a troubling scenario. Donald Kennedy of Stanford, Paul Gray of MIT, and Daniel Steiner, Harvard's general counsel, had been questioned in congressional hearings chaired by Congressman

Gore in the summer of 1981. But the most intensive grilling was reserved for Ronald Lamont-Havers, the director of research at MGH, the institution that had just signed a research agreement with Hoechst. In response to these developments Donald Kennedy decided to organize a meeting of the five universities—MIT, Harvard, Caltech, the UC system, and Stanford—"that collectively have the greatest intensity of involvement and experience with the problem [of university–corporate relationships]" (Pajaro Dunes Biotechnology Conference prospectus 1981:9). The objective of the conference was, in the words of Robert Rosenzweig (1981a:1), the then vice-president for public affairs at Stanford, "to see if agreement can be found on a set of principles that might guide the growth of biotechnology as that industry interacts with universities."

The five presidents initially were to choose five other guests (Kennedy 1981d:1) to accompany them to Pajaro Dunes, the site of the conference, but this number was later increased to six. These six consisted of two or three additional administrators, one or two faculty members, and two corporate representatives. There were also three invited guests—one of whom was from Washington University (for a complete list of participants with their titles and affiliations, see table 4.2). The group gathering at Pajaro Dunes was not unaware of its power; if anything they may have been overconfident. Robert Rosenzweig (1981a:1), in a letter to David Saxon, wrote, "There is an unusual opportunity here to shape an area of public and institutional policy before it grows beyond anyone's ability to influence, and this meeting should bring together the right group of people for the purpose."

In fact, a number of other groups felt that tremendously important decisions would be made at the conference. Albert Meyerhoff (1982a:A11), a lawyer for the Natural Resources Defense Council (NRDC), argued in a commentary that appeared in the *San Francisco Tribune* on March 26, 1982, "How decisions are made on the disposition of hundreds of millions of public research dollars from federal and state governments is at stake at this meeting. But the public has not been invited." Even the normally staid *Nature* (1982:1) cautioned: "It would be wrong for those planning to meet three weeks from now to think that what they agree among themselves about the proper relationship between universities and outside commercial interests will apply to other universities and other commercial interests." But neither the hopes of Rosenzweig nor the fears of Meyerhoff or *Nature* would be actualized at Pajaro Dunes. No cartel, code of behavior, or even applicable set of principles emerged. The signing of contracts between universities and corporations and the recruiting of faculty to work and consult for companies continued.

As if to reinforce the fact that the so-called Big 5 that met at Pajaro Dunes could not simply force their wills on other universities a meeting of eight other research universities was organized. The participants were

Table 4.2. Participants at Pajaro Dunes Conference by University and Affiliation

University	Participants	Affiliation
Stanford	Donald Kennedy	President
	Lawrence Crowley	Vice-president
	Robert Rosenzweig	Vice-president for public affairs
	Gerald Lieberman	Vice-provost and dean of research
	Charles Yanofsky	Professor of biological sciences
	Channing Robertson	Professor of chemical engineering
	Robert Swanson	President of Genentech
	Albert Bowers	Syntex
MIT	Paul Gray	President
	Francis Low	Provost
	Kenneth Smith	Associate provost and vice-president for research
	Michael Dertouzos	Professor of electrical engineering
	Phillip Sharp	Professor of biology
	Robert Charpie	President of Cabot Corporation
	David Kosowsky	President of Damon Corporation
Harvard	Derek Bok	President
	Henry Rosovsky	Dean of the College of Arts and Letters
	Daniel Steiner	General counsel
	Daniel Tosteson	Dean, School of Medicine
	David Hamburg	Professor of health policy
	Colman Mockler	President of Gillette Corp.
	Francis Burr	Fellow of Harvard College
California Institute of Technology	Marvin Goldberger	President
	John Roberts	Provost
	Donald Fowle	General counsel
	Fred Anson	Professor of chemistry and chairman of faculty
	Norman Davidson	Professor of chemistry
	Sam Eletr	President of Applied Bio-Systems
	William Simeral	Vice-president, Du Pont Co.
Univ. of California	David Saxon	President
	Ira Heyman	Chancellor
	Robert Sinsheimer	Chancellor, UC, Santa Cruz
	Julius Krevans	Dean, School of Medicine, UCSF
	William Rutter	Professor of biochemistry and biophysics, UCSF
	Herbert Boyer	Professor of biochemistry and biophysics, UCSF
	Ronald Cape	President of Cetus Corporation
Invited guests	Robert Glaser	President, Henry J. Kaiser Family Foundation
	William Phillips	Professor of chemistry, Washington University
	Arnold Beckman	Chairman of board, Beckman Instrument Co.

Source: Pajaro Dunes Biotechnology Statement 1982

Michigan, Pennsylvania, Texas, Washington University, Yale, Johns Hopkins, Princeton, and Cornell. Corporate representatives were also present at this meeting, which was held in Philadelphia and was entitled "Partners in the Research Enterprise." A number of platitudes were spoken and the meeting ended with no results and little attention from the media. In fact, Wil Lepkowski (1983:33), covering the conference for *Chemical and Engineering News*, reported that "the meeting did seem to soft-pedal worrisome conflict-of-interest problems." This conference was little more than a riposte by somewhat less prominent universities to the Pajaro Dunes initiative—undoubtedly their administrators thought it would look good to appear concerned.

The representatives at Pajaro Dunes, though important and holding powerful positions, were in no position to "carve up territory" (Donald Kennedy quoted in Hilts 1982b:A6). In the U.S. educational system the various universities are structured as competitors and even the most important universities cannot act unilaterally or organize effective cartels. Just as important, the "customers" for their research, corporations, are in bitter, free-for-all competition. These companies have little possibility of creating a consensus in their own ranks, much less of agreeing to a role for the university. Corporations attempt to secure access to a biotechnology research labor force. As long as they perceive professors as able to assist them in commodity production the problems will continue. As biotechnology becomes an industry and as new agreements begin to have a routinized format, more stable methods of interaction may develop. But whether the presidents of these universities or of all universities can effectively control the evolution of the new academic relationships is doubtful.

The university has become an important site for the production of knowledge (information) that is directly applicable to profitability. This information is being transformed into commodities, and a labor force is being created for the new industry. As the Pajaro Dunes Biotechnology Conference prospectus (1981:10) observed,

> The new commercial structures, and the form of their interaction with basic scientists and with universities, are still evolving. Until the outlines become more fixed it is probably premature to expect broad agreement about specific solutions, especially regulatory ones. But it is clearly not too soon to begin the convergence upon a set of principles—principles that will ultimately serve as the guides to more codified policy.

Pajaro Dunes was a meeting dear to the hearts of conspiracy theorists; many of the most important actors in the academic–industrial elite were in attendance. Yet agreements were possible only on the vaguest of principles. The following quotes illustrate the vague generalities of the Pajaro Dunes Biotechnology Conference Statement (1982:8):

> It is important that universities administer patent programs in a manner that conforms to the public interest and to the universities' primary commitment to teaching and research.

Universities have a responsibility not only to maintain [basic academic] values but also to satisfy faculty, students and the general public that they are being maintained.

Although we see no single "right" policy, we do believe that each university should address the problem vigorously.

This most general and bland statement was never more than an unsigned draft. MIT's Paul Gray emphasized that the ten-page statement released at the conference was not binding upon the participating institutions (Zamparutti 1982:1). Conspiracy theorists need to look elsewhere for proof of control by individuals or a conscious elite seeking to change university–corporate relations.

Pajaro Dunes was an attempt to develop certain ground rules in a chaotic situation that is threatening the ideological foundations and social function of the university. Teaching and research cannot be effectively accomplished in a frenzy of commercial activity. The need for a separation of the university's functions from corporate profit making is a point of common agreement. But in an environment in which information has become a critical input to production and biotechnology is seen by major companies as the key to the future, it is not a simple matter to maintain this separation.

Since its inception the university has been an institution that is separated from production for the marketplace. This means that it survives on transfers from the productive sector, a condition that makes it subservient yet independent. The university is not bound by the constraints operating on individual corporations in their struggle to control labor and defeat the competition. The lack of direct interest in making a profit provides a relative autonomy similar to that of the state, thereby allowing the university to produce workers trained to fill positions in industry. This training is general because the exact qualifications cannot be specified until the individual actually receives a job. Further, the university must train workers that are not merely technicians prepared for positions that industry believes it needs filled; it must also provide a pool of workers available when industries need new skills.

The agenda that NSF and industry began to tout in the early 1970s has now borne full fruit. University administrators across the United States are actively seeking opportunities to link their institutions and faculty members with the private sector. State legislators are allocating special monies to encourage university–industry partnerships. There is an increasing acceptance of industrial ethics in the university as scientists become entrepreneurs and students are viewed as hired employees. For example, the 1985 NSF Presidential Young Investigator grant promises to match any industrial grant monies the scientist receives on a dollar-for-dollar basis to a maximum of $37,500 per year. Industrial monies are becoming a source of funds.

The university as an institution is being increasingly enmeshed in everyday commercial activities. This blurring of the distinction between the university and the marketplace is seen at both the individual and institutional level. Professors cannot be expected to be neutral when they are businessmen. At the institutional level the large contracts between universities and industry, the increased exclusive licensing of innovations, and the participation by some universities in small companies encourage doubt as to whether the university as an institution is independent of industry ethically and morally. Certainly, the results of the discussion in this section indicate that relationships internal and external to the university are in the process of change.

I have examined the types of relationships being developed at the institutional level as corporations seek access to specialized workers and their knowledge. In every case companies demanded and received privileged patent rights on discoveries. In effect, all products and useful information resulting from the labor of university scientists is becoming private property owned by professors, funders, or the university. This fact transforms the university's role from that of "producing" for the general society to a function more akin to that of a leased research team. The effect this will have on the university is unclear, but obviously the academic environment is changing. The proximate impetus for the creation of the new university arrangements is the fact that professors with marketable skills are increasingly devoting more time and effort to profit-making activities.

5. Professors

as Entrepreneurs

I've examined the motivation of many of the people in this industry.... I've studied sixteen companies in exquisite detail and another ten or fifteen less exhaustively. The better, smaller, entrepreneurial companies have a quality about them that I've seen in no others, including our own—an extremely powerful entrepreneurship, more powerful for academic people than a sex attractant *(Kenneth Jarmolow, Martin Marietta corporate director for research and development, quoted in R. Johnson 1983:22).*

If you want to go into business, fine—then leave the university. We essentially lose the people who are involved in the companies, anyway.... Their attention and energy get drained off *(Professor Keith Yamamoto, UCSF microbiologist, quoted in Boly 1982a:176).*

Perhaps the most stunning aspect of the rapid growth of genetic engineering has been the absolutely critical role of university professors. E. Russell Eggers (1981:132), the chief executive officer of the now defunct DNA Science, Inc., describes their importance: "If you were to identify the twenty-five leading molecular biologists working today, I doubt that any of them work for the pharmaceutical industry. They all work on campus or in a research institution. There might be one or possibly two company scientists who are batting in a first-class league, but they would strain to make it." As Eggers points out, the university had and in most cases still has the best molecular biologists. The advent of genetic engineering has led many companies to "return to school."

The participation of faculty scientists in small startups has been a catalyst in the changing relations between the various groups that work in the biology laboratory. Many have argued that the new commercial relations are so pervasive as to be creating a new laboratory etiquette. The history of consulting in molecular biology and allied fields is short; this was merely another "basic" science before 1976. In less than a decade, however, a new industry and a new labor force have been created, and at the center of this maelstrom of activity were "pure" scientists—molecular biologists.

The creation of this new labor force is the story not of sweaty factory workers but of "think workers" dressed in laboratory coats. And, conversely, it is a story of capitalists, though not necessarily in Brooks Brothers suits; many are still in lab coats. The arrangements described in the previous chapter were in actuality a consequence of and reaction to the activities of these entrepreneurial professors. The majority of the professors are not operating in a vacuum. In a society based on achieving high salaries and a good life style, these professors' decision to participate in the commercialization of their science is only to be expected. That some professors, such as Paul Berg at Stanford, among others, resisted as long as they did is a tribute to the hold the ideology of "pure" versus commercial science has had.

Consulting—A Venerable Tradition

"There isn't a walking biochemist who doesn't have a
piece of some company in which he is a consultant,"
chortled one MIT scientist   *(Rosenberg 1981a:5).*

Faculty consulting for government, nonprofit agencies, and corporations has a long tradition. In fact, most administrators have supported consulting as an aid to teaching and research (Bok 1981:30; Giamatti 1982:1279). In hearings held to inquire into the role of oil companies in the 1969 Santa Barbara Channel oil spill, for example, the state of California was hard pressed to find professors from publicly supported universities who were willing to testify against the oil industry because they were consultants hired by these same companies (Walsh 1969:411). In the academic year 1961–62, 74 percent of faculty surveyed by the Carnegie Commission on Higher Education reported outside income (Schwartz 1975:2). And, within certain limitations, consulting probably has little effect upon the university. The specialized knowledge that professors develop has traditionally been of use to industry and is frequently called upon. For institutions such as MIT, consulting is encouraged as one aspect of being a good professor.

The traditional, though until recently unwritten, rule in universities has been that a professor may spend no more than one day per week, or fifty-two days per year, consulting (Kennedy 1981b:27; PMM 1981:51; Giamatti 1982:1279; Schwartz 1975:5). The LGUs have somewhat stricter rules owing to their government funding and to the fact that the extension organization provides free consultation for the state's farmers and agribusinesses. A further aspect of this unwritten rule was an assumption that the department chairman would discipline any gross violation of the one day per week rule, especially in cases in which it interfered with the discharge of professional duties.

Charles Schwartz (1975), professor of physics at UCB, has devoted considerable effort to documenting professorial conflicts of interest and the lack of supervision inherent in the consulting system. Schwartz (1975:1) quotes the then provost of the Professional Schools and Colleges at UCB, George Maslach, as saying, "I have no knowledge of the extent of outside consulting by faculty and others; I have no knowledge of how many people consult, nor do I know how they have spent their time. There is no indication of how I can obtain this information in any easy way." When Schwartz (1975:4) once asked his department chairman about looking into this subject of faculty consulting, "he declined, referring to it as 'a whole can of worms.' " It is quite clear from Schwartz's work and that of others (Owen and Braeutigan 1978) that consulting is lucrative, pervasive, essentially uncontrolled, and yet hidden.

In many institutions the acceptance by a professor of "a line position such as a president or director of research or other such activity" (Gray 1981:59) is the point at which the university draws the line. In other universities professors who wish to take an active role in the management of a company are asked to take a year's sabbatic without pay and then make a decision (Giamatti 1982:1279). The two most celebrated cases of professors taking year-long sabbatics "to test the water" are those of Walter Gilbert and Timothy Hall. Walter Gilbert of Harvard finally decided to resign and join Biogen as its chief executive and Timothy Hall of the University of Wisconsin, Madison resigned to join Zoecon (a Sandoz subsidiary). These two cases presented relatively easy decisions for university administrators: Gilbert was reported to have been running the company out of his Harvard office—a clear violation of policy (Bylinsky 1980:149). Recent years have been characterized by a hardening of administrators' attitudes toward professors who are spending the bulk of their time in nonscholarly activities.

PMM (1981:53), reflecting the accountant's mentality, wrote in their report to Cornell regarding consulting rule violations,

> At a minimum, institutions that have explicit policies on disclosure will have to start enforcing them. . . . But it will turn out, we believe, that those institutions which have not been enforcing their existing regulations will find a substantial resistance not only from those governed by the rules but perhaps even more so from those charged with enforcement, especially the department heads.

The university has not been structured for accountability. Whether department chairmen can effectively police consulting agreements and other extramural activities is questionable. But new rules to control professional activity are on the agenda.

President Giamatti (1982:1279) of Yale University, echoing the position of many administrators, wrote in *Science*: "The burden of mounting a teaching program and two separate research programs, where the results of one research program are to be widely disseminated and the results of the other may have to be kept secret in the pursuit of commercial success, is more than even the most responsible faculty member can be expected to shoulder." In response to President Giamatti's position, it can easily be charged that the administrators are merely trying to control the faculty to ensure that the institution prospers—that they are in effect trying to convert university professors into patent-inventing labor. To tighten up on all violations and enforce the rules could slow the process of innovation diffusion which all parties wish to foster. Also, there could be an outcry from industry, which could lose the services of a consultant who was exceeding his fifty-two days per year.

Consulting has been an important role for professors, providing income for them and productive services for industry. Yet in the last ten years consulting and other relations between professors and industry have hypertrophied in the biological sciences. The system that was meant to provide industry with access to professors and professors with knowledge of industry broke down under the pressure of the need to recruit an entire highly skilled work force. The result could be the creation of genetic engineering departments in universities as the industry becomes routinized, and corporate-oriented biologists would be located there. But it could be that the ferment produced by professors starting firms, becoming managers, etc., will continue, and the outcome will be a new norm for professors' activities.

The Beginning of the Biorevolution in the Universities

History provides numerous examples of professors becoming entrepreneurs. For example, Harvard professor Otto Eckstein converted an academic exercise in forecasting into a business he sold for $100 million. The technology driven growth of Route 128 and Silicon Valley has been predicated upon two generations of physicists, electrical engineers, and computer scientists. In this group of scientists were a number of professors who had resigned their university appointments and launched companies. Earlier academics have also emerged from the ivory tower to apply their scientific knowledge and expertise in creating businesses.

As we saw in chapter 1, the field of molecular biology had created a type of entrepreneur before World War II, but the postwar period, which saw the infusion of massive sums of NIH money, created true research entrepreneurs. These men, though not businessmen, had already become used to controlling large sums of money and to having employees. Molecular biology, with its emphasis on hardware and machines, was well prepared for commercialization.[1]

When the computer, or integrated circuit, industry began to grow, both universities and companies had researchers, but at the time the biotechnology industry began, nearly all molecular biologists were located in the universities. This is not surprising because until 1976 industry had little interest in the basic research of molecular biologists. In the pre-recombinant-DNA period, corporate interest centered on microbiologists and biochemists working with potential pharmaceuticals. The burst into prominence of rDNA literally caught industry unaware. There was insufficient trained labor available; rather than the usual oversupply of molecular biologists, now suddenly a shortage existed.

All of the earliest genetic engineering companies were founded by professors. The initial research was undertaken in university laboratories, and even when the companies secured laboratory space some of the professors did not resign their university positions. Rather, professors chose to remain faculty members and work for their companies. In a number of interviews Zsolt Harsanyi (1981:117), a former Cornell Medical School professor, former director of the Office of Technology Assessment's applied genetics report research group, and currently a vice-president at E. F. Hutton and Co., discovered that most professors for a number of reasons wished to remain on campus, and because much of the labor power remains on campus so must the research.

Genetic engineering as a commercial venture began in 1976 when Robert Swanson, a venture capitalist and ex-venture capital investment analyst for Citibank, convinced Herbert Boyer, one of the inventors of the Cohen–Boyer gene splicing process, to form a company to commercialize the new recombinant DNA techniques. Even while Congress was considering health and safety legislation in 1976 and 1977, scientists were rushing to produce the first genetically engineered hormones. Potential profit became involved in basic science questions such as what goals should be set for new experiments. For example, a new company, Genentech, was presumably started on Boyer's consulting time while he was a professor at the UCSF Medical Center. Swanson and Boyer each invested $500 in the fledgling company, and Swanson convinced six "main" investors to provide the startup capital.

1. For example, equipment such as a microscope costs $3,000, a laminar flow hood $4,000, a cell sorter $50,000–$70,000, a gene synthesizer $20,000–$50,000 (Treble 1982:5; Gebhart 1983). Not only are laboratories expensive to start up, but they become more expensive as the competition between laboratories increases. Laboratories can have capital equipment costing $1,000,000 if electron microscopes, gas chromatographs, and mass spectrometers are included.

The lead investor was the venture capital company Kleiner and Perkins, which was important in a number of West Coast startups (Petit 1977b:2). The three main ingredients in starting a firm are a professor who brings knowledge and techniques; an entrepreneur, many times a young, recently graduated MBA; and financial backers who believe the business will succeed within five to seven years.

In the early days Genentech did not have a laboratory, so Boyer's campus laboratories were used. This was facilitated by a $200,000 grant to Boyer from his company, Genentech (Meyerhoff et al. 1981:7–8). The grant provided the money needed to establish the company, and the first project undertaken was to induce bacteria to produce a small (short amino acid chain) human brain hormone, somatostatin. Of course, Genentech was not expending this money for mere scientific discovery. The *San Francisco Chronicle* put it very explicitly: "For their investment, Genentech expects to receive from UC and City of Hope [the research hospital that synthesized the artificial gene] an exclusive license to produce hormones" (Petit 1977b:2). Boyer, the officer of Genentech, contracted with Boyer, the professor, to perform research that would be proprietary, that is, patented private property at a public university.

The bacterial production of somatostatin had another purpose—to show the potential utility of rDNA. Philip Handler, president of the National Academy of Sciences and an unabashed defender of corporate funding of academic research, two months before the official press release was issued, announced this "breakthrough" in the controlling of bacterial hormone synthesis during congressional hearings on health and safety legislation. This type of breach of scientific etiquette, which demands publication in a scholarly journal before public announcement, was to become much more common in the future as biotechnology became an industry. Rules and etiquette collapsed very quickly under the pressure of events and the gaining strength of commercial motives. But it is noteworthy that the first breach was by Handler, an important proponent of scientific ethics and 'neutrality' in other fora.[2]

With the publication in *Science* of the article describing the UCSF team's success, Herbert Boyer, scientist and now marketer, announced that "the

2. In a letter published in *Science* David Perlman (1977:782), a science writer for the *San Francisco Chronicle*, questioned Handler's use of unpublished information for a political purpose. Cavalieri (1981:179), in a letter to *Science* that was not published, wrote:

I do not believe that a political debate is an appropriate forum for scientific announcements—especially when the scientific community itself purports to guard its traditional processes so zealously. The propriety of Dr. Handler's testimony, however politically useful, should, I believe, be widely discussed.

There was no debate and, of course, no censure of Handler's transgression of normal scientific protocol.

man on the street can finally get a return on his investment in science" (Petit 1977a:17). Somatostatin still remains unexploited by Genentech, though they continue to hold the patent rights. Boyer would get a return on his investment even if nothing accrued to the man on the street, but this scientific event had another result: it publicized the fact that genetic engineering could produce commodities. Even a skeptical research director within a large pharmaceutical company could not afford to ignore the outside possibility that genetic engineering was real. Furthermore, everyone knew that the next hormone on the research agenda was insulin, the sales of which in the United States alone are worth over $180 million. The implications were unmistakable—every organic chemical company needed to have a molecular biologist.

In 1977 most professors, especially those in biology, still had grave doubts regarding the propriety of commercial ties. Paul Berg, the Stanford Nobel Laureate in biochemistry, was quoted as saying, "Commercial involvement is just not to my taste. This isn't to criticize Herb [Boyer] particularly, but I just can't see it" (Petit 1977b:2). Berg is purported to have refrained from even consulting for the pharmaceutical industry. The vast majority of professors remained aloof from corporate involvement and were even somewhat contemptuous of colleagues with corporate links. Yet Genentech's success in attracting capital and the clear indications that Boyer would soon be rich began to change minds.

Professors and Entrepreneurs—A Marriage Made in Heaven

In near perfect resemblance of the frenzied founding of new firms described by Schumpeter (1964) that sets off a new upswing in the world economy, the biotechnology business was born (Kenney 1984). This time, however, the entrepreneurs had to go to the university to find the expertise needed to start a company. In 1977 and 1978 professors were reluctant to join companies because of peer pressure. But in 1977 David Jackson, tenured associate professor of biochemistry at the University of Michigan, joined in the formation of another company, Genex. Also, a number of professors sold their services to Cetus and Genentech; for example, the Cetus board of scientific advisors included Donald Glaser, Joshua Lederberg, and Francis Crick, all Nobel Laureates.

The method by which the professors and entrepreneurs make contact is not discussed publicly. In the case of Biogen the venture capital group at Inco decided to try to recruit one or two scientists from a group of approximately ten. To the venture capitalists' surprise, all the scientists showed interest (Powledge 1983a:400). Of course, the offers were very tempting, including a 3 percent block of stock, research contracts for the professors, bonuses for discoveries, and $500 per day consulting fees (Bylinsky 1980:149; Shapley 1983:83). In the early days, 1976–78, the venture capitalists actively sought out professors to attempt startups in gene splicing.

Genetic Systems, for example, was formed by a partnership between David Blech, a twenty-four-year-old stockbroker, his brother, Isaac Blech, and Robert Nowinski, previously a professor at the Fred Hutchinson Cancer Research Center. The Blechs decided to invest in starting a company. Utilizing consultants, they discovered Nowinski and upon contacting him found that he was interested in forming a company also. The contact led to the formation of Genetic Systems in 1980 (Kleinfeld 1983:D1). Genetic Systems was a later example of contact initiated by venture capitalists.

Hybritech was formed in 1978 by Brook Byers, senior partner in Kleiner, Perkins, Caulfield and Byers, Ivor Royston, an associate professor, and Norman Birndorf, a staff research associate, both of the University of California, San Diego. Royston and Birndorf conceived of the idea of forming a company to exploit hybridoma technology and contacted Brook Byers. Birndorf left the university to join Hybritech as a vice-president for corporate development. Royston has remained with the university and consults for the company (Prescott 1983a:157). Royston had received 425,000 shares (3.8 percent) in the company with a market value of approximately $10 million as of August 1983 (Hybritech 1982:29). In late 1980 the University of California invested in the company in a private stock placement (Prescott 1983a:158) at the same time that Harvard decided not to invest in one of its professors (see chapter 4).

The motivations of the professors in forming the initial partnerships are, in one sense, uniquely personal. The first and most obvious motivation is financial. Arthur Kornberg, the Stanford Nobel Laureate, has been quoted as saying, "Understandably, the scientists that provided the ideas, techniques and practitioners of genetic chemistry are reluctant to be excluded from its financial rewards by entrepreneurs and venture capitalists" (Sonquist 1981:71). Table 5.1 demonstrates that the financial rewards of being a founder of a successful company can be significant indeed. These professors also consult for the company for fees usually of $500 or more per day (Hybritech 1982:22; Shapley 1983:83). Cesar Milstein, who with Georges Köhler invented the commercially important hybridoma technologies, has been quoted as lamenting, "In this society, you're made to feel stupid if you can't make money" (J. Fox 1981a:44). The rush of investment capital into biotechnology ventures dramatically increased the value of professors' technical expertise. It must have been very difficult for professors who were receiving $30,000 to $60,000 per year to resist the lure of capital gains on the order of millions of dollars.

Conversely, the choice not to participate was also the choice to allow others to benefit from your research. The knowledge that a colleague has become rich through a company startup is ego deflating for these competitive professors, and, of course, they feel intense pressures from family

Table 5.1. Founding Professors and Equity Interests

Professor	University	Company	Shares (thousands)	Percent of total*	Value ($ million)†
D. Housman	MIT	Integrated Genetics	300	3.6	1.2
I. Royston	UCSD	Hybritech	425	3.8	10.0
J. Hansen	Univ. of Washington	Genetic Systems	215	1.6	1.5
D. Baltimore	MIT	Collaborative Research	317	3.9	1.2
F. Pass	Univ. of Minnesota	Molecular Genetics	400	10.4	2.8
A. Faras	Univ. of Minnesota	Molecular Genetics	400	10.4	2.8

Sources: Various publications
* Before public offering
† As of July 1985

and friends to benefit from their knowledge. As a result, affiliation with a company has become the norm in molecular biology departments, though the total number of professors who actually own large equity positions in companies is small.

The economic motives for participation in companies are obvious, but there are also other motives. As Boyer of Genentech said, "When the first patient gets treated with something this company makes, that's going to be a very big day for me" (Christensen 1980:27). Many of the scientists find satisfaction in moving further downstream from research to development and actually seeing their research translated into a health care product.

Another important motivation is the ennui that sets in for some professors; by age forty many feel they have already experienced their most productive years. The chance to start a company is certainly exciting, and it is even more exciting when success seems assured. For example, Walter Gilbert of Harvard seems to have relished his opportunity to manage Biogen and was willing to resign his American Cancer Society chair at Harvard. Robert Cawthorn, former vice-president of Biogen and current president of Rorer International Corporation, says of Gilbert, "[His managerial skills] should not be underestimated just because he has a Nobel Prize in chemistry" (*New York Times* 1983:31). The very different thrill of operating a small, growing company clearly can lure a professor, and in many cases professors who are heavily involved in company management leave the university completely. However, in some cases, professors accept line responsibility and have not yet resigned from the university (table 5.2).

Table 5.2. Individuals Who Have Held a Professorship and Corporate Executive Position Simultaneously*

Company	Professor	University	Department	Role†	Related with university?
Amgen	Daniel Vapnek	Georgia	Genetics	Research director	Adjunct
	Marvin Caruthers	Colorado	Biochemistry	Vice-president	Yes
Chiron	Edward Penhoet	UCB	Biochemistry	President	Yes
	William Rutter	UC Medical Center	Biochemistry	Chairman	Yes
	Pablo Valenzuela	UC Medical Center	Biochemistry	Director of research	Yes
Genetic Systems	Robert Nowinski	Univ. of Washington	Microbiology	Executive vice-president	Yes
	John Hansen	Univ. of Washington	Medicine		Yes
Genex	David Jackson	Univ. of Michigan	Biochemistry	Chairman, SAB	Yes
Immunex	Steven Gillis	Univ. of Washington	Microbiology	Executive vice-president	Yes
	Christopher Henney	Univ. of Washington	Microbiology	Executive vice-president	Yes
Integrated Genetics	David Housman	MIT	Biology	Chairman	Yes
Molecular Genetics	Franklin Pass	Univ. of Minnesota	Dermatology	President	Yes
	Anthony Faras	Univ. of Minnesota	Microbiology	Co-chairman of the board	Yes

Source: Author's compilation
* Not including those who serve as directors only
† The constantly changing nature of the industry makes it impossible to guarantee the current status of the above-named scientists.

The expanding gold rush in biotechnology diminished the disdain with which professors who had company involvement were viewed. In late 1977 Paul Berg criticized Boyer's founding of a commercial firm. But by 1980 Berg had formed DNAX, which was purchased by Schering-Plough for $29 million. When asked what made the company worth $29 million, a Schering-Plough spokesman said, "The company's assets are far and away the working scientists and the scientific advisory board" (Boly 1982a:176). This led to the observation by Boly (1982a:176) that "where Herb Boyer once endured the snubs of his colleagues [at UCSF], there are now four separate bioengineering businesses connected to members of his department (including one with the former department chairman, William Rutter)." Walter Gilbert, speaking of his department at Harvard, claims, "One half of my colleagues at Harvard are involved in companies in one form or another" (J. Fox 1981a:44). The MIT provost, Francis Low (Zamparutti 1982:1), agrees with Barbara Culliton (1982a:961), who wrote in *Science* that "most of the country's leading biologists are already affiliated with a biotechnology company."

Donald Kennedy, the president of Stanford, in congressional hearings best typified administrators' worries regarding the bioboom:

A large number of our faculty members, perhaps 2 dozen or more (at least), have recently concluded or are now contemplating individual arrangements with mostly young, new biotechnology firms.

These arrangements are on a variety of different bases, some of them involve fee-for-service, more of them involve equity participation, and some involve even quite heavy involvement in research work in the company. . . . We are not losing whole people. What we are concerned about is what the ultimate landscape will look like in terms of the loss of parts of people   (Kennedy 1981b:21).

In contrast to electrical engineers and computer scientists, biology professors have generally not resigned their faculty appointments and gone into private business (King 1981b:66). The reasons for this are unclear—perhaps they are attracted by the security of tenure or possibly they feel that the only way to remain on the cutting edge of science is to continue to be located at the university. Access to young students and their ideas is also likely to be of importance.

Professors as Consultants and Members of Scientific Advisory Boards

A major factor in luring professors to become principals and directors in companies is the provision of equity positions. These companies are, in the words of Genentech (1980a:2), "driven by science," and the small companies are dependent on the newest technology. Genentech's 1980 *Annual Report* states that "while there is a continuing effort to ensure protection of our patentable inventions and know-how, interaction with the broad scientific community is important if we are to remain on the cutting edge of science" (Genentech 1980a:2). Kay Noel, manager of Cetus Immune of Palo Alto, is quoted as saying, "The more successful biotechnology companies have learned that if you want to maintain state-of-the-art knowledge, you have to employ university scientists as consultants and fund research at universities" (McDonald 1983b:7). Cetus Immune, a branch of Cetus, is affiliated with a dozen professors. Consulting arrangements with university professors are standard practice in the biotechnology industry. The number of consultants a company retains varies. For example, table 5.3 names the consultants and their academic affiliations that Hybritech considers significant to its operation.

Scientific advisory boards (SABs) may be small, such as that of Collaborative Research (table 5.4), or large, such as that of Amgen (table 5.5). The four members of Collaborative Research's SAB are stockholders in the company (Collaborative Research 1982:11). In return for stock, options, and consulting fees, the advisors are committed to disclose to the company "any information regarding inventions, improvements, and discoveries (whether patentable or not) in the field of recombinant DNA technology" (Collaborative Research 1982:10). Further, the advisors are prohibited from disclosing any information pertaining to the company obtained while consulting for the company (Collaborative Research 1982:11). David Baltimore, chairman of the SAB and a company director, was a founder of Collaborative Research's wholly owned subsidiary, Collaborative Genetics. Baltimore also assisted Gerald Fink, another advisor, in securing a position at WI.

On the other hand, the Amgen SAB consists of ten members who operate like consultants. In the fiscal year ending March 31, 1983, the company paid aggregate consulting fees of $106,000 to thirteen individuals, including the scientific advisors. In addition, these individuals owned an aggregate of 112,500 shares of common stock and 405,111 shares of a restricted common stock (sold at $.133 per share). The company may repurchase a significant portion of these shares at cost if the holder terminates his relationship with the company. The exact nature of the duties these professors perform is not discussed, nor is it available in public sources (Amgen 1983).

Thus, an important lure tempting university professors to affiliate with a company has been the provision of equity interest. Even in cases in which the professor is not a founder, equity in these firms can lead to significant capital gains. For example, in Amgen's case the restricted common stock totally vested in the advisors will have, at current stock prices, an average net worth of approximately $400,000 (Amgen 1983). Of course, business

Table 5.3. Consultants (Hybritech 1982)

Name	Title	Affiliation
Joseph Bertino, M.D.	Professor of medicine and pharmacology	Yale
William Dreyer, Ph.D.	Professor of biology	California Institute of Technology
Richard Dutton, Ph.D.	Professor of biology	UCSD
Samuel Halpern, M.D.	Professor of radiology	UCSD
Karl Erik Hellstrom, M.D., Ph.D.	Professor of pathology Program head—Division of Tumor Immunology	Fred Hutchinson Cancer Research Center
Ingegerd Hellstrom, M.D., Ph.D.	Professor of microbiology/ immunology	Washington
Csaba Horvath, Ph.D.	Chemical engineering	Yale
Martin Kamen, Ph.D.	Professor emeritus of chemistry	UCSD
Nathan Kaplan, Ph.D.	Professor of chemistry	UCSD
John Kersey, M.D.	Professor of pediatrics and laboratory medicine and pathology	Minnesota
Norman Klinman, M.D., Ph.D.	Member, department of immunopathology Adjunct professor of biology	Scripps Clinic and Research Institute UCSD
Claude Meares, Ph.D.	Associate professor of chemistry	UCD
Alfred Nisonoff, Ph.D.	Professor of biology	Brandeis
Stanley Order, M.D., Sc.D.	Director radiation oncology Professor of oncology and radiation sciences	Johns Hopkins
Ivor Royston, M.D.	Associate professor of medicine	UCSD
David Secher, Ph.D.	Scientific staff member	MRC, Cambridge Univ., Eng.
Clive Taylor, M.D., Ph.D.	Chief of immunology Professor of pathology	LA County Medical Center Southern California

Source: Hybritech 1982

Table 5.4. Scientific Advisory Board (Collaborative Research 1982)

Professor	University	Honors
D. Baltimore	MIT	Member, NAS*; Nobel Prize, 1975
D. Botstein	MIT	Member, NAS; Lilly Award, 1978
G. Fink	MIT (formerly Cornell)	Member, NAS; NAS Prize, 1981
R. Davis	Stanford	Lilly Award, 1978; NAS Prize, 1981

Source: Collaborative Research, SEC 10-K Report
* National Academy of Sciences

Table 5.5. Amgen Scientific Advisory Board, Affiliations and Honors

Professor	University affiliation	Honors
Arnold Berk	UCLA	—
John Carbon	UC, Santa Barbara	—
Marvin Caruthers	Univ. of Colorado	—
Norman Davidson	California Institute of Technology	Member, NAS*
David Gibson	Univ. of Texas	Director of Center for Applied Microbiology
Leroy Hood	California Institute of Technology	Member, NAS
Arno Motulsky	Univ. of Washington	Member, NAS
Robert Schimke	Stanford Univ.	Member, NAS
Richard Williams	Senior scientist, International Laboratory for Research on Animal Diseases	—
Robert Wolfe	Univ. of Illinois	Member, NAS

Source: Amgen 1983
* National Academy of Sciences

results will immediately be translated into lower or higher net worth. Each scientific advisor therefore has an immediate stake in the survival of the corporation and can be expected to devote himself to its success.

Moshe Alafi, a venture capitalist and a founder of both Cetus and Biogen, speaking about the structure of Biogen, says, "This is the only company in the world where scientists have their hands on the company's jugular vein" (Bylinsky 1980:145). But nearly all of these companies—with the possible exception of Genentech, which has developed strong internal research—depend on their scientific advisors and consultants for a range of activities from research to recruitment of new workers. Another important function of scientific advisors is to act as the companies' eyes and ears in academia and to funnel information back to the applied, or bench, scientists in the company.

The consultant–client relationship is usually the first step on the path to a more intimate relationship. Consulting for industry and government has a long history in the university and has been considered to be beneficial, although occasionally it has come under attack (Walsh 1969:412). The consensus is that consulting provides professors with beneficial experience regarding real world problems (Giamatti 1982:1279; Bok 1981:30). And, conversely, scientists can bring needed new insights to industry (Bok 1981:30; Prager and Omenn 1980). Consulting relationships also allow professors to increase their salaries—a consideration in a period when professors' salaries have not kept pace with inflation—and consulting assists the professor in finding employment opportunities for his students. Obviously, the importance of each of these benefits varies in the particular case.

University professors in their role as consultants are of critical importance to all biotechnology companies. Charles Muscoplat (1982:90), initially a consultant to Molecular Genetics while a University of Minnesota professor and now executive vice-president of Molecular Genetics, Inc., in discussing the role of consultants at Molecular Genetics, has said,

> We use consultants in many ways. We use them to find names of graduating possible doctoral fellows we might want to hire or previous students who have gone off and done other work and we track them down and get information from them, are they interested in coming to work for us, or can you tell us who is doing the good work today in a certain field of molecular biology or genetics, can you get us some current literature, as well as inviting them in to give research seminars and symposia.

If a company has ties with a professor, it has a much better opportunity to secure the services of his students.

And there are other opportunities for professorial consultants. For example, James Blair, senior vice-president for New Court Securities Corporation, a venture capital group, uses "six or seven world-class scientists as outside consultants on a regular basis" to evaluate proposed biotechnology startups (quoted in Love 1981:12). Whether consulting for companies such as New Court Securities contributes to any of the laudable objectives of speeding technology transfer and/or professional growth is dubious. In a sense, it is perhaps impossible to even establish what is and is not legitimate consulting, and the one day a week rule seems impossible to define or enforce. Are professors going to be required to work at a university more than forty hours per week without overtime? This is the implication of placing a limit of one day's consulting per week. Is it legitimate for professors to work on their days off or after an eight-hour day? University administrators are not limited in this manner, and though corporate managers are, many ignore such rules. Strict rules regarding such an essentially unstructured process as scientific research are likely doomed to failure either because they are ignored or because they stifle creativity. For example, how does one judge a scientist or professor who seldom appears at the university but continues to produce articles and garner grant monies?

The tremendous wave of activity sweeping over the field as molecular biology is privatized is creating unique opportunities for certain professors to secure financial gain. These professors are bargaining from a unique position of strength owing not only to their limited numbers but also to the fact that they are tenured. The immediacy of possible unemployment does not threaten their choices, so a substantial lure is required. The environment of the small companies must be conducive to mental labor. As Robert Luciano said, speaking of Biogen's scientists, "You just couldn't hire people like that to work in industrial settings" (Bylinsky 1980:152). The new industry had to adapt to the workers it required. In 1980 Walter Gilbert said that he sees in the commercialization of gene splicing an opportunity to rewrite the traditional relationships between the university and corporations. In the case of Biogen he felt that academics would be in control: "Industry likes academics to be consultants. What we are seeing here is an attempt by academics to control industrial development!" (Wade 1980b:689).[3]

The unprecedented growth in university–corporate relationships documented in the previous chapter is one reaction by university administrators as they attempt to control the exodus of personnel, or, as President Kennedy phrased it, "parts of people." This is borne out by the results of a recent study which discovered that "the initial impulse in the majority of university–industry relationships sampled came from the university, with a significant portion of the academic researchers pursuing these relationships having had prior consulting or other employment relationships with the companies" (*Chemical and Engineering News* 1983c:18). Similarly, the refusal of these researchers to work in an industrial setting is the primary factor that has made the small firms viable.

The centrality of important scientists is obvious. For example, David Baltimore's threat to resign from MIT may have motivated the administration to approve WI. The outcome of the proposed Harvard biotechnology company was that after being forced into a position of being a commodity, labor power, to be sold by Harvard, Mark Ptashne resolved to bargain for himself. Scientists such as Baltimore, Ptashne, Gilbert, and Boyer have emerged from relative obscurity to being mentioned on the front page of newspapers (a version of the Horatio Alger story). Earlier, the grants these so-called stars were able to secure helped to support the administration, but under the new arrangements professors who take equity positions may or may not deliver as much overhead to the university.[4]

The diffuse nature of mental labor and, especially, of research makes the attribution of discoveries to one researcher or another an arbitrary decision. This is even more true when the professor is doing "basic" re-

3. Walter Gilbert, rather than making industry become more like the university, decided to resign from Biogen, N.V. in 1984 as pressure from institutional stockholders to secure more professional management increased (Bulkeley 1984:22).

4. If grants are extended to the professor's university laboratory the administration can charge overhead, and in many cases professors do bring in company monies. But, in other cases, a professor diverts his energy to his company and ceases to pursue grant money as actively, thereby decreasing the university's income.

search that is immediately "applicable"—a common phenomenon in molecular biology. Zsolt Harsanyi, paraphrasing a DNA Science, Inc. scientist, explained this lack of distinction between "basic" and "applied" in congressional testimony:

> The research on how the genetic code determines the binding of a certain enzyme to the DNA is about as basic as one can get. At the same time, the elucidation of this question could be of significant industrial value if it increases the efficiency of production. As a result much research in molecular biology is of interest to both the basic biologist and the industrialist. There is no clear line of demarcation which identifies what research is appropriate for the university or for industry   (Harsanyi 1981:121).

This lack of clear distinction also allows ideas and inventions to slip from the university to industry unnoticed. A strong pecuniary motive is behind this diffusion, and it is probably impossible to prevent. Yet even with the high potential salaries for professors who are willing to leave the university—for example, relatively inexperienced scientists receive salary offers in excess of $50,000 per year and additional fringe benefits (J. Fox 1982a:40)—large, established corporations have not been successful in attracting professorial labor. Only the provision of equity interest in startup companies combined with the ability to remain in the university convinced biology professors to become involved in private enterprise.

6. Social Relationships

within the University

The changing external environment as expressed in the new linkages between the universities, industry, and the government must necessarily impinge upon relationships internal to the university, that is, the relationships among faculty members and between faculty members and students. The fundamental cause of the social changes occurring in biology laboratories in both universities and research institutions is the blurring of the demarcations between basic and applied research. The ability of genetic engineering laboratories to produce commodities of potential commercial value quickly attracted entrepreneurial interest. However, for scientists to make commercial products these noncommercial commodities had to be privatized. Someone had to own them, and waged workers had to produce them. This required changes that affected relationships which had formerly been predicated upon the assumption that the work being done would have no market value. As we have seen, this fundamental premise broke down, and without this crucial support for traditional academic activities, the social arrangements of academe have become problematic. If the university is viewed as a location in the social system, the current changes can be viewed as a redefinition and restructuring of the university's role in society or as merely a phase in which processes now ripe for industrialization are relocated from the university to industry; if the latter is true the university will emerge unchanged when the relocation is completed.

The Myth of the Selfless Scientist

Scientists never have been as open and as dedicated to the pursuit of knowledge as popular mythology portrays. The image of the selfless scientist represents the usual human nostalgia for bygone days, when times were better and people more honest. Nevertheless, the rapid and widespread involvement of biologists in commercial enterprises has shocked the university. Confronted with important changes in university–corporate relations, university administrators have always been quick to reaffirm general, vacuous statements regarding honesty and trust.

Jonathan King, however, feels that corporate relations, especially the long-term agreements, could severely inhibit the informational networks that make possible the community of scholars. King (1981b:62), a full professor of biology at MIT, testified that

It has been American taxpayers who financed the training of biomedical researchers, the equipping of their laboratories, the salaries of support staff and the purchase of supplies and materials. In addition, somewhat contrary to corporate practice, they also supported the organization of open scientific meetings, the publishing of scientific journals, and the fiscal support for publishing papers. Not only has there been free and full exchange of information, but also of strains of organisms and materials you will get day to day in research.

The openness, the free exchange of ideas and information, the free exchange of strains, of proteins, of techniques, have been a critical component in the creativity and productivity of the biomedical research community.

King's argument is that the federally financed research system not only allowed but actually mandated a free flow of information and materials. This mandate was reinforced by the fact that journals required that experiments be reproducible and that the materials described in a publication be available to all competent investigators.

Of course, the absence of competition based on a profit motive did not mean that competition between researchers did not exist. Jonathan King testified to this ambivalence when he said in congressional hearings,

I don't mean to say there isn't professional jealousy. We have ambition and we have fame and recognition, but it is considered a departure from the normal and you are embarrassed when it comes out. It is not what you are supposed to be doing   (King 1981b:63).

In the university the competition is intense, but it also has moral strictures placed upon it by the ideals of what the university was meant to be.

The strength of the ethic of sharing of discoveries, organisms, and materials is best illustrated by an episode that occurred in 1971. James Watson, then director of Cold Spring Harbor Laboratory, accused an NIH researcher of withholding a viral strain from researchers at Cold Spring and threatened to use the following mechanisms to force the release of the organisms (Krimsky 1982:44):

1. He would personally write to the director of NIH to say there was a conspiracy to keep valuable agents from the scientific community.

2. He would write a letter to *Science* telling them, Lewis [the NIH investigator] later reported, "what kind of guy I was, and that I was sitting on these agents and had no right to be doing this when other people were interested in working with them."

3. He would write to Congress saying that "public money was being spent to develop reagents not being made available to other people."

Watson demonstrates the strength of the ethic, whose economic base lay in the fact that the government paid for the research. But there was also an ideological base, as is indicated by his threat to write a letter to *Science*. In this particular episode there were two reasons why the NIH researchers balked at delivering the requested virus: one was possible health and safety dangers, the other was a competitive one. Yet it was certain that when the pressure was put on them they would deliver—and they did (Krimsky 1982:43–45). The materials and, likewise, information did flow and, most important, no excuse could eliminate the necessity of delivering the requested materials and information.

Within department seminars and in simple personal interaction, especially in jubilation or puzzlement about results, colleagues have customarily discussed with one another the methods and implications of their respective findings. Emanuel Epstein, a noted microbiologist at UCD, has noted:

In the past it was the most natural thing in the world for colleagues to swap ideas on the spur of the moment, to share the latest findings hot off the scintillation counter or the electrophoresis cell, to show each other early drafts of papers, and in other such ways to act as companions in zealous research.

No more. Any UCD scientist with a promising new slant for [crop improvement] . . . will think twice before talking about it to anyone who is connected with either of the two Davis crop genetic private enterprises—or even with colleagues who in turn might speak to any such person. I know that this type of inhibition is already at work on this [the UCD] campus" (Meyerhoff 1982b:56).

Epstein observes that the fear of being scooped or of seeing one's work transformed into a commodity can silence those who presumably are colleagues. To see a thing that one produced turned into a product for sale by someone over whom one has no control can leave a person feeling violated. The labor of love is converted into a plain commodity—the work now is an item to be exchanged on the basis of its market price. Money becomes the arbiter of a scientific development's value.

Carl Djerassi, a professor of organic chemistry at Stanford, president of Zoecon, founder of Syntex, and a director of Cetus, finds in his experience a very different academia than the one Jonathan King described:

> There is plenty of other secrecy and confidentiality in academic life. I have been part-and-parcel of it for so many years that I am quite aware of it. I know it of my colleagues at my institution and many other institutions in my field, the desire to be first—which is an overriding one, in scientific research, perhaps unfortunately so, but realistically so—is such that the hotter the field, the less likely it is that people want to talk openly about it until they're sure of the results and until they send it in for publication (Djerassi 1981:150).

Djerassi is entirely correct in maintaining that secrecy is not new in academia—the incessant quest for grants, prizes, and status makes secrecy until publication important.[1] Yet secrecy in academia, as Watson demonstrated, has not until recently been as obsessive as that in industry.

In summation, what can be said of the precommercialization period in biotechnology? It seems legitimate to say that academia has always been characterized by strong rivalry and competition. Personal ambitions and envy have interfered with the free flow of information and, at times, forced students into difficult dilemmas and choices. Collegiality has been an ideal that sets the norms of behavior but is far from total. Nonetheless, as a center of scientific research, the university through its various mechanisms—publications, peer review, interchange of students and faculty, "old boy" networks, and departmental seminars—has been uniquely suited to the rapid transmission of information and materials.

In the rush to purchase access to professors and their laboratories, traditional social relationships involved in information and materials transmission are being transformed. The transformation is still in process, making it difficult to predict its outcome, but certainly the traditional values of openness and freedom will be replaced increasingly by obsessive secrecy

---

1. See Siekevitz (1980) for an eloquent plea for a return to traditional values.

and attempts to patent any and all discoveries considered commercializable. Scientific results that are private property have the feature of allowing the patenter to control the access of others to his work. The days of "science for science's sake" are disappearing in areas affected by biotechnology, and with them some unique social features, such as scientific openness.

A New Research Agenda

The most basic criticism of the developing corporate–university arrangements regards the decisions as to who controls the university's research agenda (Pajaro Dunes Biotechnology Statement [PDBS] 1982; Noble 1982; Kenney and Kloppenburg 1983). F. M. Scherer, the Northwestern University economist, commenting on recent trends in academia, wrote in 1980, "I have the impression that more recently emboldened by [success in giving grants to conservative scholars], business donors have become more confident and more strident . . . in attempting aggressively to 'turn' scholars, as John Le Carré might put it, in the direction of research with probable pro-business implications" (Scherer 1980:6). Scherer was writing about social scientists, but in fields such as biotechnology that are directly related to profitability this attempt to "turn" the research agenda is even more pronounced. Certainly the social and intellectual climate for these research-channeling activities has recently been superb.

It is most important to understand that the research agenda, because of its emergent and novel aspects, cannot be simply set. Yoxen (1981:74) has referred to the setting of the research agenda as being carried out in a condition of "directed autonomy," in which research scientists believe they retain—and do retain—a degree of autonomy over the planning of research. The strength of this belief of scientists is illustrated by the statement of a head of one of the laboratories that is involved in the Monsanto–WU agreement. The scientist said, "I do not feel pushed or directed or influenced in what I do" (Freeman 1983:9). Professor David Kipnis (1982:45), testifying in a congressional hearing regarding the Monsanto–WU agreement, placed the previous professor's statements in context:

We [the project review committee] have distributed to our faculty a description of the kinds of experimental approaches, as well as fields in which basic science should be encouraged.

We have not defined the projects because we don't have the applications to review.

But we have defined a very broad area from the point of view of gene expression to the point of where these materials act and how they act and clinical studies.

Kipnis has acknowledged that the research agenda at WU's School of Medicine is directed. Monsanto provides the funds, which quite naturally will attract researchers. Notice that the scientists are not *required* to work in these areas or *pushed* into them; they will choose freely to conduct research on the topics of interest to Monsanto.

Now, of course, other universities are less concerned with problems such as corporate influence of the research agenda. The *Cornell Communiqué* (1979:10), an alumni newsletter, describes the benefits of the Technology Transfer Program (in addition to the $600,000 it contributed to university income in 1978–79) in this manner: "Other, less tangible benefits also accrue: Faculty exposed to the industry's market for ideas are far more likely to apply themselves to problems reflecting the concerns of commerce, and are more able to draw corporate sponsorship of their research projects." Cornell does not mince words regarding its new Biotechnology Institute. An issue of *New York's Food and Life Sciences Quarterly* (1983:26), an official publication of the Cornell University Agricultural Experiment Station, in listing the institute's benefits to corporate sponsors, spelled out that "collaborating corporations will have [among other benefits]... a role in the guidance and development of academic biotechnology."

Of course, in the public press university administrators provide other justifications. Theodore Hullar, director of research for the College of Agriculture and Life Sciences, is quoted in the *Cornell Daily Sun*, the campus newspaper, as saying, "It's not for profits, it's not for patents, it's just for knowledge" (Jaschik and Kuntz 1982:9). This quote, published in September 1982, proved to be somewhat sanguine because in September 1983 legal negotiations were still under way, with a major point of contention being patents (Blodgett 1983). The companies feel that the research agenda of the Biotechnology Institute will provide things of potential commercial value.

The previous two examples are symptomatic of a much larger process by which research is increasingly being skewed to targets of greater commercial interest. This distortion takes place through a number of distinct patterns. In the first, the professor as an individual begins to orient his research toward specific products that have or could have potential value. In most cases this professor will already have an equity position in a company, and his university research is in an area that already may be close to a commercial application. The scientist's and the company's objectives will be closely aligned, and the scientist will quite understandably attempt to ensure his company's success. Also, his university research agenda can be subtly affected through the extension of corporate grants for specific research projects. For example, by choosing and funding scientists whose work is useful, a competitive advantage is provided, and this particular research topic expands. A more blatant influence is the letting of a contract to the scientist to do a specified piece of work—his agenda is then clearly specified.

Long-term contracts and research centers provide further opportunities for influencing the research agenda. Under these arrangements corporations choose projects to fund, and professors not funded will in relative terms lag behind their funded competitors. To recoup their position in such a competition they must conform—the purchaser of the research is king. The basic principle of science management is to provide funding opportunities in the topic of interest. So, for example, the current effort to incorporate plant molecular biology into plant breeding is convincing scientists to add a molecular biology component to funding proposals in plant breeding. In some cases this is merely decorative—but students and young faculty will learn molecular biology. Thereby the new desired paradigm gains adherents and begins to colonize the area through the wielding of its control over research funds.

Conflicts of Interest

Ordinarily the term *conflict of interest* is used in relation to the interests of individuals. In most cases it is not considered a conflict when an institution such as a university signs a contract to do specific research for a corporation. The notion of a conflict of interest individualizes what is in actuality a systemic problem regarding the desire of individuals to increase their income and remain competitive. The emphasis upon the danger of conflicts of interest assumes that decision making should be untainted by "money" or "politics." In many cases, however, supposed conflicts of interest are used politically to defuse and disperse public ire regarding the workings of the economic system by providing scapegoats, that is, immoral individuals. When the problem is presented at the individual level, it appears that the solutions are simply to compel disclosure and enforce legislation regarding the proper type or amount of interest conflicts.

What are these potential conflicts of interest? Conflicts of interest in biotechnology stem from the fact that nearly all of the biotechnology researchers have university appointments and yet work for and sometimes own substantial interests in companies that are commercializing biotechnological research. Among the manifestations of these conflicts are the use of students and university equipment for private gain, the division of working time in such a way as to slight the university, the shifting of research to accommodate corporate sponsors, the transfer of patentable inventions from the university to private laboratories, and the suppressing of research results. These are not unusual in the corporate world or, more correctly, are standard operating procedure for profit-making entities; but they have been rare in university social relations.

David Noble and Nancy Pfund (1980:252), writing in *The Nation*, summarize these conflicts thus: "Once priorities have shifted from social need, the ostensible concern of government, to potential return on investment, which is business's main criterion, patents, proprietary interest and secrecy will no doubt replace open debate, peer review and publication as the norms of the academic scientific community." This type of change is "natural" when the branch of knowledge becomes part of the production process. Conflicts of interest have always been a feature of universities and merely express the fact that certain branches of research are closely related to commerce. Yet biotechnology is a special case because of the rapidity of the growth and the pervasiveness of university–industry interactions.

Perhaps the simplest and most ingenious method for avoiding conflicts of interest was expressed by Anthony Faras, a professor at the University of Minnesota and cochairman of Molecular Genetics, Inc.: "He [Dr. Faras] takes pains to avoid any conflict of interest between his academic and corporate work. 'We were very careful not to move even a pipette between my lab and the company,' he says. 'The only thing we moved was the expertise to apply the technology to a commercial application' " (*Business Week* 1982d:59). It is strange that Faras believes that conflict of interest is nothing more than mere theft—which is what removal of university property is. In fact, if the expertise being produced in his university laboratory is moved without compensation to Molecular Genetics Faras might be liable to charges of conflict of interest. Faras's simple formulation negates any reason for concern as long as nothing physical is removed. The key to biotechnology, as Dr. Faras well understands, is not physical instruments but knowledge. And his laboratory, where the knowledge was created, was supported by government funds. To be conducting research for two separate institutions with quite different missions may make it impossible not to be confronted with conflicting duties (Faras remains a professor at the University of Minnesota but in 1984 resigned as cochairman of Molecular Genetics).

If conflict of interest is more than not stealing pipettes or perhaps benefiting unfairly from government research monies, it must be accepted that being a professor or university scientist is somewhat more than a "job." If "the academic seeks knowledge and learning for its own sake" (Linnell, quoted in Inman 1983:1), then certain other behavioral rules are to be expected. These behaviors include ensuring free and open flow of information, not exploiting students, spending the requisite time with students, not exploiting or appropriating university research for private use. On the other hand, if a professor is not seeking learning for learning's sake, then it is only proper to treat him as an employee and seek greater control over his work activities.

The simplest case of interest conflict—it is by no means unusual—occurs when a professor has a significant equity interest in the company, receives consulting fees from the company, and simultaneously has been awarded a research grant from the company. Cases of conflict of interest are very difficult to discover because securing access to accountings of professorial grants is very difficult. The classic case of this type of multiple linkage in the biotechnology industry involved Herbert Boyer, the founder of Genentech, who also received a $200,000 Genentech grant to clone bacteria to produce somatostatin. A postdoctoral student in Boyer's laboratory describes the changes that occurred with the creation of Genentech:

> "I remember that first day. . . . There were only twelve of us in Boyer's lab, and one guy was singled out to have a confidential meeting with Herb and Bob Swanson [Genentech's financial overseer and cofounder]. We all wondered what was going on, and he came back out and couldn't tell us. Right then, that very moment, things changed in the lab, and it sort of all fell apart from that point"   (Boly 1982a:174).

Boyer's UCSF laboratory became a corporate laboratory producing in secret for commercial gain.

Yet rather than being unusual, these types of relationships have become quite the norm, especially for small biotechnology companies. The state of California, as a result of a lawsuit filed by CRLA, has compelled professors to file financial documents regarding equity interests and potential conflicts of interest (Meyerhoff et al. 1981; Hilts 1982b). The disclosures revealed a number of conflicts. One of the most salient was that of a UCB plant pathology professor who not only was on the Advanced Genetic Sciences' scientific board, but also had received consulting fees of more than $10,000 from the company. The circle was completed by his serving as principal investigator on an $82,302 grant from the company to his laboratory at the university (Sward 1983:4). After questions were raised regarding this problem, the president of Advanced Genetic Sciences, Daniel Adams, is quoted as saying, "Much of the publicity in these kinds of cases is unfair. We were not dictating the subjects of research in any way" (Sanger 1983:22). As another example, California Biotechnology, Inc., formed by E. F. Hutton, has provided equity interest to John Baxter and John Shine. These two professors "will be retaining their laboratories, and much of the research [for the entire company] will be contracted to them at their institutions" (Finn 1982:3). These types of research arrangements are pervasive and are evidence of a new genre of interrelationships.

The relative strictness of UC, Yale, and Harvard is matched by a liberality at other universities that have less to offer academically and therefore must offer even more control to companies. But even prestigious universities such as MIT have comparatively lax standards for the prevention of conflicts of interest. For example, the Damon Corporation formed a subsidiary, Damon Biotech, Inc., and appointed five MIT professors as consultant/advisors. These professors received equity positions and consultant fees; whether they have also received research grants is unknown. The potential for conflicts of interest is clear (*The Tech* 1982:4). But MIT officials say they see no possibility of conflicts of interest. John Kinsey, the

Table 6.1. MIT Biology Department Faculty and Corporate Affiliations

Professor	Corporation
David Baltimore	Collaborative Research
Eugene Bell	Damon Biotech
David Botstein	Collaborative Research
Herman Eisen	Damon Biotech
Gerald Fink	Collaborative Research
Leonard Guarente	Biotechnica International
David Housman	Integrated Genetics
Har Gobind Khorana	Damon Biotech
Harvey Lodish	Damon Biotech
Irving London	Damon Biotech
Salvador Luria	Repligen
Alexander Rich	Repligen
Paul Schimmel	Repligen
Philip Sharp	Biogen
Susumu Tonegawa	Damon Biotech

Sources: Various publications

chemistry department chairman, has said, "I don't see that the area itself defines any conflict." Robert Byers, the director of the MIT news office, is paraphrased as saying, "There is no conflict of interest inherent in the situation." Kimball Valentine, an MIT attorney, agreed, saying, "The forming of firms by professors is a time-honored practice. . . . I don't see any conflicts of interest in forming a company in one's own field of specialty" (Fong and Scofield 1981:1). The liberality of MIT is well known. Table 6.1 lists MIT biology professors who are known to hold equity positions in biotechnology companies.

Conflicts of interest may be present in a number of activities and relationships that a professor may be involved in. Important specific relationships are being transformed, as we shall see below in discussing the implications for the university as a community. Individually, any one of these changes might be unimportant, but viewed in totality they seem likely to usher in a drastic change, and these changes will in all probability be reproduced in other academic disciplines of commercial interest.

Students

I recently visited a major teaching department in biophysics and molecular biology at a major university. This was a department with a distinguished record of Ph.D. production. The faculty of the department appeared, on my visit, to be split sharply down the middle between those who had not and those who had commercial affiliations. Those who had commercial affiliations had a particular charm for the incoming graduate students because they seemed to offer to

graduate students a fine opportunity for employment, once the Ph.D. degree was earned.
    The dissertations . . . , I was told, which were being handed out, had deteriorated in quality and some of these were purely developmental product-oriented studies of little basic importance, but of considerable possible monetary value. This was happening in a department where the university was, in fact, not actively participating, as far as I could tell, in this commercial venture. . . . Regrettably, in some cases, some of the most famous faculty members in the department are rarely seen on campus. They are much too busy with other things. I hear tales of graduate students who claim that their preceptors do not even know their names because they meet them so rarely, the preceptors spending much time in the industrial facility, whether in this country or, on occasion, in Europe   *(Stetten 1981:63–64).*

The actual laboratory work of biotechnology, especially in molecular biology, is not performed by the professors. Quite the contrary, postdoctoral students and graduate students perform the bulk of the actual work (Hopson 1977:61; J. Fox 1981a). Both postdocs and graduate students are vulnerable to pressure from professors as to the type and direction of their research. Jonathan King at MIT has described the possible fate of graduate students when their preceptors become businessmen: "In the contract work the graduate students are still kind of cheap labor; they are cheap labor and the post-doctoral fellows are cheap labor, et cetera. And they are very often changed to something that has to be done for the marketability of that project" (King 1981b:73). The cheapness of labor and their high skill levels make these workers most desired by professors. The salaries of university postdoctoral students are in the $15,000 to $20,000 range, but for the granting agency the overhead and benefits could build their salary costs to $25,000 to $30,000 (typical overhead is approximately 50 percent). The importance of postdoctoral students is indicated, for example, by the rumor that Biogen built its new research facility in Cambridge, Massachusetts, because of the difficulty of obtaining Swiss work permits for American postdoctoral students (Dickson 1980b:769).
    The fact that students are so dependent upon their thesis chairman means that they are easily exploited, although Walter Gilbert, the former Harvard biology professor and now president of Biogen, has said he has no such concern, believing that any commercial exploitation of a student will be exposed and the exploiting professor doomed, "since commercially motivated work is often not academically meritorious and so [the professor] will not attract top flight graduate students and government grants" (Aisenberg 1982:617). In actuality, professors with money for fellowships and

assistantships will attract graduate students and postdoctoral students in the same way that a company with money is able to hire workers. This edge in the competition for the vital laboratory work force confers an advantage on the well-endowed professor. Concomitantly, money garnered by one faculty member pressures the others to also secure industrial support.

Abuse of students is best documented at Stanford and UCD. Even in these locations, however, actual facts are difficult to obtain, as students who criticize their professors place their entire career in jeopardy (see figure 6.1). The weapons for disciplining a talkative graduate student or postdoctoral student are many, and the student has little recourse. The academic affairs committee of the Stanford Graduate Student Association (SGSA) issued a statement documenting abuses. A National Public Radio reporter describes one incident of faculty abuse:

> A Stanford post-doc was upset when her advisor told a company which the advisor consulted for about the project she was working on and her approach to its solution. The company then assigned a large number of personnel to an identical project and rapidly solved the problem. The post-doc had nothing to show for months of work and was forced to begin a new project from ground zero   (SGSA 1982b:1).

In another case, "a Stanford Master's [degree] student complained that he had been hired as a research associate to design and build a system using only industrial standard parts, and that at some point in the future he might be hired directly by the faculty member's company to package the units for sale" (SGSA 1982b:2). By all standards university students are not supposed to be merely inexpensive labor, yet the commercialization of research is increasing the possibility of such misuse.

Perhaps the most detailed case of ethically suspect student–professor interactions concerns Ray Valentine's linkage with Calgene (discussed earlier in the section on the linkage between UCD and Allied Corporation). Students accused the company of exploiting their ideas. William Boly (1982a:172) quoted one of Valentine's postdocs as saying, "Calgene gets first crack at all our ideas." The suspicion that consultants for Calgene were raiding students and postdocs for ideas increased, and eventually JaRue Manning, the then graduate advisor in microbiology, felt compelled to write a memorandum to the graduate group chairman detailing the gravity of the situation. Manning (1982:82) wrote:

> Four of the five students [working in Valentine's laboratory] have expressed a desire to transfer out of Professor Valentine's laboratory. Although each student has concerns that are unique, there are at least two factors common to all of them. First is the statement by Professor Valentine that it is the student's responsibility and not his [Professor

Conflict of Interest?

Students experiencing

1. Research directed toward capital gain rather than scientific advancement,
2. Corporate work done under the guise of research,
3. Unfair patent and copyright policy.

You can help. A study is being done to focus the problem and formulate solutions.

Contact the Ombudsman's Office

John Goheen
Building 260
Room 261
497-3682

If names are given, anonymity is assured. Anonymous letters will be accepted. ——————————————

Source: Stanford University n.d.

Figure 6.1. Stanford University Conflict of Interest Notice

119

Valentine's] to meet with CalGene personnel and establish that their graduate research project is not being conducted at CalGene. Second is the switching of student research projects as a condition for continued support after students have spent up to two and one half years on a project.

Due to the scandalous situation that had developed, Manning suggested to the chairman "that until items 1) and 2) above [conditions in the previous quote] have been satisfactorily resolved that Professor Valentine not be allowed to accept any graduate students" (Manning 1982:82). For all intents and purposes this memorandum can be interpreted as censure by colleagues. It has been standard practice for professors to exploit graduate students (see Conrad 1982:167). Valentine took this practice one step further in trying to exploit students for commercially valuable ideas.

The situation at UCD is probably being repeated in molecular biology laboratories across the country. Jeffrey Fox (1981a:44), the well-known science writer for *Chemical and Engineering News* and *Science*, reported an example of the types of events that may occur: "Several postdocs describe an informal bull session convened by one professor. 'Let's have a discussion of practical projects,' he reportedly suggested without telling the lab group that he was involved with a private company." The importance of students as generators of new ideas cannot be underestimated— and ideas are crucial to improving biotechnological production methods. The presumed noncommercial relationship between a student and his mentor is easily violated and quickly destroyed. A professor may find it difficult to keep knowledge or ideas produced at the university separate from those produced while he or she was working in an industrial lab. Information and ideas created by graduate students could thus flow to a professor's company, purposefully or inadvertently. Henry Kaplan, a Stanford professor of radiology, feels it is possible to "imagine perhaps graduate students or post-doctoral fellows who do research for professors with company connections, finding themselves under pressure to do work of direct benefit to the professor's company" (Andreopoulos 1981:2).

The commercial ties of one faculty member may conflict with those of another, thereby complicating students' selection of dissertation committees and inhibiting the sharing of the knowledge necessary to carry out research. In one case at Stanford, "students were told that a faculty member's close ties with an industrial concern meant that he would have to leave a project involving several faculty and students before another firm would contribute funds" (SGSA 1982b:2). In this case the "typical" collegial relationship of interfaculty cooperation was interrupted and the potential benefits to students of a faculty member's advice and direction were lost. In another case at Stanford, a professor forming a company based on research in his laboratory "filed a patent disclosure on a group project without informing or including other faculty or student group members" (SGSA 1982b:2). While not technically illegal, the action certainly damaged cooperation between members of the research team. Numerous potential conflicts arise when a professor is also a businessman, and there seem to be few effective means of protecting students in the existing structure.

The above problems stem from professors' involvement with students, but the opposite situation can also occur—faculty who become increasingly involved in managing a company can begin to neglect their duties. J. Fox (1981a:41) quoted a postdoctoral student as saying, "It's definitely, absolutely happening; people are neglecting their labs because they're spending time for their companies." Increasingly, universities are invoking the one day per week consulting rule to ensure that professors are discharging their duties as faculty members (Giamatti 1982; Bok 1981). Whether regulations such as these will ensure that students receive adequate attention is doubtful. At major research universities students are also neglected by professors for other than commercial reasons.

The crux of the problem for the university is that the student–teacher relationship is not a commercial one, that is, one of employer–employee or salesman–client. The obligations between the two are personal and idiosyncratic—yet simultaneously asymmetric. The exploitation of students for a faculty member's academic advancement is traditional; on the other hand, the professor's potential to profit financially from a student's work places the relationship in a very different light. The problem has perhaps been best summarized by the SGSA's academic affairs committee (SGSA 1981a:1): "Many graduate students are also uneasy when their advisors take equity and managerial positions in firms closely related to their research. Are they now working for their advisor the Professor, or their advisor the Entrepreneur?"

The Free Flow of Information

The flow of information and material has been crucial to the progress of biology, and, as mentioned earlier, this has been undergirded by the pervasiveness of governmental support. Because the bulk of biological research had no commercial utility, there was little reason for researchers not to share information or materials or both after receiving due recognition through publication. It is somewhat artificial to separate information from materials, but the two do present somewhat different problems, so the next section will concentrate on the free flow of materials. Obstruction of information flow strikes at the essence of the university—both the ideal of collegiality and the goal of providing well-trained students. The obstruction of material flow will disrupt research and the ability to reproduce results (the specific organism is required to ensure replicability). In the field of biotechnology, "products" of the university—information and materials—are undergoing a transformation in status.

Success in the university has traditionally been predicated upon publication, collegial estimation, and scholarly awards. An indication of the prestige of a university has been the number of its publications and active seminars. Visibility and prestige among peers were translated by the peer review system into funding. At a more micro level, internal, or departmental, discussions have been a source of ideas and inspiration. Discussion and debate have been an essential characteristic of the university.

The arrangements described in the previous chapters have placed constraints upon the type, amount, and destination of information disseminated. Information flow has not been halted; rather, the flow has been redirected. For example, in the MGH molecular genetics department, information now flows to Hoechst, bypassing academic journals and the other forms of scholarly communication. Similar flows are directed by other university–corporate agreements or by the entrepreneurial interests of professors. Professors who are corporate equity owners naturally direct the products of their research toward their companies, and, of course, this redirection excludes others from receiving information.

The objection by most critics of university–corporate relations has been that they may stifle the free flow of information. The response has been that the contracts with universities guarantee publication rights after short delays for patenting. Modeling information flow on a flowchart indicates that university information is merely taking new paths. Further, what has occurred is that the timing of the flow has changed. The sponsoring company gets the information first. In a fast-moving field, speed is all-important; the spoils go to the fastest. If a competitor must wait two or three extra months, the company that is the first recipient of the important information will have the important initial advantage and, in all probability, will have reinforced itself with patents.

The redirection of information flows with the objective of securing private profit is having the effect of increasing secrecy on campus. Inside departments, secrecy has grown. Jonathan King (King 1981b:63), the MIT biology professor, testified as follows before a congressional committee: "I will tell you that the atmosphere around biology department coffee pots has changed in the last few years. It is clear this is a new element coming in there." So many MIT biology professors are linked to commercial operations that the department can hardly be as open and freewheeling as it was earlier. Having a commercially valuable idea adopted by one's university colleague would be infuriating and would lead to tremendous ill will. One former postdoctoral student who worked in Boyer's laboratory during the formation of Genentech described his relationship with fellow researchers who were working for the company: "You knew they weren't free to talk about their work. They were your friends, so you didn't want to make them feel awkward. So you sort of censored yourself'' (Boly 1982a:174). Secrecy is increasingly the norm among biology professors who possess valuable information.

Professors must also limit the topics of public discussions, especially of research for which patents might be issued. An article by two lawyers published in a trade journal in 1981, entitled "To Publish or Profit" (Misrock and Stern 1981), actually discussed whether certain academic work should be kept a trade secret. In Europe, discussion prior to the filing of a patent can lead to the loss of patent rights, thereby discouraging prepatent discussion. The possibility that others might steal an invention led Albert Halluin, then an Exxon patent attorney and now Cetus chief patent counsel, to advise members of the American Society for Microbiology as follows:

In the future when you come to scientific meetings and you are going to give a presentation, consider going to a notary public to have notarized [the material] you are going to [present, giving] the date when you wrote it down and the colleges you are going to visit and have a professional conversation about what you are doing, consider not telling them certain things because then if they go run with what you told them, they are not in violation of any law   (King 1981b:76).

Such a message delivered to the prestigious American Society for Microbiology served to raise the level of scientists' awareness as to the value of information. That the relative merits of secrecy are being discussed indicates its increasing prevalence.

The fact that most biotechnology scientists are now connected to various companies implies that most professors are competitors. H. J. Kooreman, a research and development specialist for Gist-Brocades, a Dutch multinational company, stated that at a recent international conference "people [were] always trying to get information out of you. . . . But . . . nobody here [was] really talking. Even the university people [were] being extremely secretive, and that's new" (Lancaster 1981:25). DeWitt Stetten (1981:65), in a presentation at the 1981 Battelle Conference on Genetic Engineering, presented a similar anecdote:

I spoke to two friends. One, an academic biologist, the other an industrial biologist. I asked both of them the same question, the question one always asks: "What are you doing? What are you going to do next?" The academic biologist bubbled over and gave me a list of products he and his colleagues were trying to make. The industrial man said, "I've got a list but unfortunately I can't tell you what's on it."

University scientists are increasingly being transformed into industrial scientists, and the corollary is that new paths of information flow are being developed.

The entrance of patent considerations into the biological sciences has been decried by some as increasing secrecy (Noble and Pfund 1980; Wade 1980a:IX). Yet others have argued that patenting contributes to information flow through protecting disclosures (Hart 1983; Djerassi 1981:151). The key to understanding these two contradictory positions is to see patenting as a legal mechanism to create private property. The system requires secrecy until the patent application is filed. Therefore during the research process maintaining secrecy in order to prevent preemption by competitors has high priority. Further, any disclosure of work in progress could invalidate the patent (see appendix 2 for a discussion of Cohen–Boyer and challenges), and therefore the research process becomes cloaked in secrecy. The ideal patent is one that emerges out of total secrecy to catch competitors unaware.

The fact is that secrecy in research becomes standard, and information flows only to corporate colleagues. The argument that patenting facilitates information flow is true only insofar as in the absence of patenting trade secrecy would shroud everything. Publication of research results becomes somewhat trivial when the patent filing precedes publication. Charles Weissman, a senior scientist at Biogen, said "he would quit his company before he would allow the suppression of a publication of his for secrecy reasons. 'The only difference [between the university and Biogen] is that we put some of our work in a patent application before we publish in scientific literature. But then, it's quicker to write a patent application than to publish' " (*GEN* 1981b:4). The fact that company scientists are allowed to publish is not so important; publishing is good advertising for the company and improves employee morale.

The favor with which commentators have received the idea of company scientists publishing exhibits either naivete or an attempt to propagandize (Hart 1983:100; Benner 1981:68). The actual result of these changes will be that the openness that characterizes industrial disclosure through patents will become the norm for free information flow. The cross-fertilization that occurs in the lab during informal conversations over coffee will end or at least be curtailed. Paul Berg, professor of biochemistry and Nobel Laureate, put it very well: "No longer do you have this free flow of ideas. You go to scientific meetings and people whisper to each other about their companies' products. It's like a secret society" (Dunner 1981:60). This reaction by Berg—similar to that we saw expressed earlier by Stetten—is related not only to secrecy but also to a lack of spontaneity in answering questions. For example, I have been to biotechnology meetings where, upon close questioning, the presenters have had to refuse to answer a question because it might reveal proprietary information (see also Kennedy 1982). Such evasions indicate that, patents or no patents, certain previously accepted norms of openness and congeniality have changed.

Another new circulation pattern coming into existence is citing in such a way as to protect proprietary rights. Mark Ptashne, the key scientist in the proposed Harvard company, claimed that as early as 1980 colleagues were beginning to write papers and cite references in such a way as to ensure their patent claims were valid (Dickson 1980a:388). Ptashne is seconded by Sidney Pestka of the Roche Institute, who is quoted as saying, "The quality of what's published has also become suspect. People aren't putting all the information necessary for science in the papers, and reviewers aren't picking it up" (Lancaster 1980:20). The statement has the ring of truth. Pestka, incidentally, was central in the so-called hijacking of UCLA KG1 cell line for transfer to Roche.

Not all of the information channels are closing; an important new one has been opened: the press conference (Andreapoulos 1980). Biogen used this ploy to announce their victory in the race to be the first company to produce interferon bacterially. Companies use it to increase the value of their stock before its issue, doing so subtly, however, to avoid violating certain laws regarding stock issuance. In some cases, press conferences are held before a discovery is published in scientific journals—a practice considered to be somewhat disreputable. Previously the announcement to the public coincided with the journal's appearance. The objective of scientific disclosure has thus been transformed into a method of advertising a company. The information offered emphasizes commercial potential rather than scientific achievement. This method of disclosing scientific results will likely increase as the salutary effect on stock prices is noted.

The channels of information flow in biology are being adapted to the reality of the market. The patent and the press conference are becoming the chosen instruments of universities as well as industry for releasing information. The research process by implication will be less open because of the need to prevent premature disclosure or preemptory patenting by a commercial competitor. The previous information flow patterns guaranteed by federal funding are being undermined by the new corporate monies.

The Free Flow of Materials

The flow of information is inextricably linked to the flow of biological materials, which are the tools of both university and industry research. An etiquette had developed that biological materials should be freely passed to all scientists presumed competent to use them. As it became obvious in the late 1970s that these research materials could have commercial value, a number of universities developed forms to be signed by investigators from other universities who were requesting materials. Figure 6.2 is an example of the form Harvard University developed to accompany requests for plasmids. It specifically states that the recipient must not pass the plasmids on and must periodically report on their use. But the most im-

Date

Name
Title
Address

Dear

In answer to your inquiry, we are willing to provide you with plasmid   (here-
after the "plasmid") subject to the following terms and conditions:

1. The plasmid and any and all progeny or mutants made through the use of such plasmid
are to be used only for research purposes. Any use of such plasmid or any and all
progeny or mutants thereof for the production of goods or products for sale shall
be subject to a separate agreement between   and Harvard negotiated in good
faith and containing terms affording appropriate compensation to Harvard for such
use and   agrees such goods or products will not be sold before formalization
of such agreement.

2. The plasmid is to remain the property of the President and Fellows of Harvard
College.   shall report to Harvard every twelve (12) months as to whether it
is using and intends to continue using the plasmid. In the event   is no longer
using or does not intend to continue using the plasmid, it shall be returned to
Harvard. It is understood that you will be in periodic contact with   at Harvard,
as mutually agreed between you and him, to report on   work which utilizes the
plasmid.

3. No specimens of the plasmid are to be given or made available to any other person
(other than   employees), firm, or corporation, but are to remain under your
immediate and direct control.

If you find these terms and conditions to be acceptable, kindly indicate that fact by
signing in the space provided below and returning this letter to us.

                                                  _____
                                                  Stephen H. Atkinson
                                                  Executive Secretary

ACCEPTED:

_____for _____   Date:_____

Source: Harvard University n.d.

Figure 6.2. Harvard University Plasmid Form Letter

portant clause prohibits commercial use unless Harvard receives a share of any revenues.

The incident that provoked a major effort to improve control over the flow of biological materials involved UC, the National Cancer Institute (NCI), the Roche Institute of Molecular Biology, Hoffmann-La Roche (the Swiss transnational), and Genentech. In this case two researchers at UCLA developed a cell line (KG1) that they used for experiments that were described in *Science* in 1978 (Koeffler and Golde 1978).[2] Robert Gallo, an investigator at NCI, requested KG1 from the researchers and after receiving it noticed that it produced interferon. Sidney Pestka, of the Roche Institute, a research center "wholly funded by, but generally considered as scientifically independent from, the drug firm of Hoffmann–La Roche" (obviously an erroneous assumption) (Wade 1980c:1492), requested and received KG1 from NCI and set to work inducing it to produce greater quantities of interferon.

Unbeknownst to Gallo and the UCLA researchers, Roche had contracted Genentech to reprogram KG1 to superproduce interferon and had filed a patent on KG1 (*GEN* 1983b:4). But when the UCLA researchers discovered that KG1 had been passed on to commercial producers they objected that no permission had been granted to Roche for the use of the cell line. The UC system agreed and litigation ensued between UC and Roche (Wade 1980d).

According to etiquette, Gallo should have passed the cells only after receiving permission to do so from the original investigators. But Gallo had no idea that Pestka and Roche had a commercial proposition in mind. Of course, little trouble would have ensued if KG1 had not become a valuable interferon producer (Wade 1980d). The final disposition of the various lawsuits was that Roche paid an undisclosed sum of money to UC and UC withdrew its claims (Culliton 1983:372).

The actual guilt or innocence of the various parties is not as important as the lesson the incident provided to researchers that these formerly merely useful research materials now have market value. Previous to this, Gallo believed that "passing around cell lines to serious investigators [was] the way ethical scientists [were] supposed to behave" (Boly 1982a:173). After the incident Gallo insisted that he would not "send anything out of [his] lab unless it's 100% [his] or [he had] written approval from everyone involved" (Lancaster 1980:20).

Nicholas Wade (1980d:1493), writing in *Science*, found it

harder to explain...why [Pestka]—or someone on Roche's behalf—apparently neglected to observe the scientific courtesy of asking per-

2. This speculation is based on the fact that Genentech wrote into the contract that Roche would protect Genentech from all liabilities (Genentech 1980a). However, this clause probably appears in many contracts between startups and MNCs.

mission to clone the cells and to file patents on the clones. . . . The handling of the cells by Roche and Genentech after they had come into Pestka's possession was a secret process, allowing Roche alone to benefit at the expense of others.

Wade himself partially explains why Roche chose to ignore scientific etiquette, but a more complete answer is also possible. Roche probably realized that it might eventually have to pay for KG1, but it was compelled to act in the manner it did to ensure secrecy during the development process. As Wade (1980d:1474) wrote in *Science*, "The powerful forces of the profit motive clearly have the capacity to strain and rupture the informal traditions of scientific exchange." Roche probably was eager to prevent competitors from knowing what it was doing—secrecy and the "hijacking" of KG1 was justified in their cost-benefit calculus.

The tremendous profit potential in biotechnology has led to a number of other significant incidents regarding material flows, and in each case profit-making entities are involved. In at least three cases commercially interesting cell lines were removed from universities to industry in violation of normal etiquette. In each case it was postdoctoral students who were the culprits. In defense of these postdocs, Bertram Rowland (1982:4), the attorney who handles UC and Stanford patent litigation, has written: "When graduate students and postdoctoral researchers left their universities, it was commonplace that they would take with them materials with which they had worked, so as to be able to continue their research. . . . From the point of view of the profit motive, the information and materials had no value." Although students have been known to take cell lines, professors likely have had much greater opportunity to move cell lines with little possibility of exposure; in fact, such transference is probably pervasive.

In one case, a postdoctoral student in John Baxter's laboratory at UCSF removed a cell line adapted for human growth hormone production to Genentech, his new employer. This led to an intense competition between Genentech and UCSF to be the first credited with synthesizing the growth hormone (Andreopoulos 1980:744). Both institutions announced success in press releases issued on the same day, though in neither case was it "on the basis of published data" (Andreopoulos 1980:744). Published data would come later. The result of the misappropriation of this cell line was that Genentech achieved a publicity coup and retained the cell line. UCSF was paid a $350,000 lump sum and given the right to royalties (Boly 1982a:176).

A similar event occurred when Calgene hired a postdoctoral student from Ray Valentine's laboratory and he took a cell line with him. Valentine granted permission to transfer the line to the company, but UCD requested that the line be returned and it was (Boly 1982b). However, the information had already been transferred to Calgene. Policing the flow of materials is as difficult as guaranteeing a free flow and, as commercial opportunities are developed, reciprocal flow will dwindle.

The last incident involved a Japanese postdoctoral researcher, Hideaki Hagiwara, who took a monoclonal antibody–producing cell line back to Japan to treat his mother, who was dying of cancer. Numerous complications cloud this incident, including the fact that Hagiwara's father operates a commercial health care research institute in Japan (Sun 1983b:393). Further, the research had been conducted in a laboratory funded by Hybritech, a firm which Royston founded and in which he owns an important equity interest. Table 5.1 indicates that the *Science* article which declared that "Royston is a minor shareholder" (Sun 1983b:394) was incorrect. The ultimate settlement was an agreement between Hagiwara's institute, Royston, and UC in which UC retained patent rights but would extend an exclusive license to the Hagiwaras to sell any products derived from the cell line in Japan and other Asian countries. UC also receives royalties on these sales. "Royston and Hagiwara also agreed to exchange information generated from future research on the cell line" (Sun 1983b:394). Likely this means that Hybritech will have access to any information and uses generated in Japan. The satisfaction of Royston and, presumably, of Hybritech is indicated by the fact that Royston and Hagiwara are coauthoring two articles (*GEN* 1983d:27). Still, this incident almost certainly will lead to greater constriction of freedom of access and less trusting of fellow scientists with cell lines.

The times have changed even since 1975, when Cesar Milstein and Georges Köhler invented monoclonal antibody–producing hybridoma (defined in appendix 1) and decided not to patent it. To some extent Milstein and Köhler did not recognize the commercial value of their discovery (Wade 1980c:693), but they did not neglect to ask recipients of their cell line to also refrain from patenting the line (Milstein n.d.). Wade (1980c:693) described the way these scholars handled their research materials thus: "Milstein did not apply for a patent on his technique. He gave away his plasmacytoma cells in the usual scientific tradition of free exchange, asking only that recipients should not patent any hybridomas made from the cells and that they should not pass them on to third parties." The new property relations developing in biotechnology are ensuring that the information flow patterns for materials will also change. Many research materials that formerly would have been placed in circulation are now being withheld.

Industry is caught in a difficult situation—ideally they would rather keep all their materials and information in-house; however, their need to be able to tap into the information and material exchange network means that they must be prepared to circulate materials and information. Thus, Genentech has drawn up a form that it requires requesters of biological materials to sign. The form has largely the same stipulations as other such forms with the exception of one clause. The clause reads, "I understand I may publish the results of my experiments using (a named plasmid), but only with the consent of Genentech; such consent not to be untimely or unreasonably withheld" (Genentech n.d.). The Genentech form opens with the salutation, "Genentech is happy to supply you with a sample of (a named plasmid)" (Genentech n.d.). Quite obviously these types of stipulations do not qualify as being in keeping with a free flow of information or materials. In fact, the early transmission of results to Genentech could result in an outside researcher's discoveries being patented by Genentech.

The ultimate effects of this privatization are unclear. The university could merely transform and adjust. However, it is not certain that the university can continue to satisfy its functions of training and doing general research for society with such restricted information flow. However, if the current frenzy to secure professors abates it is possible that new lines between commercial and basic research will be drawn, but information and materials will flow freely only when no commercial possibilities exist. On the other hand, the constriction and rechanneling of information and materials flow could severely handicap the entire research system. If such practices spread to other departments, they could destroy the university as an institution dedicated to the open and free pursuit of knowledge— essentially killing the goose that laid the golden eggs.

Changing internal social relationships have accompanied the new commercial links, both individual and institutional. Leslie Glick (1981:145), founder and president of Genex, has testified regarding joint ventures between a university and faculty that "Not only will commercial considerations influence decisions about thesis topics and research proposals, but they will likely also influence the employment and promotion of professors. We have seen that the commercialization of academic biomedical research is fraught with potential hazards." Though Glick was referring only to joint ventures such as MGH–Hoechst and Washington University–Monsanto, it seems highly probable that the fact that professors are becoming equity owners in companies also poses dangers for the university.

The idea that a worker (scientist) could have a conflict of interest presumes assumptions regarding the role of the university as a producer of research accessible to the entire society. The business relationships preclude this because of the centrality of the requirement of privatization. Yet it seems as though the problem of conflicts of interest is insoluble. Probably new rules will be confined to forcing professors to continue to acquire overhead-producing grants. Generally administrations can be expected to respond only when their interests are threatened.

The networks of information flow have now been reoriented in such a way as to ensure that financiers and corporate managers quickly get access to information. Also, we saw that a new information channel has been opened by the judicious use of press conferences to tout scientific "breakthroughs," many timed to precede stock offerings. This rechanneling has led to charges that there is an increase of secrecy in the university. The distinction between secrecy of results, which the patent mechanism adequately addresses, and secrecy in research, which must be strengthened due to the fact that disclosures destroy patent rights, has not been made. Increasingly information is made public now with commercial, not academic, requirements in mind.

The once relatively open exchange of biological materials is becoming more formalized and selective. Similarly, sharing of equipment and willingness to perform certain tasks for other scientists is increasingly based on financial remuneration or linkage to the same company. Increasingly the materials of research are regarded as commodities and therefore no longer acquired on the basis of need but rather for money.

The role of students, and especially of postdoctoral researchers, is also changing. In some cases, mentors are guiding students toward commercial research, and in other cases their ideas and research topics are being transferred to companies without financial compensation for the students. This practice formerly was considered unethical. More and more biology students are being used as workers while still being classified as students. The student–professor relationship, which must, at least partially, be based on trust, cannot long survive when obvious monetary interests are involved. The rampant commercialization and commodification of the previously nonmarket professor–student relationship may not be good for the long-term health of the U.S. university system.

The earlier fragile system of peer pressure and "old boy" networks is collapsing under the assault of commercialism. Behavior that is normal in industry or the professions—secrecy, evasiveness, and invidious competition based on pecuniary motives—threatens to disrupt the social relationships based on noncommercial motives that are expected of and have characterized the university. This rapid demise indicates that a number of the forces that had held the postwar research system in place weakened simultaneously. The changes are due to a slackening in the growth of public funding, NSF and NIH pressuring universities to link with industry, a shift in the political climate toward increased sympathy for industry, and an industrial push into new production areas. Finally, the science of molecular biology has developed to a point at which materials and information from basic research have acquired potential commercial applications.

7. Venture Capital

Startups

I found it just as rewarding, too, to see a
group of investors' eyes light up over
these commercial possibilities as to see a
group of students' eyes light up
*(Herbert Boyer, UCSF professor and
cofounder of Genentech, quoted in
Christenson 1980:27).*

These firms are not comparable to the
small electronics firms, their independence
is purely formal. Behind each is one or
more large groups   *(Chesnais
1981:228, translated by author).*

It's in everyone's best interest to protect
basic research. But, the university and
industry are different organisms, with
different nutrients and metabolism. A
corporation must run on a profit-making
basis: its revenues are split among the
government (through taxes), the
shareholders, and its own future
operations. Particular university projects,
on the other hand, are not judged on a
return-on-investment basis, nor should
they be. However, in that the product
revenues and taxes of industry help create
funds to feed back to the universities,
industry has a right to a share of university
products. There's no rip-off involved
*(Thomas Kiley, Genentech vice-president
legal affairs, quoted in Pfund 1983:49).*

The Corporate Connection

The formation and development of the modern biotechnology industry, though not
immediate or unifocal, took but eight chaotic years, and only in the last
five has this business begun to expand. The growth of the industry is due
to the recognition by investors that biotechnology could well disrupt old
markets, create new products, and cheapen current manufacturing processes. Two distinct types of corporate players pursue the commercialization
of biotechnology—small venture capital startup companies and large trans-

132

national pharmaceutical and chemical industries. I will examine the strategies of both types of companies regarding personnel recruitment, university interactions, product development, and financing. These two economic institutions are distinct, and the evolutionary trajectory of the U.S. biotechnology industry is dependent on the interactions between them (Office of Technology Assessment 1984a).

As noted previously, startup companies were perhaps the only private entity to which professors could be lured from the university. The environment provided in these knowledge-intensive organizations is considered by academic scientists to be desirable, and these companies have the ability to provide significant economic compensation to scientific workers. The discussion of the role and development of startups will provide insight into the operations and organization of some of the leading competitors in a global race to secure profits from biotechnology.

The Role of Venture Capital

Biotechnology has emerged as an industry largely because of one economic institution: venture capital. Venture capital funds, venture capital firms, and corporate venture capital divisions[1] have invested the monies necessary to start companies. In a sense, venture capital has an old history in the United States; there have always been financiers willing to invest in fledgling companies, hoping thereby to garner large capital gains with corporate success. But during the last fifteen years venture capital has become formalized, with special partnerships or divisions in large companies devoted entirely to financing new ventures. The current venture capital pool in the United States has been estimated to be $6.7 billion (Office of Technology Assessment 1984b:42). The most lucrative area of venture financing has been "high technology."[2] But venture financiers have also been willing to risk investment in any venture that may offer possibilities of large gains. Molecular biology, as it discovered potentially marketable products, was just such an opportunity.

The venture capital system is largely an American phenomenon. In England small venture capital–financed companies have been launched, usually with some government backing (Yoxen 1984:8). In most other

1. Likely some parallels exist with the small computer companies that have been launched with venture capital. This conjecture has been briefly examined in an OTA (1984) report and found wanting. However, thus far these comparisons have been cursory and usually done by persons unfamiliar with the biotechnology industry.

2. For example, Kleiner Perkins invested $100,000 in Genentech for 13 percent of the stock. The stock went public at $35 per share, and the investment valued at that price was $34 million. This was, of course, an unusually productive investment, but overall returns for venture capitalists have been in the neighborhood of 20–30 percent per year (J. Fox 1982a:10). This rate of return significantly outperforms more conservative investment strategies.

Table 7.1. Location of Biotechnology Startups*

State or region	Number of companies	Important startups
California	35	
San Francisco Bay Area	22	Genentech, Cetus
Los Angeles	6	—
San Diego	4	Hybritech
Davis	2	—
Thousand Oaks	1	Amgen
Massachusetts	10	Biogen, Collaborative Research
New York City Area	13	
New Jersey	8	—
Connecticut	3	Bioresponse
New York	2	Enzo Biochem
Maryland	6	Genex
Colorado	4	Agrigenetics
Wisconsin	3	Subsidiaries of Cetus and Agrigenetics
Washington	2	Genetic Systems
New Mexico	2	—
Florida	2	—
Pennsylvania	2	—
Minnesota	1	Molecular Genetics
Utah	1	Native Plants, Inc.

Source: *Genetic Engineering News*, Third Annual Guide to Biotechnology Companies 1984b
* The companies selected include only startups dedicated entirely to biotechnology. The list is not exhaustive.

countries, such as Japan, for example, the venture capital system of encouraging and financing innovation is unimportant or nonexistent (Katzenstein and Tanaka 1984). The overall social benefits of this system of commercializing new products and services may be debatable. But in a system of risk-averse large corporations, venture capital provides a mechanism for introducing the new technologies that are so crucial to ensuring continuing economic growth.

The United States has two poles of venture capital investment concentration—San Francisco and Boston (table 7.1). The reasons for this concentration include the large pool of scientifically skilled laborers, the academic environment, and desirable urban environments.[3] In both regions growth has been based on the computer and integrated circuit industries, although Massachusetts relies upon defense contracts whereas San Francisco (in particular, Silicon Valley) has been built upon civilian sales. In electronics these two regions are centers for creative work and for the foundation of new companies. Both areas are becoming biotechnology startup centers, but others include the Washington, D.C.–Maryland area around NIH, Madison, San Diego, and Seattle.

3. I will not attempt to explain why certain cities are considered desirable or to disentangle whether the academic environment influences the city or vice versa.

The San Francisco and Boston regions were also centers of debate over the safety of rDNA, and the public scientific declarations of the potential utility of rDNA that issued from this discussion attracted the interest of some of the many venture capitalists in the two areas. Further, San Francisco, Boston, and Maryland were already the primary locations of small biological supply companies such as New England Biolabs, Bethesda Research Laboratories, Collaborative Research, and Peninsula Laboratories. These supply houses were already successfully selling biotechnology tools such as enzymes, reagents, and DNA sequences to scientists who were working on NIH and NSF grants. Other companies such as Cetus, founded in 1971 to produce superior antibiotic producing bacteria through natural selection, were venture funded. These companies were small in total dollar sales but gave financiers some experience in funding biologically oriented companies. Acting upon the promises made by scientists during the rDNA debate that they would be able to synthesize valuable products, some venture capitalists began to take the plunge.

The Biotechnology Companies

The biotechnology companies give their scientists two things, [Jarmolow] says: First, the potential to get rich. Second, an opportunity to make an "enormous, direct contribution by providing real products—such as a herpes vaccine—to real people" *(Kenneth Jarmolow, Martin Marietta's director for corporate research and development, quoted and paraphrased in R. Johnson 1983:22).*

One can develop an understanding of biotechnology startups by examining their stages of growth. (See figure 7.1 for a visual representation of these stages.) The central themes of this growth are the two intertwined problems of recruitment of labor and the creation of a viable corporate structure to ensure that products emerge. The biotechnology companies are quite varied and have set different and in many cases contradictory goals. But every company must, as rapidly as possible, bring a product to the market. However, generating saleable products is very difficult for biotechnology companies because the techniques they use are state-of-the-art and have not been routinized. Nearly everything is being done for the first time. In contrast, electronics companies are making improvements in a technology that is already proven and manufacturing products that already have a market. Some genetic engineering companies have immensely powerful tools but no commercial products; others have products but no markets for them.

The practitioners of genetic engineering before 1978 were almost without exception located in universities and research institutes; there were no im-

Stage 1		
$100,000–$500,000 Business plan formation, hire first professional manager	Entrepreneur and professor form partnership	Venture capitalist and professor form partnership
Stage 2		
$1–$10 million Acquire facilities, recruit staff	Possibility of multiple offerings to other venture capitalists or institutions	
Stage 3		
Research contracts can be simultaneous with Stage 2. With or without equity, both long-term and short-term	In-house research for large multinational corporations	
Stage 4		
Realizing of investment, build commercial production and marketing facilities	Public equity offering	
Alternative or Supplement		
Issue industrial revenue bonds	Funds to build production facilities	
Stage 5		
To finance products being prepared for market. Can be simultaneous with Stage 4	Research and development limited partnerships as tax shelters for investors	
Stage 6		
Internal cash flow from products sold	Ship products	

Figure 7.1. The History of a Biotechnology Company

portant corporate scientists (Eggers 1981:132). This is in marked contrast to the computer industry, where most venture startups have been based on the work of independent engineers who had already left operating companies, especially IBM, Digital Equipment Corporation, and Hewlett-Packard. Thus, the key to starting a genetic engineering company is securing a labor force. Recruiting workers for biotechnology is not a simple task; desired workers such as senior professors are tenured and receive substantial salaries from their universities. These scientists, as discussed earlier, have had no interest in joining large companies; but as Michael Klagsbrun, an associate professor in Harvard University's department of biology and a staff surgeon at Children's Hospital, is quoted as saying, "Nobody thinks badly of working for the small startups because the work is challenging and you are working for the brightest guys in the field" (Rosenberg 1981b:8).

In the late 1970s the formation of a genetic engineering company nearly always involved an entrepreneur soliciting various professors until he discovered one who was interested in forming a company. This search usually took six months to a year in the 1976–78 period. The length of the search was at least partially due to the fact that debates regarding the safety of rDNA research were still under way. Thus, founding a biotechnology company appeared very risky.

For example, the founding of Genentech in 1976 by Robert Swanson and Herbert Boyer was the fruition of Swanson's search for a scientist-cofounder. Swanson, a Harvard MBA, was initially employed by Citibank in the venture capital business financing section and then left to join Kleiner Perkins, the most important independent venture capital company. While at Kleiner Perkins, Swanson became acquainted with Cetus. Upon leaving Kleiner Perkins, Swanson approached Cetus with an offer "to help push genetic engineering" but was rebuffed (R. Lewin 1978a:924–25). Because Cetus was at that time the only operating biotechnology company, Swanson's only alternative if he wanted to participate in a biotechnology company was to found a genetic engineering company. But for this he needed to secure technical talent. His talent search eventually led to Herbert Boyer. In the case of Advanced Genetic Sciences, the president and founder, Daniel Adams, had previously been with Inco, setting up their venture capital fund, which created Genentech, Cetus, and Biogen. Adams left Inco, secured the services of Harvard professor Lawrence Bogorad, and formed Advanced Genetic Sciences (Kania 1982:10).

An outsider—financier or otherwise—finds it difficult to know which scientists are doing good work and should be approached to become corporate participants. Swanson's tactic was to compile a list of top professors and approach each with a partnership proposal; Herbert Boyer accepted (Lewin 1978a:925). In the case of Genetic Systems, the entrepreneurs David and Isaac Blech, after reading an article on monoclonal antibodies (described as "magic bullets"), decided to form a company. Their tactic was to hire the writer of the magazine article and certain scientists to assist in the search for a chief scientist (Kleinfeld 1983:D1). To form Biogen, Inco's venture capital group, feeling that many of the best U.S. scientists had already entered into corporate agreements, compiled a list of scientists in both Europe and the United States. The venture capitalists approached and coaxed these scientists until they had secured a scientific team (Bylinsky 1980:149). Another company, Immunogen, was started by TA Associates, a venture capital fund, asking Biogen's board of scientific advisors to list top scientists in various fields. The venture capitalists then approached and secured the cooperation of the top scientist on the list, Baruj Benacerraf of the Sidney Farber Cancer Institute. Benacerraf then compiled a list of scientists needed for the company (Rosenberg 1981b:8). In each of these cases the entrepreneurs or venture capital companies approached the scientists after referral from other scientists.

Table 7.2. BIL Consultants and Their Academic Affiliations

Consultant	Academic affiliation
Sydney Brenner	Director of Medical Research Council's Laboratory of Molecular Biology, Cambridge
John Davidson	Department of chemical engineering, Cambridge University
Peter Dunnill	Department of chemical and biochemical engineering, University College, London
Richard Flavell	Plant Breeding Institute, Cambridge
Charles Lane	Formerly at the Laboratory of Developmental Biochemistry, National Institute of Research, London
Edward Ziff	Department of biochemistry, New York University Medical Center

Source: Biotechnology Investments Limited 1983:4

The other method of launching a company has been for scientists to approach venture capitalists with their business plans. An example of this method is Hybritech—where Ivor Royston and Howard Birndorf, researchers at UCSD, contacted Robert Byers of Kleiner, Perkins, Caulfield, and Byers to discuss the possibility of creating a monoclonal antibody venture (McDonald 1983b:1). Understandably, in the gold rush atmosphere that prevailed from 1979 to 1981 many scientists performed the role of entrepreneurs and directly approached venture capitalists with business plans. By 1980 this had become the prevalent pattern as scientists became sensitized to the value of their results.

Venture capitalists are in many cases not sufficiently knowledgeable to evaluate the technology being proposed, and so nearly all have retained consultants. Table 7.2 lists the academic affiliations of the consultants retained by the British venture fund Biotechnology Investments Limited (BIL). Additionally, "reports are also commissioned from other experts" (BIL 1983:4). These examples illustrate that scientists are not only taking their work one step closer to application, but are becoming increasingly enmeshed in commercial activities. BIL is only one example, and all venture capital funds have consultants that perform similar tasks.

The Business Plan

The business plan is the key to securing the first round of financing because it is meant to describe the course the company will take. Financiers are being asked to buy a piece of paper; therefore, the business plan undergoes rigorous scrutiny. Raugel (1983:9) estimates that only 25 to 30 plans of the 200 to 300 submitted get serious study. For example, CW Ventures, a U.S. venture capital fund, reviewed more than 250 investment proposals, but made financial commitments of just $1.7 million to five companies and verbal commitments to only three more (BIL 1983:10). The selection process for funding must be rigorous to ensure against bad investments.

A business plan is crucial; it is the document upon which the birth of the company depends. The plan must address a number of concerns, including the originality of the technology, the potential products and competitors, the size of the market and possible sales, patent protection achievable, employees and their curriculum vitae, and the prospective method of realizing the investment, for example, a public stock offering. Charles Sager, a vice-president of Rothschild, Inc., a venture capital fund, has said:

> We're not interested in just research proposals. . . . We want a concept that evolves into a business with customers. We expect to see a business plan which incorporates marketing people who have learned in the school of hard knocks how to take a product from the research stage to a customer. We want to know who they will sell to, for how much, why these people will buy it and who their competitors will be (A. Brown 1982:10).

The scientist's focus on research for research's sake must be replaced with the more detached calculations of the accountant. BIL (1983:4) requires that "the company under review not only employ scientists of high calibre but also first rate business managers such that the team is ready and able to establish a successful venture."

Frederick Adler, a prominent venture capitalist, sums up the corporate perspective thus:

> In every industry, growth and success are measured in real terms: in units shipped, in headcount, and in values added and in long-term profits per share. The companies that succeed will be those that consistently measure up in this respect. This means that biotechnology companies must now pay as much attention to top quality management as to state-of-the-art technology. All the technology in the world is worthless if the company cannot take advantage of it, market it, earn a profit with it. Increasingly, the emphasis will be on management competence as much as on market potential (*GEN* 1982b:4).

The quote succinctly describes the orientation a successful business plan must exhibit. *Business Week* (1982c:91) summarizes the faults of small biotechnology companies: "The most common problem, venture capitalists say, has proved to be bad management: Either the managers have a poor business plan, or they are unable to follow a reasonably good one." The business plan is so important because it is the "product" that secures

Table 7.3. Startup Dates of Biotechnology Firms: Important Companies and Total per Year*

Year	Number	Important companies
1971	2	Cetus
1972	1	Bioresponse
1973	3	—
1974	1	—
1975	1	—
1976†	2	Genentech
1977	3	Genex
1978	6	Biogen, Hybritech, Collaborative Research
1979	9	Molecular Genetics, Monoclonal Antibodies
1980	18	Calgene
1981	33	Genetic Systems, Integrated Genetics
1982	11	—
1983	4	—

Source: *Genetic Engineering News* Third Annual Guide to Biotechnology Companies 1984b
* Not every firm is listed, but rather a selection of the most important companies directly involved in biotechnology.
† Genentech is the first company to be devoted entirely to genetic engineering.

funding and also provides a benchmark by which investors will judge the company in the years before it makes profit.

Genentech, as the first company completely devoted to genetic engineering, had certain unique problems, the most important of which was the fact that genetic engineering was not only practically unknown, but also had never produced anything marketable. To accomplish their goal of launching a company Swanson and Boyer spent several months developing a business and science plan that laid out their objectives and strategies for the first five years (Benner 1981:66). Swanson developed the criteria for commercial feasibility and Boyer provided the knowledge of what was possible scientifically. Genentech set out as part of its business plan the manufacture of a product that potentially could be commercialized; hence the somatostatin experiments. This business plan received financing from Kleiner Perkins to fund the research to produce somatostatin. Thomas Perkins, recalling his decision to fund Genentech, said "it was the first time [he had] knowingly funded basic research" (Benner 1981:66). Table 7.3, which lists the founding dates for startups, shows that Genentech's success with somatostatin in 1977 and insulin in 1978 awakened venture capitalists and scientists to genetic engineering's commercial possibilities.

In the case of Genetic Systems, the entrepreneurs, the Blechs, were required by Robert Nowinski, the scientist, to show that they could raise money. They promised to have $1 million in six weeks and $3 to $4 million in six months. In return, Nowinski promised a marketable product in one or two years (Kleinfeld 1983:D3). Each business plan has unique characteristics, but the critical need for an early product is universal.

Genentech is a dramatic example of a startup being initiated by the principals. In other cases a scientist has come to the attention of the venture capitalists and they have assisted in preparing the business plan. For example, BIL assisted Corale Brierley of New Mexico Institute of Mining and Technology, "a leading researcher into the application of biotechnological processes to mining and pollution control industries" (BIL 1983:7), in starting a company. BIL describes its role thus:

> We introduced Dr. Brierley to a firm of business development consultants and provided her with seed capital ($300,000 in exchange for 25 percent equity) to finance the preparation of a detailed business plan covering an analysis of potential markets, a survey of prospective customers and joint venture partners, and initial research into the feasibility of specific processes. This plan has now been completed and the initial product target has been selected as a water purification system which will absorb heavy metals onto microorganisms. The system should be available for test marketing by 1985. The second target will be the development of microbial processes for the recovery of precious and strategic metals from ores which are either low-grade or difficult to leach   (BIL 1983:7).

BIL was intimately involved in founding this company. As chief executive officer for the new company, BIL brought in Raymond Decker, former vice-president of research and development and corporate technology at Inco. Notice that the business plan has given the new company a short-term project that will be close to marketability by 1985 and a president from the "school of hard knocks." The "doable" project will generate income for the company, thereby lessening its dependence on capital inflows. The business plan also has a long-term project that if successful will become the basis of the company's future.

Venture Capitalists

After the preparation of the business plan, the next step in launching a company is to secure financing. Although the approach to venture financiers can be intermingled with the earlier stage, as we have seen, nonetheless the venture financier has somewhat different goals from the corporate founders. The founders generally wish to give up as little equity as possible in exchange for financing because the capital appreciation of the company is where the money will be made. Founders also want to secure as large and solid a commitment as possible from the venture financiers. If the company can secure a significant commitment from a venture financier, then the financier will try to help make it a commercial success. Stanley Pratt, editor of *Venture Capital Journal*, says, "The venture capitalist, unlike the traditional banker, joins the board of the company he invests in and actually participates in its management" (Butterfield 1982:5). Usually if the company is successful the venture capitalist will support management. On the other hand, in financial crises the venture capitalist's role on the board makes it easier to remove corporate officers.

The venture capitalist's goal is simple: to make an investment for five to seven years that will provide 500 to 1,000 percent capital gains when the company's stock is offered publicly. For example, table 7.4 itemizes the unrealized capital gains BIL made from its venture investments. Similar and even greater gains can be cited for other venture capital companies. An estimate of Kleiner Perkins's unrealized capital gains from Genentech is $32.8 million on an investment of $300,000. The gain on Hybritech was $66 million on an investment of $1.7 million. A successful public stock offering can result in significant capital gains for its preoffering owners.

As has been indicated, the business plan and the share of corporate ownership that can be extracted are the two most important considerations in the bargaining. Venture capitalists must also take other steps to protect their investment. The simplest of these is an agreement stipulating that the company accept an outside member on its board of directors—usually a representative of the lead venture capital investor. So, for example, Franklin Johnson, a general partner of Asset Management Partners, sits on the boards of Amgen, California Microwave, Coherent, SBE, Tandem Computers, and Teradyne (Amgen 1983:23). Demanding a seat on the board is a standard practice, but venture capitalists can also become active in shaping corporate policy.

Another provision that is included in most financing agreements is registration rights. These allow the venture capitalists to register certain portions of their stockholdings for sale to the public. In many agreements the stockholder can "piggyback" his shares onto a corporate offering, either bearing a portion of the offering expenses or not depending on the contract. The registration provisions are critical because they determine the venture capitalist's costs as well as the conditions by which he will realize any capital gains. Registration rights are also important to the company's founders because the offering of more shares publicly may dilute share values or provide opportunities for takeovers. In some cases the possibility of takeovers is addressed by a clause that allows the company or current stockholders rights to purchase a certain percentage of any corporate stock registered. This can also be used as dilution protection (which is explained below).

Other common financing terms include provisions for special voting rights to prevent mergers or sales of assets that would materially affect the investor's investment decision. In some cases a clause is added requiring a company to buy back shares if it does not meet certain benchmarks. These clauses are demanded by investors to protect themselves in an inherently insecure financial venture (Burstein and Adler 1983:18). The small

Table 7.4. Description of Public Venture Capital Investments by BIL

Company	Date of purchase	Number of shares	Purchase price ($)	Date went public	Public issue price ($)	Current price (July 1985) ($)
Amgen	June 1981	515,000	4.00	June 1983	18.00	7.25
Applied Biosystems	Sept. 1981	700,600	2.38	May 1983	17.00	25.50
Integrated Genetics	Feb. 1982	300,000	3.33	July 1983	13.00	4.00
Immunex	Oct. 1982	300,300	2.50	May 1983	11.00	6.00

Source: Biotechnology Investments Limited 1983

startup, on the other hand, will push for clauses that will prevent venture capitalists from cutting and running if the company has problems. The exact wording of the contract and the responsibilities of each party are of vital importance to both management and venture capitalists.

The venture capitalist's investments are usually accompanied by high risks. In the event of corporate failure, bankruptcy proceedings usually yield very few tangible assets. Much of the original capital has been spent on research salaries and uncompleted products that are difficult to sell. Even with clauses protecting the venture capitalist, corporate failure would mean the loss of a significant percentage, if not all, of the investment.

If the venture capitalist agrees with the concept of the corporation's business plan, he will provide initial seed money in the range of $100,000 to $500,000. This money may be combined with monies the founders' friends and relatives invest, which makes the entrepreneur even more eager to succeed.

Now, the business plan must be polished and further financing secured. Typically, other venture capital companies are approached to participate in financing the actual corporate startup. For example, Hybritech started with a seed money investment of $300,000, but the initial stage research was funded by a $1.6 million private placement from Kleiner, Perkins, Caulfield and Byers, Sutter Hill Ventures, and Asset Management Corporation (Prescott 1983a:157).

In addition to money, the venture capitalist brings to the company a vast network of connections with business development consultants. The startup needs legal services ranging from drawing up the company's legal structure to setting its patent policy; specialists are required for all of these needs. Industrial executives experienced in corporate finance, personnel management, and marketing are identified and hired to place the fledgling company on a businesslike basis. These individuals, usually vice-presidents from MNCs, must be contacted, and the venture capitalists can assist in this process. This fleshing out of the corporate structure is critical because these personnel will be the ones that ensure that the company will make money. Julian Davies, until recently director of Biogen's Geneva laboratories and formerly Steenbock Professor of Biomolecular Structure at the University of Wisconsin, in discussing Biogen's movement into production, puts it very succinctly:

> There is no doubt that getting into the question of production and [clinical] trials involves a totally formal and structured aspect of the company that we will have to accept. . . . We now are looking for people who are experts in this kind of area, and they're very, very different from the kind of people we're looking for in research. We need different capabilities, we need different training, and to some extent we need people with totally different attitudes (Powledge 1983a:404).

Davies is expressing a most important fact: biotechnology startups are companies, and they must focus on the bottom line to be successful. At this early stage of setting the company up, the venture capitalists will set goals for the company to achieve before it receives further financing. Charles Sager of Rothschild, Inc. says, "Most deals are in a spending mode. ... We will finance people to checkpoints we set up—not necessarily a product, maybe just a lab prototype" (J. Fox 1982a:11). Essentially the venture capitalist performs the role of the market in evaluating a company's progress. Unacceptable performance could inhibit future funding or increase demands for greater equity in return for funds.

Assuming that the seed money stage has been successful, professors or scientists will begin conducting initial research, although sometimes this early stage research has already been undertaken in university laboratories. A competent business executive, preferably from an MNC, will be hired to start building a management team. The company at this stage is little more than a president, a few scientists and technicians, a secretary, and an idea or two. But its first five years of growth have been plotted.

Takeoff

The next step for the fledgling company is to actually establish itself as an independent entity with laboratories, offices, and a staff. Again, most information is proprietary, but some cost estimates have been revealed in the press and in congressional hearings. Nelson Schneider (1980:45) of E. F. Hutton estimated that in 1980 first-class laboratory facilities cost $150 per square foot equipped and the carrying costs for a single Ph.D. were $100,000 to $125,000 annually. Each Ph.D. would require 500 to 1,000 square feet of laboratory space. Thus even for a modest genetic engineering (rDNA) facility of 10,000 square feet a capital outlay of $1.5 million would be required. Additionally, ten to twelve Ph.D. scientists would be required to staff the facility at a cost of $1 to $1.5 million annually. The last major expense would be approximately $500,000 annually to support corporate administration. Therefore a minimal research operation would require $6 to $7 million in its first two to three years of operation. A more viable operation would require 20,000 square feet and twenty-five Ph.D.s at a cost over the first two to three years of $10 to $12 million.

The rDNA industry was less expensive to enter in 1977 because of the lack of competition. Further, Genentech was able to do its first projects in Herbert Boyer's UCSF laboratories (Yamamoto 1982). Therefore the large capital investments were not needed at the front end. Also university postdoctoral students could be assigned projects whose results would benefit the company, thereby saving the company the costs of supporting a Ph.D. researcher.

A hybridoma venture would be somewhat less expensive to start. Space requirements for a minimal startup are estimated to be 5,000 square feet, at a cost of $30 per square foot through a lease arrangement. Construction of laboratory facilities would be approximately $100 per square foot. Personnel expenses, including three Ph.D.s, a general manager, a production process manager, and ten other employees would be at least $483,000 per year. The total startup costs for a minimal venture would be at least $3.5 to $4 million over the first three years. Any smaller investment would be unlikely to succeed because it would lack the critical mass for marketing and would not have a full complement of scientific expertise. To develop products for human diagnostics the investments would be a factor of five or ten greater—that is, a minimal investment of $18+ million over two to three years (Treble 1983).

The seed money is spent quite rapidly as the company conducts research. Therefore another round of financing is launched. This larger investment of $1–$10 million dollars will not be provided by any single venture capitalist but will be spread among a number of investors—both venture capitalists and MNCs. For example, Hybritech, as mentioned earlier, first secured $1.6 million from various venture capitalists but later (1980) made a private stock placement of $10 million to a number of other investors, including the University of California, the University of Rochester, and several additional venture capital firms (Prescott 1983a:158).

Again at this refinancing stage corporate management must make decisions regarding the percentage of stock it wishes to sell. On the one hand, investors want the capitalized value of the company to be low so that they can purchase a bigger percentage of the equity for less capital. These investors are naturally comparing this investment with other potential investments and their returns. The company's principals, on the other hand, want the value of the company to be high. Burstein and Adler (1983:18) offer the following perspective on the matter: "This discussion must be conducted with a view to the ultimate objectives of the company and the investors—the sale of the investment at capital gains rates in the future." Donald Kennedy (1981a:2), president of Stanford University, affirms Burstein and Adler:

It used to be that one built one's business and then, if one was fortunate, one made some money. A lot of people now are making money before they've built their business because people are recognizing that there is potential value in ideas. These firms are being capitalized so that much of the incremental value is being realized before a product is on the market or before it is even very sure there will be one.

The fact that these companies are being bought to make a capital gain in five to seven years makes the pricing strategy for the equity sold very important.

The monies from these private equity placements provide the capital to build the company. Biotechnology companies during stage 2 exhibit explosive growth in personnel (table 7.5), but personnel growth levels off when the essential corporate structure is in place. The completion of stage 2 financing leaves a company that is ready to sign research contracts with larger companies and has certain high priority products in the pipeline. And if the research goes well, the company is now preparing for its initial public stock offering.

In stage 2 the vast majority of these small startups claimed to have no interest in making public offerings in the near future. For example, Peter Farley (*WSJ* 1980a:20), president of Cetus, said in August 1980 that the company would not go public until the mid–1980s, but it did so four months later![4] Walter Gilbert, Biogen's chairman and chief executive officer, said as late as November 1982 that a public stock offering was not likely for at least two years—the stock offering came less than four months later (Ashbrook 1982:48). During stage 2 all of the companies are spending money but have little revenue except for research contracts with large MNCs (discussed in the next section). The amount of money being expended per month is commonly termed the *burn rate*. Moreover, venture capital sources can be tapped only so many times before a company's welcome is worn out. The venture financiers want a market developed so as to be able to realize their paper profits.

Yet there are advantages to remaining private. As late as May 1980 in congressional testimony, Nelson Schneider (1980:54) of E. F. Hutton gave Senator Adlai Stevenson the following reasons why he continued to advise companies to remain privately held:

> The problem is, some of the regulations of a public company's responsibilities could really inhibit the freedom of activity . . . of smaller initial stock option companies. For example, suppose a joint venture might want to be announced or entered into by a Cetus or Bethesda Research Lab, with a very large company. It might not be in that large company's interest to see it publicly disclosed, but under SEC regulations of course from the small company's standpoint if it were publicly owned it would have to be a material event.

For publicly traded corporations any event that materially affects the company's profitability must be disclosed. This is true also for companies such as Monsanto, but few discoveries will *materially* affect Monsanto because of its enormous size. The disadvantage therefore lies in the fact that an

---

4. It takes two to three months merely to prepare the registration statement and get it approved by the SEC, so this was, in all likelihood, a deliberate deception.

Table 7.5. Annual Employee Populations of Selected Biotechnology Startups, Doctoral Level, Nondoctoral, and Total

	Cetus*			Genentech†			Genex			Biogen‡			Molecular Genetics		
Year	Doctoral	Nondoctoral	Total	Doctoral	Nondoctoral	Total	Doctoral	Nondoctoral	Total	Doctoral	Nondoctoral	Total	Doctoral	Nondoctoral	Total
1976	13	107	120	—	—	—	—	—	—						
1977	14	106	120	—	—	—	1	0	1						
1978	21	142	163	2	5	7	1	2	3	1	2	3			—
1979	31	168	199	—	—	56	6	13	19	—	—	3	1	2	3
1980	43	230	273	49	117	166	21	49	70	—	—	41	5	9	14
1981	62	398	460	74	244	318	41	150	191	—	—	154	23	33	56
1982	82	398	480	89	342	431	48	153	201	79	172	251	25	42	67
1983	77	450	527	114	429	543	48	171	219	90	241	331	24	77	101
1984	97	516	613	133	541	674	48	216	264	87	289	376	26	98	124

Sources: Interviews, annual reports, and various sources

* Cetus was already an operating company.

† Genentech was unable to provide personnel populations for its earliest years. I have also omitted full-time employees that Genentech had in H. Boyer's laboratory at UCSF.

‡ Biogen was unable to provide as much information as other companies.

important discovery by a small startup will have to be reported, whereas a similar event in a large company need not be disclosed. However, despite Schneider's advice, during the next three years a deluge of companies moved to public stock offerings.

Corporate Structure

In order to allocate scientific resources optimally . . . scientists must be supported and guided by professional business managers concentrating on project implementation and marketing   *(Eagle and Coyman 1981:2).*

The organizational structure of biotechnology companies is unique. In contrast to computer and other electronics startups, biotechnology companies remain dependent on senior university professors. As discussed in chapter 5, some professors are recruited to leave their university and join the staff, while others only join the company's scientific advisory board. The key to biotechnology startups has been to secure the services of the best professors, and the structure of the companies reflects their dependence on intellectual labor power. This dependence on scientists is reflected by Swanson's observation on Genentech's future: "If the research goes well . . . we can handle the rest of the problems of the world" (Benner 1981:68).

Of course, the research cannot be allowed to go undirected—these companies are not universities. In fact, one analyst has evaluated academic scientists thus: "Academia places a clear premium on irrationality and antisocial behavior. Many of our best scientists have spent little time developing their interpersonal skills and can be very difficult to control" (Kania 1982:17). The creation of this scientific work force requires direction. Therefore the company brings in managerial expertise for the staff positions from the large pharmaceutical companies.[5]

The Scientific Advisory Board

The scientific advisory board (SAB) was a mechanism developed to provide the scientific leadership that the small startups require in order to be commercially successful. Many biotechnology companies have a formal SAB that has close links to the corporate board of directors or director of research. Figure 7.2, an organizational chart for Cetus, indicates the importance Cetus attaches to its SAB. Other aspects of the organization of biotechnology companies are not significantly different from those of other

5. Perhaps this means scientists are not yet trained to be a docile labor force.

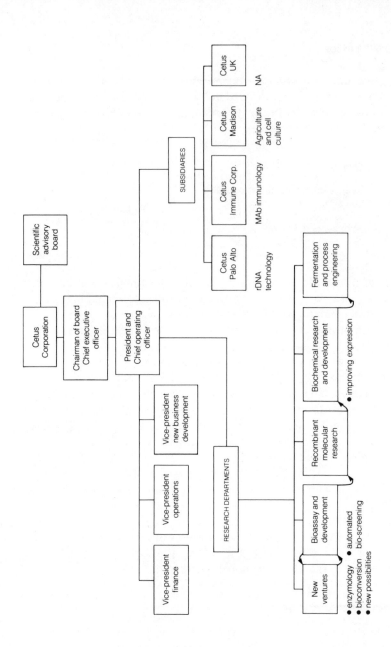

Source: Ellis 1982:89

Figure 7.2. Cetus Organization Chart

companies, except that many biotechnology companies have one or more individuals designated to handle university relations. The vital difference between these companies and venture startups in electronics is the common use of formal SABs.

Why would a professor join an SAB? The first incentive is clearly monetary—in nearly every case the scientist is granted an equity interest in the company. The recruitment of SAB members often depends on the "invisible college" from which the founding scientist or SAB member comes or on other scientists with whom the SAB member has collaborated. For example, when David Katz, the department chairman of cellular development and immunology at Scripps Clinic and Research Foundation, left to form the company Quidel, three professors from Scripps and one from UCSD joined him (Prescott 1983c:28). This invisible network provides the recruits for a SAB and, in turn, helps define a company's research targets.

Another important benefit for professors who join a company's SAB is that the company may provide research funds for his university laboratories. For example, Myron Essex, professor of virology at the Harvard School of Public Health, owns 208,000 shares of Cambridge BioScience and has received a three-year, $333,722 grant from the company to continue his research (Cambridge BioScience Corporation 1983:40; *Harvard Gazette* 1983:2). In return, Cambridge BioScience has been granted a nonexclusive, worldwide license to commercialize any patents from the work. Arrangements whereby the scientific advisor secures grants from a corporation in which he owns significant equity interest are common. The circle is completed by Essex's status as a member of the Cambridge BioScience corporate board of directors and a once-a-week consultant for a salary between $15,000 and $40,000 per annum (Cambridge BioScience Corporation 1983:35). The research for which Essex is being funded yielded two articles in *Science* in 1983 (Essex et al. 1983a; Essex et al. 1983b), the first of which coincidentally was published one month before the stock was issued. Research monies are patently the lifeblood of research professors because new funds allow expansion of research, thereby propelling their careers forward.

Finally, at a time when large numbers of molecular biology professors are affiliated with a company, the pressure on those who remain unaffiliated is intense. A professor who has no corporate connections has numerous disadvantages, such as fewer research funds, a more difficult time placing students, and less access to the modern equipment corporate monies can provide. The pressure to cash in on the gold rush also comes from government officials, university administrators pressing for patents, and a constant stream of offers from entrepreneurs. The SAB has become an accepted institution through which professors may derive monetary gains from their research.

The SAB also makes a venture startup believable. The senior professors who make up the SAB are the key to inducing young scientists to join the company (Rosenberg 1981b:8). Cetus, which has the largest and most prestigious SAB (thirty-one members, including five Nobel Laureates), describes the SAB's corporate role thus:

The Company [Cetus] views its Board of Scientific Advisors as an important resource. . . . The ways in which its members interact with Cetus scientists and management vary widely. Some serve as day-to-day advisors to Cetus scientists, critiquing experiments and giving continuing advice; others visit Cetus periodically and review several programs or disciplines; some have increased their commitment to the point where they have become founders of new Cetus subsidiaries. Some concentrate on surveying scientific developments and communicating to Cetus the state of the science of genetic engineering. All assist the Company in finding and employing the best possible scientific talent and participate in periodic Cetus retreats of several days' duration during which they review Cetus programs and possible future directions with Cetus scientists and management   (Cetus 1981b:11–12).

At Cetus the SAB is involved in all of the science-related aspects of the functioning of the company. In many companies the SAB or its chairman communicates directly with the top management.

Advanced Genetic Science's (AGS) SAB operates in a slightly different manner (members of AGS's SAB are listed in table 7.6). The SAB meets four or five times per year for three to six days

to discuss candidates for full-time positions, to review and direct individual research projects both at AGS laboratories and at other locations, and to set priorities for the overall research effort. Research projects are selected by the Scientific Board and are funded if approved by the board of directors. The Scientific Board has a representative on the board of directors who is responsible for insuring complete information flow between the two boards. Thus, the AGS Scientific Board performs an important line management function for the Company   (Kania 1982:15).

The SAB at AGS has a formal communication link with the board of directors, which is somewhat different from, say, Amgen, where the chairman of the SAB, Daniel Vapnek, is the director of research.

In some companies the SAB's function is purely advisory, as at California Biotechnology, Inc. (1983), or is an addendum, as at Biotechnica International, Inc. (1983), where most of the scientists are either employees or consultants. Finally, a few companies have no SAB at all. These include Genentech and Hybritech, both of which rely very heavily on consultants; at Genentech the names of consultants are not listed in any official documents. Yet even if they are not members of a formal SAB, senior scientist-consultants play a leading role in all startups.

Table 7.6. Advanced Genetic Sciences' Scientific Advisory Board with Institutional Affiliations

Member	Institutional affiliation
John Bedbrook	Formerly, CSIRO, Australia
Lawrence Bogorad	Maria Coors Cabot Professor of Biology, Harvard University
Nils Olof Bosemark	Director of research and development, Hilleshog AB
Howard Goodman	Chief of the department of molecular biology, Massachusetts General Hospital, and professor of genetics, Harvard Medical School
Pal Maliga	Section head, Institute of Plant Physiology, Biological Research Center, Hungary
Jozef Schell	Director, Max-Planck Institute for Plant Improvement, Germany, and codirector, Genetic Research Laboratory, University of Ghent, Belgium
Milton Schroth	Professor of plant pathology, University of California, Berkeley
Marc Van Montagu	Codirector, Genetic Research Laboratory, University of Ghent, Belgium

Source: Advanced Genetic Sciences 1983:23

Because scientific advisors have access to proprietary corporate information companies are prompted to structure the advisors' contracts in such ways as to ensure their loyalty. The first technique for ensuring loyalty has been to accord scientists a gradual vesting of the stock given to them. For example, at DNA Plant Technology (DNAPT) SAB members are granted stock options that "become exercisable in five cumulative installments of 20% of the total number of options granted and expire . . . after 10 years" (DNAPT 1983:35). Vesting arrangements, commonplace throughout the industry, are useful because the scientist's equity position gives him a stake in the growth of the company. Conversely, by leaving the company before vestiture the scientist forgoes significant capital gains.

The SAB members have confidential knowledge regarding the projects and trade secrets of the company and, therefore, in most cases have agreed to contract clauses limiting their future employment opportunities for specified periods after termination. For example, scientific advisorial contracts typically

prohibit the disclosure of any trade secrets or other confidential information pertaining to the Company which may be obtained by the members of the Scientific Advisory Board from the Company and prohibit them from associating with another commercial organization which is engaged in research, development, and manufacture or sale of products related to any specific or ongoing projects of the Company during the term of the contract and, *at the Company's option*, for a 24 month period thereafter [emphasis added] (Integrated Genetics 1983:26).

Obviously, clauses such as these link the advisor to a company and help reduce the constant danger that scientists may leave and join a competitor, taking secrets with them. Protection clauses also are a relatively effective antiraiding insurance.

The role of the SAB is multifaceted because usually management is not equipped to evaluate what is possible scientifically. Further, the prominence of a company's SAB has a direct influence on the caliber of scientists willing to accept full-time employment with the company. The type of work undertaken in startups is predicated on high levels of skills, which occur in only a few individuals—ten mediocre scientists do not equal one brilliant scientist. Scientific advisors are the key to making the important scientific advances needed to manufacture products. Finally, an illustrious SAB provides credibility to a company as it enters the equity market. A company (somewhat like a sports team) touts its stars.

Going Public

Investment in the shares of Common Stock offered hereby involves a high degree of risk. Before deciding to purchase any of the Common Stock offered hereby, prospective investors should carefully consider the following factors, among others set forth in this prospectus *(DNAPT 1983:5)*.

I have discussed the building of the company, the selling of equity to private investors, and the establishment of a business plan. An important factor, stage 3, the signing of research contracts with large MNCs, has been deferred until the next section because it is an activity that overlaps both stages 2 and 4. Characteristically the small startup has now been in existence for two or three years, has grown to fifty to eighty people, and is fully structured. Marketing and production, though as yet only skeletal, are prepared for planned growth. The research and development component has also made important progress, but the company has yet to be evaluated in the market. Finally, the transfusions from venture capitalists have become more difficult to obtain because they want to start to realize their investments. The company needs more money to expand—and the stock market is one place to get it.

Becoming a public corporation requires that the company provide enough information about itself so that the investor can judge the merits of the company. Such disclosure was viewed by many companies with considerable trepidation, as they would have to openly discuss their activities and display their cash flow (or lack thereof). On the other hand, as

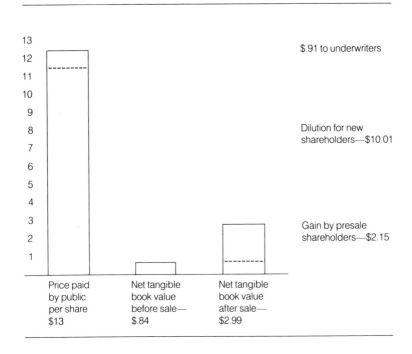

13
12    $.91 to underwriters
11
10
9
8   Dilution for new
7   shareholders—$10.01
6
5
4
3   Gain by presale
2   shareholders—$2.15
1

Price paid   Net tangible   Net tangible
by public   book value   book value
per share   before sale—   after sale—
$13 $.84 $2.99

Source: Integrated Genetics 1983:9

Figure 7.3. Dilution after Public Stock Offering of Integrated Genetics

Genentech would show in 1980, the public was willing to exchange a substantial sum of cash for very little equity. The hype surrounding biotechnology was put to good use in inflating stock prices.

The decisions regarding a stock's price are made in bargaining and consulting with an underwriter, preferably a large brokerage firm, if they will agree to underwrite the offer. But any brokerage firm will do if a large one is not willing to lead an offering. This brokerage firm then allots stock to other companies that wish to participate. If everything goes as planned, the stock opens and sells on the over-the-counter market on the chosen day, the company receives a capital infusion, and the brokerage firm receives a commission, usually of about 7 percent.

The very moment the public purchases the stock, their investment undergoes an immediate and radical dilution of value. This dilution is graphically illustrated in figure 7.3. Dilution occurs because the public buys shares of common stock at a substantially higher price than the present owners of the stock paid for their shares. In the case of Integrated Genetics, Sutter

Table 7.7. Biotechnology Company Stock Offerings: Date and Price

Company	Date	Price ($)
Enzo Biochem	June 1980	1.50
Genentech	October 1980	35.00
Cetus	March 1981	23.00
Biologicals	April 1981	15.00
Genetic Systems	June 1981	2.00
Hybritech	October 1981	11.00
Collaborative Research	February 1982	11.00
Molecular Genetics	June 1982	9.00
Genex	September 1982	9.50
Hybritech	November 1982	26.75
Centocor	December 1982	18.00
Genex	March 1983	14.82
Molecular Genetics	March 1983	15.75
Biogen	March 1983	23.00
Genetic Systems	April 1983	15.00
Applied Biosystems	May 1983	15.00
Amgen	June 1983	18.00
Chiron	June 1983	15.00
Damon Biotech	June 1983	17.00
International Genetic Engineering	June 1983	never offered
Integrated Genetics	June 1983	13.00
Advanced Genetic Sciences	September 1983	15.00
California Biotechnology	October 1983	—
DNA Plant Technology	December 1983	—
Agrigenetics	January 1984	—

Sources: Various journals

Hill Ventures purchased 1,182,000 shares at $.33 per share and another 418,000 shares at $3.33 per share for a total investment of $1,782,000. Even at this early stage at the then-current valuation of the company Sutter Hill's investment was worth $5,661,000 (Integrated Genetics 1983:90). If Integrated Genetics has any success, Sutter Hill will have made a tidy profit.

The first major company to go public was Genentech. (For a chronology of biotechnology stock offerings, see table 7.7.) Genentech's October 14, 1980, public offering of 1 million shares as $35 per share set off a buying frenzy that sent the share price to a peak of $89 before it subsided to $70 at the close of the market day (Gartner 1980:20). Genentech was the beneficiary of an interest and enthusiasm for genetic engineering that contrasted sharply with the earlier cautious attitudes that the safety debates engendered. A sampling of articles written in the months preceding the Genentech offering included "Cloning gold rush turns basic research into big business" (Wade 1980b in *Science*); "The miracles of spliced genes" (Clark et al. 1980 in *Newsweek*); "Biotechnology: research that could remake industries" (*Chemical Week* 1980); and "The hunt for plays in biotechnology" (*Business Week* 1980a). For a company that was unprofitable and going public in the midst of the deepest recession since the Great Depression, the offering was a spectacular success.

Cetus, Genentech's archrival, recognizing that a public stock offering was an excellent way to secure funds, offered 5 million shares at $23 in March 1981. Cetus's offering was compelled by the failure of a consortium led by E. F. Hutton and Northern Trust Company of Chicago to privately place $50 million worth of stock (D. Dorfman 1981:D1). The success of this stock sale—the largest single stock offering by a new corporation in history—by a company that openly claimed that it would not be profitable until 1985 at the earliest, emboldened other companies to prepare stock offerings. But Cetus was not a spectacular issue like Genentech's, and the underwriters even had to step in and repurchase some shares to maintain the offer price (M. Johnson 1981). Table 7.7 indicates that the bulk of the biotechnology companies were unprepared in 1981 to go public, as they were not yet fully structured. One observer declared, "The biotechnology boom has largely resisted that malaise, giving the appearance of some special immunity, in part because of its reliance on money sources that are amazingly resistant to the impact of recession" (J. Fox 1982b).

The offerings of other companies received relatively bad receptions in 1981 and 1982, two well-known companies, Genex and Collaborative Research, having disappointing debuts. Collaborative Research expected to receive a price between $13 and $17 per share but was forced to settle for $11. Genex attempted to sell 2.5 million shares at $11–$12 each but was able to place only 2 million at $9.50 per share (*Chemical Week* 1982e:34). Additionally, venture capital was becoming increasingly scarce for the already established firms, prompting articles prophesying a coming shakeout (see Feder 1982 or C. Johnson 1982, both in the *New York Times*, or Lancaster 1982 in the *Wall Street Journal*). Needless to say, there was not a shakeout; rather, the period of the predicted shakeout was a bull market in which many biotechnology companies were able to float stock.

The soaring stock market of 1983 allowed public offerings of more biotechnology stocks than in the previous three years combined. Peter Dorfman (1983), the editor of *GEN*, observes that companies went public because venture capitalists were refusing to extend further funds to these risky "me too" companies. M. Kathy Behrens, assistant vice-president for research and finance at Sutro and Sons, a venture capital fund, agrees:

It's a pretty routine scenario. . . . First, the breakthrough technology. Everyone gets excited. The money starts rolling in. Not too many companies around. Everybody and his brother starts jumping into the pool with "me-too" companies. Competition becomes intense. Company evaluations either decline or level off. The money gusher begins to dry up   (Patterson 1983:50).

This apocalyptic, Schumpeterian forecast has yet to be borne out. But many companies are issuing stock that can be best characterized as "fluff," so much so that the California commissioner of corporations has ruled that purchase of these "blue-sky" companies is to be restricted to investors earning over $40,000 per year (Powledge 1983b:555). The public stock offering has proved to be an important source of funds and, simultaneously, has put the venture capitalists and company founders on the road to financial success. Whether public purchasers of the stock will be so fortunate is another matter. The valuation of Cetus at $11 per share indicates that the market believes that it has 20 percent of the value of Upjohn. The success of these many offerings prompted Nina Sigler, the biotechnology analyst for Paine Webber, to comment in 1982, "When you consider that only one product has reached market, this industry has shown a greater tenacity for financial survival than any other nascent industry. . . . I believe this gives the industry a high probability of weathering the current tough financial times" (*Chemical Week* 1982e:33). The public offering has provided the biotechnology industry with a major source of capital, but the stock market is easily saturated with offerings. Nearly all 1983 and 1984 stock issues have been little more than a way for investors to lose money through rapid and massive dilution.

Contracts Between Venture Startups and Multinational Corporations

In those early days . . . we were thrown out of some of the finer offices in the chemical and pharmaceutical industries. This was before recombinant DNA; but recombinant DNA was absolutely predicted by our scientific advisors   *(Peter Farley, one of the founders of Cetus, quoted in* Chemical Week *1982a:49).*

For us, research contracts provide a convenient bridge between start up and operations in the agricultural marketplace   *(Molecular Genetics 1983:1).*

Research contracts are imperative for every small biotechnology startup because of the large capital outlays required to develop a viable company. The startups are without revenues except the interest on unused capital. Research and then scale-up rapidly draw down financial reserves, forcing the company to continually sell pieces of itself to secure financing. In this environment it can be advantageous for the company to sell its technical services to another company—in most cases a multinational pharmaceutical or chemical manufacturer. (Table 7.8 provides a list of the announced contracts Genentech has with other companies.)

The wholesale signing of research contracts between startups and MNCs

Table 7.8. Genentech's Research Contracts by Product with MNCs (1982)

Product	MNC	Company's nationality	Type of contract	Cost
Insulin	Lilly	U.S.	Exclusive (world)	Royalties
Human growth hormone	Kabi	Sweden	Exclusive (except U.S.)	Royalties
Human interferon (α)	Hoffmann-La Roche	Switzerland	Exclusive (world)	Royalties, right to supply
Human interferon (γ)	Daiichi Seiyaku Toray Industries	Japan Japan	Exclusive (except U.S.)	Royalties, right to supply
Bovine growth hormone	Monsanto	U.S.	Exclusive (world)	Royalties
Tissue plasminogen	Mitsubishi Kyowa Hakko	Japan Japan	Exclusive (Japan)	Royalties
Human serum albumin	Mitsubishi	Japan	Exclusive (Japan)	Royalties
Bovine interferon	Granada	U.S.	Exclusive	$20 million

Source: Genentech 1982

is somewhat unusual in venture capital–financed companies. In computers a new startup works for itself and does not usually contract its research capability out (contracting does occur in the software industry). The most important reason for doing contract research in biotechnology is the long product lead times, which have been in the area of four to five years; in computers lead times are between six months and two years.

The dilemma for the startup is how to secure the needed monies without selling the company's future products.[6] These research agreements are different from normal subcontracts because the large MNC is trying to purchase access to the knowledge and the skills needed to operate independently. Therefore, any cooperative relationship also has an antagonistic aspect, and the startup must approach contract research very cautiously.

Genentech's experience is very instructive because it used contracts to strengthen the company. Genentech's first contract was to provide genetically engineered insulin-producing bacteria to Eli Lilly, the world's largest insulin producer. Under terms of the contract signed with Lilly in 1978, Genentech received payment for research performed and an unspecified royalty on all of Lilly's bacterially produced insulin sales, while Lilly re-

6. This is commonly referred to as "the selling of the company's birthright." In other words, the company's reason for being—to eventually sell proprietary products—would be lost in these contracts.

ceived exclusive worldwide rights for manufacturing and marketing (Genentech 1982:4–5). Lilly then spent an estimated $100 million taking the bacterially produced insulin through clinical tests and production scale-up (Shapley 1982:101). In this case Genentech did not retain manufacturing rights, but these would have been of dubious advantage for a market as dispersed and dominated by a few firms as that for insulin. Lilly began to pay royalties in late 1983 as the product entered the marketplace, but due to the high price of artificial insulin the sales have been small.

The next Genentech contract was to produce human growth hormone (HGH) bacterially. Genentech concluded a contract with AB Kabi, a Swedish company that is the world's largest supplier of HGH. Kabi received worldwide exclusive manufacturing and marketing rights excluding the United States. In return, Kabi funded the research. Under this contract Genentech secured the right to manufacture HGH and sell it in the United States—a major step in its quest to be more than a contract research company.

In 1980 Genentech and Hoffmann-La Roche reached an agreement to jointly develop alpha and beta interferons.[7] Genentech developed the bacteria and will supply a portion of the interferons needed for clinical trials. In return Roche sponsored Genentech's research. Further, Roche is sponsoring the clinical trials. The contract gives Roche worldwide exclusive marketing rights in return for payment of royalties. Genentech also secured the right to supply Roche "with a substantial percentage of Roche's marketing requirement" (Genentech 1982:5).

For gamma interferon, Genentech retained the rights to produce for the U.S. market while selling rights to overseas markets. Bovine and porcine growth hormone were contracted to Monsanto for research revenues and royalties. The rights for a vaccine for foot-and-mouth disease, which had been sold to International Mineral and Chemicals (IMC), were repurchased in 1983 with the proviso that IMC would receive a profit share on any sales (Genentech 1983). In the case of tissue-type plasminogen activator, Mitsubishi Chemical and Kyowa Hakko were merely given marketing rights in Japan in return for research funding. Finally, Genentech has "other projects which, for proprietary reasons, are not discussed" (Genentech 1982:4). An example of contract secrecy is Genentech's $20 million agreement with the Granada Corporation to produce bovine interferon. The contract was signed in January 1982 but not announced until August 22, 1983 (*Wall Street Journal* 1983b:36).

In Genentech we see a company on a steady drive to become less and less dependent on contract research and more and more desirous of producing tangible products. An important aspect of Genentech's pursuit of

7. These products were the object of a suit by the University of California that was discussed earlier.

profitability has been its constant emphasis on the need to manufacture products and gain important experience in conducting clinical trials and scaling-up to commercial production levels. HGH was the first product that Genentech chose to produce and market because few doctors specialize in human growth disorders, and HGH could thus be easily distributed. HGH will permit Genentech to expand its experience in all aspects of the pharmaceutical industry without requiring the immediate building of a large marketing network.

Genentech's goal from the outset has been to become a freestanding corporation. To reach this end it has had to be an innovator in nearly every area. Most important, it has rarely sold its technical know-how—it has sold prepared bacteria, not the ability to make them. Genentech has not allowed scientists from other companies to work in its laboratories, thereby minimizing information leakage.

If Genentech has linked with a number of companies, yet kept all at arm's length, AGS has adopted a different strategy:

> In contrast to many genetic engineering start-up ventures which are happy to take money from anyone willing to invest, Dan [Adams, president and founder of AGS] has very specific goals in his efforts to secure financial backing for AGS. He wanted a limited number of investors. And he wanted those investors to be philosophically comfortable with his own management style and with the concepts behind AGS. He was also looking for investors who would be easy and fun to work with. Finally and most important, he wanted investors who could make a substantial contribution to AGS, in terms of expertise, perspective, manufacturing and distributions systems and commitment. Hilleshog and Rohm and Haas met these criteria. According to the company, "These stockholders were chosen for their ability to assist AGS in achieving its goals"   (Kania 1982:13).

AGS has effectively made an alliance with the two companies that fund much of its research, Rohm and Haas and Hilleshog.

The weakness of depending on only two companies is that these companies exert great influence by virtue of their economic clout. Rohm and Haas provided 87 percent of AGS's research and development income ($2,646,000) in 1982, owned 14.9 percent of the stock, controlled a seat on the board of directors, and also had the right to have a representative at all meetings of the SAB.[8] Hilleshog provided 9 percent of AGS's income ($268,000), held 14.9 percent of the stock, controlled a seat on the board of directors, and had a member on the SAB. Rohm and Haas has a right

---

8. AGS, as discussed above, has an SAB that is intimately involved in all facets of company operations and, therefore, is an excellent location in which to collect information regarding the company's goals.

to negotiate with AGS regarding any "research and development in the fields of biological pesticides, plantation, field and orchard crops, vegetables and diagnostic products" unless these are funded by another entity (AGS 1983:29). In consummating such close relationships the company may have sold its birthright because the contract also gives Rohm and Haas first option upon any agricultural technology developed with AGS's own money.

The original strategy for AGS was to sell research projects that would develop the knowledge base for other projects (Kania 1982:18). For this strategy to be effective would seem to require (to take a hypothetical case) that while doing contract research on soybeans the company would be developing expertise that could be readily applied to chickpeas. Therefore, the company, while ensuring its near-term financial survival, positions itself better for the next set of products that it will take along the commercialization path. This strategy is ultimately based on the company's business plan and its goals in the mid-term. The company that becomes a mere contract research organization will continue to reap income only as long as it can remain on the forefront of science. Whether AGS is able to emerge from its status as a contractor for Rohm and Haas and Hilleshog may be determined by its successes outside agriculture—especially its bacteria to be used for snowmaking.

No startups have been able to avoid committing themselves to contract research, and in most cases they have deliberately courted contracts with MNCs. For example, Cambridge BioScience Corporation (CBC) states its interest in seeking corporate contracts:

> The company is pursuing joint venture partners to share the risk and cost of new technological endeavors that appear to have significant commercial application, but require major investment and long development time.... Such joint venture agreements, if consummated, may provide the company with a mechanism of sharing the risks and costs associated with these research and development projects and may allow the Company to make better use of its limited financial and personnel resources. If the Company enters into any such agreements, it expects to receive revenues from joint development contract funding, and may receive royalty payments as well   (CBC 1983:21).

CBC, with total assets of a little over $6.5 million, including a recent stock issue, must rapidly secure funding to pay for its research program, which consumed $500,000 in 1982 alone. As its research operation expands to prepare for product development there will be even larger expenditures. The "burn time" will force CBC to secure "deep pocket" partners.

If certain companies have had problems following their strategies and business plans, others have been very successful. For example, Genetic Systems, a manufacturer of monoclonal antibodies for diagnostic and therapeutic purposes, has entered into a number of joint ventures with MNCs but in most cases merely provides a finished product.[9] The engineering knowledge and experience acquired from that contract are then transferable to another monoclonal project. Therefore, even as Genetic Systems sells its opportunities in some product areas, it develops its potential in others. Genetic Systems has managed to secure research funding and marketing assistance without allowing itself to be overly dependent on any one company or selling all of its interesting commercial projects (Genetic Systems Corporation 1982:2–3).

The contract clauses that allow cancellation can prove to be a company's undoing. For example, International Plant Research Institute (IPRI) had a nearly $1 million per year long-term contract with Eli Lilly to breed drought- and salt-tolerant wheat. A year after signing, Lilly changed the goals to disease resistance and attempted to abridge the contract. IPRI refused to cancel the contract, but agreed to change its scope. However, at the first opportunity to terminate the contract, Lilly opted for termination. Various reasons are offered for Lilly's actions, but most important was that "Lilly scientists were said to believe they had learned enough to conduct the research themselves" (Dwyer 1983b:319). The most dangerous risk of a startup relationship with an MNC was realized: IPRI lost its monopoly on the knowledge.

In many cases the research contracts contain specific terms under which either party may withdraw. Usually these contracts provide little security to the startup. For example, DNAPT signed a contract with Koppers Company whereby the latter would provide $360,000 per year until August 1988 for DNAPT to conduct research on plant disease diagnostic kits, "but [the contract] may be terminated by Koppers Company, Inc. on December 31, 1985, and thereafter, upon completion of specified phases of research" (DNAPT 1983:21). DNAPT has another research project with General Foods for $594,000 over two years with a three-year renewal clause.[10] Yet, as DNAPT (1983:21) writes in the prospectus, "There can be no assurance that General Foods will not terminate the contract after one year." In the event of cancellation, no money is returned, and in nearly all cases all rights revert to the startup company (for example, see Genentech 1980b:9).

In certain cases an MNC will purchase an equity interest in the startup in addition to signing a research contract. Of course, ownership increases MNC leverage, though in many cases this is counterbalanced by other corporate owners. Perhaps the best example of this is AGS, in which

9. Monoclonal antibodies offer many advantages to small companies. First, they are much less expensive to produce than rDNA products because of the small quantities needed and the relatively simple technology involved. Second, there are thousands of antibodies that can be produced, and the production of each antibody can be done with similar techniques.

10. DNAPT would receive $250,000 in 1984, $344,000 in 1985, and a total of $1,069,000 for 1986–88 inclusive if the contract is renewed (DNAPT 1983).

Hilleshog and Rohm and Haas both own 14.9 percent.[11] In a few cases thus far there have been disputes between MNC funders and the startups. But the details of the settlements are not publicly available (Amgen 1983:15; Genex 1982b:21–22).

The success of a startup hinges in good part on the contracts it can make with MNCs. Management must balance the immediate need for income against the loss of future revenues. These decisions will determine whether the company will have self-generated revenues when the contract research monies expire. Overdependence on contract research provides the startup with a very unstable income base and can monopolize researchers' valuable time to the detriment of corporate projects. The problem is compounded if management sells all of the bread-and-butter projects that could yield revenues in the near-term. The MNCs with their enormous cash reserves are always willing to purchase products that can be commercialized, but no startup can survive merely on *potential* royalties. (The viewpoint of the MNCs is presented in chapter 9.)

Research and Development Limited Partnerships

The insatiable appetite of the startups for capital has led to the invention of new financial mechanisms to secure more capital. The most widely used innovation was invented by a Wall Street lawyer and is called a research and development limited partnership (RDLP) (J. Fox 1982a:14). These partnerships are used in most cases not to fund research and development but rather to fund clinical trials or production scale-up. The startup essentially is contracted by the partners to perform the tasks needed to bring the product to market. This financial arrangement is an important method of securing increased funding and shifting the risks of launching a new product to the limited partners. RDLPs have been adopted very rapidly by a number of startups. (Table 7.9 provides a list of the important RDLPs.) The partners, in return for accepting these risks, receive a varying package of tax breaks, royalties, and options to buy stock at a discount or at a set price. Tax provisions allow the direct expensing of all research expenditures. If the product is successful, partners receive royalty payments that are taxed as capital gains (20 percent). The RDLP also provides options for investors to purchase stock at varying discounts up to 50 percent.

Investors in the Genentech RDLP, for example, were required to have "a minimum net worth of $1 million or a $200,000 per year income in the

11. The fear of being swallowed up by their larger partners is an important reason for acquiring more than one large sponsor—they will tend to balance each other. Also, this fear of takeover makes foreign sponsors attractive because they are usually interested only in securing a specified product rather than in taking over. While this may be optimal for the startup, it may have adverse consequences for U.S. industry's competitive position in the world economy.

Table 7.9. Research and Development Limited Partnerships by Company, Value, Date, and Product

Company	Value ($ million)	Date	Product
Genentech	55.6 34.0	October 1982 June 1983	Tissue plasminogen Gamma interferon and Human growth hormone
Agrigenetics	55.0	March 1982	Plant genetics
Molecular Genetics	11.1	October 1982	Hybrid corn and animal healthcare
Hybritech	6.0	December 1982	Monoclonal antibodies for cancer treatment
Genetic Systems	3.4	January 1983	Monoclonal antibody diagnostics
Cetus	75.0	July 1983	Interferon and cancer diagnostics
California Biotechnology*	27.5	October 1983	General research

Sources: Various publications
* The entire company is a research and development limited partnership structured by E. F. Hutton Company.

two years prior to the offering and expectations of that income in the next year" (*Chemical Week* 1983d:55). A single unit of an RDLP usually costs between $100,000 and $150,000, but half-units are also available. If the product achieves commercial success there is a possibility of substantial royalties. The tax shelter coordinator for E. F. Hutton (a salesman) was quoted in *Chemical Week* (1983d:55) as saying, "There are very few stocks which provide people with the 300%, 400%, or 500% return on their investment a partnership might provide." Of course, if the product is unprofitable the company owes nothing to the partnership and there is no return at all, there is only the tax write-off.

Genentech has formed a $55 million RDLP to bring to commercial production HGH and gamma interferon.[12] Due to the secrecy surrounding

12. The HGH research effort is an example of how a small startup must operate. Genentech sold Kabi the rights to manufacture and market HGH for most of the world with the exception of the United States (Genentech 1982:5). Then Genentech made "rapid preparations for commercial production," surprising Kabi (Walgate 1980:528). With Kabi funding the research, the cost of the research to Genentech was minimal—with the exception of the opportunity cost of the staff time committed to the project. In essence, Kabi funded the research of a company that would be its major competitor.

Gamma interferon appears to have been internally funded initially, but then research contracts were negotiated with two Japanese companies, Daiichi Seiyaku and Toray, and a German one, Boehringer Ingelheim. These companies received exclusive licenses to market Genentech's gamma interferon outside the United States (Genentech 1982:5–6). The RDLP will provide the money for the development of sustainable commercial production.

Table 7.10. Genentech's Clinical Partners Limited Budget ($ million)

Year	Research Applied	Clinical	Development	Total
1982	0.9	2.4	1.3	4.6
1983	1.4	6.0	3.2	10.6
1984	0.8	10.3	3.3	14.4
1985	0.1	11.4	1.7	13.2
1986	—	5.4	0.8	6.2

Source: BioEngineering News 1983

the details of these partnerships, it is impossible to ascertain the level of royalties that investors can expect. In the Genentech RDLP investors are guaranteed 22 percent of any profits that accrue (*Bioengineering News* 1983). Table 7.10 indicates the proposed uses to which the funds of the Genentech RDLP will be put over a five-year period. The years 1984 and 1985 will be important ones for the partners because Genentech will be testing for wider uses of HGH, and gamma interferon will also be used in clinical tests (*Bioengineering News* 1983). The successful conclusion of these tests is critical for ensuring that royalties will accrue to the limited partners. The large sum to be devoted to clinical testing, $35.5 million, illustrates the hurdles that a startup must overcome to generate a cash flow from manufacturing and simultaneously one of the reasons the startups must contract out so many products to large MNCs that have the deep pockets to be able to afford clinical testing. Scale-up and refinement are expected to require only 21 percent of the total placement.

The RDLP is an important mechanism for enabling startups to tap the capital of private individuals who are looking for returns not available from common stock. The RDLP is insurance against the risk that one unsuccessful product will bankrupt the company. Essentially all of the costs and risks of commercialization are borne by the limited partnership. Moreover, the startup acquires greater control over its fate—neither becoming a passive recipient of royalties nor risking the entire company on one go-it-alone product.

The RDLPs are the last step between these startups and the market.[13] The RDLP allows the companies to tap the large amount of investment monies in the United States and amass the capital needed to become commercially viable. The RDLP can be considered to be a creative use of tax law to encourage economic innovation. The results of this new form

13. Some startups have brought products to market without RDLPs. The need for RDLPs is the greatest for human pharmaceuticals such as interferon and new hormones, which must pass rigorous and expensive Food and Drug Administration safety and efficacy tests. Much less testing is required of animal pharmaceuticals and "in vitro" diagnostics. Therefore, a few of these have already been brought to market without the aid of RDLPs.

of financing will become apparent in the next five or six years as the partnerships' products approach the market.

Commercialization

Next year [1983] is the year all good companies must prove themselves. People won't invest in professors any more   (Brook Byers, chairman of Hybritech, quoted in Business Week 1982a:37).

The final goal that most companies have striven for is the commercialization of products.[14] In the six months to a year before selling its first product, the company actively adds sales and management personnel recruited from the large MNCs. No longer does the company organization chart resemble a university biology department onto which a couple of staffless vice-presidents for production and marketing are grafted. For most companies the first year for transformation from a research startup to a true company that needs marketing strategies, salesmen, and delivery systems was 1983.

The fateful product development choices made by management in 1978, 1979, or 1980 have now developed into the company's ticket for survival. For the more successful companies a number of products have emerged (table 7.11). The bulk of these products are diagnostics using monoclonal antibodies (MABs). MABs are high-value, low-volume pharmaceuticals that are relatively simple to manufacture. The scours (a young animal diarrheal disease) vaccine being marketed by both Molecular Genetics and Cetus is also made with MABs. The reason the first biotechnology products were developed for agriculture is that agricultural products are not subject to as stringent health and safety testing as products applied to humans.

Genex adopted a unique strategy and was manufacturing l-aspartame and l-phenylalanine (amino acids) for G. D. Searle's aspartame using genetically engineered microorganisms. In fact, Genex moved production to a newly acquired fermentation plant where full-scale phenylalanine production will take place (*Wall Street Journal* 1983d:8). However, in late 1985 Searle canceled its contract with Genex in favor of producing the aspartame with in-house capacity. Genex has sued Searle but in the meantime Genex

---

14. There are exceptions, such as Applied DNA Systems, which intend to maintain their status as service companies providing expert consulting and doing specific contract research. This type of company sometimes serves as a clearinghouse that subcontracts projects to university professors. Another model of service company is Techniclone, which employs seven full-time employees, seven university contractors, and four consultants. Techniclone's major income was derived from contracts to supply Beckman Instruments, Baker Instruments, Fujizoka, and Hoffmann-La Roche. Techniclone is pursuing further contracts and at this time is not considering developing in-house marketing and production (Prescott 1983b:23).

Table 7.11. Startup Company Products, Introduction Dates, MNC Partner*

Startup company	Introduction date	Product	Partner
Biogen	May 1983	Hepatitis diagnostic	Green Cross Hoffmann-La Roche Behring Werke
Cetus	July 1983	Blood virus diagnostic	—
Centocor	January 1983	Hepatitis diagnostic	Warner-Lambert
Genentech	October 1982	Human insulin	Eli Lilly
Genetic Systems	January 1983	Chlamydia diagnostic	Syntex
	August 1983	Herpes diagnostic	—
Genex	1982	l-aspartic acid	—
	1983	l-phenylalanine	—
Hybritech	July 1981	Monoclonal antibodies	—
Molecular Genetics	March 1983	Scours vaccine	—
Monoclonal Antibodies	November 1982	Pregnancy test	—

Sources: Author's compilation, various journals and annual reports
* Research products have been omitted as have producer goods, i.e., inputs to other companies' production processes.

has been decisively weakened. Finally, Eli Lilly is selling human insulin produced with Genentech's bacteria (Genentech is only a royalty beneficiary). The genetic engineering industry at the end of 1984 was still largely confined to the sale of research inputs, some monoclonal diagnostics, an animal vaccine, and human insulin. Yet the products of biotechnology are beginning to appear. In 1985 a number of animal therapeutics and more MAB-based diagnostics entered the marketplace, and Genentech's genetically engineered HGH received final FDA approval. The product pipeline is beginning to fill up.

A number of companies will soon become profitable. Howard Greene, Jr., the president and chief executive officer of Hybritech, describes his company's imminent move to profitability:

But we see the revenue and expenses lines finally crossing in the next couple of quarters [quoted August 17, 1983]. . . . Our general feeling is that chugging along for five years without making money is long enough. . . . What is important to note is that we will finally be at a breakeven level on our operations; our revenues finally cover our significant research and development and other operating expenses   *(Wall Street Journal* 1983a:16).

Table 7.12. Selected Recombinant DNA Products and Corporate Research Teams*

Product	Startup	Multinational corporation
Bovine growth hormone	Amgen Collaborative Research Genentech Molecular Genetics	Upjohn Akzo (Netherlands) Monsanto American Cyanamid
Alpha interferon	Amgen Biogen Cetus Collaborative Research Genentech Genex	None Schering-Plough Shell Oil National Patent Development Corp. Hoffmann-La Roche Bristol-Myers
Interleukin 2	Immunex Genex Cetus Biogen	Hoffmann-La Roche Yoshitomo Pharmaceuticals None Shionogi
Human serum albumin	Genex Collaborative Research Biogen	Green Cross (Japan) Kabi-Vitrum (Sweden) Warner-Lambert Shionogi
Gamma interferon	Amgen Biogen Genentech	None Shionogi Daiichi Seiyaku Toray Industries

Source: Author's compilation
* Excluded from this list are MNCs conducting in-house research on these products. Also, the specific products listed are possibly the most competitive. Finally, this is only a partial listing, as much work remains proprietary; therefore, it is likely that a number of other alliances are in effect.

Genentech, Genex, Biogen, and the others are all aiming for that point where revenues begin to permanently outweigh expenses and profit is generated.

Because biotechnology products have been on the market only two years at most, the industry's structure is hard to outline. However, there is intense competition between various startup and MNC teams regarding many of the major products (table 7.12). In many cases MNCs currently supplying the product or its substitute have purchased access to genetically engineered products to ensure that they will not be outflanked. As one can see from table 7.12, the industry is international, as every MNC has rushed to buy access to biotechnology products and techniques.

The startups' ability to muscle their way into potentially lucrative markets is not assured. In product areas now supplied by the large MNCs, the competition will be fierce; price cutting and patent infringement could destroy the startups. A more viable strategy for startups might be to enter the animal vaccine business, which has smaller markets, smaller competitors, and less required testing. Molecular Genetics is pursuing this strategy most avidly, as is Cetus for its first product, a scours vaccine. The essence of the plan is to carve out niches within which the startup can develop cash flow to finance expansion. The MAB firms have actively pursued just such a strategy because MABs, with their extremely high target specificity and relatively simple production technologies, lend themselves to it. For the MAB companies, the interests and expertise of key professors provided the initial corporate products and applications. For example, Genetic Systems' first product, a diagnostic, has targeted a sexually transmitted disease (chlamydia). The second generation of products includes respiratory disease diagnostics, the formation of a subsidiary with Syntex for cancer diagnostics, and blood cell typing kits (Genetic Systems 1982). Monoclonal Antibodies, Inc. (1982) has specialized in sexual hormones, and its first product was a pregnancy test. Centocor, which does no marketing, was started by scientists from the Wistar Institute (Philadelphia) on the basis of inventions regarding the diagnosis of hepatitis B virus, which became the company's first product (Centocor 1982:10). Centocor, Hybritech, and Genetic Systems are all planning to expand into the lucrative area of cancer diagnostics and therapeutics.

Each startup chose to develop MAB-based diagnostic tests for different pathological conditions, and coincidentally all are now developing cancer diagnostics. As the startups have developed diagnostic products, large, deep-pocket competitors such as Johnson and Johnson, Abbott, Baxter-Travenol, and Warner-Lambert are also entering the marketplace. In fact, segments of the MNCs' product lines are licensed from the startups. For example, research and development contracts between Centocor and Warner-Lambert, Monoclonal Antibodies, Inc. and Johnson and Johnson, Hybritech and Johnson and Johnson, and Genetic Systems and Syntex have already been signed. And in late 1985 Hybritech and Genetic Systems were acquired by Eli Lilly and Bristol-Myers, respectively. Obviously, the current situation in the diagnostics field is very fluid, and predictions of success are premature.[15] Production and marketing strategies will be as vital as technical superiority, and perhaps more so.

---

15. Diagnostics are an important market because of the growth in medical testing that can be performed by technicians rather than doctors. The use of MABs would permit these tests to be performed and interpreted by workers who are less highly paid than doctors, the value of whose labor time is high. Further, unlike previous tests, many of the new ones do not require expensive, specialized detection instruments. These tests will probably deskill the doctor, who will no longer need to diagnose diseases on the strength of his "craft" knowledge. Rather, "simple to use" kits will be sold to doctors and hospitals for diagnostics. Or in some

The lack of a proper commercialization strategy can significantly retard a company's development. Easily the richest genetic engineering company, Cetus, with its superior staff and scientific advisors, has made little headway. In the late 1970s Cetus developed a different strategy from that of most other companies—it decided to attempt to biosynthesize bulk chemicals such as fructose, ethylene, and ethanol and secured industrial sponsors for the three projects: Chevron for fructose, National Distillers for ethanol, and Standard Oil of Indiana for ethylene glycol. These companies acquired 49.6 percent of Cetus's stock—Standard Oil of Indiana owns 21.3 percent, Chevron 17.3 percent, and National Distillers 11 percent (Cetus 1981a; *Chemical Week* 1982e:34).

Peter Farley—a Cetus cofounder, then vice-president, and soon to become president and chief operating officer—commenting on Cetus's strategy in 1978, said, "We're building another IBM here. . . . We see ourselves as far and away the number one company doing what we're doing. . . . As a company applying modern biology to industry we are the major game in town. And with Standard Oil money behind us now, we can reach an optimum exploitation of that opportunity even faster" (R. Lewin 1978b:18). In 1980 Farley (1980:55) reiterated his ideas on how Cetus would go about becoming the IBM of biotechnology: "As you begin to move into the commercialization phase, then the question is: What is the most appropriate source for this money? In our own case, we have chosen to go the large, corporate stockholder route because we feel that they have the proper perspective, in the sense of being able to look out ten or fifteen years for the returns."

What was the outcome of this strategy? Choosing the wrong products can prove to be an extremely serious miscalculation. The National Distillers project was successful, but there is so little demand for gasohol that scale-up plans have been scrapped—a loss of a significant royalty potential for Cetus (Nossiter 1982:24). In May 1982 Chevron withdrew from the fructose project, causing Cetus to furlough eighty-nine employees in the next six months (Potter 1983:7A). Nevertheless, Cetus has large capital resources and has been able to recover. To facilitate the new focus, Robert Fildes, then president of Biogen U.S.A., was hired to replace Farley. Cetus's new concentration became high-value, low-volume products currently being pursued by the rest of the industry, but Cetus had lost a five-year head start.

Successful commercialization is based upon the corporate business plan laid out at the startup stage. If the target products were the proper ones and the company's scientists were successful, the company should either already have products on the market or expect them soon. Successful execution of the business plan should have developed unique areas of

---

cases diagnosis of conditions such as pregnancy and infertility will be done through the use of kits purchased over the counter at pharmacies.

expertise; the company should not merely be a "me-too" company. The commencement of a product-generated cash flow is the first step to becoming a successful corporation in the marketplace.

Shakeout, Retrenchment, and Bankruptcy

> The people [management at Armos] turned down capital. . . . It was the biggest mistake they made, but you can't blame them. . . . The pricing [the amount of equity management was willing to surrender for more capital] was too high from a wrong perception of the market for investment money   *(Frederick Adler, a venture capitalist, quoted in J. Fox 1982b:9).*

The history of biotechnology ventures contains failures as well as successes. Because the startups have yet to enter the marketplace, failures such as the one that overtook Osborne Computers have not occurred. The lurid press reports of an impending shakeout (Feder 1982; Lancaster 1982) have proven premature.[16]

Even respected analysts from brokerage firms such as Dean Witter Reynolds were quoted in the *New York Times* as predicting that the shakeout would come in the later part of 1982 or early in 1983 (Feder 1982). Table 7.7 flatly contradicts these prognostications, indicating that during 1983 more companies went public than in any other year. Some analysts believe that this stampede of companies offering shares to the public is an expression of the lack of private capital (P. Dorfman 1983). However, this interpretation is open to doubt, because going public is also a way to get more money for less equity.

Corporate retrenchments have occurred at firms such as Cetus, IPRI, and Bethesda Research Laboratories. In all three, retrenchments were accompanied by important management changes resulting from venture capital pressure.[17] When a startup has a financial crisis, the interaction between its financiers and its corporate founders and managers can become strained.

---

16. No shakeout has occurred, but there have been many fewer new startups. The startup window was from 1978 to 1980 for rDNA and was intermingled with the hybridoma startups from 1980 to early 1982. Whether there will be another startup wave in areas such as lymphokines, liposomes, or neurology is difficult to predict. The biology industry has likely seen a peak in sheer number of startups.

17. An important social scientific technique is to examine unusual cases to gain insight into the normal case. In bankruptcy or severe corporate crisis the antagonisms between corporate founders and financiers become evident, and their contradictory interests are highlighted. Furthermore, the internal workings of the company are more accessible to outsiders because the principals are willing to make recriminations and describe relationships. Bankruptcy removes the need for secrecy.

Only one significant startup, Armos, has actually declared bankruptcy.[18] Armos's two principals, Brian Sheehan and Sharon Carlock, were previously employed by Genentech before forming Armos. The initial startup investment was $2.5 million, $1.5 million from Carlock and Sheehan and $1 million from Adler and Company, a venture capital firm. Armos targeted animal vaccines and bovine interferon as product areas because of the ease of entry (fewer health and safety restrictions, etc.). The research team and facilities were judged to be of high quality, and they actually had some research success (J. Fox 1983b:9). However, the problem at Armos was that their burn rate was too fast, and they were unable to secure any corporate contract revenues.

Armos began to sink when it sought to secure another round of financing. Sheehan and Carlock were reluctant to proffer enough equity to attract second-round investors because they would have lost control of the company.[19] Frederick Adler, the initial venture capitalist who invested in the company, puts it bluntly: "If someone refuses [to make a 'reasonable' offer of equity] . . . [they can] retain control but lose the company" (J. Fox 1982b:12). Adler tried to arrange meetings with investors, but when Armos's management refused to offer sufficient equity, the company's demise became inevitable. Unless it can continue to secure capital transfusions, bankruptcy is the ineluctable fate of any company that is spending more than it takes in.

Armos's management had a point when they resisted losing control of the company. A recent *Wall Street Journal* article describes the role the venture capitalists may play in a company:

Venture capitalists often hold seats on the board of a startup company, and if they find that the person who started the company doesn't have

18. Another bankrupt company, Southern Biotech, is a peculiar case because it started as a blood processing laboratory that was extracting interferon from white blood cells by means of the Kantel process. The company was initially called the Southern Medical and Pharmaceutical Corporation but then renamed itself Southern Biotech and started biotechnology research. Southern Biotech's first move was to hire William Stewart, an interferon specialist at Sloan-Kettering Institute for Cancer Research, and he formed a research team. Shearson/American Express made an initial stock offering that realized less capital than the company expected. However, the company management continued to make significant expenditures for life-style amenities even while its laboratories were only partially equipped. Southern Biotech, its capital exhausted, filed Chapter 11 bankruptcy in June 1982, less than four months after its stock issue (Norman and Marshall 1982:1076–82). Southern Biotech is a unique case of a company that merely constituted itself to secure a share of the biotechnology "gold rush" that was under way in 1980 and 1981. Its demise offers little insight into the operation of venture capital (there was none involved), the biotechnology industry, or the alleged "coming industry shakeout."

19. For example, Herbert Boyer and Robert Swanson, the founders of Genentech, together own less than 20 percent of the company. A common feature of many larger biotechnology startups is that the founders have a minority interest.

the knack to build it up, they may advise him to step aside, frequently to oversee technical or creative operations. Sometimes they get tough. "The hardest part of the job is firing the president," says Mr. Lucas [a venture capitalist], who says he has done that many times   (Dolan 1983:1).

Armos's management was probably correct in assuming that a coup like the one described in the above quote was being prepared for them, as Adler had been urging them to slow their burn rate (J. Fox 1982b:12). If management lost control of the board of directors, they, Carlock and Sheehan, would have been displaced. With no slowdown in the burn rate, no investors, and an inability to control the company Adler had only two choices: invest on management's terms or pull the plug. Armos was only one percent of Adler's portfolio—they needed his money worse than he needed their company. So he pulled the plug.

Armos is a rare example of an instance when management decided it was better to destroy the company than to secure a portion of their investment by giving up corporate control. Certainly emotional attachment to a company is understandable, but at the prospect of losing their entire investment most entrepreneurs become flexible. Armos is a unique case in which management and their venture partners were so completely at odds that no compromise could be struck.

A restructuring and removing of previous management is common when cash flow problems beset a company. In some cases the entrepreneur forgets the company must make money and cannot simply expand in an uncontrolled manner. Perhaps the most dramatic example of corporate restructuring and scaling back of projects occurred at Bethesda Research Laboratories (BRL) in 1982. BRL was founded in 1976 by Stephen Turner to sell restriction enzymes to researchers in the biomedical research institutions in the Washington, D.C., area. BRL was uniquely situated to participate in the biotechnology boom, and both sales and employees doubled nearly every year (J. Fox 1982a:12). But the 1982 downturn surprised the corporation, which had been expanding recklessly. BRL was caught in a cash flow squeeze, and within a few months the company was on the brink of bankruptcy.

As a price for saving the company, Turner had to allow the appointment of an outsider-dominated board of directors. An executive committee of the board was formed to cut costs and increase cash flow (J. Fox 1982a:12). Finally, over 150 employees were terminated in the cost-cutting drive. In saving his company, Turner had to lose control of it, and within two years the company was sold to the Dexter Company (*Chemical Week* 1983e:34).

A similar case occurred at IPRI. In March 1982 the operating duties of the company's founding president, Martin Apple, were transferred to a chief executive officer. Writing at the time in *Chemical and Engineering*

News, Jeffrey Fox (1982a:13) said, "Such changes [the shift of power] can be overemphasized and overinterpreted, of course." In IPRI's case it was not overemphasized; by May 29, 1982, Apple had left IPRI to form a new company (*GEN* 1982d:3). To make IPRI "a business in fact, not only in spirit," a vice-president of Hunt-Wesson Foods, Raymond Moshe, was made president (*Chemical and Engineering News* 1982a:6). By November 1982 the company could not meet its payroll and between 20 and 50 percent of the employees had been laid off (*GEN* 1983a:3). In June 1983 Bio-Rad Laboratories purchased 70 percent of IPRI's stock, and the company had recovered sufficiently to sign research contracts. At IPRI the founder was replaced and over 60 percent of the staff was terminated to bring the company in line with its finances (*GEN* 1983e:14).

   In each of these troubled companies the burn rate was too fast, and when management was unable to control it they were eased out by the venture investors. Armos was the only example in which the founders controlled sufficient equity to resist the other owners. The cost of resistance was the demise of the company. The venture capitalists take seats on the company's board of directors to ensure that their investments are protected. As long as the startup is on target as set out in the business plan, a management shakeup is unusual. But in cases in which the value of their investment is threatened venture capitalists will take action.

   What is most amazing about the biotechnology industry is the number of new corporate entries that remain viable through receipt of capital infusions. That only the few mentioned here and probably some much smaller companies have shaken out in the last five years is unusual in a period marked by runaway inflation and the worst slump since the early 1930s. Business failures were at all-time highs, yet biotechnology expanded into the recession. In general it is valid to say that the problems experienced by the companies I have discussed were due to bad management; the environment was favorable to corporate survival.

   There will probably never be a shakeout in the form of numerous bankruptcies. Rather, the shakeout is more likely to consist of a buyout by large MNCs that can use the technical expertise assembled in the startups. Clear examples of this are the earlier mentioned purchases of Hybritech by Eli Lilly and Genetic Systems by Bristol-Myers. At risk will be the startups' low- and mid-level sales and marketing personnel who will be redundant. The scientists will see no change in their tasks. They will merely be assigned tasks and projects by their new employers.

8. The Internal

Relationships of

Startup Companies

It's a matter of trying to keep science
basic enough to make sure that the
scientists feel that they're doing good
science, and to make sure the company
and stockholders are guaranteed that what
they're doing is going to be relevant and
have social impacts   *(David Martin,
former professor at UCSF and now vice-
president of research at Genentech,
quoted in* Chemical Week *1982d:16)*

Startups are founded upon the scientific skills that their employees bring to the company from the university. Yet the norms of "doing science" in the university are very different from those necessary for economic success. The biotechnology startups must be able to reconcile the world of the university with that of industry. To become overly hierarchic and bureaucratic might stultify scientific creativity, destroying the commercial advantage the startups have had in creating a superior innovative environment, but a lack of focus on products that are able to be commercialized will almost certainly inhibit the cash flow that is crucial for commercial survival; this was an important factor in IPRI's financial problems (IPRI 1982). The internal relationships of the startup companies have unique features that separate them from both universities and MNCs.

Research life in the universities also entails competition for money, but the products are papers and other research materials that are traded for recognition, status, and scholarly position. These can be understood met-aphorically as capital that is accumulated in terms of publications and recognition in the field. This capital is expressed in research monies and in the building of a research empire, which reinforces a scientist's ability to secure more results, that is, published papers that are influential in the discipline (Latour and Woolgar 1979: chapter 4). The academic environ-ment is highly competitive—even many postdoctoral students are building their positions so as to be able to start their own research empire—but depends ultimately on cooperation among members of the research team.[1]

A company requires more structured behavior from its employees. The laboratory workers and even the senior scientists cannot be allowed to pursue scientific research merely because they think it is important. The excitement of discovery must be subordinated to the need to create mar-ketable products. The relationships and operating methods that prevail in university laboratories must be transformed in order to be integrated into an institution geared to producing marketable research and/or manufac-turing products. I shall synthesize the available information about what goes on inside the biotechnology startups, although the story is necessarily incomplete because of the secrecy that cloaks biotechnology companies and their activities.[2] This secrecy is difficult to penetrate because it is an integral part of the production relations that are critical to success.

Internal Organization

Nearly all of the biotechnology companies are organized "in a collegial manner, with scientific staff positions parallel to post-doctorate through tenured rungs on an academic ladder" (Eagle and Coyman 1981:3). Bio-technica International, Inc. (1983:18) describes the three levels of scientists on its staff thus:

The Company's current full-time scientists include eight Senior Scien-tists, five Research Scientists and eight Assistant Scientists, all of whom

1. Other people in the laboratory, such as technicians, and secretaries, are not a part of this competition, though they are crucial in providing its underpinnings.
2. The biotechnology companies, large and small, are extremely secretive because the commodity created by research is information. Information is a unique commodity because its reproduction costs are essentially zero and yet its application can yield tremendous profit or cost savings. Because information production is inherently a social process, information tends to leak, and all companies are very security conscious. At the same time, of course, tremendous efforts are made to get information. A Harvard Business School case study of AGS opens with the president of the company, Daniel Adams, searching for his key to lock the door at night. Adams then is paraphrased as asking, "What was the use of locking it? He had to assume that regardless of his precautions, AGS, like most high-technology firms, had its phones tapped and its trash searched" (Kania 1982:1). Secrecy can be obsessive, with some companies tapping their employees' telephones.

are parties to employment agreements with the Company. During 1983, the Company intends to increase its scientific staff, primarily through the addition of approximately ten Assistant Scientists. All Senior Scientists and all but one of the Research Scientists hold doctoral degrees in their scientific disciplines. Assistant Scientists hold Bachelor's or Master's Degrees and work under the direction of the Senior and Research Scientists.

Biotechnica International also has senior research consultants who are faculty members at either MIT or Harvard but are intimately involved in at least one of the company's projects.

Biotechnica International's senior scientists most nearly resemble university faculty members, the research scientists parallel postdoctoral researchers, and the assistant scientists are akin to graduate assistants or junior technicians. In the startup's hierarchy the senior scientists are sometimes on the boards of directors. In contrast to the university, where a peer group of scientists makes collegial decisions and each faculty member has an equal vote, a company is characterized by clear hierarchy, and control is vested in the corporate owners. The lines of authority are vertical: from management down to workers (scientists). Although some of the university's lines of authority are certainly vertical—though seldom involving the power to terminate subordinates (a faculty member cannot fire a student or even his secretary, for that matter)—they are also horizontal (collegial) when it comes to deciding many departmental matters.

In biotechnology startups, scientists from various disciplines are brought together for a project, and outside consultants—in many cases members of the SAB—are brought in to provide expert assistance to the senior scientists. Company research has a chief scientist directing the technical aspects of the research effort, his role in many ways resembling the role of the principal investigator on a university grant. However, the university principal investigator holds the ultimate authority in "his" laboratory; the money comes to the university in the investigator's name. The university scientist has tenure as well as complete control of his fund allocations, whereas the corporate scientist has neither. The scientist in a corporation is simply a highly skilled worker (though he may own a part of the company) and cannot be conceived of as an independent operator. Any activities are measured by the progress they make toward commercialization. If good science or university-like conditions are the key to commercial success, then they will be present, but the corporate goal is and must be commercial success.

Bringing a genetically engineered product to marketability is a process that involves more than one scientist or research group. Merely to prepare a product for marketing requires "interacting teams of molecular biologists, immunologists, virologists, biochemists, chemists, clinical doctors, process engineers, fermentation experts, and others" (Eggers 1981:107). One of the attractions of working for a biotechnology firm is the opportunity to work with scientists from other disciplines on a common problem—something that occurs infrequently at universities.[3] These small biotechnology startups are organizationally suited to facilitate the interaction and cooperation among various scientists that is needed to manufacture products.

Atmosphere

The startups must remain on the cutting edge of the biological sciences— to lose this edge will mean losing the highly competitive race to the market. Genentech describes its position thus:

> We are a company driven by science. We encourage our scientists to interact with the academic community and to receive credit for their achievements through publication. While there is a continuing effort to ensure protection of our patentable inventions and know-how, interaction with the broad scientific community is important if we are to remain on the cutting edge of science   (Genentech 1980a:2).

A reporter who toured Genentech's laboratories wrote that "the atmosphere [at Genentech] actually feels more like a university than a business" (Benner 1981:68). Julian Davies, then director of Biogen's Geneva laboratories, describes their laboratories similarly (quoted in Powledge 1983a:402):

> We [Biogen] set up the research unit here in the same way that it was set up in Cambridge, to allow people the flexibility and time and ideas to be able to express themselves. The labs don't close. We want people to be able to work at night and weekends, and they do. . . . In general, we wanted to provide a scientific utopia.

The startups are predicated on providing an environment in which the creativity of the university can be directed into economically valuable channels. Leslie Misrock, the lawyer who invented the RDLP as a financing instrument, terms the environments in both companies and universities "a hothouse atmosphere." Quite obviously, the intellectual workers must enjoy a proper environment in which to be productive. In 1981 Genentech's ratio of laboratory space to office space was more than two to one (Benner

---

3. Recently large MNCs have been stressing that universities need to do more interdisciplinary research in biology (for example, Sohio provided a grant for interdisciplinary centers). Universities are responding very rapidly—Cornell, for example, has already formed an institute for this effort. One can only speculate as to whether these are a competitive response to the startups by universities whose grant monies may be threatened by the success of the startups or whether they are a response to corporate demands.

1981:68). The scientist-workers who are crucial to ensuring the success of the companies demand a certain ambiance.

The most interesting discussion of the startup's atmosphere—more correctly the desired atmosphere—is an article by an architect, Peter Shaffer, who specializes in designing buildings for biotechnology companies. Shaffer (1983:23) writes,

> To reinforce management's philosophy that the company is a synthesis of science and business, . . . we designed several informal meeting areas—for coffee, reading, etc.—where staff could gather and exchange ideas. Meeting rooms are glass enclosed to convey a sense of open communication. Even the major conference room has informal "living room" ambiance.

The overriding objective is to create an atmosphere of openness and comfort that allows information to flow freely.

Biogen's architect, too, sought to encourage communication by his design:

> At Biogen, communication between administration and technical staff had high priority. In addition, proximity of staff scientists to their work and to daylight was of paramount importance. Senior scientists, on the other hand, needed to communicate more actively among themselves and could therefore have offices near each other but remote from the laboratories   (Shaffer 1983:23).

At Biogen apparently the role of senior scientists is not in the laboratory but more administrative, thereby resembling that of the principal investigator on a large university research team. These senior scientists are the interlocutors between corporate management and working scientists. In Biogen's facility the first floor is administrative, and the second contains laboratories. The connection between the two was accomplished by a central atrium where communication between scientist and management is encouraged by the presence of informal meeting rooms.

The attraction and retention of highly qualified scientific personnel is critical for corporate survival. Biotechnica International (1983:6) describes this need succinctly in its stock prospectus:

> The Company's primary asset, at this stage of its development, is its employees. Few scientists have the skills needed for sophisticated molecular genetic research and competition for such employees is intense. With the increased opportunities for such individuals, there can be no assurance that the terms of employment, compensation, working environment and stock ownership given by the Company to its employees will be sufficient to retain them as the Company's employees.

Because for most startups the creation and retention of a scientific staff is so crucial, nearly all of the companies, no matter what management might prefer, allow scientists to publish articles. For example, Genentech's scientists have published articles in *Science, Nature,* and the *Proceedings of the NAS* (Genentech 1980b:4). Of course, before the articles are submitted corporate attorneys review them for patentable ideas. The larger startups also have many in-house seminars (Genentech 1980b:13; Cetus 1981a:22). At Genentech these seminars are attended by patent attorneys on the alert for any patentable ideas (Yoxen 1983:134).

As mentioned above, the campuslike atmosphere is designed not only to attract skilled scientists and provide an environment that enhances intellectual productivity, but also to induce effective communication between management and scientists. Management must be able to gauge effectively the potential and the value of ongoing research. These evaluations of research are vital to management as they make decisions regarding investments of scarce funds and the selling of contract research.

In some companies such as IPRI an overriding desire to maintain secrecy is believed by some to have been linked with commercial setbacks (Munger 1983). At Armos, personal mail was opened and telephone conversations were monitored (J. Fox 1982b:10). If management operates in this fashion, the information that it receives will become skewed toward what management wants to hear. Jeffrey Fox (1982b:10) discusses the types of dysfunctional communications that can result:

> It's easy enough for management and a scientific team to feed one another half-truths without realizing it or understanding the consequences. Management wants to hear that certain projects are progressing, and so do scientists. . . . This tendency [of management to praise success] becomes accentuated if some scientists become infatuated with preliminary results. . . . Unfortunately for management, which cannot or may not appreciate the flimsy underpinnings of such hasty announcements, the task of sorting out the real from the hoped-for can become increasingly difficult. This is especially true if the good-news messengers are deemed not only praiseworthy but accurate, thus prompting management to set new and more-ambitious-than-ever deadlines.

A company that conducts its business through internal spying and fear or that is managed on the basis of misinformation, inflated expectations, and ignorance is flirting with disaster.

Little is known about the internal communications among scientists, but it is fair to assume that the employees do not freely discuss corporate secrets. Daniel Adams, the president of AGS, seems confident regarding AGS's scientists: "Scientists never give away information for free anyway, and we feel that the value of the inflow of information is greater than the value of the outflow. Also, we couldn't hold on to top scientists if we kept them locked up" (Kania 1982:18). This estimation of the ability or desirability of controlling information flow also seems more likely to ensure honest scientific evaluation of ongoing research.

A good physical working environment is certainly to be desired, but it is not as important as a good informational environment. Scientists must be immersed in a constant flow of information and must be active participants in this process. Moves to stifle this flow are likely to be self-defeating for the company. This constant need by both scientists and management conditions the types of buildings built to house the company. Whether the internal creative environment of the university science laboratory can be transferred to a profit-making entity is, of course, not yet clear.

What If Employees Resign?

Information is invaluable in the biotechnology industry. All employees sign contracts regarding their rights and obligations upon termination. Already a number of employees have left Genentech to form other biotechnology companies or to join management at other companies. For example, the founders of Armos were former Genentech executives (J. Fox 1982b). Nowell Stebbing, Amgen's vice-president of scientific affairs, was director of biology at Genentech (Amgen 1983:22), and Robert Crea, research director of Creative Biomolecules, was formerly a Genentech manager. Personnel turnover has been common in the other high-tech industries and will no doubt continue to be so in biotechnology.[4]

Little discussion of the corporate consequences of the resignations of key individuals has ensued—though every stock prospectus has a section cautioning that retention of key personnel is important for the success of the company. Most companies are already large enough to be able to compensate for the loss of any single researcher, but due to the lack of products a development stage company's value still resides in its research team. Douglas Rogers, an investment banker of Kidder, Peabody, and Company, describes the importance of the employees thus: "[The startup company's] main assets are the scientists. . . . The problem is, those sci-

---

4. Whether continued executive mobility will be for the purpose of initiating new startups or will simply be a method of climbing the career ladder is impossible to predict. What does seem obvious is that the continued increase in the sheer number of biotechnology startups is not assured: first, significant investments are required because of the long lead times before marketing. The barriers to entry are increasing because there are already established firms and research projects. Needless to say, the established companies follow the scientific literature and are usually able to mobilize to take advantage of any opportunities. Only companies formed to exploit certain niches will be able to secure financing—for example, Advanced Mineral Technologies for mining. Second, most of the available scientists are already linked to companies in one way or another.

entists have legs and can walk" (*Chemical Week* 1982a:52). Any company in which few skilled laborers occupy such an important role is inherently unstable.

The importance of highly skilled scientists to corporate success has prompted the practice of raiding scientists. Officials from an unnamed California biotechnology company are quoted in *Bio/Technology* as saying, "The headhunters are very active. We are seeing a lot of raiding going on" (Dwyer 1983c:644). To lose such personnel is dangerous not merely due to the loss of their skills but also because these workers take with them the knowledge they gathered while working for the company. Perhaps the most devastating raid thus far was Cetus's recruitment of Robert Fildes, then president of Biogen, Inc., the U.S. subsidiary of Biogen (*Chemical Week* 1983c). Little is currently known regarding compensation or restraints that Biogen may have imposed or demanded from Fildes for allowing him to break his Biogen contract.[5]

The loss of trade secrets and proprietary knowledge is potentially damaging to a company's competitive standing. Recently a suit brought against Cetus Corporation by Bio-Rad Laboratories alleged that Cetus, by hiring two former Bio-Rad employees, had misappropriated trade secrets. Bio-Rad claims that the two researchers "constituted the heart of Bio-Rad's research team working on the subject of cancer diagnostics, Blakemore providing marketing analysis and Loor providing clinical research" (Elman 1983:4). The complaint against Cetus charges that the two former employees broke their employment agreements, which pledged secrecy and confidentiality. Cetus, a company which had unwisely emphasized high-volume, low-value molecules, needed to change directions, and these new employees could assist in that process. The newly acquired expertise could constitute a major step forward in Cetus's race to commercialization.[6]

Raiding will likely continue as the competition in the industry increases. The more successful companies will find themselves forced to protect their prize employees, many of whom will become subjects of bidding wars. This type of raiding, which is deplored by nearly every company and all personnel managers, is probably uncontrollable in the context of U.S.

5. The first concrete information regarding this raid was contained in the appendices of Biogen's and Cetus's 10-K filing with the Securities and Exchange Commission in 1984.
6. I do not discuss the implications of the transience of these highly skilled, key personnel. For companies in a startup stage the loss of presidents, vice-presidents, and key scientific personnel can lead to stalled programs and losses of proprietary information. Whether this will benefit the large MNCs, which have more stable staffs, is questionable. As indicated in table 8.1, their young, aggressive middle- and upper-level management are deserting to the startups. The U.S. biotechnology industry is developing a highly mobile, career-oriented labor force. Further, this mobility means that everyone is searching for a quick payoff—including the MNCs. The success of this uniquely American method of organizing industry is not guaranteed, especially when compared with the more stable, measured Japanese effort (Kenney 1985).

industry. For example, Gabriel Schmergel, president of Genetics Institute, was quoted regarding the move of Robert Fildes from Biogen to Cetus as saying, "Bob Fildes is a highly respected professional manager and a very tough competitor. . . . We always took Cetus seriously, and we're going to take them a lot more seriously now" (*Chemical Week* 1983c:41). Further, the raiding and retrenchments that have taken place at Biogen and Bethesda Research Laboratories may have negative impact on the esprit de corps of the startups.

The Forgotten Workers: Nonscientific Managers

One might imagine that the startups are the exclusive domain of scientists—scientists as workers, scientists as managers, scientists as consultants on the SAB—with perhaps a couple of Stanford or Harvard MBA entrepreneurs added. In the early days this caricature was not far from the truth. Certainly a company without products, which is precisely what the startups were, had no need for a marketing network. However, the research progress made by the companies soon made it imperative for them to start implementing a marketing strategy. To do that, experienced managers from large chemical and pharmaceutical companies were needed.

The motivations of the young (thirty- to forty-five-year-old) middle- and upper-level managers to leave seemingly secure positions in large multinational companies to join biotechnology startups are diverse. A major consideration would appear to be the lack of challenge within the multinationals. Many of the businessmen that make the switch to the startups are aware that they have been on the corporate fast track but also recognize that further advancement inside the company will be slower because the corporate pyramid narrows drastically near the apex. Further, the MNCs, with their large bureaucracies and numerous vice-presidents, offer little sense of accomplishment and increasingly less security.

Robert Byrnes[7] (quoted in Benner 1981:68), Genentech's former vice-president for marketing, describes his role thus: "You have to be flexible . . . and not overly concerned about what you do day-to-day—whether it's running out to get a liver for a scientist or playing the role of vice-president in a negotiation. It doesn't matter. The point is, I'm a resource. We, as managers, have to demonstrate it daily. Then everyone else in the organization will adopt it." For managers the situation in small startups presents new challenges daily and there is no constant routine. (To cite a dramatic example, the first human test of Genentech's HGH was by injection into twelve company executives [Chase 1983:14].) Such an environment draws the more energetic entrepreneurial managers from the MNCs. These man-

7. Robert Byrnes came from American Hospital Supply Co. to Genentech and then returned to American Hospital Supply (Jones 1984).

agers are brought in to provide expertise in actually producing and marketing products. Table 8.1 shows the source of key management personnel of the startup companies.

The remuneration of managers of the startups compares to that of their counterparts in larger companies. Startup company executives usually receive a block of stock or options to purchase stock in the company. From the company's viewpoint this is both an inexpensive form of payment and a method of giving the manager a stake in the corporation's success. The potential economic gains for executives in startups are great, but the risks are commensurate. Yet if the company grows and prospers, these managers will have an opportunity to structure an entire section of a corporation, and the value of their equity share will grow. For an ambitious businessman in the chemical or pharmaceutical industry, the opportunities presented by becoming a manager in a biotechnology startup are tremendous.

The recruitment and organization of a competent, motivated support team has as much or more bearing on the success of a company as does good science. The ongoing development of the biotechnology startups will increasingly be influenced by the salesmen who will be marketing their products. The corporate managers (profiled in table 8.1) are the people organizing these companies for the long haul to self-sufficiency and are responsible for developing marketing staffs that must operate in a fashion similar to those of any other pharmaceutical or specialty chemical company.

Table 7.5 shows that the percentage of employees holding Ph.D.'s decreases significantly as the company grows. For example, the percentage of employees holding Ph.D.'s at Genex dropped from over 30 percent in 1980 to approximately 22 percent in 1983 (Genex 1982a:2). At Hybritech the research staff is already a mere 12 percent because of the tremendous growth in production and marketing personnel (Prescott 1983a:160). These changes will gradually transform the internal corporate atmosphere from one that is somewhat collegial to one more formal and production oriented. Such a change may be occurring already at Cetus, where the new president, Robert Fildes, intends to bring in professional managers for research groups. It is reported that some senior scientists are unhappy about being subordinated to nontechnical personnel and are planning to depart (Dwyer 1983a:314). This change in atmosphere and emphasis could disrupt the research process.

Jobs, Labor Shortages, and Unemployment

Commentators who examine biotechnology startups persistently tend to focus entirely on the professors and corporate management. But every company has many technicians as well, usually with bachelor's or master's degrees, who do the innumerable and mundane tasks so necessary to efficient laboratory operations, such as preparing solutions and counting

Table 8.1. Startup Companies' Management Personnel and Their Former Positions in Multinational Corporations

Manager	Current title	Former title	Multinational corporation
Genentech			
James Gower	Vice-president, pharmaceutical marketing	Vice-president marketing and sales, American Cri-Care Division	American Hospital Supply Corp.
Fred Middleton	Vice-president, finance and corporate development, and chief financial officer	Vice-president, planning and corporate development	Chase Manhattan Bank
Integrated Genetics			
Robert Carpenter	President and chief executive officer	President, Fenwal Division	Baxter-Travenol Laboratories
Patrick Connoy	Vice-president, sales and marketing	Vice-president, marketing, nursing products division	American Hospital Supply Corp.
Robert Erickson	Vice-president, technical director	Vice-president, R & D for the biotechnology group	Miles Laboratories, subsidiary of Bayer AG
Evan Lebson	Treasurer	Controller, dialysis services	National Medical Care, Inc.

Thomas Smith	Vice-president, operations	Operations manager, physiological diagnostics	Abbott Laboratories
Amgen			
George Rathman	President, chief executive officer	Division vice-president, R & D	Abbott Laboratories
Gordon Binder	Vice-president and chief financial officer	Vice-president	United Geophysical Corp., a subsidiary of Bendix Corp., a subsidiary of Allied Corp.
Robert Weist	Vice-president, general counsel, and secretary	Senior strategic planner	Abbott Laboratories
Philip Whitcome	Manager of strategic planning	Manager of corporate development, medical products	Bristol-Myers Co.
Genetic Systems			
James Glavin	President and chief executive	Vice-president, sales and marketing	Oximetrix Corp.
Max Lyon	Vice-president	Director of planning for transportation	Weyerhaeuser Co.

Source: Various annual reports

colonies. As we saw in chapter 2, these technicians are now being trained at a number of universities. They will likely remain an unorganized, relatively weak, semiskilled labor force. A recent report (Feldman and O'Malley 1982) indicates the numerical importance of technicians—48 percent of the biotechnology labor force falls into the technician class, and only 12 percent are in "leadership" positions. Additionally, of course, jobs will be available for secretaries, janitors, and security men.

California expects that the biotechnology boom in the 1980s will have yielded nine thousand jobs by 1990 (Pfund 1982:31). Clearly, biotechnology will not provide any great relief from unemployment, despite the promise of articles such as "Wanted: More Genetic Engineers—and Soon" (*Chemical Week* 1981c:29), "Genetic Engineering's Manpower Problem" (N. Howard 1982 in *Dun's Business Month*), and "Endless Possibilities for Ideas—and Jobs" (Cooke 1981 in *Boston Globe*). No doubt the genetic engineering and fermentation production processes will be highly automated.[8] Further, technicians trained in today's techniques will become obsolete rapidly because of the constant changes engendered by the intense activity of the company and university researchers. Biotechnology is unlikely to replace the "sunset" industries.

Nevertheless, some positions have opened, and salaries in 1983 were estimated for three levels of professional scientists. For the first level, a newly graduated Ph.D., the starting salary was from $23,000 to $32,000. The second level, a Ph.D. with three years of postdoctoral experience, received between $28,000 and $40,000 per year. The typical scientist with five years of experience earned between $32,000 and $44,000 per year (Dwyer 1983c:642). An executive recruiter claims "it was a buyer's market for Ph.D. scientists, but now the tables are turned" (Dwyer 1983c:641).[9] Increasingly, companies have reported receiving hundreds of applications for advertised positions (Dwyer 1983c:645). In a hybridoma company salaries of skilled technicians were approximately $18,000 per annum. The unskilled animal handlers and office help received perhaps between $12,000 and $14,000 per annum (Treble 1982). Skilled technicians have had some

8. The implications of the employment and labor processes of biotechnology have been studied little but there is every reason to believe the product manufacturing will be automated (Gaden 1981; Atkinson and Sainter 1982).

9. These salary estimates seem low. A listing of positions from Kalvert Personnel Service (1983:209), a headhunting firm, that was published in *Bio/Technology* showed no salaries under $30,000–36,000 per annum starting. Personnel managers may believe it is in their interest to underestimate salaries and overestimate the number of applicants. Treble (1982:5) estimates the full burden costs for Ph.D.'s necessary to launch a hybridoma company would be between $45,000 and $55,000 per annum. One-third or one-quarter of this salary is presumably indirect costs; therefore, the salaries received by the scientists are $30,000+. But it is plausible that salaries for more ordinary biochemists and molecular biologists have leveled out.

mobility in companies, but in general appear to be a permanent caste of sub-Ph.D. employees.

Ex-professors are not prone to work willingly under a non-Ph.D. scientist or manager. For example, in reorganizing Cetus Robert Fildes is seeking commercially oriented research and development directors for Cetus subsidiaries "which are presently overseen by senior scientist consultants" (Dwyer 1983a:314). However, allowing scientists great influence in corporate decision making is probably not a viable strategy for ensuring the survival of the firm.

The startups have thus far managed to provide an environment conducive to doing applied research without becoming overly bureaucratized and stifling individual creativity. The two structures in startups include management, sales, and production in one pyramid and the various levels of scientists in another pyramid. The scientific hierarchy is arranged very much like that of a university, with senior scientists directing projects— often two or more scientists will collaborate, each bringing a special skill— and one or more research or staff scientists making up the core of the project team. The popular press has portrayed these startups as companies made up of professors and has tended to downplay the commercial side.

Biotechnology corporations have structured their organizations so that information flows freely internally between scientists while external flow is restricted. This information flow can be disrupted by the loss of key personnel. The phenomenon of corporate personnel raids can debilitate a research team and even gut a corporate research program, as occurred at Bio-Rad following Cetus's raid. The interaction of relatively free scientific information flow inside the company and an extremely competitive market for experienced personnel produces unstable corporate personnel complements.

The university-like atmosphere of the startups will probably diminish in the future. As ever-increasing numbers of executives and managers, formerly from large MNCs, are brought in to make the companies profitable, internal social relations will reflect these management directives. Increasingly, scientist-founders are being replaced by professional managers recruited from large companies; for example, in December 1984 Walter Gilbert, formerly a Harvard biology professor, was replaced at Biogen by Mark Skaletsky, a nonscientist. Further, as the novel techniques of genetic engineering become routinized, the startups conceivably may become specialty chemical companies operating in similar fashion to other chemical and pharmaceutical companies, and their environments will reflect this shift.

9. The Multinational

Corporations and

Biotechnology

The real innovation comes out of the hothouse atmosphere at universities and small companies, but is somehow stifled at large companies *(Leslie Misrock, lawyer for the biotechnology industry, J. Fox 1982a:14).*

Recombinant DNA is just a way to synthesize things. . . . As soon as you've inserted the gene, it's identical to what you would do in the chemical industry anyway. [The small firms will] play an important role in the early years, but less so down the line. They have no expertise in the development of materials once they've got them. Development costs 20 times as much as research. In the early years, people will buy discoveries, but why buy from somebody and share the profits when you can do it all yourself *(Dr. Howard Simmons, Du Pont director of central research, quoted by A. Brown 1982:9).*

The response of MNCs to biotechnology has ranged from neglect to multimillion-dollar investments. Nearly every chemical and pharmaceutical manufacturer is investigating what biotechnology means for its particular market situation and its corporate strategy for the 1980s and beyond. In the current chaos of possibilities, hype, and promises, the large, relatively ponderous corporate bureaucracies (with a few exceptions) have had difficulty responding quickly to biotechnology's potential. Yet the rapid maturing of biotechnology as a profitable manufacturing technique has brought an increasing number of MNCs into the industry.

As alluded to earlier, biotechnology is providing the technical tools to erode the barriers between a number of industries. This was not immediately recognized but now has become accepted wisdom. Very important in galvanizing the rush into biotechnology was the *Diamond vs. Chakrabarty* Supreme Court patent decision, which allowed the patenting of novel living organisms and genetic sequences spliced into new organisms. Now living organisms and their DNA could be privately owned—allowing the extraction of monopoly rents. Finally, the immense possibilities of biotechnology provide opportunities for many new products in the food, chemical, pharmaceutical, and energy fields.

What strategies are the MNCs using to further their corporate goals of ensuring that they do not miss out on the opportunities presented by biotechnology? Every MNC must develop a strategy that at a minimum ensures that currently profitable business lines are not undermined by competitors using biotechniques. In essence, a company must decide what strategies will be most effective in ensuring its survival if the new biorevolution is as significant as reports indicate it might be. To understand the motivation for MNC investment, it is necessary to briefly outline the economic context in which biotechnology is being promoted and evaluated.

The Context

Until recently, two largely separate industries comprised the bulk of the MNC competitors in biotechnology—the chemical and the pharmaceutical industries. Both can be conceived of as producers and marketers of molecules—in one case in massive quantities with "industrial" purity, in the other in smaller quantities with "pharmaceutical" purity. Until recently these industries were highly distinguishable in the United States. The first group is made up of companies such as Allied, American Cyanamid, Celanese, Dow, Du Pont, Monsanto, and Stauffer—to name some of the major U.S. players. The other includes Abbott, Baxter-Travenol, Johnson and Johnson, Eli Lilly, Merck, SmithKline, Beckman, and Warner-Lambert.[1] But the 1970s transformed the entire worldview of the chemical industry, for the chemical industry stagnated while the pharmaceutical industry seemed impervious to serious problems.

In the 1950s and early 1960s chemical sales had boomed as the growing economy fueled demand for plastics, fertilizers, and herbicides, and industry continued to bring ever larger and more efficient production units on stream. More recently, however, although the chemical industry has continued to develop new products, the research has tended to develop look-alike products, and innovation has slowed. The industry has increas-

---

1. The names of foreign firms have been omitted only for reasons of length. Chemical companies such as Asahi Chemical, BASF, Ciba-Geigy, Hoechst, ICI, Mitsubishi Chemicals, and Mitsui Petrochemicals and pharmaceutical companies such as Akzo, Glaxo, Hoffmann-La Roche, Kabi, Novo, Sandoz, and Takeda indisputably will be important global competitors. Nonchemical and nonpharmaceutical companies such as Ajinomoto, Gist-Brocades, Shell, Snow Brands Milk, Suntory, and perhaps Unilever and Tate and Lyle could also play a significant role. Obviously, any company that manufactures products based on carbon (organic chemistry) has the potential to become a significant factor in biotechnology.

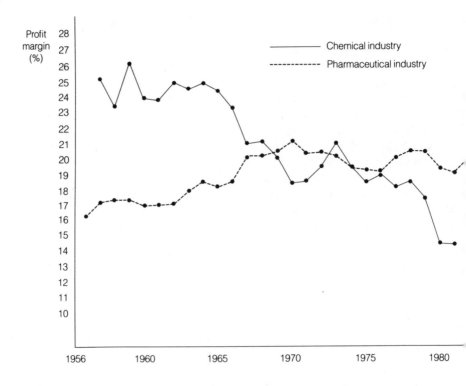

Source: Standard and Poors Company, *Industry Surveys*, various years

Figure 9.1. Pharmaceutical and Chemical Industries' Profit Margins, 1956–1982

ingly become a low profit commodity producer. Furthermore the chemical companies, already plagued by overproduction, were devastated by the 1974 and 1978 oil crises, which drove their major variable cost, energy, up sharply. Keegan (1979:30) summed up the effects of energy price rises on industry: "The chemical industry is the largest industrial consumer of energy and has the highest level of cost dependency [of any industry] on energy for its products." Figure 9.1 indicates the drop in the profit margins of chemical corporations in the 1970s, after being for many years higher than those of the drug industry. Both drugs and chemicals have had higher-than-average profit margins for nonfinancial corporations, although 1980 to 1982 saw the chemical industry's margins drop to the average for all industries. This drop will become even more pronounced as new Third

World petroleum producers begin to enter the world market in the late 1980s with bulk commodity chemicals.

The oil crises have forced the petroleum industry to examine its future role. The current strategy of the oil MNCs is to penetrate the basic chemical industry as OPEC countries build integrated refineries and basic chemical production facilities. *Forbes* (Gibson 1978:38) describes the situation thus:

> As they [chemical companies] scramble to develop new strategies in a business that is growing more slowly than in the Fifties and Sixties, the chemical firms basically have two choices: They can integrate backward and secure their own energy and feedstock materials to enter into a slugging match with the oil giants. Or they can quit the bulk commodities end of petrochemicals and move downstream.

In the long run, downstream movement is the only viable alternative, and it will be accelerated as natural gas, the primary feedstock, is deregulated in 1985 and the chemical industry loses its last major subsidy.

Increased competition and overcapacity are not the only problems weakening the chemical industry. Increased public concern and political action regarding environmental issues have also had an impact upon profitability. The operating cost alone of chemical waste management has increased from $643.3 million in 1974 to $1,864.8 million in 1980 (nominal dollars) (Chemical Manufacturers' Association n.d.:11). The seemingly infinite amount of pollutants and their dispersion at countless sites are also discouraging for the industry.[2]

The environmental and workers' safety movements have put intense pressure on companies in a number of ways. The image of the chemical industry is very negative—as is that of most MNCs.[3] But most important, the lawsuits springing from this pollution and the increasing costs of cleanup are calling into question profits that these companies had already banked. That is, the corporation ended its production cycle and sold the product— supposedly the transaction was complete. But now five, ten, and fifteen years later those profits are being called into question and sometimes lost completely due to cleanup costs and damage settlements. From a stockholder's viewpoint, the most fearful occurrence is an unforeseen liability

2. The disclosures of serious pollution problems at Love Canal in Buffalo, New York, Times Beach in Missouri, and the Stringfellow Acid Pits in southern California are threatening companies with massive cleanup costs. The reason that companies are acquiescing to pollution controls is not a new environmental consciousness among managers but rather the vigorous public protest that has been transformed into a potent political force. Rarely has the knowledge of the harmfulness of a product deterred a corporation from continuing profitable manufacturing and marketing activities.

3. The best evidence of this is the increasingly large damage settlements being awarded by juries to plaintiffs in lawsuits alleging corporate misconduct. Recent awards to asbestos workers, to contraceptive users, and to servicemen exposed to dioxin are evidence of this.

because he has not anticipated this cost. When these liabilities become generalized, the outcome of investments becomes increasingly unpredictable. For these reasons product and production process safety have become a major concern in all industry, but perhaps most acutely in the chemical industry.[4]

In recognition of the seriousness of these challenges, chemical companies have developed strategies to circumvent the problems. Du Pont bought Conoco, integrating into coal and oil; Dow has bought oil and gas properties and has launched a massive energy efficiency effort; and Monsanto has divested a large proportion of its commodity chemical operations. Each company is using a mix of the various strategies in a multifaceted effort to cope with the profitability crisis. Yet capital growth does not stem from defensive moves.

To overcome stagnation, chemical executives saw the importance of owning proprietary rights to molecules. The patenting of a chemical gives the company a seventeen-year monopoly on that particular molecule, which allows the company to ensure lucrative returns on it. The agricultural chemical divisions are a prime example of commercial success on the basis of patented compounds. For example, Monsanto's patented herbicide Roundup earned nearly $500 million in 1982, a year of severe recession (*Chemical Week* 1983a:47). As we shall see, patentable agricultural pesticides and herbicides are drawing ever greater investment by chemical companies.

The chemical industry also sees the pharmaceuticals as an ideal area to expand into. The smaller volume of products handled translates into smaller, more manageable pollution problems.[5] Likewise, the majority of the pollutants are not as toxic or persistent because the products must be safe for humans. Finally, the pharmaceutical industry, because of its technical similarities to the chemical industry, does not offer insurmountable barriers to entry.[6]

The projected growth of the pharmaceuticals market is a further investment incentive to the chemical MNCs. Reasons for this growth include the aging of the population and an increasing emphasis upon health. Fur-

4. The organic chemical production process is based on high temperature, high-pressure reactions that have numerous toxic and noxious by-products. It is these and the products themselves that are new and sometimes very persistent in the biosphere.

5. An example of this "less is better" philosophy is a new group of agricultural chemicals offered by Du Pont under the trade names Glean and Oust (Garrison 1982). These require smaller application quantities, which is supposed to be better for the environment. However, it could be that these chemicals are simply more toxic. Quantity applied has no immediate correlation to safeguarding the public.

6. The distinction between pharmaceuticals and chemicals is more blurred in Europe, where companies such as Hoffmann-La Roche, Sandoz, Ciba-Geigy, Hoechst, and Novo have already integrated the two branches. Similarly, an integration process has been under way in Japan, with companies such as Asahi Chemical making a major effort in pharmaceuticals.

ther, government spending on health does not appear to be easily controlled or cut, which also bodes well for market growth. And, finally, little opportunity exists for producers in developing countries to penetrate the U.S. market.

The pharmaceutical industry is composed of both MNCs and smaller specialty companies that produce only a few patented products. The barriers to entry in pharmaceuticals are not very high because of the possibility of patenting new drugs. It is relatively easy to develop a product that will allow a company to create a niche. The large number of pharmaceutical companies also provides the cash-laden chemical companies with many takeover targets. The importance attached to acquiring a pharmaceutical company was evidenced by the recent bidding for Richardson-Merrill's ethical drug business which was eventually purchased by Dow Chemical (*Chemical Week* 1983a:46). Another example was the purchase by Monsanto of G. D. Searle Company, a major pharmaceutical concern, for $2.7 billion. Prices for drug companies are naturally high, given the number of chemical companies that are interested in purchasing a pharmaceutical company (Alsop 1983:33).

Why Biotechnology?

Biotechnology, as we have seen, holds the promise of an enormous number of new products and of breaking down the technical barriers between the pharmaceutical and chemical industries. However, Nelson Schneider of E. F. Hutton had things backward when he was paraphrased as saying that "chemical firms face the prospect of a well-financed, highly capitalized [pharmaceutical] industry coming in and possibly taking away some of the traditional chemical markets" (*Chemical Week* 1981a:37). As we shall see in this section, the actual process is quite the reverse, as the well-financed chemical industry will use biotechnology as a wedge to open pharmaceuticals.

The relevant industrial branch by the year 2000 may be not chemical or pharmaceutical but chemical–pharmaceutical (Schneider 1981:4). Biotechnology's impact will not be in bulk commodity chemicals, according to Robert Thomas (quoted in Pfund 1983:7), the president of Chevron Research Company: "Today we are much less optimistic in this area [bulk chemicals] because biotechnology does not create anything *unique* in these markets, nothing that petroleum-based sources can't satisfy. Where we see biotechnology having the major impact is in the healthcare/pharmaceutical and agricultural markets, because, there, biotechnology enables you to do things you can't do any other way." The point that Thomas is making is that these are the new products that can be patented, that is, for which exclusive property rights are available. In the 1950s the invention of synthetic textiles such as nylon, orlon, and rayon offered similar profitability and in so doing propelled the petrochemical revolution. In 1980 it is recognized that similar opportunities are available in the areas of health care and agriculture.

The first assumption that a naive observer might make is that the traditional pharmaceutical companies would have an overwhelming advantage in pharmaceuticals. Given the diminishing returns of research that uses traditional techniques, one would certainly expect the pharmaceutical industry to have moved very fast in biotechnology (Steward and Wibberley 1980:118; Brunings 1979). But biotechnology, and especially rDNA, which could reverse this stagnation, are new technologies, so pharmaceutical companies based on traditional technology have no inherent advantages.

The chemical companies will have some important advantages in their struggle to survive in the pharmaceutical–chemical industry. The first is that they have strong screening programs for chemical activity, and the results of these programs are in easily accessible form, having been stored on computer tapes. The second is that there will be synergies between the skills developed in applications of biotechnology to agriculture and medicine. Third, the chemical companies, as larger financial entities, have more money to devote to research than do the pharmaceutical companies. The entry of the chemical industry should not be viewed apocalyptically, but it does mean that a new group of financially strong and increasingly research-oriented competitors are emerging in the pharmaceutical industry.

A final desirable characteristic of biotechnology is its low entry costs. For example, the cost of access to an individual researcher can be in the $10,000 to $100,000 region. To purchase significant research from a startup costs $2 to $5 million over two to five years plus royalties on any products derived. Finally, a small in-house operation can be started for $2 million per year. Obviously these investments might not be large enough to support a commercially viable operation, but for an investment of a few million dollars an MNC's management can make a more informed decision regarding the desirability of a more significant commitment in biotechnology.

Multinational Corporations and Biotechnology—History and Strategy

The pharmaceutical and chemical companies—though slow to enter the biotechnology industry—were not unaware of the emergence of molecular biology, rDNA, and biotechnology. In fact, James Watson had received a Merck fellowship from the National Research Council (NRC) for his study at Cambridge, where he and Francis Crick theorized DNA's structure (Judson 1979:68). From the beginning corporate scientists were aware of the developments in molecular biology, but there was little commercial interest until the mid 1970s. For example, industry received with interest but no serious objections the promulgation of the initial NIH guidelines in 1976.

A survey by the Pharmaceutical Manufacturers Association[7] said in 1977 that "all the major companies were interested in [rDNA] but only six were actively engaged—Hoffmann-La Roche, Upjohn, Eli Lilly, SmithKline and French, Merck, and Miles Laboratories" (Wade 1977:559a). Schering-Plough also was aware of genetic engineering's possibilities and may have been using the technique (surmise based on the fact that they were heavily involved with Cetus). Significantly, at this early stage the chemical industry was much less aware of biotechnology's implications. Ralph Hardy, Du Pont's director of life sciences, was quoted in 1977 as saying, "I'd be surprised if any of this [prospects of rDNA] came about before the Twenty-First Century" (Bronson 1977:16). Monsanto, Allied Chemical, and the other chemical companies were similarly skeptical and remained passive observers.

The first clear public statement of interest in rDNA by a pharmaceutical company occurred in 1977. Commenting on revisions of the rDNA guidelines, Lilly requested that if the guidelines were extended to private companies, proprietary information should be held in confidence and that certain organisms be exempted (Eli Lilly 1977:A37). In the hearings regarding guideline revisions in 1978, Upjohn joined Lilly in asking for the protection of proprietary information (Upjohn 1978:A258). Lilly also objected to requirements that "outside" members be appointed to institutional biosafety committees. Further, Lilly asked for exemption from the rule forbidding experiments of more than ten liters (Eli Lilly 1978:A272).

The production of somatostatin (Itakura et al. 1977) and rat insulin (Ullrich et al. 1977), both in 1977, spurred Eli Lilly to push very aggressively in 1978 and 1979 for relaxation of the ten-liter guideline (NIH 1979:34). Lilly, the supplier of 80 percent of the insulin consumed in the United States, was actively seeking to secure its predominant position in insulin manufacturing and marketing. In 1978 it signed a contract with Genentech for rights to its insulin-producing bacteria, and to further protect itself signed contracts with a UCSF team consisting of William Rutter and Howard Goodman to engineer an insulin-producing bacteria (Douglas 1978:170; Dickson 1979:495). David Dickson (1979:495) noted that Eli Lilly gave $250,000 in research funding to the Rutter-Goodman team. This grant allowed Rutter to conduct experiments in France which at the time were forbidden in the United States (Douglas 1978:170). Eli Lilly's quick response allowed it to commence marketing bacterially produced "human" insulin in 1983, beating its competitor, Novo Industries, by six months.

The pharmaceutical companies were the first industrial group (except for Inco) to recognize the significance of molecular biology and biotech-

---

7. The Pharmaceutical Manufacturers Association not only had been involved in the initial congressional hearings in 1976, but continued to follow and occasionally participate in RAC meetings, representing the pharmaceutical manufacturers as an interest group.

nology.[8] In large part this early recognition was due to the fact that molecular biological research was funded by NIH and was concentrated in the medical schools and biology departments of U.S. universities, where pharmaceutical companies fund much research. However, it was not long before the chemical industry became aware of biotechnology's potential. The attraction for the chemical industry centered on the possibility of using the products of biotechnology to find new human health care drugs and as a tool to create new products for agriculture (Kenney et al. 1982; Kloppenburg and Kenney 1984).

The Multinational Corporations React

The bus [biotechnology] is moving . . . and if you want a ticket you'd better get with it now   *(Edward Johnson, chief executive officer of Du Pont, quoted in* Business Week *1980b:89).*

[Every company in the health care business] is going to have to have bio-technology capabilities just to maintain its position in existing markets   *(Parker G. Montgomery, chairman and chief executive officer of Cooper Laboratories, quoted in the* Wall Street Journal *1980b:16).*[9]

Biotechnology fever gripped not only Wall Street and MNCs in the United States but also MNCs around the world. New drugs such as interferon were portrayed as veritable panaceas for everything from the common cold to cancer, and companies invested. In a 1982 survey six MNCs in the United States (in addition to a multitude of small companies) were reported to be involved in interferon research and development: G. D. Searle, Bristol-Myers, Burroughs-Wellcome, Du Pont, Hoffmann-La Roche, and Schering-Plough (Kramer 1982:17–19). The most bitter competition in interferon is between Schering-Plough and Hoffmann-La Roche. Each company is spending approximately $40 million, that is, 15 percent of its research budget, to begin production of a drug which, as of December 1984, had not been proven to have important therapeutic benefits (Wald-

8. Inco's role is unique because its interests in biotechnology were not technical but rather entrepreneurial. In the early 1970s Inco established a free-standing venture capital unit that has invested in Cetus, Genentech, and Biogen—to name the best known. Inco's effort was more in the nature of a financial investment and was not motivated by a desire to use biological techniques in its own production processes, so Inco is little different from a venture capital fund. In the five years 1976–81, when Daniel Adams, now president of AGS, was head of Inco's venture capital fund, its value increased from $8 million to $140 million—a respectable capital appreciation (Kania 1982:10).

9. Cooper Laboratories has begun funding contract research at Zymos Corporation to develop a protein to counter a respiratory disease (*Drug and Cosmetic Industry* 1982).

holz 1983:1). Schering-Plough is already constructing a $106 million fermentation plant in England so as to be prepared to commence manufacturing as soon as health clearances are received (*Journal of Commerce* 1983a:22B). Biotechnology research is proceeding at a frenetic pace. Irving Johnson, vice-president at Eli Lilly, described the corporate view of biotechnology's potential as follows: "Potential applications of recombinant DNA techniques are limited only by the imagination of people using them" (Wade 1979:663).

In 1977 very few pharmaceutical companies, much less chemical companies, had made any important investments in biotechnology. By 1980 many MNCs had made initial commitments, and more were contemplating making a move. However, an example of the small scale of these investments is the fact that in 1980 Du Pont's genetic engineering investment was only $2 million. By 1983 every large chemical and pharmaceutical company had made a multimillion-dollar investment in biotechnology. These investments can be grouped into four quite distinct investment patterns:

1. The company can develop an in-house research capacity. This can be autarchic or it can be formally linked with an outside institution which may do research and development while the in-house group does industrial scale-up tasks. It can also buy a biotechnology startup, thereby securing an in-house research team.

2. The MNC can contract with universities to do directed or undirected research and merely secure a license to commercialize any discoveries.

3. Research and development contracts can be let to biotechnology startups or the MNC can secure exclusive marketing rights to a startup's product.

4. The MNC can purchase equity in biotechnology startups.

Each company uses a combination of strategies, and some such as Monsanto and Allied are using all four.[10]

Before I discuss these strategies it is useful to briefly examine the individuals who have been brought onto management teams to oversee the corporate biotechnology effort. These scientist–managers are critical to corporate planning of diversification into this new industrial field. For example, in 1983 Du Pont appointed Mark Pearson as associate director of life sciences for molecular biology. His previous experience was as director of the Laboratory for Molecular Biology and head of the Developmental Genetics Section at the National Cancer Institute (*Journal of Commerce* 1983e:22B). In 1979 Monsanto recruited Howard Schneider-

10. Allied has recently pulled out of nearly all of its biotechnology investments.

man, the dean of the School of Biological Science at the University of California, Irvine, to serve as senior vice-president for research. With the tremendous investment these companies are planning in the life sciences, it is imperative for them to secure highly skilled research managers.

Building an In-House Research Staff

Any MNC intent upon entering the biotechnology industry must build an in-house research capability and ultimately produce and manufacture products. To do this efficiently and effectively the MNC must understand and control all the parameters of its production process. In-house research allows the company to control the scientists developing the manufacturing process. Further, all information regarding costs of production can be kept as trade secrets. If external contracts are let, the company has the staff to evaluate and supervise the contract's progress; in-house capability allows the MNC to take full advantage of contracted research. No company could seriously contemplate launching a major biotechnology effort without building its own research apparatus.

The importance attached to the new possibilities and markets offered by biotechnology has caused chemical companies to restructure radically.[11] Monsanto, for example, restructured itself into five divisions, with biotechnology becoming a part of the agricultural products division (*Chemical Week* 1983a). Du Pont's restructuring created two new departments, agricultural chemicals and biomedical products, to carry forward the company's introduction of biotechnology products (*Journal of Commerce* 1983c:22B). The rise of biology as a productive force has in both Du Pont and Monsanto strengthened agricultural products. Further, both companies are also building their in-house pharmaceutical operations.

Many MNCs are rushing to complete life science research facilities to increase their competitiveness in the race to commercialize biotechnology. Table 9.1 contains a partial listing of major corporate investments in biotechnology facilities. In-house research is usually (but not always) not expected to be at the frontiers of knowledge, but rather to transform state-of-the-art science into state-of-the-art technology. John Hanley, chairman and CEO of Monsanto, describes the status of Monsanto's genetically engineered bovine growth hormone–producing bacteria in these terms: "We have our first product possibility—the [bovine] growth hormone—on a critical path. It looks for all the world like a development project, and

---

11. Whether these restructurings are of the magnitude, scale, and importance of those discussed by Chandler (1962) that resulted in the divisional structure is difficult to estimate. But in the current internal restructurings entire layers of middle management have been eliminated. Through the use of automation and computerization command and control functions are increasingly being centralized. The numerous divisions that previously characterized chemical companies are being merged into a few megadivisions.

Table 9.1. In-House Corporate Life Science Research: Description and Location*

Company	Area of research	Location	Description
Monsanto	Biological sciences	Missouri	$185 million
Du Pont	Life sciences	Delaware	$85 million
Chevron	Agriculture	California	$38 million
Lilly	Biomedical	Indiana	$60 million
Ciba-Geigy	Agriculture	North Carolina	$7 million
Pfizer	Agriculture	Missouri	20 researchers
ARCO	Agriculture	California	15 scientists, 57 employees
Allied Corp.	Agriculture	New York	50 employees

Source: Adapted from Buttel et al. 1985
* These data are accurate according to the best of currently available information.

not basic research" (Storck 1983:13). The bovine growth hormone–producing bacteria were purchased from Genentech, but Monsanto designed a fermentation system compatible to the bacteria.[12] Design and scale-up is the kind of activity in which the MNCs have a comparative advantage in that they can invest large sums of capital and labor.

The caliber of research personnel the MNCs are able to hire has been questioned by certain observers (Harsanyi 1981; Eggers 1981), especially in the area of molecular biology, where the excitement of the startup combined with equity interest attracts many scientists. But Robert Kunze, the senior vice-president for technology at W. R. Grace, said, "We've been showing up on campuses and we've been hiring what we believe are the best people from the best schools—with very little competition" (*Biol Technology* 1983:30). Kunze's statement must be taken circumspectly because, as explained earlier, the best students are placed—they are not hired by companies "showing up" on campuses. Yet MNCs have had some success in recruiting active researchers. For example, Mary Dell Chilton, a well-known professor of plant biology at Washington University, resigned to become the head of Ciba-Geigy's agricultural research station in North Carolina (*Journal of Commerce* 1983d:22B). Her move was a blow to

12. In this early stage of genetic engineering, fermentation processes are being designed to handle the newly engineered bacteria. *E. coli* is a bacteria relatively unsuited to large-scale fermentation. The reason for *E. coli*'s pervasive use is that it was the bacterium that had been used in research work. The advantages of *B. subtilis* and other microorganisms are now becoming increasingly apparent, and success in inserting foreign genes into *B. subtilis* is starting to be achieved (Franklin 1983). The increasing ability to use microorganisms that have better fermentation properties than *E. coli* could allow the designing of bacteria for the fermentor rather than the current process of designing fermentors for bacteria.

Monsanto's agricultural operations because Monsanto provided major funding for her work at Washington University and had drawn significant benefits therefrom. Still, the labor power hired by the MNCs to date does not appear to be of the same caliber of talent found in the biotechnology startups.

Perhaps what is missing in these large research facilities is the "hot-house" atmosphere that comes from intimate linkage between the startups and the university. This could be due to geographical location. Most corporate facilities are not situated in close proximity to centers of startup activity nor are the neighboring universities the peaks of research activity. For whatever reasons, the MNCs have been unable to stay at the forefront of research. For example, Howard Schneiderman, a Monsanto senior vice-president, said in February 1983, "I don't see that we will have to invest in biotechnology outside the company except perhaps with one company, Genentech of San Francisco" (Sanford 1983:C1). But by October 1983 Monsanto had contracted Biotechnica International to develop genetically engineered *B. subtilis* strains to produce proteins. The key to this reversal is Biotechnica's scientists—Drs. Richard Losick and Janice Pero, both of Harvard University (*Journal of Commerce* 1983f:22B). Obviously, Monsanto still does not feel that its technical independence or competence is complete.

One other important way for an MNC to increase its in-house competence is to purchase the company with the desired technical competence outright. A classic example of this strategy was Du Pont's purchase of New England Nuclear (NEN) for $430 million in 1981.[13] NEN produces diagnostic tests using radioisotopes and has been doing research on monoclonal antibodies (Du Pont 1983). With the acquisition of NEN, Du Pont's expertise in diagnostics took a quantum leap, and the company had an important base for expansion into MAB diagnostics. And, in fact, research done at NEN allowed Du Pont to bring out its first MAB-based clinical diagnostic (*Financial Times* 1983:6).

In another buy-out, Schering-Plough purchased the privately held company DNAX for $19 million and 340,000 Schering-Plough common stock shares (*GEN* 1982e:3). Finally, Lubrizol purchased Agrigenetics, a seed company that has invested heavily in biotechnology, for $110 million. This purchase will be added to Lubrizol's ownership of Sigco Research, Inc., a hybrid sunflower seed company; Lynnville Seed Co., a soybean seed company; investments in Sungene Technologies, Inc., a plant genetic engineering company; and a major investment in Genentech (*WSJ* 1984b:8). These and the previously mentioned Hybritech and Genetic Systems buy-

13. NEN was not a startup but rather a thriving business with 1,700 employees worldwide (Du Pont 1983).

outs are the only important takeovers to date, but more will occur in the future as some companies fall behind in the commercialization race. Biotechnology companies are not inexpensive; venture capitalists and the founders will sell only if the buy-out guarantees significant capital gains or if the company is weak. The purchaser is thus in the position of having to pay a significant premium for a startup's hopes (see the earlier discussion of dilution). Allied Corporation's senior vice-president for technology, L. J. Colby, Jr., describes his company's desire not merely to buy equity but rather to acquire "the whole enterprise. 'We're trying to build our scientific healthcare area, where we don't have a good research base' " (Lancaster 1982:26). In 1983 Allied invested in Genetics Institute. In most cases the biotechnology startups are too expensive to justify an outright takeover.

The building of an in-house research staff is obligatory for any MNC that expects to play an important role in the biotechnology industry. But these in-house staffs usually have neither the mandate nor the connections to remain, like the universities and the startups, on the cutting edge of biotechnology. Most companies feel they must build in-house research capabilities even while going outside to secure specialized expertise. In-house laboratories form the base upon which every MNC builds its overall research effort.

Long-Term Affiliations with Universities

The importance of long-term contracts between universities and industry was discussed in chapter 3. Here I will touch upon the subject again from the viewpoint of corporate planners. Why has corporate management been willing to commit such large amounts of money to university research (see table 3.1)? The answer lies in a unique confluence of circumstances.

The company usually is buying access to an entire operating research laboratory—the startup, organizational, and capital costs are already sunk costs, a tremendous savings that should not be underestimated. Further, these expenditures for research can be immediately expensed from corporate income tax with the current research 25 percent tax credit.[14] Yet the corporate decision to fund university research is not a simple economic decision based on cost.

As important as cost is the fact that top university researchers are usually not willing to join MNC research staffs. As described earlier, there is a widespread belief that good basic research is stifled in corporate labs. Therefore, researchers wish to remain in universities to continue their

14. The expensing of corporate-funded research at universities is not unique, and internal corporate research expenditures can also be expensed.

interaction with other faculty members and students. MNCs sign long-term contracts with the university to secure formalized rights to any commercially useful discoveries.

These long-term arrangements provide an MNC with privileged access to a certain line of investigation. Research success gives the MNC favored access to the discovery and even the potential of royalties if the discovery has commercial potential. For example, if the seminal Cohen–Boyer patent had been discovered by research sponsored by Hoechst at MGH, then Hoechst would have held the rights to the most basic process of genetic engineering. The entire genetic engineering field would have been paralyzed, as Hoechst would have controlled the price of entry into the biotechnology industry. The economic implications cannot be underestimated. The possibility of great or even moderate success justifies MNCs' making selected investments in university researchers.

Even if no product is generated, university–industry agreements carry a number of intangible benefits, such as access to graduate and postdoctoral students, a location from which to tap into scientific networks, opportunities to discuss scientific problems encountered by company scientists, and sometimes the chance to read manuscripts before they are published. In this early stage of the industry's growth companies stand to gain numerous advantages by investing in university research.

As table 3.1 indicates, a number of companies—especially chemical companies, which are keen to build their biological expertise—have made at least one such investment. Other companies, however, such as Dow Chemical, for example, have seen no need to make any significant investment in university research. Stauffer Chemical, intent on pushing into plant molecular biology, has also opted not to invest in long-term, large-scale arrangements.[15] In fact, Ralph Hardy, formerly Du Pont's director of life sciences, has said (1982) that industry will not get its money's worth from its funding of university research, and Du Pont has signed only the one contract with HMS. In all probability Hardy's sentiment is predominant— the gold rush for academia is over.[16]

Monsanto, on the other hand, seems resolved to continue its funding of what it deems worthy projects, though perhaps on a smaller scale. As recently as December 15, 1983, Monsanto signed a research contract with Oxford University for $1.5 million over five years. Any patents deriving from the research into oligosaccharides would be held by Oxford, with Monsanto receiving an exclusive, worldwide license (*Journal of Commerce* 1983h:22B). Monsanto has not deviated from its course of funding poten-

15. All companies have funded the research of specific professors, but many have chosen not to make the bigger, long-term commitments.

16. In 1984 Ralph Hardy left Du Pont and became president of Biotechnica International; he also affiliated with the Cornell University Biotechnology Institute.

tially valuable university research and, in fact, seems ready to cast its net further and further afield. Overall, however, the race to fund universities has slowed down, in large part because most research with potential applications has already been purchased. But any commercially valuable research will undoubtedly quickly secure funds from industry.

Contract Research with Biotechnology Startups

Ten years from now, there will only be two or three "biotechnology" firms left. There's a certain naivete out there now and many of these firms lack a clear track of exactly what they are in business to do. If they want to sell their technology, that's fine, but that means they have to stay on the forefront. If they want to sell *products*, they need a lot of resources over a long period of time, which they currently don't have, including lots of money. That's why acquisitions and mergers will become more attractive   *(Al Weitz, vice-president of Schering-Plough and president of DNAX, quoted by Pfund 1983:27).*

The small companies of every new industry start out running circles around the old companies, but they still need size to do certain things. Don't think [rDNA] will revolutionize the way business is done. The technology is revolutionary, but it will get sorted out in the end *(John Donalds, Dow Chemical's director of biotechnology, quoted by A. Brown 1982).*[17]

MNCs have taken two paths in their approach to biotechnology startups: they have signed research contracts with them or bought equity in them; and in many cases they have done both. What strategies and motives will the MNCs employ in letting contracts to the small startups? In some cases an MNC desires simply a tailor-made process or bacteria and is not interested in making a significant commitment to the startup.

The managers of the MNCs believe that they will ultimately dominate biotechnology and that the small startups will fail. The MNCs' advantages are located not in research but in production scale-up, clinical testing, and marketing. For example, Lilly has built two synthetic insulin plants, one in the United States and the other in England, at a cost of $60 million each. That amount would represent an enormous outlay for a small startup (A. Brown 1982:11). Further, MNCs already have the in-place marketing networks or, as in the case of Du Pont, are in the process of building one (Harvey 1982). As indicated in the section on RDLPs, health and safety

17. John Donalds is now president and chief executive officer of Collaborative Research, Inc. (Collaborative Research, Inc. 1984:3).

testing is neither inexpensive nor brief. A company that needs revenues badly may become insolvent while waiting for tests to be concluded. For companies such as Du Pont, building a marketing network or taking over a company that has a network provides no financial obstacle. These realities provide some justification for the MNCs' beliefs that the small startups will never prove to be truly competitive.

As MNC biotechnology laboratories become increasingly involved in competitive races to develop biotechnological products, it will be necessary to bring in outside expertise. The reasons for contracting startups could be several. In many cases these startups have access to the world's top experts (usually university scientists) on specific topics.[18] So John Donalds (quoted in A. Brown 1982:14), then Dow Chemical's director of biotechnology, states his company's approach thus: "Our approach . . . leans towards outside research contracts while doing development work in-house. . . . If [the small firms] have the researchers, I'm not against giving them money to do the work." Significant savings of time and money can be made through the judicious use of outside contractors.

Another advantage for the MNC is that contracts with startups can, if the company is privately held, be kept confidential. And even contracts with public firms can be kept relatively secret. For example, Genex's 10-K filing with the Securities and Exchange Commission (1982b) describes projects with headings such as "a plasma protein (Schering AG)," "a therapeutic protein (AB Fortia)," or "a fibrinolytic agent (Yamanouchi Company, Ltd.)." These short descriptions in prospecti and 10-K filings provide only the outlines of a company's projects.[19] Information regarding specific research topics is very valuable and is guarded. A university contract based on publication and relatively open access cannot provide this secrecy.

A research contract with or without an equity component can be used by an MNC to secure "a window on the technology" at relatively low cost. However, contract research can be a low-risk, low-benefit strategy when compared to establishing an in-house research operation or purchasing equity in a startup. In many research contracts the MNC is investing money merely to discover the potentials of biotechnology. Therefore, the contract results are not critical. For corporate management this probationary in-

---

18. For example, Chiron and Collaborative Research are especially skilled in the use of yeast, whereas Biotechnica International is skilled with *B. subtilis*.

19. Businessmen and scientists conversant with the particular industry or company would likely be able to identify the exact product being investigated. But outsiders have no such privileged information, and there is a concerted effort made to keep these research goals secret. On the other hand, the flow of personnel from one company to another provides a ready vehicle for information transfer. Even companies as security conscious as IBM have plan and data leaks. This is even more true in a venture capital–financed industry with its higher-than-average rates of employee turnover.

vestment will lead to a corporate decision to either seek greater involvement or to abandon any further efforts to enter the field.

As table 9.2 and chapter 7 indicate, startups require these research contracts in order to survive. But even if the MNCs want to strangle the startups financially, the intense competition with other MNCs forces them to extend contracts to startups for highly skilled tasks. Contract research is a relationship fraught with tension. The MNC doesn't want to fund its competitor, and the startup does not want to sell its technological superiority—the major advantage the startup has over the MNCs.

Equity Participation in Biotechnology Startups

The startups are very short of capital and are actively searching for investors; an obvious source of capital is the MNC. For the MNC's management, simply paying contract fees to the startup provides little insight into the production process and no control and no possibility of equity appreciation. In many cases MNCs have purchased enough equity to be awarded a seat on the startup's board of directors—an ideal position from which to ensure that the MNC's interests are not harmed by the startup's activities and to establish a base for a possible takeover in the future.

The MNC's willingness to commit significant sums of money to the startup enables it to secure large blocks of stock at relatively low prices. Therefore, many of these investments have experienced significant appreciations when the stocks went public (table 9.3). For companies such as Inco capital appreciation is the raison d'etre of their investments in biotechnology, and successful investments have become important sources of income.

Other MNCs had less immediately commercial objectives; they needed and desired an internal perspective on the evolving biotechnology. As a condition for making a major equity investment many MNCs demand a seat on the startup's board of directors. This allows the MNC not only to insure its investment but also to discover what opportunities the company feels are worth pursuing. The knowledge gleaned may be important for MNC in-house research, especially during the stage in which the MNC is still groping for commercial targets. Even after the MNC has its in-house research facility operating, the informational nexus of the biotechnology startup, with its scientific advisors—full-time university faculty members— and research scientists, offers ready access to information about the latest research breakthroughs.

Perhaps the most prescient investment in a biotechnology startup was made by Lubrizol, an oil additive company that in 1979 bought 24 percent (1,555,200 shares) of Genentech for $10 million (Gartner 1980:20). This investment cost $6.43 per share, and a year later Genentech went public for $35 per share. Donald Murfin, president of Lubrizol, described his

Table 9.2. Selected Startup Companies with Multinational Partners and Various Contract Features

Startup company	Multinational corporation	Nationality	Value ($ million)	Duration	Board of directors	Equity (%)
Integrated Genetics	Silliker Labratories	U.S.	—	—	No	—
	Toyobo	Japan	—	—	No	—
	Connaught Laboratories	Canada	—	—	No	—
	Serono Laboratory	Netherlands	—	—	No	—
Amgen	Abbott Laboratory	U.S.	19.0	5	Yes	11.9
	Tosco	U.S.	—	—	Yes	8.4
Genetic Systems	Syntex	U.S.	3.9	3	No	3.1
	Cutter Laboratory	Germany	1.6	3	No	—
Hybritech	Johnson & Johnson	U.S.	2.1	4	No	—
	Baxter-Travenol	U.S.	2.9	—	No	—
	Teijin	Japan	7.5	3	—	—
	Baker Instruments	U.S.	—	—	No	—
	American Cyanamid	U.S.	1.9	3	No	—
Genex	Allied Corp.	U.S.	16.5	5	No	—
	AB Fortia	Sweden	—	—	No	—
	Bristol-Myers	U.S.	2.5	3	No	—
	Green Cross	Japan	—	—	No	—
	Kabi-Vitrum	Sweden	—	—	No	—
	Koppers	U.S.	2.5	3	Yes	29.0
	Schering AG	Germany	—	1.5	No	—
	Yamanouchi	Japan	—	—	No	—
Advanced Genetic Sciences	Rohm and Haas	U.S.	5.0	2	Yes	14.9
	Hilleshog	Sweden	1.9	2	Yes	14.9

Sources: Various publications, including SEC 10-K filings and prospectuses

Table 9.3. Equity Investments in Startup Companies by Multinational Corporations at Stock Cost and Issue Price

Startup company	Multinational corporation	Percent shares outstanding	Price per share paid ($)	Price to public ($)
Chiron	Martin Marietta	18.5	5.59	12.00
Genetic Systems	Syntex	2.8	1.00	9.875
Advanced Genetic Sciences	Rohm and Haas Hilleshog	15.5 15.5	3.97 1.17	15.00 15.00
Collaborative Research	Green Cross Dow Chemical	— —	10.00 10.00	11.00 11.00
Genentech	Lubrizol Corning Glass	21.0 6.0	9.60 35.03	35.00 35.00*
Cetus	Standard of Indiana Standard of California National Distillers	21.3 17.3 11.0	— 3.60 2.72	23.00 23.00 23.00
Enzo Biochem	Johnson & Johnson	14.6	16.47	6.50*
Biogen	Inco Schering-Plough Monsanto	20.1 12.6 12.5	.39 3.97 10.00	23.50 23.50 23.50

Sources: Various annual reports and corporate prospectuses
* Stock bought after first offering.

reasons for investing: "We thought—and still think—they're the finest game in town. . . . If it [the investment] didn't work out . . . it was still considerably less risky than launching our own in-house research effort in this area" (*Chemical Week* 1982a:50). Paradoxically, the investment has yet to yield any new chemical products or less expensive processes for Lubrizol. Murfin later averred, "I have grave doubts that this technology can be used for commodity chemicals" (*Chemical Week* 1982a:50). But one can hardly say that the investment "did not work out," for Lubrizol managed to more than quintuple its investment by the time the stock was first publicly traded. The market price per share has increased a further 50 percent in the four years of public trading. A risky "insurance" type of investment became a tremendous capital gain.

Martin Marietta (39 percent owned by Allied Corporation) developed another strategy for making equity investments in biotechnology startups. Marietta has purchased more than $25 million of equity in three biotechnology startups: Molecular Genetics (21 percent), Chiron (10 percent), and Native Plants (20 percent) (R. Johnson 1983:1). The company has not disguised the fact that it intends to further increase its investment. The keystone of Marietta's strategy is to draw these three companies together in cooperative research—a unique and difficult goal because each of the companies has other important corporate investors. The consortium concept—merging these three companies into Marietta—could result in the company having a potent agricultural biotechnology division. Kenneth Jarmolow, Marietta's corporate director of research and development, plans to maintain a "hands-off policy" for now (R. Johnson 1983:22), but obviously Marietta is positioned to make a takeover bid at a propitious time in the future.[20]

The larger the amount of capital a MNC is willing to invest in a startup, the greater the benefits it can demand. In some startups corporate investors have demanded and secured ex-officio membership on the SAB. For example, at AGS both Rohm and Haas and Hilleshog have a member not only on the board of directors, but also on the SAB (AGS 1983). Since both of the MNCs have large in-house research staffs working on problems similar to those being worked on by AGS, this right is extremely valuable. From their positions on the SAB, MNC scientists will be able to observe much more intimate details regarding the decision-making process than any minority board director could. Obviously, the deeper the MNC is involved in the startup, the more information it can glean on the state of the art in biotechnology.

The purchase of equity interest in a startup provides a number of distinct benefits. The first are the capital gains that accrue from a successful equity investment. For Inco and other companies in economically depressed industries these capital gains can offset the losses incurred in their traditional products (see table 9.3). For MNCs whose products may be undercut or displaced by biotechnology, equity investment insures a share in any profits or capital gains that will accrue to the biotechnology company as it erodes the MNC's market. Just as important, a significant capital investment provides a solid base from which to launch a takeover attempt if the biotechnology startup begins to grow into a full-fledged competitor. A takeover might not be too difficult because of the large percentage of stock held by venture capitalists who would likely sell out if a high enough premium were offered.

The final practice, perhaps the most prevalent one, is for the MNC to purchase equity in the startup while simultaneously funding contract research. The equity participation allows the MNC a return on any break-

20. Regarding the possibility of a Marietta takeover Franklin Pass, the president of Molecular Genetics, Inc. is quoted as saying, "I don't see any special risk from Martin Marietta. . . . Sure, it's my understanding that they are cultivating an acquisition of the one or two companies that emerge as attractive" (R. Johnson 1983:22). The president of Chiron, Edward Penhoet, also is aware of the implications of Marietta's investment: "There's no commitment from any of the companies to be increasingly or wholly owned by Martin Marietta. . . . We're neither desirous nor adamantly opposed to [Martin Marietta buying majority interest in Chiron]" (R. Johnson 1983:22). Probably none of the companies are presently interested in being acquired, but if they were to suffer serious financial setbacks their outlook could change.

through made as a result of its contract funding. A seat on the board of directors and voting privileges ensure that the MNC can oppose any decision that is inimical to its interests, especially such occurrences as an attempted takeover by one of the MNC's competitors. Having input into a startup's decision is important for protecting an MNC's proprietary interests.

The strategy of purchasing an equity interest has led some observers to charge that the independence of startups is purely illusory (Raugel 1983). This assertion is not justified by the evidence. In very few cases does any one MNC have an equity stake greater than 20 percent. Acquisition of the entire startup would in many cases be resisted by other shareholders and perhaps by the scientists themselves. There is no evidence to indicate that MNCs control the firms they have invested in or that they are as yet considering a complete takeover. Equity involvement should rather be seen as an attempt by MNCs to secure some of the biotechnology "action."

The Overall Strategy of the Multinational Corporations

We're up to the eyeballs in molecular biology"   (John
Hanley, then chairman of Monsanto, quoted in Dickson
1981:397).

MNCs can use any number of possible strategies to secure a market position in the coming biorevolution. Each large pharmaceutical or chemical company is placing its investments in accordance with its particular market niche and its particular vision of its market in the 1990s and beyond. In the avalanche of investment that began with one or two MNCs placing small investments, followed with a few more, and ended with every company rushing to find a place in the new industry, clearly one will find varying motives and types of investment. I will examine the responses of a number of MNCs, especially with reference to the previous four general categories of involvement.

Eli Lilly and Kabi AB of Sweden were among the earliest investors in Genentech. Lilly bought the worldwide rights to genetically engineered insulin-producing bacteria, and Kabi, in exchange for research funding, secured the non-U.S. rights to HGH. Lilly and Kabi were the leading sellers, respectively, of insulin and HGH. Both of these companies immediately began to build in-house research groups while purchasing contract research.[21] Their investments were both defensive and potentially cost minimizing—to protect themselves the companies acquired products rights.

---

21. Lilly is reported to be working on bovine and porcine growth hormone (*Drug and Cosmetic Industry* 1982:36). Further, Lilly is reported to have made a small equity investment in a recent private stock placement by Genetics Institute (*Journal of Commerce* 1983g:22B).

With the exception of Johnson and Johnson, Bristol-Myers, and Mal-linkrodt (table 3.1), the pharmaceutical industry has not invested in large formal agreements with universities. Even the investment in rDNA start-ups, especially strong in the 1978–80 period, has slackened, in large part because most of the viable projects have already been bought. On the other hand, the pharmaceutical companies have rushed to invest in MAB startups, acquiring marketing rights and research. MABs offer business opportunities in the rapidly growing diagnostic business, and competent scientists were in short supply.

The chemical companies, in contrast, entered biotechnology with little experience in fermentation or health care. In fact, the bulk of their life science capability came in crop protection chemicals and, in some cases, animal production inputs. The science of molecular biology had not been perceived as being relevant to the chemical industry. Chemical companies were more comfortable in the agricultural colleges and chemistry and chem-ical engineering departments than in medical schools. However, biotech-nology provided a unique opportunity to adopt new production processes, and a number of chemical companies took the plunge.

The company that has made the largest investments in biotechnology is Monsanto. To quote Union Carbide's vice-president for research, S. Tinsely (1983), "They have bet their company on biotechnology."[22] The president of Rohm and Haas, in discussing risk-aversive behavior in the chemical industry, mentioned Monsanto as an exception because of "the tremendous investment it is making in genetic engineering for the 1990s" (*Chemical and Engineering News* 1983d:16). Monsanto has made the largest investments in biotechnology of any company and, most surprisingly, is continuing to increase them. Table 9.4 presents the entire gamut of Mon-santo's biotechnology and agricultural chemical investments.[23]

Monsanto's push into biotechnology is motivated by the tremendous success it is having in agricultural chemicals, which provided over 80 percent of its profit in 1982 (Kenney and Kloppenburg 1983:7). The need to find successors to the lucrative Roundup and Lasso herbicides compelled Mon-santo to invest in biotechnology (Bers and Warren 1981:32), as did its desire to enter the pharmaceutical industry, which was frustrated by an inability until recently to acquire a pharmaceutical manufacturer. Mon-santo's management has expressed the importance of biotechnology to Monsanto's future very bluntly: "This technology [biotechnology] is a must for companies such as Monsanto" (Monsanto's vice-president for economic and financial analysis, quoted in *Wall Street Journal* 1982:23). Monsanto's first molecular biology investment (in 1974) was with HMS. In addition to

22. Of course, with the Bhopal, India, tragedy we discover that Union Carbide was also betting its company on a certain technology.
23. Agricultural investments will be discussed more specifically in chapter 10.

Table 9.4. Monsanto—Anatomy of a Biotechnology Company

In-house investment
—$185 million invested in biological sciences research center

Pharmaceutical companies
—Purchased G. D. Searle Co. for $2.8 billion

Biotechnology companies (equity investments and important contracts)
Collagen—artificial bone powder
Biogen—tissue plasminogen activator
Genentech—bovine growth hormone
Genex—venture capital investment
Biotechnica International—*B. subtilis* protein expression

University contracts
Harvard University—biomedical research ($23 million)
Washington University—biomedical research ($23 million)
Rockefeller University—photosynthesis research ($4 million)
Oxford University—sugar chains ($1.5 million)

Seed company subsidiaries
Jacob Hartz   Monsanto Seed
Hybritech Seed Co.   Farmers Hybrid Co.

Fertilizer
Fifth largest U.S. producer of nitrogenous fertilizers

Pesticides
58 percent share of grass herbicides market in corn (1978)
Roundup—revenues of $500 million
Lasso—revenues of $200 million

Source: Adapted from Buttel et al. 1985

being the very first multiyear industry–university contract, this venture was Monsanto's introduction to molecular biology. Whether Monsanto foresaw the rDNA revolution is somewhat immaterial; the company was prepared mentally and financially to participate and in fact to take a leading role in rDNA.

Monsanto's first participation in genetic engineering was through its venture capital subsidiary, Innoven (jointly owned with Emerson Electric). "The original Genentech investment was made in 1977 and the original Genex investment was made in 1978" (Monsanto Public Relations 1983:3). The success of these investments and the growing recognition of the potential importance of biotechnology for the chemical industry and especially for agriculture led Monsanto in 1979 to hire Howard Schneiderman, then dean of biological sciences at UC, Irvine, as senior vice-president of research and development. Schneiderman has said that his job was to make Monsanto "a significant world factor in molecular biology" (*Chemical Week* 1983a:47).

In 1979 Monsanto contracted Genentech to bacterially produce bovine growth hormone. In 1980 Monsanto purchased a 12.5 percent stake in Biogen and a 30 percent share in Collagen. The next step for the company was the opening of its Molecular Biology Laboratories in 1981 "to provide a major new skill base for Monsanto" (Monsanto Company n.d.:5) In 1982 and 1983 other contracts were signed with universities and startups to provide needed expertise (table 9.4). Simultaneously, Monsanto was completing a $185 million research center in which to gather its research operations. And by 1983 Monsanto scientists were making important discoveries in plant science (*Chemical and Engineering News* 1983a:6).

Monsanto's financial commitment to biotechnology is now in the hundreds of millions of dollars and has until recently centered in the agricultural and animal nutrition industries.[24] To accomplish its goal of becoming a world leader in biotechnology, the company is using all four of the strategies listed earlier and is making larger investments than other companies. In 1983 the president of Monsanto, Richard Mahoney, described Monsanto's strategy:

> The biotechnology targets are newer and we are still in a phase of collecting lots of activities and grouping them. We've painted broad targets and we're still defining the specifics.
>
> Now there is no doubt in our minds that we know the areas we want to be in. But we want to give the scientists enough freedom in the early stages to be more definitive. There's an expression around here that you must avoid picking up the flower once a week to see if it's still growing. That's deadly in the new technology   (Storck 1983:13).

In the next few years analysts will be able to evaluate whether Monsanto's investment in biological research is justified and determine which investment strategy has been most effective in establishing a presence in biotechnology.

All of Monsanto's chemical industry competitors are making investments in biotechnology as a part of their diversification programs, but no company is making as concerted an effort. Perhaps the closest parallels are Du Pont (table 9.5) and Allied (table 9.6).[25] Allied's initial efforts were focused on developing products for agriculture, but in 1984 this focus was shifted to pharmaceuticals. Du Pont's focus, building on its NEN investment, will probably be in the area of MABs. Except possibly in the field of nitrogen fixation, the chemical companies will be in direct competition with pharmaceutical companies.

24. This may be changing, as in June 1983 Monsanto signed a contract with Biogen providing Monsanto with global (except for the Far East) production and marketing rights for tissue plasminogen activator. The Washington University School of Medicine–Monsanto contract is also for human health care.

25. In early 1984 Allied pulled out of the liquid fertilizer business and retreated from its nitrogen fixation–related biotechnology investments such as Calgene (*Journal of Commerce* 1984:22B).

Table 9.5. Du Pont—An In-House Operation

In-house investment
  —Two new agricultural research facilities ($60 million)
  —Life science center ($85 million)
Biotechnology company affiliations
  —Purchased New England Nuclear, a totally owned subsidiary ($345 million)
University contracts
  —Harvard Medical School ($6 million)
Pesticides
  —One of the largest pesticide producers in the U.S.

Source: Author's compilation

The MNCs, especially pharmaceutical companies, became aware of rDNA, genetic engineering, and biotechnology in late 1975 and 1976. But it took Genentech's success with somatostatin to provoke Lilly and Kabi to make their first investments. Though the pharmaceutical companies were the first to contract the new startups, the chemical industry quickly followed. In most cases the decision to invest in biotechnology was taken at very high levels and is an expression of corporate managements' efforts to diversify into new, more profitable areas.

Four strategies have been used to implement an MNC's decision to diversify into biotechnology. Most MNCs have adopted more than one strategy because of the need to spread risks and to insure that they will have a strong position in the coming biorevolution. In many cases the small startups possess certain expertise that is impossible to reproduce, and

Table 9.6. Allied Corporation—The Aborted Push Into Biological Nitrogen Fixation

---

In-house investment
  —Major research effort in Syracuse, New York, comprising over fifty employees
Biotechnology company affiliations
  —Calgene, formerly 20 percent, now canceled
  —Biologicals, 7.3 percent equity held through Allied Canada
  —Genetics Institute, $15 million investment
  —Genex, now canceled
University contracts
  —University of California, Davis, $2.5 million now completed
  —Contract research at numerous other universities
Agricultural input companies
  —Nitragin Co., a legume innoculant company recently purchased for undisclosed sum
Fertilizer
  —Allied was one of the five largest fertilizer companies in the United States, but now
    has divested major segments of its fertilizer lines

Source: Author's compilation

MNCs are forced to let contracts to the startups, though Du Pont, for example, until recently refusing to invest in startups, has conducted nearly all of its research in-house (*Business Week* 1980b:86).[26] No consensus has yet developed on which strategies will be most successful, but it is clear that industry–university long-term contracts can no longer play such an important role because few important researchers are uncommitted to a company and because product-oriented research is becoming the norm.

The funding of a startup either through equity participation or through contracts is a questionable strategy because the funder is making possible the growth of a potential competitor.[27] But the inability of many MNCs to recruit the most talented researchers will continue to retard in-house research and force them to go to outside researchers. The only MNC that has demonstrated excellent expertise is the Monsanto plant molecular biology group, which is credited with a number of scientific achievements. Interestingly, Monsanto, even with these in-house scientific successes, continues to contract for certain specific tasks (*Journal of Commerce* 1983f:22B).

The MNCs may ultimately become the dominant actors in biotechnology—most probably absorbing the small venture capital–financed startups. This is not to say that some startups—such as Cetus, Genentech, and Biogen—may not become independent, viable companies. Nevertheless, the vast resources of Monsanto, Lilly, or Du Pont will probably prove fatal to the undercapitalized startups.

26. In 1984 Du Pont invested $4.5 million in Biotech Research Laboratories (BRL) and received an approximately 7 percent equity. Du Pont also can appoint one member of BRL's SAB and board of directors. Further, Du Pont has the right to acquire rights on any future BRL projects (*GEN* 1984a:7).

27. This creation of a competitor, of course, assumes that the funding contract doesn't force the small company to sell its birthright.

10. Agriculture and

Biotechnology

A revolution in biological research is occurring—one that promises to transform the industries that serve agriculture, and thus, eventually, farming. The innovators are companies like Monsanto, Stauffer Chemical, Dow Chemical, Eli Lilly, Rohm and Haas, Merck, Du Pont. Each is in the business of selling new products and services to modern farmers and cattlemen. Many of these corporations, through links with top geneticists, biochemists, and molecular biologists in universities in the United States and, increasingly, abroad are sowing the seeds for what they hope will be a new industrial revolution in agriculture   *(Lepkowski 1982:8).*

I think it is important to note that these sorts of technologies historically have not improved the financial position of the farmer. Where the impact has been is to lower food cost in the end because of the competitive nature of this society and so on   *(George Seidel, Jr., associate professor of physiology and director of the Embryo Transplant Laboratory at Colorado State University, in congressional testimony, 1982:166).*

The opportunities that biotechnology opened in agriculture were discovered a few years after its applications to medicine were recognized. This lag is due to the fact that molecular biology was largely confined to medical schools and to non-land-grant universities (non-LGUs)—institutions that until recently were uninterested in agricultural problems. In the 1976–78 period biotechnologists' interests were chiefly human health care products such as insulin, HGH, and interferon. As the implications of biotechnology for human health care became clear, it was only natural that veterinary applications should also become obvious. This awareness probably came first to companies such as Lilly and Upjohn, which already had significant animal health and nutrition divisions. The introduction of biotechnology to agriculture will change the agricultural production system and has already set in motion changes in the agricultural research system.

Biotechnology's impact on agriculture has unique aspects. I will examine the increasing role of non-LGUs in plant molecular biology, the technical impetus biotechnology is providing toward concentration in the agricultural inputs sector, and the unique development of high technology biotechnology firms specializing in agricultural applications. There is an ongoing shift in emphasis in the agricultural inputs industry from an applied, routinized technology such as fertilizers to advanced technologies that produce patentable materials. The technical basis of this shift is researchers' increased ability to rigorously characterize the activities of plant–chemical interactions.

Biotechnology is providing a common technical base on which the pharmaceutical, chemical, agricultural, and food processing industries can be united, and in agriculture this fusion is taking place. The public institutions currently providing research support for agriculture are already evolving to provide support for new clients. In addition, new public and private institutions or old institutions that have changed focus are beginning to find agriculture a fruitful research area. These new institutions include Harvard, MIT, Rockefeller University, Caltech, Scripps Clinic and Research Foundation, and Washington University. Further, the entire chemical–pharmaceutical industry is mobilizing to participate in the impending agricultural biorevolution. Finally, genetic engineering companies specifically targeting agricultural biotechnology have been founded to take advantage of the new market opportunities in agriculture.

What is Technically Possible in Agriculture?

Obviously, the $50–100 billion market value for the most radical group of genetically engineered [agricultural] products in the third time frame [1990 and beyond] does not include overall price effects or any synergisms currently inestimable   *(Murray and Teichner 1981:119).*

The above quote makes quite clear the enormous size of the agricultural market that could be impacted by biotechnology. Contemplation of the essential role of agriculture in producing the food, fiber, and wood so necessary for civilization indicates the profound impact that biotechnology will have on our lives. World agriculture in the year 2000 will be transformed, and our food will be produced with new techniques in a changed social environment.

Animal production has been the first industry to receive new production techniques from biotechnology, and the animals affected range from cattle to abalone. Total U.S. animal health sales were $1.9 billion in 1982 and had risen to $2.3 billion by 1984 (Anderson 1983:8). Large mammals have received the greatest attention—in large part because in the United States livestock rearing is a $70 billion industry. The poultry industry also is receiving greater research attention and will be another area of innovation. The growth of global meat consumption, much of which will come from the adoption of modern production techniques, may increase the size of the animal health market even more.

Biotechnology's first impacts are already being felt in beef and dairy cattle farming. The life cycle of the cow will be more rigorously controlled by the new biological techniques. For example, new reproductive technologies have made it possible to induce a cow to produce an average of eight and up to twenty ova at an ovulation (superovulation). It is now possible to "twin" embryos to produce identical twins, quadruplets, octuplets, etc. These ova are artificially inseminated and then flushed from the cow after six days. These embryos can be sexed so that dairy farmers need only implant female embryos—cattlemen would choose males—into "surrogate mothers." The surrogates have had their estrus synchronized with the donor cow so as to be prepared to receive the embryos. The embryos can also be frozen for transportation or future use. Bovine reproduction is being completely transformed through the application of new biomedical knowledge (*Business Week* 1982b; Genetic Engineering, Inc. 1982; Pramik 1983a; 1983b). Indeed, in the near future bovine reproduction will be an entirely managed process, and the calf will be a genetically select individual.

The next step in the life cycle is the healthy growth of the calf to maturity. The newly born calf is subject to a diarrheal disease, scours, that affects 16 to 17 percent of calves in the United States, with a 30 percent mortality rate (Cane 1983:14). A new vaccine has been developed by Molecular Genetics, Inc. to prevent scours. Companies are also developing vaccines for other bovine diseases, including foot and mouth disease (Molecular Genetics, Inc. 1982). Bovine interferon is being tested for efficacy against shipping fever, which occurs when cattle are shipped to feedlots and costs the cattle industry more than $250 million annually (Hoozer 1982:15; *WSJ* 1983b:36). The cumulative effect of these vaccines will be to shorten animal turnover time and to allow cattle raising to be carried out under less sanitary conditions and with increased population densities. Also, there are possibilities of developing farmer-administered diagnostics based on MABs, thus lessening the need to use expensive veterinary services.

Feed is a major cost factor in the bovine production system, and it too will be affected by biotechnology. The two major constituents of animal feed are carbohydrates and proteins. In the United States these proteins are largely provided by soybean meal. Biotechnology may make it possible to meet this need with single-cell protein (SCP), consisting of bacteria or yeast grown on a feedstock such as methanol, or, perhaps, agricultural wastes. Currently SCP is not cost competitive with soybean meal if the carbon-based feedstock is purchased on the world market (Yanchinski 1981). However, in countries that are flaring natural gas the process could be quite economical. The other bovine feed innovation is the possibility of genetically engineering yeast or bacteria to superproduce the amino acids lacking in most feed. A final possibility is to genetically engineer maize (the major animal feed) to produce amino acids such as lysine and tryptophan that must be added to cattle feed as a supplement (J. Fox 1981b).

Another intriguing commercial possibility created by genetic engineering is the microbial production of bovine growth hormone (BGH). When administered to dairy cows BGH has been shown to increase lactation more than 10 percent with no increase in feed consumption (Peel et al. 1981). Although a hormone delivery system has not been perfected, it has obvious economic potential. Genentech estimates that the global market for BGH is $500 million (*Business Week* 1982b:130). If an oral delivery system can be perfected, BGH could become a standard feed additive, and a number of companies are currently scaling up for commercial microbial BGH production.

The pork industry is only slightly behind the beef and dairy industries and will experience similar technical change. In fact, growth hormone, interferon, and various vaccines are already in preparation for pork. On the other hand, for a number of technical and economic reasons reproductive technologies are not as developed for the pork industries. The poultry industry has traditionally been deficient in basic research (Smith 1982). But already Amgen has successfully cloned a gene to produce chicken growth hormone, which Amgen hopes will decrease broiler turnover times by 15 percent—from eight to seven weeks (Amgen 1983). Finally, there are many other biotechnological applications such as in cloning salmon (Johnstone 1983:328).

Animal-based food production systems offer opportunities that are only now becoming apparent. Over the next decade the invention of new products and processes for animal production will create still more new markets. Some of these new products such as a foot and mouth disease vaccine will be very important in Third World countries. Preventing foot and mouth disease could make the cattle export trade in countries such as Argentina and Brazil much more lucrative and simultaneously affect U.S. cattle producers. The market for animal biotechnologies is already worldwide in scope, and countries such as Argentina and Brazil could become important markets.

Even though biotechnology for mammals is presently more advanced, plant biotechnology offers the greatest long-term agricultural potential. Biotechnologically produced inputs will affect arable agriculture in various ways. The most important markets center upon the seed—that little pack-

age of genetic information that determines a plant's agronomic characteristics. Other areas of corporate interest in biotechnology include manipulation of soil microorganisms or other microorganisms that live on plants
either symbiotically, parasitically, or neutrally and the production of plant
diagnostic kits to assist in the identification of diseases. The range and size
of these markets is unlimited.

Plant diagnostics will not be an important market but on a smaller scale
could be a lucrative one. The types of plants for which diagnostics might
be useful are, for example, turf grass and citrus (DNAPT 1983:21)—that
is, markets in which customers are not likely to be price conscious; country
clubs and owners of expensive homes would be willing to pay relatively
high prices for healthy turf, and high value orchard crops require assured
diagnosis—mistakes are very expensive. An orange tree at its productive
peak is very valuable, and in groves with diseased trees the extra cost of
an easy-to-handle reliable diagnostic might be perceived as neglible. The
size of the plant diagnostics market is undetermined, and thus far there
have been few entrants in this field.

The first plant-related agricultural biotechnology to be marketed will
probably be genetically engineered bacteria to prevent crop frost damage
(Tangely 1983; P. David 1983). No estimates of the market size are available, but in Florida alone the December 1983 frost cost $500 million. The
potential for frost damage preventative bacteria on a global scale could be
several billions of dollars annually. Another commonly discussed use of
genetically engineered microorganisms is to fix nitrogen more efficiently.
The USDA estimates that U.S. farmers spent $10 billion for fertilizers and
soil conditioners in 1980 (J. Marx 1982:67), so the market potential is
enormous, and the applications of genetically engineered microbes to arable agriculture are still largely unexplored.

The most intriguing possibility that biotechnology opens is that of genetically engineering the whole plant or linking the plant's growth to certain
specified inputs such as pesticides or desired fertilizers.[1] Research in plant
genetic engineering is receiving ever-greater investment and is advancing
rapidly. For example, in 1983 a bacterial gene was spliced into a plant but
was not expressed in the whole plant (*Chemical and Engineering News*
1983b). By 1985, however, a number of research teams had successfully

---

1. This linkage has already been partially developed in traditional plant breeding. For
example, Green Revolution rice varieties require irrigation—in this case the required input
is controlled, measured, and expensive water. Further, to perform economically the rice
requires fertilization, a commercial input. This is not to say the rice will die without fertilizer,
but the purchase of the seed would be economically unjustifiable without it—and economics
is the only justification for adoption of the new varieties. Finally, new seeds and changed
agricultural practices in the United States have required ever greater pesticide use to merely
keep abreast of evolving pests (for further discussion, see Kloppenburg and Kenney 1984).

expressed transferred genes at the whole plant level. Currently, the process of excising desired genes and transferring them to another species is still rudimentary, but technical capability is constantly improving.[2]

The techniques of protoplast fusion and plant tissue culture have even more immediate application to plant breeding (Evans et al. 1983). Plant tissue culture techniques make it possible to regenerate exact replica plants from single plant cells, though, in fact, the tissue culture process itself gives rise to unique variation, that is, somoclonal variation. Cell fusion and tissue culture will soon provide breeders with new material and new techniques for rapidly scanning plant cells for desired characteristics.

Farther in the future, the discoveries of plant molecular biology will make it possible to understand how herbicides and plant growth regulators operate. This knowledge would make it possible either to design better chemicals or perhaps design plants that would respond to crop chemicals in a desired fashion. Conversely, it might be possible to design plants with better natural pest defenses. But all plant design work begins with reprogramming DNA; the ability to reprogram DNA will mean the ability to determine the characteristics to which a particular plant responds. This suggests that with proper engineering a plant could be produced that would respond only to particular proprietary chemicals. The market for these "packages" could be in the billions of dollars.

Obviously tremendous markets and market shifts will occur because of biotechnology, and this in turn will profoundly alter the social arrangements and the actors in agriculture. Old institutional actors in the food and fiber system will, in some cases, atrophy, while others will increase their strength. I will examine the response of these various actors to the increasingly obvious fact that biotechnology is forming a new technical base for agriculture.

Industry, Biotechnology, and Agriculture

It's no coincidence that companies involved in herbicides get into biotechnology.... What's happening is, they're trying to cover themselves   (Chemical Week *1982c:40*).

[Corn seed] is not nearly as big a market potential—we have a lot narrower focus—as a company the size of Monsanto foresees. They can span the range from the crop all the way to animal growth hormones, to some process that would enhance their chemical operations. Monsanto could use a biological product, an enzyme or a culture for fermentation to do something that they are now using expensive fossil fuels on, thus they can afford to expend a lot more dollars because they have

2. In plant biotechnology the ability to transfer genes will probably come before sufficient knowledge has developed regarding which genes or gene complexes are worth transferring.

larger potential payoff than Pioneer, who only sells seed
of six agronomic crops. The markets are just different
*(Nicholas Frey, Pioneer Seed's Coordinator of Johnston
Research, 1982:121).*

In contrast to biomedical applications of biotechnology, which originated
in the university, the use of biotechnology in agriculture has been pressed
by MNCs whose executives grasped biotechnology's potential applications
to agriculture even earlier than the university administrators.

The implications of the trajectory of biotechnical change offer many
possibilities, but even the best innovations need a market. Agriculture
provides numerous commercial opportunities. In 1980 farmers spent $128
billion for operating costs, including outlays for fuel, oil, and fertilizer of
nearly $17 billion (Budiansky 1983a:19). As mentioned earlier, Monsanto's
Roundup herbicide alone had sales that approached the $500 million mark
in 1982 (*Chemical Week* 1983a:47). Finally, increasing world food demand
means that agricultural markets have important future growth potential.

The seed will become the proprietary nexus for plant genetic engineering.[3] The seed is a vehicle for conveying the fruits of molecular biological
research to the farmer and thereby realizing a profit on the incorporated
research.[4] The large-scale drive by MNCs to develop in-house molecular
biology staffs has overlapped and accentuated a movement already under
way among them to purchase seed companies (Mooney 1979; Kenney et
al. 1982; Kloppenburg and Kenney 1984). Table 10.1 is an illustrative listing
of a number of MNCs that have purchased seed companies and that also
have in-house biotechnology research capabilities.

In agriculture every MNC is staking out a market sector where its competitive position appears to be strong. Monsanto has placed its emphasis
on two different aspects—animal nutrition and health and pesticide-plant
interactions (Storck 1983:11). Allied Corporation, on the other hand, had
initially embarked upon building expertise in biological nitrogen fixation

---

3. Biotechnology (molecular biology) offers the possibility of removing or inserting desired genes into a plant's DNA, thereby making possible specific, controlled mutations. A
seed could then be programmed to respond to environmental conditions in particular ways.
But molecular biology offers even more subtle possibilities. For example, a herbicide by
definition in some way inhibits a plant's life functions—that is, the molecules of herbicide
bind with plant molecules, disrupting their activities and causing the death of the organism.
A more rigorous understanding of the molecular activity will make it possible to design, or,
more properly, to engineer, plant resistance to herbicides. This new knowledge allows rationalization of the herbicide–plant interface, and this technical union facilitates a commercial
union that would capture the synergies of this design process.

4. It is no exaggeration to say that nearly every company from every industry with an
interest in agriculture has made an investment in agricultural biotechnology—input producers,
food processors, and even Martin Marietta (the possible exception is the farm machinery
industry).

Table 10.1. Multinational Corporations, Product Lines, and Seed Company Subsidiaries*

Multinational parent	Primary products	Seed subsidiaries
Sandoz (Switzerland)	Pharmaceuticals	Ladner Beta Seed (Canada) Zaadunie (Netherlands) Northrup King (USA) Rogers Brothers (USA) National-NK (USA) Sluis en Groot (Netherlands)
Shell (UK/Netherlands)	Oil, chemicals	International Plant Breeders (UK) Compañía General de Semillas (Spain) Rothwell Group (UK) Interseeds (Netherlands) IPB Japan (Japan) Nickerson P. Gmbh (West Germany) Zwaan (Netherlands & Belgium) North American Plant Breeders (USA; with Olin Chemical)
Ciba-Geigy (Switzerland)	Pharmaceuticals, chemicals	Funk Seeds International (USA) Stewart (Canada) Louisiana Seeds (USA) Ciba-Geigy Mexicana (Mexico)
Celanese (USA)	Textiles, chemicals	Celpril (USA) Moran (USA) Joseph Harris (USA) Nugrain
Cargill (USA)	Grain marketer	ACCO (USA) Dorman (USA) Kroeker (Canada) PAG (USA)
Occidental Petroleum (USA)	Oil, petrochemicals	Ring Around Products (USA) Excel Hybrid (USA) Missouri (USA) Moss (USA)

Source: Adapted from Buttel et al. 1985
* All information is accurate to the best of my knowledge, but it should be kept in mind that the proprietary nature of these firms makes it difficult to keep abreast of the latest data.

but retreated from this area in 1984 (*Journal of Commerce* 1982:22B). Du Pont is investing in pesticide development. Each company must acquire a protectable niche or an area in which it will be competitive.

The first important agricultural product development project launched was the 1979 Genentech–Monsanto alliance to produce BGH. Other MNCs that were producing animal nutrition products rapidly formed alliances to develop their own BGH production processes. These included Biogen–International Mineral and Chemicals, Molecular Genetics–American Cyanamid, Amgen–Upjohn, and Collaborative Research–Akzo. If effective, simple-to-use delivery systems can be developed, the BGH market will be very competitive. On the other hand, smaller feed companies that are unable to develop and produce BGH may be displaced because their feed packages do not contain the growth-speeding hormone. BGH may be a technical change that contributes to and speeds consolidation of the smaller feed additive producers.

The biorevolution also provides important commercial opportunities for food processors. Specially engineered microbes can convert wastes or low-value products to those of much higher value. For example, whey, a waste from cheese production, can be converted into marketable lactose (*Food Engineering* 1979). French researchers are attempting to develop a microbial process to transform inexpensive vegetable oils into oils with a flavor similar to that of expensive oils such as cocoa oil (Cantley and Sargeant 1981:331).

Companies such as General Foods, Ralston Purina, Campbell Soup, Nestle, Hershey, and Frito-Lay are actively developing in-house research capacities and are also funding university and biotechnology startup research (*Food Engineering* 1983:21). Jose Pellon, of the Institut de Gestion Internationale Agro-Alimentaire, and Anthony Sinskey, of MIT's department of food sciences, have commented on the role biotechnology will play in the food industry:

> The impact of genetic engineering in the food processing industry will be piecemeal rather than industry-wide, mainly because of the inability to identify commercially significant functions. This inability stems from insufficient biochemical and genetic knowledge, the low profitability of products and the resistance of the food industry to investment in research and development. In the next decade we will probably see a number of companies with a high-technology base entering the food processing field. Also, some food processing industries [companies?] will invest in genetic engineering firms to strengthen their inadequate in-house research capabilities   (Pellon and Sinskey n.d.:16).

The threat that the large chemical and pharmaceutical companies may become involved in food processing has spurred processors to make investments in genetic engineering in-house research and in biotechnology startups (DNAPT 1983; *GEN* 1983f:50; Morris 1983).

Food processing companies have production processes and markets that are very different from the chemical and pharmaceutical companies, but biotechnology is increasingly providing all three industries with a common technical base. Furthermore, the strategic moves of the food industry companies in regard to biotechnology have roughly paralleled those of the chemical industry—only the food industry moved approximately three years later. Perhaps the most involved food processor is General Foods, which has followed the example of the chemical industry (see table 10.2). Bob Carbonell, Nabisco's executive vice-president for technology, de-

Table 10.2. General Foods and Biotechnology

In-house investment
—Unknown but have set up a biotechnology group
University research
—Engenics (University of California, Berkeley, and Stanford)
—Cornell Biotechnology Institute
—Funds project-grants at a number of universities
Biotechnology startup investments
—DNA Plant Technology ($1 million for three years)
—International Plant Research Institute
—Plant Research Venture Fund

Source: Author's compilation

scribes Nabisco's reasons for investing in Cetus: "Genetic engineering probably will demonstrate its potential worth in food processing in the next three to five years. . . . We're involved in the research venture with Cetus primarily because, when the value of biotechnology becomes apparent, we want to be there" (*GEN* 1983f:50). This reasoning is almost verbatim that of chemical industry spokesmen in 1978.

The final group of investors in biotechnology are farmers—not just any farmers, but rather big farmers. These large integrated farmers could derive great benefits from plants designed to their specifications. Thus, Boswell Farms, a large California cotton grower, has funded and now purchased Phytogen to produce new and better varieties of cotton (*GEN* 1983c:3; Miller 1985:26). Similarly, Brown and Williamson Tobacco Co. has contracted with DNAPT (1983) to produce improved tobacco varieties. Only the largest farmers (actually plant-growing corporations) can afford to fund this type of research. Most farmers either depend on public research or merely buy finished inputs.

Agriculture provides an ideal market for the MNCs' biotechnology investments for a number of reasons. First, the agricultural MNCs already have marketing networks in place; any new products are merely new lines. And where seeds and chemicals can be linked in a package, the separate marketing networks for seeds and chemicals can be combined, thus decreasing overhead. Conversely, the dispersion of farmers and the consequent need for large marketing networks are an important barrier to entry for smaller firms. Second, farmers are an ideal market in that they rapidly adopt innovations. In the United States any innovation promising increased profits has a ready reception from farmers.

As discussed earlier, a primary reason corporate managers are emphasizing agricultural applications is to secure the large profit margins to be had from a proprietary molecule. Most of the large MNCs view biotechnology as merely another tool in their diversification away from bulk commodities. For example, Allied Corporation recently divested its liquid fertilizer business (*Journal of Commerce* 1983i:22B). Monsanto has undergone a similar restructuring and rationalization, shedding products in which it did not have a strong competitive position. At the same time, these companies have begun massive efforts to further build their in-house agricultural research staffs.

But the building of research operations has been difficult because of the lack of skilled plant biologists. The responsibility (or blame) for this shortage was quickly placed upon the LGU system—America's agricultural universities—for not doing basic research and training the labor power that the companies desired (to be discussed in the next section). In actuality competent scientists in plant molecular biology were unavailable because there was no important constituency demanding their training or providing for their employment. The blame for the unpreparedness thus should not be placed on the servants of industry, the university, but rather on the master, the chemical industry. It is not difficult to remember that less than ten years ago there was a glut of molecular biologists.

To secure the necessary agricultural biotechnology research expertise the MNCs both raided universities and signed long-term research agreements with universities. These arrangements were in addition to normal grants of various types. For example, until 1983 Monsanto funded Mary Dell Chilton's Washington University plant molecular biology laboratory. But in a stunning raid, Ciba-Geigy acquired Chilton's services in appointing her director of its new agricultural biotechnology research center in North Carolina (*Journal of Commerce* 1983d:22B).[5] The rush to secure the services of the few available plant molecular biologists paralleled that which occurred five to six years earlier in the medical area.

The other corporate strategy has been to sign contracts with agricultural biotechnology startups. The MNCs' motives here are similar to those presented in chapter 9—that is, to secure access to expertise not available through other channels. Because the MNCs moved rapidly in plant agricultural applications, the growth of startups was limited. In veterinary applications the startups are more important because animal health products are direct spinoffs from human health—for example, HGH–animal growth hormones, human monoclonal diagnostics–animal monoclonal diagnostics, and various human and animal vaccines.

Agricultural Biotechnology Startups

The number of startups specifically dedicated to agriculture is comparatively small. Table 10.3 lists these companies and their principal scientists,

5. A year earlier Chilton had been quoted in *Newsweek* (1982:69–70) as saying, "The biggest danger [to science] is that the best people will be directed to applied research in industry."

investors, and research goals. A few other smaller agricultural biotechnology firms exist, but none of these have gone public and they maintain a relatively low profile. Additionally, the large biotechnology startups have research under way that has agricultural applications—for example, Genentech, BGH; Cetus, scours vaccine; and Collaborative Research, rennin. A more unique distinguishing feature of truly agricultural biotechnology startups is that their research concentrates upon plants. Plant biology is distinctly separate from mammalian and microbial biology and requires special expertise.

The first company dedicated to plant biotechnology was IPRI, which was founded by a UCSF professor, Martin Apple, in 1978. The other important companies were formed in the next three years. All of these companies survive on contract research, with the exception of Agrigenetics (now part of Lubrizol Corporation), which has purchased thirteen seed companies and thereby secured revenues with which to finance its research. Molecular Genetics, Inc. conducts research in both animal and plant biotechnology and has begun sales of its scours vaccine (Molecular Genetics, Inc. 1982), which is already generating product revenues.

The staffs of these companies are partially drawn from the LGUs, such as the University of California at Berkeley and at Davis, the University of Minnesota, the University of Wisconsin, Kansas State University, Cornell University, and Michigan State University. Other universities also have a number of important plant molecular biologists. For example, at Harvard, scientists such as Lawrence Bogorod (AGS) and Frederick Ausubel (Biotechnica International) are faculty members. However, the shortage of plant molecular biologists is so acute that a number of European and Third World scientists, including Hungarians and Brazilians, have been recruited into U.S. companies (AGS 1983; DNAPT 1983).

With certain exceptions, the agricultural biotechnology startups (for example, Calgene, Phytogen, and Plant Genetics, Inc.) will find it difficult to survive in the seed-agricultural chemical industry, as the long-term nature of plant biotechnological research condemns these companies to contract research. The tremendous investments and market power of the MNCs will in all likelihood overwhelm these smaller companies, though their ability to secure critical patents could negate corporate market power. Calgene, for example, has secured a patent on a gene that confers in vitro cell resistance to Roundup, Monsanto's herbicide, to soybean plant cells (Comai et al. 1983). Calgene now owns that DNA sequence. Calgene's ability to regenerate the whole plant and express the Roundup resistance gene would be extremely valuable. Otherwise, the startups must acquire relatively sheltered niches in which to survive. An example of this is DNAPT's strong emphasis on tomatoes through its linkage with Campbell Soup and its strong tropical commodity orientation. AGS is developing expertise in frost protective bacteria, and Molecular Genetics has devel-

Table 10.3. Agricultural Biotechnology Startups: Selected University-Based Researchers, Financial Linkages, and Areas of Research

Company	Principal university-based researcher and researcher's university affiliation	Financial linkages	Areas of research
Agrigenetics	Jack Widholm, Univ. of Illinois Paul Kaesberg, Univ. of Wisconsin Vernon Gracen, Cornell Univ.	Purchased by Lubrizol	Seed-related biotechnologies
Advanced Genetic Sciences	Lawrence Bogorad, Harvard Univ. Milton Schroth, Univ. of California, Berkeley	Rohm and Haas, Hilleshog	Cloning of disease-resistant potatoes
Calgene	Raymond Valentine, Univ. of California, Davis	FMC Corp., Continental Grain	Plant genetics
Genetic Engineering Co.	Edwin Adair, Univ. of Colorado Thomas Wagner, Ohio Univ.	Johnson & Johnson	Animal reproduction
DNA Plant Technology Co.	Norman Borlaug, Texas A&M Philip Ammirato, Columbia Univ. Melvin Calvin, Univ. of California, Berkeley	Campbell Soup (40%), Koppers Co., General Foods	Tomatoes, tobacco, forestry products
Molecular Genetics	Anthony Faras, Univ. of Minnesota Charles Green, Univ. of Minnesota Lynn Enquist, NIH	American Cyanamid, Moorman Manufacturing, U.S. Dept. of Defense	Corn, scours prevention, and nonagricultural applications
Sungene	Roy Curtiss, Washington Univ. William Dreyer, Caltech	Lubrizol, Mitsubishi, Aambrecht & Quist	Sunflowers, corn hybrids

Source: Buttel et al. 1985
* All information is accurate to the best of my knowledge, but it should be kept in mind that the proprietary nature of these firms makes it difficult to keep abreast of the latest data.

oped numerous animal vaccines. Startups that secure a niche early and can protect it with patents and strategic alliances do have a possibility of surviving.

The survival of agricultural startups is predicated on a relative lack of accomplished scientists being available on the job market. The startup companies' SABs, which contain the top university scientists, can secure preferential access to the products and scientists produced in SAB members' laboratories. And the startups' laboratories are, in fact, located conveniently close to major universities. For example, AGS has a Berkeley, California, laboratory;[6] Agrigenetics' main laboratory and Cetus's agricultural laboratory are located in Madison, Wisconsin; and Plant Genetics and Calgene are in Davis, California—in each case close to the vital professors.

Biotechnology and the Agricultural Research System

The seriousness of this situation [the state of the U.S. agricultural research system] highlights two major issues: (1) there is a critical need for more high quality, perceptive leaders of national stature in agricultural research; and (2) it is unclear who represents and can speak for the various components of the agricultural research system. The resulting leadership vacuum leaves agricultural research with inadequate, confused, and often contradictory representation at the national level during a critical period for the country, for agriculture, and for agricultural research (Rockefeller Foundation 1982:1).

The U.S. agricultural production system has had its own publicly funded research system for over one hundred years. The mission of this research system has been to provide applied research for the various clientele groups that are of the U.S. food and fiber system. This arrangement has translated into close connections between producer groups and research institutions as agricultural scientists undertake problem-specific research (Hightower 1973; California Rural Legal Assistance 1981). Scientists respond to immediate needs or, as in the case of seeds, there is a division of labor between what the private and public sectors undertake in the entire process of producing a marketable seed (National Association of State Universities and Land-Grant Colleges 1982:26). The mission of the agricultural research system is to provide applied research "for the farmer."

This very "applied" emphasis would prove to be detrimental when the

6. A Kansas laboratory was abandoned by AGS once James Shepard and other important Kansas State University scientists left AGS (*WSJ* 1984:25).

formerly "basic" science of molecular biology became applied because traditional agricultural researchers were not expert in this new applied science. The few LGU scientists who were skilled in plant molecular biology were quickly recruited by companies, while the changing technical base made universities from outside the LGU system important competitors in the plant sciences. Simultaneously, various LGU constituencies experienced shifts in knowledge and labor power needs. Some constituencies such as the small private seed companies and the farm block were weakened, and other constituencies such as the large multinational agribusiness input companies became more assertive. The latter began to apply pressure on the LGUs to retreat from applied to basic research.

The agricultural research system as early as 1972 was severely criticized in a National Academy of Sciences (1972) report for being parochial and doing too much marginal research (Marshall 1982:33). The criticisms were ignored throughout the 1970s but surfaced again in 1982 as the research system was again denounced in separate reports by the Office of Technology Assessment (1982) and the Rockefeller Foundation (1982). The latter's criticisms included the charge that the system does not do sufficient basic research.

The central research pivot in the LGU and in agricultural research in general has been the plant breeder. The breeder was the person who integrated the knowledge of the meteorologist, soil scientist, plant pathologist, entomologist, etc., into the seed. The breeder produced plants that were able to respond to the particular environments and various inputs and cultural practices. The breeding process has traditionally been a time-consuming, craft discipline tracing its roots back through Mendelian genetics to prehistoric times.

Now genetic engineering threatens to change the plant breeder's position because genetic engineers try to develop techniques to design new plants by simply deleting or adding genes. If this becomes possible, the plant breeder's role would be less central; breeders (privately or publicly) would grow the plant and polish it for release. The creative and important role would increasingly be that of the gene splicer. Consequently, the brash boasts and threats of the molecular biologists has led some plant breeders to resist molecular biology (Sprague et al. 1980). How this resistance will be overcome is as yet unclear—perhaps it will be overcome by attrition due to retirement.

The LGUs that conduct important molecular biology research are limited to large universities such as the University of Wisconsin, the University of California at Berkeley and Davis, the University of Minnesota, and Cornell University. In fact, in a recent poll only Wisconsin and UCB were ranked among the top ten universities in cellular and molecular biology. With these few exceptions, the large private universities and medical schools have the greatest expertise in molecular biology.

The emergence of the biotechnology industry in the late 1970s therefore largely bypassed the LGUs, and many of the best LGU molecular biologists left for other universities or entered industry. For example, Wisconsin's Timothy Hall and Julian Davies went to Agrigenetics and Biogen, respectively, Michigan State's Peter Carlson went to Zoecon, and Kansas State's James Shepard went to Advanced Genetic Sciences and, eventually, to Allelix. For the LGUs, already weak in molecular biology, the losses were severe.

The corporations flocked to the universities to purchase access to molecular biologists, and from table 3.1 it can be seen that the bulk of these institutions were not the LGUs. As MNC interest turned to agriculture and plant molecular biology, the LGUs were lacking in expertise, and a large amount of the funding for plant research went to universities that were not traditionally known for agricultural research, for example, Rockefeller University, Harvard Medical School, MIT-Whitehead Institute, and Washington University. This corporate funding is building the expertise of these universities and making them de facto competitors with the LGUs.

Plant molecular biology is still a fledgling science, requiring a large amount of "basic" (that is, not immediately profitable) research before commercial products can become available. The corporate sector is not willing to bear the financial burden of paying for this research; it feels that universities should shoulder the load. The logical agency to undertake this research is the USDA, but its funds are allocated in such a way that it does not provide sufficiently large quantities of capital for launching a concerted effort in this capital-intensive research. The current grant allocation system provides money only to the agricultural research system and not to outside institutions, and the USDA competitive grant system, as practiced by NIH and NSF, allocated only about $17 million (FY84) (Lepkowski 1983:15). Agricultural research funding in the USDA is regional, which has guaranteed that research is decentralized and, in many cases, underdeveloped, but the nearly $470 million that the USDA disburses annually for research is an inviting target for non-LGUs that are seeking increased research funding. The MNCs also feel that their funding would be better leveraged if USDA monies were available to non-LGUs.

The clearest expression of the strategy of opening USDA funds to more competition comes in the report *Science for Agriculture*, issued after a two-day conference held at the Winrock International Conference Center in 1982. The conference sponsors were the Rockefeller Foundation and the White House Office of Science and Technology Policy. The fifteen participants included representatives from industry, the LGUs, the USDA, the Rockefeller Foundation, and the OSTP (see table 10.4 for a list of participants and their affiliations).

The Winrock report bluntly indicted the agricultural research system for its parochialism and lack of "cutting-edge" basic science (Rockefeller

Table 10.4. Participants in *Science for Agriculture* Workshop

Dr. Perry Adkisson Deputy Chancellor for Agriculture Texas A & M University System	Dr. Lowell Lewis Director, Agricultural Experiment Stations University of California
Dr. James T. Bonnen Professor of Agricultural Economics Michigan State University	Dr. Judith Lyman Visiting Research Fellow, Agricultural Sciences Division The Rockefeller Foundation
Dr. Winslow R. Biggs Director, Department of Plant Biology Carnegie Institution of Washington	Dr. James Martin President, University of Arkansas
Honorable George E. Brown, Jr. U.S. House of Representatives	Dr. John Marvel General Manager, Research Division Monsanto Agricultural Products Company
Dr. Irwin Feller Director, Institute for Policy Research and Evaluation Pennsylvania State University	Dr. John A. Pino Director of Agricultural Sciences The Rockefeller Foundation
Dr. Ralph Hardy Director, Life Sciences Central Research and Development E. I. Du Pont	Dr. Denis J. Prager Assistant Director, Office of Science and Technology Policy Executive Office of the President

Dr. James B. Kendrick, Jr.
Vice-President, Agriculture & University
  Services
University of California
	Dr. Peter van Schaik
	Associate Area Director, Agricultural
	  Research Service
	U.S. Department of Agriculture

Dr. Terry B. Kinney, Jr. Administrator, Agricultural Research Service U.S. Department of Agriculture	

Foundation 1982:12). The report, acknowledging political reality, recommends that formula funds should not be diminished, but that all future real increases in funding should go to the competitive grants program to be used to fund "basic" research. The competitive grants program is intended to be the cutting edge of a new method of funding agricultural research.

Further, the report urges the USDA and the LGUs to sponsor "workshops, seminars, symposia, etc., designed to bring together experts from all relevant research settings to discuss the state-of-the-art of various basic science areas, identify research needs, and explore collaborative arrangements for meeting those needs" (Rockefeller Foundation 1982:2). The entire thrust of the report is to have the agricultural research system learn from industry and universities outside the system.

Finally, the report makes it very clear that agricultural research should find a new constituency:

Private sector expertise should be fully utilized in efforts by the public sector to identify future research needs, estimate future demand for scientific and technical manpower, and define appropriate, complementary roles and responsibilities for the various sectors and institutions involved in science for agriculture.

Mechanisms should be developed for strengthening the linkages between the findings of basic and applied research performed in the public sector and their development and commercialization by industry.

Public-private sector relationships should be actively promoted by including industry scientists in symposia, consultants, and research review teams, and by seeking the contributions of such professional scientific associations and organizations as the Industrial Research Institute (Rockefeller Foundation 1982:26).

The only mention of farmers and consumers in the report alleges them to be the groups diverting the USDA's attention from "basic" research to political concerns.

The Winrock report can be viewed as the opening salvo in a campaign to accomplish two objectives: the first is an attempt to restructure the agricultural research system into a few "peaks" or "centers of excellence" more amenable to direction from the national level (Kenney and Kloppenburg 1983). This process is similar to the effort pioneered by Flexner (1910) and the Rockefeller Foundation with reference to the medical schools (Kohler 1976; Yoxen 1981). The second objective is to allow non-LGUs to compete with LGUs for the USDA research monies, which would weed out the weaker LGUs and experiment stations. The smaller institutions would be left to survive on state monies and whatever other income they could generate.

The obvious, "ideal" model that many of the conferees had in mind was that of NIH (Hardy 1982). The NIH funding structure allows the top ten institutions, 0.8 percent of all those funded, to receive 19.8 percent of the total NIH grants (NIH 1981). The desire to reproduce the NIH model in agriculture is understandable—it is hoped that commercial successes similar to those of biotechnology can be attained in agriculture. Obviously, corporate representatives are pushing in this direction.

The media reaction to the Winrock report was immediate and overwhelming. Though the report itself makes no mention of creating a National Institutes of Agriculture, the *New York Times* (1982:A30) in an editorial called explicitly for such a change. Similarly, *Science* weighed in with editorials applauding the report and especially defending the USDA competitive grants program (E. Marshall 1982:33; Walsh 1982; Norman 1982:1227). Similar laudatory articles appeared in *Chemical and Engineering News* (Lepkowski 1982), *Chemical and Engineering News*

(1982b:23), and *Chronicle of Higher Education* (McDonald 1983a). The immediate assumption appeared to be that change was at hand. Yet within the agricultural research system reaction to the report was generally negative. Obviously, the smaller, weaker institutions were vehemently opposed to its recommendations. And, in fact, the presence of representatives from the agricultural research system at Winrock had prevented the report's recommendations from being even more harsh. Further, even for the large LGUs—with the possible exception of the UC system, Wisconsin, and Cornell—the prospect of competing for funds with Harvard, MIT, and Stanford for research funds was daunting. Moreover, the funding mechanism for agriculture is political, and the smaller states have no intention of sacrificing their research facilities for what certain groups claim is the good of the country. Even these attacks have not caused the agricultural research system to change radically or speedily.

The new biotechnology offers a technical wedge and an inducement to transform the agricultural research funding system. But the agricultural research system can also import the techniques of biotechnology to do applied research for the public. Certain sectors and groups in the LGUs will resist any change, but other applied scientists could use biotechnological techniques to develop, for example, more efficient conservation-oriented agricultural techniques (Pfund 1983; Buttel and Youngberg 1982).

The Land Grant Universities and Biotechnology

Even if there has been little change at the national funding level, the LGUs are investigating ways of increasing their income from industrial sources. LGU administrators and faculty have seen the gold rush in the private universities and, spurred by the public funding crunch, have decided to secure a piece of the action. The LGUs have also developed some unique university–industry arrangements: the Allied–UCD arrangement, the Cornell Biotechnology Institute, and WARF's arrangements with Cetus Madison, Agrigenetics, and AGS, to name the most important (see chapter 3). Cornell's Biotechnology Institute, WARF's arrangements, and MSU's Neogen were purported to be uniquely designed to keep industry at arm's length. Yet some questions remain regarding the ethics of entirely publicly supported institutions entering into arrangements with profit-oriented entities.

In general, the LGUs as a group have not formulated a separate or explicit policy for dealing with the impacts of biotechnology on their institutions, and perhaps, given the wide diversity in the LGUs, no single policy is possible or desirable. The National Association of State Universities and Land-Grant Colleges (1982) issued a report that provided little concrete guidance, possibly because it was doubtful that any guidance would have been accepted. The LGUs are in the process of redefining their mission and searching for their constituency. The new chemical and pharmaceutical heavyweights centralizing the agricultural inputs industry are replacing former clients and demanding different services. For example, the MNCs that are buying seed companies want the LGUs to abandon traditional seed breeding and newly bred seed variety release and move to areas of basic research (Kloppenburg and Kenney 1984). Constituencies such as farmers and small independent seed companies rely on LGUs to perform relatively applied tasks; large integrated MNCs feel that they can accomplish these tasks profitably and would rather rid themselves of non-profit competitors.

The LGU system is being pressured to transform itself and simultaneously is being raided for its "hot" plant biologists. Pressure is also being applied for these universities to form multidisciplinary research teams to tackle problems—teams quite obviously parallel to corporate research teams. These university research teams will be more able to provide the type of research the corporate teams need. The LGU research agenda is currently in flux, and its ultimate shape is still uncertain.

> The trend [manifested in the attendance at a recent plant genetic engineering conference held at UCD] towards involvement of primarily non-agricultural industrial companies in plant breeding and related "biotechnology" (including, ultimately, genetic engineering) is clear enough in the USA, but less obvious elsewhere *(N. Simmonds, professor at Edinburgh School of Agriculture, 1983:69).*

> The major benefits from improving cereal grains are likely to be economic (production of cheaper animal protein in developed countries) rather than idealistic (feeding the malnourished populations of developing countries). Nevertheless, cheaper or more efficient animal protein production is a worthwhile aim as people in many societies would like to eat more meat but are constrained by economic factors *(Bright and Shewry 1983:84).*

Even at this very early date in the application of biotechnology to agriculture it is becoming clear that agriculture may provide the largest market for new or less expensive biotechnologically manufactured products. And, in fact, many of biotechnology's first products will have impacts on agriculture—for example, Lilly's microbially produced insulin displaces bovine and porcine insulin, a slaughterhouse by-product. Even at this premature stage, there is no doubt that agriculture as we know it will be greatly changed in the next thirty years.

The chemical and pharmaceutical industries that already had important positions in agricultural inputs are consolidating these positions by purchasing other input producers (with the exception of farm machinery) such as seed, bioinsecticide, and innoculant companies. At the farm output purchasing end, large food processors are examining biotechnology as a technique that can create new, lucrative markets and provide future profits. The ever-increasing importance of large MNCs in agriculture and in producing inputs for the agricultural system will inevitably affect the other social institutions of agriculture.

In the last three years the role of the LGUs and of the entire agricultural research system has become an issue of intense debate. The debate is expressed not in terms of whose interests will be served but rather in dichotomies such as "basic" versus "applied" or "politically" based funding versus "scientifically" based funding. The MNCs want the LGUs to increase "basic," "scientifically based" research, that is, the type of research that does not produce marketable commodities. The MNCs feel that they have the financial muscle to breed new plants and want to end competition from the public sector.

Other new and increasingly important players in the agricultural research arena are universities such as Harvard, MIT, Washington University, and Stanford that traditionally have regarded agriculture and plant biology as peripheral and even "backward." These private universities have begun to see the "intellectual" value of this area. A concerted attempt is under way to open USDA research funding to these new entrants—most of whom regard their constituency as national, not merely regional. Biotechnology and its potentialities are being used as the lever to create new constituencies for the LGUs and to ensure that biotechnology's technical possibilities are actualized in a manner suitable for commercialization by MNCs.

Farmers, a vital group in our food and fiber system, have been largely ignored in this discussion because the debate about the research system has treated them as mere consumers of technical innovation. And, in fact, farmers have—with the exception of Boswell Farms, the giant California cotton grower, and perhaps companies such as Bud Antle—been unable to afford the investments in research needed to secure the benefits of biotechnology for themselves. Because of its current applied emphasis, the public research system, which observers have charged is preparing the conditions for capitalism in agriculture (Lewontin 1982; Perelman 1977), may now in part be a barrier to that further penetration. The system has therefore come under severe attack. What the ultimate effects of biotechnology will be on the farmer is a question that remains unasked, much less answered.

One obvious conclusion is that the large farmers will continue to grow at the expense of their smaller neighbors. The larger farm will be able to adopt biotechnology more rapidly and reap the benefits of early adoption. The transformation of the agricultural production process will be gradual but nonetheless revolutionary. In fact, the various biotechnologies will probably compete with each other, thereby quickening the pace of change. For example, one technique allows production of a single cell protein (for animal consumption) from hydrocarbon feedstocks; protoplast fusion may allow breeding of more productive soybeans (the meal is a protein supplement for animals); genetic engineering may create microbes that more efficiently fix nitrogen, thus cheapening production; and through biotechnology less expensive herbicides may be developed, thereby lessening production costs.

I have presented an overview delineating the unique aspects of biotechnology's application to agriculture. Although the transformative process is already under way, it is neither inevitable nor entirely directed. The purposes and social consequences of biotechnology are presently quite open to public input. The shaping of the research agenda in the LGUs need not be determined by the MNCs alone. Research is not a free good—it costs money. And as with any human activity, the person who controls the purse strings has the power to set the agenda. As the Rockefeller Foundation proved many years ago, research agendas and entire disciplines can serve the purposes of different social groups, and there is no reason to believe that this is untrue in agriculture.

Epilogue.

Thoughts on an

Industry's Birth

he birth of the biotechnology industry is a salient example of the dynamism of the capitalist system—in less than eight years a thriving, highly competitive industry has been created. Companies as large as Du Pont, with over 100,000 employees, and as small as Gametrics, with one employee (Pramik 1983b), are seeking a niche in biotechnology. The rapidity of corporate growth is illustrated by Genentech, a two-person partnership in 1976 that by the end of 1985 had grown to over 600 employees (Genentech 1982:8). The tremendous pressures for commercialization are speeding the research and development process, as companies can ill afford to lag behind competitors. In this competition new processes and products are constantly being invented and then quickly routinized as newer, more efficient techniques are developed.

Whether biotechnology will prove to be as important as its proponents claim cannot be answered. But, with its ability to affect so many facets of the natural world, biotechnology could become one of the locomotive technologies that will pull the global economy from its present doldrums. Biotechnology has been the cutting edge of new institutional arrangements that are evolving to facilitate the flow of information from the university to industry. These types of arrangements are already spreading from biology to other departments. If the next upswing in the world economy is to be based on information, then building new channels of information flow is crucial. But even given that information flow must be enhanced, it is not certain that the new channels being created in U.S. society are "functional." The new arrangements between university and industry may possibly undermine the university research process and only marginally speed the transfer process. Moreover, the pervasive secrecy of the industry, characterized by a lack of cooperative arrangements between companies, will further inhibit information flow.

Regardless of whether biotechnology ultimately survives as an industry as opposed to being merely a new tool in traditional industries, it is undeniable that in the United States at the present moment it is a distinct industry with its own peculiar problems. It is as yet unsettled whether the giant chemical and pharmaceutical companies will be able to absorb the startups, or whether a biotechnology industry separate from chemicals and pharmaceuticals will be created. The answer to this question will probably depend on the speed and success the startups have in marketing their products. Biotechnology companies may be successful in establishing themselves in the pharmaceutical industry but unable to survive in agricultural chemicals. In chapter 7 I described the excitement and intense speed of this building process. It is fascinating that in the United States this industrial creation occurred in the middle of the deepest depression since the 1930s and with no planning or even directional assistance from the state.

In this history of biotechnology, I have traced the transformation of an academic science into a technology and of scientists into a work force. The basic science of biology at a certain historical moment had matured sufficiently to be transferred from the university and transformed into a force of production. The large university–corporation contracts were a response by university administrators and corporate executives to the loss of their scientists and their information to small biotechnology companies. University administrators felt that much of the knowledge created at the university was being smuggled out and desired to retain a share of the value of these inventions. Corporate executives perceived biotechnology's potential for creating a new industry that would directly compete with their existing processes, and therefore they needed to recruit a labor force for their research efforts. One solution for business has been to purchase access to these scientists in the university—the long-term university–corporate contract constituting the means to this end.

The small startups have had an important advantage because of their ability to provide their key employees with a share in a company that is subject to rapid capital appreciation. Also, the research environment is structured to be similar to that of a university, thus stimulating, it is hoped, the productivity of this academic work force. The desire is that researcher creativity remain high. The startups have also been able to attract top-flight corporate managers. Again, stock equity provides a major incentive. Also, the challenge and excitement of operating a small "high-tech" company is an important inducement to these young corporate vice-presidents and project managers.

The outcome of the struggle between the startups and the MNCs is by no means settled. The valuable patents, access to better personnel, and innovative management of the startups are pitted against the financial power and marketing power that provide the MNCs with tremendous endurance. Additionally, the MNCs can purchase entire startups outright. However, such buyouts have drawbacks because the most important corporate asset of the startups is their labor power, highly qualified scientists who may resign and thereby devalue the investment. Scientific labor is so critical because the point of greatest value added is the research and development stage. For example, the profit comes not from the production of monoclonal antibodies, but from the ownership of a particular monoclonal antibody. The biotechnology industry is not sufficiently routinized to allow the application of financial muscle to pragmatic, plannable goals to be entirely successful. In this period of flux, speed in developing (and patenting) the newest technique could prove to be a key to successfully outflanking the slower MNCs. As the industry stabilizes, the advantage should shift back to the MNCs if they become more capable of performing innovative research.

The State

The state, largely in the form of the federal government, has had an important background role in providing the environment in which the biotechnology industry could be created. Numerous state interventions made the formation of the biotechnology industry possible. Federal government funding of NIH and NSF research built the basic scientific knowledge from which commercial biotechnology developed. The entire history of molecular biology is that of federal funding of "basic" research that was meant to create the technical base necessary to understand and cure diseases. The campaigns undertaken by NIH to find cures for diseases such as cancer have also turned out to be projects that prepared commodities to the point at which they were ready for commercialization by industry. Upon these techniques and commodities the biotechnology startups were founded.

No corporation or group of corporations could have undertaken the research effort necessary to provide the knowledge base to create an industry. The uncertainty of payoff and long investment lead times were prohibitive. The importance that startups attach to "basic" research is evidenced by the testimony of startup presidents at Senate hearings in 1980 (Farley 1980; Turner, 1980). Federal government funding under the rubric of improving the health of Americans has resulted in the opening of tremendous new possibilities for industry, and for many companies it continues to provide the knowledge so necessary to continuing their in-house research.

The role of the state in regulating corporate activities is well known. The charter of the NIH Recombinant DNA Advisory Committee (RAC) provided for minimal control and no direct monitoring of corporate use. Industry has been delighted with this federal quasi-regulatory committee that provides an aura of regulation while undertaking no enforcement activities (Miller and Amatniek 1984). Nonetheless, the RAC is a focal point for public protests and can thereby be used to increase public concern. The genetic engineering regulatory activities of the federal government continue to provide a vehicle for raising public awareness of increasing corporate activities in biotechnology. Dedicated activists can use these agencies to conduct a "guerilla campaign" against what they see as abuses of biotechnology. Guerilla warfare has already been successful against such technologies as nuclear power. However, biotechnology, in contrast to nuclear technology, is diffuse, with a great variety of projects occurring simultaneously around the world. Therefore, regulation of the growing, changing biotechnology industry is very difficult. No nation dares to put its national economic interests at a comparative disadvantage, and thus instead of imposing stringent and uniform regulations each country vies to ease its regulations slightly more than other countries hoping to secure an advantage.

Another crucial role for the state is that of validating new areas of the natural world as private property. The patent system makes certain production knowledge and combinations of matter ownable. The state's authority is the ultimate guarantor that these monopoly positions will not be infringed. In this role the state affirms an individual's ownership of man-made combinations of the natural world. The significance of the *Diamond vs. Chakrabarty* decision was that it permitted the patenting of a living organism *sui generis*, that is, it need not be part of a process.

The importance of the U.S. federal government in the creation and nurturing of the biotechnology industry cannot be underestimated. Two major themes seem worthy of detailed consideration. The first is the role of patents in creating an industry. Is patentability a type of signal to industry or an expression of the ripeness of a particular aspect of the natural world for ownership? The second concerns the process by which regulations are developed, that is, the manner in which various interest groups interact when confronted with an open-ended, unanswerable situation. For example, why did the scientists win the struggle over rDNA regulation? The answer to these questions could be used to illuminate important aspects of political theory. Clearly the state has had a pervasive presence in many aspects of the process of creating biotechnology, and this in turn will affect the social arrangements that currently exist. The role of the federal government in the biotechnology area, from regulation to research funding, provides an excellent opportunity to examine the role of the state in assisting industrial growth.

The International Context

I have limited my discussion to the particular and peculiar characteristics of biotechnology in the United States. I believe such confinement to be justified on the basis of practicality and the global preeminence of U.S. industry. However, the nature of the international competition for world markets can be seen, for example, in the bitter struggle to commercialize microbially produced human insulin between Lilly (United States), Novo (Denmark), and Hoechst (West Germany). It is probably unreasonable to discuss the efforts by MNCs to commercialize biotechnology solely in national terms. For example, whether Denmark is an important country in biotechnology will have little effect on the success of Novo Industries, which is an internationally important biotechnology company. Similarly, Switzerland is not an important research leader; but Hoffmann-La Roche, Sandoz, and Ciba-Geigy make Switzerland's industry as important as that of France. Nevertheless, the emphasis of this study on the U.S. biotechnology industry to the exclusion of foreign companies was necessary to provide a boundary within which to examine the evolution of the U.S. industry.

If there are leading nations, they are clearly the United States and Japan. Japanese firms, though trailing U.S. corporations, are determined to become world factors in biotechnology (M. Tanaka 1983). The Japanese companies—like other MNCs, domestic and foreign—have provided significant sums of capital to certain U.S. startups for production of organisms and technology transfer. Very clearly this transfer process is speeding the Japanese drive to become a world class competitor in biotechnology. Increasingly, observers are contrasting the American model of commercializing new technologies with that of the Japanese (Office of Technology Assessment 1984). The U.S. lead, based upon the lavish government research expenditures and large numbers of researchers, is being whittled away by the better organized Japanese effort (*Journal of Commerce* 1983b:4C; Katzenstein and Tanaka 1984). In contrast to the U.S. biotechnology industry, which is characterized by extremely chaotic competition replete with tremendous redundancy, the Japanese enterprise is more highly structured and consequently less redundant.

The actions of the Japanese government have been vital in building the industrial infrastructure that is so necessary to sustain an industry (Garner 1983; S. Tanaka 1984). Even with governmental organizing of companies and assistance in the development of a technical base, the Japanese effort boasts an intense competition between the various corporate groups. In reaching their goal, which is to match and surpass the American effort as biotechnology becomes routinized, the Japanese feel that their advantages will become more telling as scale-up and process efficiency become important for profitability (Samejima 1984).

The other developed nations do not have the large, mutually reinforcing integrated biotechnology industrial structure so necessary for capitalizing on biotechnology. A truly unified Europe could produce such a structure, but it seems more likely that the European industry will be based on individual companies and countries rather than on integration. Companies such as Ciba-Geigy, Hoffmann-La Roche, and Sandoz of Switzerland; BASF, Bayer, and Hoechst of Germany; Akzo, Gist-Brocades, Shell, and Unilever of the Netherlands; Kabi and Pharmacia of Sweden; Novo of Denmark; and Burroughs-Wellcome and Imperial Chemical Industries of the United Kingdom are certain to become important international competitors, but their respective nations will probably not be able to organize significant national efforts rivaling those of Japan and the United States. This is true even though some European countries have important molecular biology research establishments, such as Cambridge University, the Max Planck Gesellschaft, and the Institut Pasteur.

Another international aspect is the potential that biotechnology has for changing the relative status of the less developed countries. Increasing numbers of biotechnology companies are interested in using biotechnology to produce seeds and other inputs for Third World agriculture. However, despite the tremendous liberating potential of biotechnology, the ultimate result of biotechnology's usage in less developed countries (LDCs) may be greater dependence (Kenney 1983; Buttel et al. 1985; Kenney et al. 1983). The LDCs could increasingly fall behind in the furious technological race and thus receive biotechnology's benefits only as consumers of developed country imports.

The ultimate contest in biotechnology will be between the United States and Japan to see which system can diffuse innovation more quickly. The United States still has an early lead and the most advanced biotechnology companies because of the entrepreneurial process described in the previous chapters. But the test will come as the "sprint-to-market" mentality is replaced and the "marathon" nature of the competition is understood. This marathon aspect is where the Japanese and the MNCs will have an advantage over the startups (Kenney 1985). The result of the competition to commercialize biotechnology could be an important factor in deciding the relative economic positions of the United States, Japan, and Europe in 1990 and beyond.

In the short time since rDNA was commercialized, a number of other aspects of biomedical research have been privatized. The most important newly commercialized areas include monoclonal antibodies, gene probes, and immunology, and other areas such as neurobiology may be only a few years away from privatization (Siekevitz 1984). In a society that allocates its products by the market, privatization is the "natural" manner of distributing products.

The biomedical funding system created an entire research structure based on grantsmanship and the building of research empires. The most successful researchers have built empires with annual revenues in excess of $1 million. For the empire to keep functioning, products in the form of journal articles and prizes awarded are crucial (Latour and Woolgar 1982). In this bitter competition, research monies from any source are welcome because they could provide the competitive edge. The constant need for new machines and more labor is clear; one is required to have gene sequencers, improved high-pressure liquid or gas chromatographs, nuclear magnetic resonators, and mass spectrometers, for example, if the competition has them. The entrepreneurial system and its reward structure ensure that only the most competitive survive, and these survivors are the very scientists who are critical assets for biotechnology startups.

It seems paradoxical to condemn individuals for profiting from their inventions when corporations will gladly appropriate these inventions to secure a profit. A professor who chooses not to commercialize his discovery will see someone else capture the benefit from it. The case of Mark Ptashne is instructive; Harvard University was willing to sell him, his inventions, and its name. Under such conditions it hardly seems strange that Ptashne would decide to secure a more favorable financial position for himself. The professors who join companies have made rational choices, given the alternatives presented. Moralizing about their activities is hypocritical, since any group of individuals presented with the concrete historical choices that faced these university scientists would have made similar decisions. Professors are also creatures of their social milieu. However, taking an understanding view is not to excuse the more egregious exploitation of students, the betrayal of the public trust, and even the theft that have occurred in the creation of this industry. Yet has any industry come into existence unsoiled by chicanery and outright crime?

The activities of university administrators in sanctioning the rental of a university laboratory, along with the students and the researchers therein, may constitute a more serious danger to the university. Many laboratories, formerly institutions producing knowledge of use to all in society—consumers, workers, farmers, and business people—have become captives of a single corporation. The result is that the freely usable knowledge base is shrunk, and this could lead to a lack of information for those unable to purchase it. The frenzied courting of industry by university administrators and faculty willing to sell nearly anything seems particularly inappropriate, since these same administrators are charged with the responsibility of acting for the good of the greater university community, and the university has a self-proclaimed obligation to serve the greater good of society.

The point is not only that the knowledge being sold was paid for by the public but, even more important, that the university, a peculiar and fragile social institution that can trace its history back to early feudalism, is being subsumed by industry, one of the very institutions with which it should, to some degree, be in conflict. When university and industry become partners, the entire society is endangered, for the demise of the university as an independent institution will lead to the crippling of the tradition of an independent university.

The rush to employ biology in production has caused strains in traditional social relations. I have documented the social process of transforming scientific knowledge into technology, a process that has included the transformation of old institutions and the creation of new ones. The speed of this process has been stunning. And the development of biotechnology as a productive force continues unabated; far greater changes than those already under way should be expected.

The answers to the questions that I have raised will not be easy. To be fully serious the debate must ask the question of what can and cannot be privatized and done for profit. Industry cannot answer this question—the managers have a duty to maximize profit; if they fail they will be replaced by the company's stockholders. Government and the universities have an obligation to debate these issues. This requirement for unbiased debate raises the question of whether the universities and their professors are capable of carrying on this debate. I have documented here the increased subservience of the university to industry. In most cases, university professors and administrators would rather opt for silence—Socrates would have interrupted the multimillion dollar plans for the new biotechnology institute.

Perhaps the cruelest irony will be experienced by U.S. industry itself. As the university is bought and parceled out, basic science in the university will increasingly suffer. The speculative, noncommercial scholar will be at a disadvantage, and the intellectual commons so important for producing a trained labor force and the birthplace for new ideas will be eroded and polluted. Industry will then discover that by being congenitally unable to control itself and having no restraints placed on it by the public sector it has polluted its own reservoir.

Finally, a more comprehensive issue looms. The entire manner in which man conceptualizes interaction with the natural world will change as we begin to create new life forms—making "natural" selection a planned rather than random process. Our world will be filled with genetically engineered organisms: if DNA is a "program" then these are "living robots." Ultimately, we will need institutions to deal with the fact that we can engineer ourselves. As an aspect of preparing for the scientific and technological impact of biotechnology in our world, questions must be answered as to which institutions will have control over these techniques. Is private ownership and sale for profit necessarily the best system to control activities that will lead to human genetic engineering? Should the immense power of transforming and changing life forms be transferred to groups merely seeking a return on investment? What are the "correct" moral and ethical positions regarding biological breakthroughs?

The fact that U.S. society has not debated the difficult social, economic, and ethical issues that confront the human race because of the advances in the biological sciences is surprising, given our traditions. This book is an effort to provide the factual underpinnings of this debate. In other words, when the ethical questions of genetic engineering and biotechnology are discussed, we must remember that we are also discussing social and economic relationships. Finally, biotechnology is *our* technology: all of us have contributed to its genesis and we must therefore have a say in its development and use.

Appendix 1.

Biotechnology

Briefly Explained

DNA

DNA is a very long molecule consisting of nucleotides (made up of one sugar, one phosphate, and a nitrogenous base molecule) connected in a spiral-shaped stack of double helices. A simple bacterium typically has three or four thousand genes per cell, while higher organisms such as man can have three or four million genes per cell, with each gene being about 1,500 base pairs in length (Jackson 1979:43). The actual genetic information is contained in the sequences of the base pairs: thymine (T), which links only to adenine (A), and guanine (G), which links only to cytosine (C). So, for example, a sequence of one strand of DNA could read A-T-G-C-C. The DNA is able to reproduce because the DNA is a double chain of nitrogenous bases and the strand A-T-G-C-C is matched by the strand T-A-C-G-G. But DNA does more than merely reproduce. DNA also contains the code for the production of the cell's proteins and enzymes (for further discussion see Watson 1970; OTA 1981). This code is transcribed to RNA, which actually codes for the necessary amino acids to build proteins (for further discussion see Watson 1970; Watson and Tooze 1981; Sylvester and Klotz 1983).

Single-Cell Organisms

The most studied microorganisms have been single-cell bacteria such as *E. coli* and *B. subtilis*, molds, yeasts, and actinomycetes (Demain and Solomon 1981:69). Research is farthest advanced in the single-cell organisms. Because single-cell organisms reproduce very rapidly, selective breeding of mutations is rapid and results of experiments are correspondingly quickly available. Microorganisms have only one chromosome, thus eliminating the need to understand the interaction effects that occur in higher organisms having more than one chromosome, such as plants and animals. Also, the DNA of higher organisms contains noncoding sequences which complicate research and their use in production (Hopwood 1981:94). Microorganisms are simpler to work with.

The biotechnologies have not focused on procaryotes (single-celled organisms) to the exclusion of the eucaryotes (multicelled organisms). An industrially important discovery was the ability to transfer eucaryotic genes coding for products such as somatostatin, insulin, and human growth hormone to procaryotes, which would then produce (express) the proteins (Cohen et al. 1973; Itakura et al. 1977; Goeddel et al. 1979b; Goeddel et al. 1979a). The discovery that this was feasible is the basis of the Cohen–Boyer patent. For example, the gene coding for human insulin has been spliced into bacteria and yeasts, providing a nearly unlimited source of insulin. The ability to induce procaryotes to produce eucaryotic substances creates the possibility of manufacturing many new products.

Tissue Culture and Cell Fusion

Tissue cultures were first developed in the late 1890s by biologists, and these techniques were gradually improved throughout the twentieth century. Tissue cultures of living material allow the propagation of mammalian and plant cells in vitro—a very useful property in scientific and industrial processes. In a tissue culture, eucaryotic cells continue functioning in a nutrient medium as independent, reproducing living organisms. Thus, very specialized animal or plant cells can be produced in enormous quantities. With improvements in tissue culture technology scientists have even learned how to propagate complete plants from a single plant cell (Evans et al. 1983).

Much of the biotechnological research using higher organisms is related to reproduction. For example, in the plant seed industry protoplast fusion, a technique that combines two cells into one, provides the important potentials for transferring desirable traits across natural boundaries. Protoplast fusion allows much greater exchanges of genetic information than could previously be achieved through plant breeding. The result is that improved plant varieties have been created. Tissue culture and cloning techniques then make it possible to rapidly grow these improved plants in vitro, thereby truncating the period necessary to breed new seeds.

Similarly, animal cells can be tissue cultured to produce desired biological materials. These tissue culture techniques are especially important in the production of MABs. This area of research is being avidly pursued because mass production is the last, but most vital step to the market.

Monoclonal Antibodies

MABs were discovered by Cesar Milstein and Georges Köhler in 1975, and this invention is already producing commercial products. The MABs producing cell, or hybridoma, is the product of the fusion of a cancer cell, a myeloma, and a cell that produces a desired antibody. In a successful fusion the hybridoma receives from the cancer cell the ability to reproduce rapidly and the other cell provides the antibody production capacity. These antibodies are commercially interesting because they react to only specific antigens; thus the antibodies can be targeted. This specifically allows the MAB to make its identification at very low concentrations, so the first use of MABs has been as diagnostics.

It has been speculated that the MABs' extraordinary specificity may allow them to be used as "guided missiles" to attack malignant cells by delivering a toxin to them. Although the efficacy of MABs for drug delivery is still uncertain, MAB-based diagnostic kits for pregnancy, sexual diseases, and hepatitis are already being successfully marketed (Genetic Systems 1982; Monoclonal Antibodies 1982). MABs will certainly become a major tool in the diagnostic market, where ease of use and extraordinary specificity offer unique advantages over the current expensive chemical-based detection techniques.

Fermentation

The technical definition of fermentation is, in its broadest sense, "the chemical transformation of organic compounds with the aid of enzyme(s)" (Demain and Solomon 1981:67). Fermentation is a process by which most of the organisms created in laboratories will actually be put to use. The commercial products of fermentation "fall into four major categories: (1) the microbial cells themselves; (2) the large molecules, such as enzymes, that they synthesize; (3) primary metabolic products (compounds essential to cellular growth); and (4) secondary metabolic products (compounds not required for cellular growth)" (Demain and Solomon 1981:70).

Cells may eventually become commercially valuable as a source of protein. For example, Imperial Chemical Industries (ICI), an English corporation, was uneconomically producing single-cell protein (SCP) as an animal feed (Yanchinski 1981:1). The Soviet Union is also producing SCP on an industrial scale (Rose 1981:138). Another use of whole cells is to convert simple energy-rich feedstocks into more sophisticated organic chemicals. Future technological advances and the discovery of more efficient bacteria may make it possible to substitute substrates such as cellulose for the methanol presently used in ICI's SCP process. The engineering of bacteria that are able to digest less expensive waste substrates could make SCP competitive with soybeans and other products.

More lucrative products of fermentation are large molecules such as enzymes, hormones, and biological factors. Enzymes, which control the rate of metabolic process in an organism, may provide lucrative markets. Prior to the recent upsurge of interest in genetic engineering, the most important area of biotechnology was immobilized cell and enzyme technologies. Immobilization of enzymes or the cell reduced the cost incurred by losing valuable enzymes in batch processing and facilitated the conversion of industrial processing to a continuous basis. The high fructose corn syrup industry is predicated upon enzyme immobilization techniques that conserve expensive enzymes (Casey 1976). A number of enzymes can be used in a kind of assembly line where the raw material is worked up by a series of biochemical processes.

Primary metabolites are molecules that are important for the growth of cells. The most important molecules in the fermentation industry are amino acids, purine nucleotides, vitamins, and organic acids (Demain and Solomon 1981:72). Commercial production of primary metabolites necessitates the creation or breeding of organisms producing metabolites in quantities greater than is necessary for the microorganisms' reproduction. In the past, overproduction traditionally has been induced by the use of mutation breeding programs. The new genetic engineering techniques make it possible to engineer the changes rather than depend upon fortuitous circumstances such as mutation.

The last group of products, the secondary metabolites, are the most varied and interesting. These cell products are termed secondary metabolites because they are not absolutely vital to cell growth and usually occur in small quantities or are produced in highly specialized cells or are produced only during particular phases of cell growth. The secondary metabolites, which can include antibiotics, pigments, fragrances, and flavors, provide very specialized compounds uniquely suited to a particular task. Formerly these products were painstakingly extracted from raw materials, but biotechnology offers opportunities to produce them much more cheaply and efficiently.

Appendix 2.

Biotechnology

and Patents

This is a patent-intensive industry right now. . . . A patent is an umbrella under which a small company can grow up *(Thomas Kiley, Genentech vice-president for legal affairs, quoted in T. Lewin 1982:3).*

The basic objective of the patent system is to induce inventors who have created a useful item to make it public. Individuals hold the patents, but in most commercially valuable patents the rights are assigned to companies, and companies hold the bulk of useful patent rights. In exchange for disclosure the law provides the patentee seventeen years' exclusive use of the invention. The societal objective is to ensure that the information in the patent application is made public to allow others to improve upon the invention. The lack of a patent system in a capitalist economy could conceivably result in every production process being cloaked in trade secrecy. In fact, many processes are not patented because of a corporate decision that trade secrecy is preferable to patenting.

The key section of the U.S. code with regard to patenting is the following sentence: "Whoever invents or discovers any new and useful process, machinery, manufacture, or composition of matter, or any new and useful improvement thereof, may obtain a patent therefor, subject to the conditions and requirements of this title" (Section 101 of Title 35 of the U.S. Code, quoted in Biggart 1981:113n). Anything for which a person is seeking a patent must fall under one or more of these categories, and the item must be reducible to practice, that is, it must work. The patent must also be enabling, that is, any knowledgeable practitioner in that field of endeavor must be able to reproduce the invention from the patent description (Ditzel 1982).

There are two important classes of chemical and biological patents—product patents and process patents. Product patents protect a new product—for example, a chemical, microorganism, machine. A process patent is used to protect a new method of producing or using a known chemical product or product of nature. Human insulin, for example, cannot be patented, but the genetically engineered bacteria and the process for producing insulin can be protected (Beton 1982). The ideal patent position is to secure both product and process patents and to do each as broadly as possible. A product patent is usually more valuable than a process patent because most products can be manufactured by various processes, that is, someone can design around a process patent, whereas a patented product cannot be reproduced. The knowledge in the patent has the same property status as real estate or any other private property. The greater the amount of the natural world or, more specifically, combinations of natural things that can be claimed, the larger the number of possible products that are protected.

In addition to patent law, laws have been passed allowing the patenting of plant varieties (1970 Plant Variety Protection Act). In this appendix I will discuss plant variety protection along with general patenting, though plants were the first living organisms to be provided explicit patentlike protection. In agricultural biotechnology, plant variety protection may be used in conjunction with a process patent to protect novel plants. Little analysis of how to maximize protection for plant biotechnology has yet become available publicly. However, Agrigenetics has already been granted a process patent on a hybridization technique that is crucial for breeding new plant varieties (Elman 1982). Agricultural genetic engineering will use both patents and plant variety protection.

The *Diamond vs. Chakrabarty* decision to allow the patenting of microorganisms was decided on the basis of Section 101, Title 35, as is any other patent application. Ananda Chakrabarty, then a General Electric scientist, was denied a patent on an organism that metabolized crude oil (and therefore could clean up oil spills) which he had isolated in a pure culture. In denying the application, the patent examiner and the government attorneys argued that Congress had not included living organisms (as products) in patent law because of their essential difference from inanimate objects (Biggart 1981; Dunner 1981; Gershman and Scafetta 1982). General

Electric appealed the Patent Office's decision, thereby leading to the court decision.

The U.S. Court of Customs and Patent Appeal (CCPA) handed down the first reversal of the patent denial. The government then appealed and lost in the Supreme Court. The CCPA defended its decision by referring to the aforementioned Section 101, Title 35, saying,

We look at the facts and see things that do not exist in nature and that are man-made, clearly fitting into the plain terms "manufacture" and "compositions of matter." We look at the statute [patent law] and it appears to include them. We look at legislative history and we are confirmed in that belief. We consider what the patent statutes are intended to accomplish and the constitutional authorization, and it appears to us that protecting these inventions, in the form claimed, by patents will promote progress in very useful arts   (CCPA quoted in Gershman and Scafetta 1982:24).

The criteria of utility, nonobviousness, and novelty required of these "compositions of matter" by the law were met by the new microorganisms. If DNA is mere chemicals, there is no reason for not patenting life forms.

CCPA continued in its opinion: "[There is] no *legally* significant difference between active chemicals which are classified as 'dead' or organisms used for their *chemical* reactions which take place because they are 'alive' " [emphasis in original] (Gershman and Scafetta 1982:22). The gist of the Supreme Court's decision on a 5–4 vote to uphold the CCPA was that the quality of being alive does not prohibit patentability (Dunner 1981:56). *Diamond vs. Chakrabarty* established that society would recognize a person's claim to own a living thing, in this case a microorganism. In a 1985 patent approval full patent rights were extended to plants; whether animals can be patented is at this point untested.

The Supreme Court ruling on the Patent Office's appeal to overturn the CCPA decision that man-made life forms could be patented elicited two responses. Some industrially oriented groups believed it was not extraordinarily significant. Public interest groups, conversely, viewed the decision as fundamental. These different perspectives are best understood by first summarizing the arguments against patenting and then examining the reasons used to oppose patenting.

Sheldon Krimsky (1981) succinctly summarized the major objections to patenting, and the crux of the case is based on extralegal issues. Jonathan King (1981a:40–41) argued that patents should not be granted because of the potential ecological damage that released organisms could cause. In an article entitled "New Disease in New Niches," King (1978) fully articulates the possible dangers of unrestricted release of engineered organisms. This appeal against patenting is essentially an argument that possible dangers and social costs far outweigh any social benefits that may be derived from permitting such organisms to be patented.

The other important argument is that life forms were not intended by Congress to be patentable (with the exception of plants) (Gershman and Scafetta 1982:8). In public debate this has been a very potent argument—especially because many religions see life as sacred and not "ownable" (T. Howard 1979; National Council of the Churches of Christ 1982). These religious concerns had no impact on the court, but political struggles may be important in future decisions regarding the limits of what is patentable.

Among propatent groups such as patent lawyers, industry, and universities there were two schools of thought—one that believed patentability was crucial and another that believed it was less important. Peter Farley, then president of Cetus, testified: "Unquestionably, this [patentability] is a very important issue in that at least one-third and, perhaps, as many as one-half of the developments stemming from this new technology will be enhanced from an industrial point of view if life forms can be patented" (Farley 1980:27). In a 1980 Senate hearing on the industrial application of rDNA, every business representative explicitly underlined the importance of patenting for the growth of the industry. The explicit threat was that the lack of patent protection would result in all biotechnical knowledge being treated as trade secrets (Hardy 1980:33; Dunner 1981:58).

Donald Dunner, a patent lawyer, has argued that "the decision [*Diamond vs. Chakrabarty*] is important but it is not life or death of the industry, and even had it gone the other way, it probably would not have been" (Dunner 1981:56). Without patents the industry would have been based on trade secrecy to an even greater extent than it currently is. Leslie Misrock felt that the legal issue decided was "trivial law" (Zoler 1981:8). Mitchel Zoler (1981:8), a patent lawyer, observed:

> The decision [*Diamond vs. Chakrabarty*] in fact, may be having a profound effect while at the same time being "trivial law," simply because it is perceived by both Patent Office and public as having allowed patenting of microorganisms for the first time. Under this perception, more applications are being made and more are being approved by the Patent Office.

What Zoler is referring to is the sanction that the Supreme Court gave to microorganisms as being an aspect of the natural world that could be privatized. Zoler makes the important observation that the significance of the Supreme Court decision was not in breaking legal ground. Rather, the decision signaled that this new technology was open to economic investment and corresponding ownership.

Diamond vs. Chakrabarty did not solve (or address) a number of very difficult questions that arise when a living, reproducing organism can be owned. Sheldon Krimsky (1981) compiled a list of unanswered problems regarding the operation of microorganism patents:

1. Who owns bacteria that have escaped containment? "Except for the initial manufacture, human intervention plays no role in subsequent replications of the organism" (Krimsky 1981:12). How will these progeny be owned?

2. How much novelty in the organism qualifies it as being patentable? Can minor changes in a natural organism or an already patented organism qualify for a patent? This is especially important because there is so-called useless DNA that does not get expressed.

3. How can the organism, etc., be described exhaustively? What if the organism undergoes change in the depository?

4. Can a product of nature, e.g., interferon, formerly essentially unavailable in commercial quantities be patentable? That is, can a product patent be obtained for a product that occurs in nature?

5. Are multicellular organisms patentable? If so, then genetically engineered animals or even humans could be patentable. What is the line of demarcation?

Each item raised by Krimsky poses profound legal and ethical questions that have not yet been seriously addressed. There will be a tremendous demand for life science lawyers over the next twenty years to shape the law and to restructure the legal system to be compatible with this new area of private property.

The Supreme Court decision established the right to own living organisms, plasmids, and gene sequences. The objections by public interest groups were overruled because the legal aspects of patent law clearly defended product patenting for microorganisms as compositions of matter. There was no *legal* (in the narrow sense) reason to differentiate animate and inanimate products of human manufacture. Biotechnology was recognized as a field of endeavor in which inventions could secure monopoly rewards.

The Fundamental Patents—Cohen–Boyer

The parties with greatest interest in the Supreme Court ruling are the universities—especially Stanford and the University of California, San Francisco—and the scientists who work in them   *(Gurin and Pfund 1980:544).*

Stanford and the University of California share patent applications that claim ownership of the basic process for rDNA. These patent claims issue from the invention by Stanley Cohen of Stanford and Herbert Boyer of UC of a method of using plasmids to insert recombined DNA into a cell. Any entity desiring to sell products using this process must pay a license fee and royalties to Stanford–UC (Goldstein 1982:180–81). The Cohen–Boyer patents are extremely broad and central to genetic engineering. Through the two patents Stanford–UC have proprietary ownership of one of the core techniques in the biotechnology industry.

Stanford decided not to grant an exclusive license to one company, a move that would have created a probably unenforceable monopoly (because any company wanting to get into genetic engineering would be forced to infringe). Instead, Stanford, which is handling the licensing for both schools, has chosen to offer licenses to all interested companies. The important contract stipulations of the Cohen–Boyer patent include:

1. The license is nonexclusive and royalty bearing.

2. The licensee guarantees to follow NIH guidelines.

3. The licensee will pay a license fee of $10,000 per annum, but five times this fee will be deductible from royalties owed on future products— up to 50 percent of any year's royalty payment.

4. Sliding scale royalty fees have been set (for further information, see Stanford University Patent Licensing Agreement 1981).

The conditions for using the Cohen–Boyer patent are reasonable according to normal industry standards (Goldstein 1982:186). The comparatively low price was, in part, a strategy to avoid incurring interferences, that is, legal objections to the patent award. In 1982 Stanford was able to sign licenses with seventy-one companies for a total of $710,000 in the first year (*GEN* 1982a). The patent will provide an enormous cash flow for the two universities, regardless of any policing difficulties. Albert Halluin, formerly a patent lawyer with Exxon Research and chief counsel at Cetus, has estimated the value of the Cohen–Boyer patents, the process claim and the products claim, at between $250 and $750 million (*New Scientist* 1983:923), enough to excite any university administrator.

The Cohen–Boyer process patent was awarded in December 1980, and the product patent (the more valuable) was to be awarded in July 1982, but a number of objections to the patent application were raised at a biotechnology patent conference at Cold Spring Harbor Laboratory, N.Y., so the Patent and Trademark Office withdrew both patents (Halluin 1982; Budiansky 1982a; Goldstein 1982). Halluin's objections to the patent are, quite interestingly, somewhat similar to those that some critics have voiced regarding the commercialization of biology. The first objection concerned the possible disclosure in print of the technique more than a year before the patent was filed in a *New Scientist* article commenting on the 1973 Gordon Conference (Ziff 1973). Information cannot be allowed to flow freely until the patent has been filed. Second, a University of Michigan professor, Robert Helling, claims that his name was unjustifiably omitted from the patent (Dickson 1980a:388). Finally, questions regarding whether the patent was enabling and the fact that no materials were deposited at publicly accessible depositories until much later have been brought forward (Goldstein 1982). The patent was finally issued in 1984, by which time Stanford had already collected nearly $2 million in license fees.

Why is the right to patent life forms so important to universities? The most salient reason is that the university is not constituted as an institution that sells products in the market. If the university cannot patent inventions it would have nothing to sell because the university cannot use its inventions to become a company. The inventions would be a public good. In the case of the Cohen–Boyer patents it is impossible to argue that this invention would not be practiced without an exclusive license or patent. The Cohen–Boyer techniques were being used long before the patent was granted (Goldstein 1982). If there were no patenting, all corporate inventions would remain a trade secret, but even under these conditions companies could profitably use their inventions, while universities could not use them, and, absent patenting, could not sell them.

The role of the federal government in encouraging university patenting deserves special attention. Before 1977 it had been normal for the federal government to hold and license most inventions developed with federal monies. However, the government's success in licensing was limited, even though NIH did permit nonprofit institutions to own patents on NIH-funded research. This privatization of governmentally funded research was formalized by the Government Patent Policy Act of 1980, which permitted nonprofit organizations and small businesses to retain title to inventions and to secure the benefits of commercialization. This important change encouraged universities to become much more aggressive in marketing faculty members' inventions that were created under governmental sponsorship (Office of Technology Assessment 1981:251).

The potential income from patents has led to a deluge of patenting as universities develop in-house patent offices. University patent offices must justify their existence by collecting enough money from patents to cover their expenses. Consequently, increasing numbers of biological research tools such as restriction enzymes, MABs, and plasmids are becoming university property to be sold to the highest bidder or bought in advance by a corporate funder. A "gold rush fever" has gripped universities, each of which hopes it will be the lucky patenter of another Cohen–Boyer type technique. But, of course, a university would now file correctly by keeping the discovery secret, filing globally, and more adequately meeting all the other requirements. The university could then sell the exclusive patent rights to a single company for a large sum or devise other stratagems.

The possibility of large gains has resulted in headlines such as "Yale

Bungles Patent Claim" (Budiansky 1983b). In this particular instance Yale and its licensing agent, Research Corporation, did not recognize the value of a DNA probe invented by a Yale professor, David Ward. Enzo Biochem, a biotechnology startup, did understand the invention's value, after the inventor convinced them of its value, and secured an exclusive license from Yale in return for paying the cost of patenting. Yale's response has been to establish its own patent office in the hopes of not repeating the mistake. The Yale incident indicates the uncertain nature of the biotechnology licensing business. There is a distinct possibility that university patent lawyers will not be as competent as those in private practice. If this is true it can be expected that some of the best patents will still end up in corporate hands with little compensation for the public that provided the research funding.

Ownership of biological products and processes, as we have seen, is playing a key role in the development of biotechnology. Both universities and the small startups hope the patent system will provide financial opportunities. In industry there can be little doubt that without a patent system trade secrecy would become the norm. But, on the other hand, the patentability of biological materials is extending industrial style secrecy to the university.

The *Diamond vs. Chakrabarty* decision has made possible private control over living, mutating organisms. As I have indicated, this poses important challenges to what is recognized as private property. For example, if a company releases its own *E. coli* and it takes up residence and reproduces in someone's stomach, do the bacteria still belong to the company? These and other difficult issues regarding ownership of biological materials will undoubtedly lead to much litigation until satisfactory definitions are developed. Patenting will play an important role (how important remains unclear) in the evolution of the genetic engineering industry.

References

The following abbreviations are used in the references:
CEN   *Chemical and Engineering News*
CW   *Chemical Week*
GEN   *Genetic Engineering News*
JOC   *Journal of Commerce*
NYT   *New York Times*
WSJ   *Wall Street Journal*

Adelman, A. K.
   1982a "Institutions report increasing dependence on foundation funding for genetic research." *GEN* 2 (July/August): 18–19.
   1982b "Biotechnology growth spawns generation of new university technical training programs." *GEN* 2 (November/December): 1, 27.
   1983a "Michigan's genetics center makes recombinant vaccines." *GEN* 3 (March/April): 1, 11.
   1983b "Biotech training at SUNY colleges filling projected demand for Bachelor's technicians." *GEN* 3 (July/August): 11.
Advanced Genetic Sciences, Inc.
   1983 *Prospectus*. Greenwich, Connecticut: Advanced Genetic Sciences, Inc.
Aisenberg, J.
   1982 "So far . . ." *Nature* 297 (24 June): 617.

Alsop, R.
1983   "After a slow start, Du Pont pushes harder for a bigger share of pharmaceutical sales." *WSJ* (16 June): 33, 42.
Amgen, Inc.
1983   *Prospectus*. Thousand Oaks, California: Amgen, Inc.
Amatniek, J. C.
1983   "College biotechnology programs on the rise." *Bio/Technology* 1 (August): 46–47.
Anderson, W.
1983   "Animal health sales outlook bright." *Feedstuffs* (13 June): 8.
Andreopoulos, S.
1980   "Gene cloning by press conference." *New England Journal of Medicine* 302 (27 March): 743–46.
1981   "No microbial monsters." Stanford University Medical Center News Release (30 March).
Ashbrook, T.
1982   "Biogen to help explore biotechnological uses in industry." *Boston Globe* (2 November): 48.
Atkinson, B., and P. Sainter
1982   "Downstream biological process engineering." *Chemical Engineer* (November): 410–19.
Atkinson, S. (Patent Officer, Harvard University)
1982   Personal interview. (15 February).

Baltimore, D.
1982   "Interview with David Baltimore." *SIPIscope* (March/April): 11–18. *SIPIscope* is published by Scientists' Institute for Public Information.
Barker, R. (Director, Division of Biological Sciences, Cornell University)
1982   Letter from Robert Barker to Dean Greison. (7 April).
1983   Personal communication. (19 August).
Barrett, P. M.
1981   "Med school receives $6 million grant." *Harvard Crimson* (30 June): 1, 6.
Benner, S.
1981   "Genentech: Life under the microscope." *Inc.* (May): 62–68.
Berg, P., et al.
1974   "Potential Biohazards of Recombinant DNA Molecules." *Science* 185 (26 July): 303.
Berg, P., D. Baltimore, S. Brenner, R. Roblen, and M. Singer
1975   "Asilomar conference on recombinant DNA molecules." *Science* 188 (6 June): 991.
Berlowitz, L., R. A. Zdanis, J. C. Crowley, and J. C. Vaughn
1981   "Instrumentation needs of research universities." *Science* 211 (6 March): 1013–18.
Bers, J., and A. Warren
1981   "Biotechnology." *Design News* (7 June): 32–34.
Beton, J. L.
1982   "Patents in the chemical industry." *Chemistry and Industry* (24): 988–93.

Biggart, W. A.
1981   "Patentability in the United States of microorganisms, processes utilizing microorganisms, products produced by microorganisms and microorganism mutational genetic modification techniques." *IDEA* 22 (2): 113–36.
BioEngineering News
1983   "Genentech partnership closes—a detailed look." *BioEngineering News* 4 (7 January). Willits, California.
Biotechnica International, Inc.
1983   *Prospectus.* Cambridge, Massachusetts: Biotechnica International, Inc.
Bio/Technology
1983   "W. R. Grace: A slow-moving giant leaps into research." *Bio/Technology* 1 (March): 30–31.
Biotechnology Bulletin Report
1983   "W. R. Grace." *Biotechnology Bulletin Report* 30 (July).
Biotechnology Investments Limited
1983   *Report of the Directors and Accounts for the Year ended 31st May, 1983.* London: N. M. Rothschild Asset Management Limited.
Blodgett, D. (Administrative assistant at Cornell Biotechnology Institute)
1983   Personal communication. (19 August).
Bok, D. (President, Harvard University)
1981   "President's Report: Business and the academy." *Harvard Magazine* (May–June): 23–35.
Boly, W.
1982a   "The gene merchants." *California Magazine* 7 (September): 76–79, 170–76, 179.
1982b   "Strained relations." *California Magazine* 7 (September): 78.
Bonner, J.
1981   "New bridges between academic and commercial organizations." In *Proceedings of the 1981 Battelle International Conference on Genetic Engineering*, Volume 1, pp. 28–30, held in Rosslyn, Virginia. June 6–10, 1981.
Brenner, S.
1974   "New directions in molecular biology." *Nature* 248 (26 April): 785–87.
Bright, S. W. J., and P. R. Shewry
1983   "Improvements of protein quality in cereals." *Critical Reviews in Plant Science* 1 (1): 49–93.
Bronson, G.
1977   "Controlling gene transplants." *WSJ* (11 May): 16.
Brown, A. S.
1982   "Can the gene splicers survive commercial success?" *Chemical Business* (26 July): 9–16.
Brown, E. R.
1979   *Rockefeller Medicine Men.* Berkeley: University of California Press.
Brunings, K. J.
1979   "The role of basic research in development of medicinal products." *Research Management* 22 (4): 19–23.

Buchanan, J. M., and A. P. French
1981a "Letter to MIT faculty regarding the proposed Whitehead Institute." (6 November).
1981b "The Whitehead Institute and MIT." Memorandum circulated to MIT faculty (4 November).
Budiansky, S.
1982a "Key biotechnology patent delayed." *New Scientist* (29 July): 409–10.
1982b "Mass General placates Hoechst." *Nature* 300 (25 November): 383.
1983a "Growing pains for U.S. agriculture." *Technology Review* (January): 19–22.
1983b "Yale bungles patent claim." *Nature* 305 (13 October): 568.
Bulkeley, W. M.
1984 "Biogen's chief, Walter Gilbert, quits top posts." *WSJ* (18 December): 22.
Bull, A. T., G. Holt, and M. D. Lilly
1982 *Biotechnology: International Trends and Perspectives*. Paris: OECD.
Burstein, L. S., and A. W. Adler
1983 "Structuring the private investment agreement for bridge funds." *GEN* 3 (May/June): 18.
Business Week
1980a "The hunt for plays in biotechnology." *Business Week* (28 July): 71.
1980b "Du Pont: Seeking a future in bioscience." *Business Week* (24 November): 86–98.
1982a "Biotechnology is now survival of the fittest." *Business Week* (12 April): 36–37.
1982b "The livestock industry's genetic revolution." *Business Week* (21 June): 124–25, 130, 132.
1982c "A chill grips high-tech venture capital." *Business Week* (23 August): 91–92.
1982d "Business and universities: A new partnership." *Business Week* (20 December): 58–60.
Buttel, F., and I. Youngberg
1982 "Implications of biotechnology for the development of sustainable agricultural systems." Paper presented at the Fourth International Conference on Resource Conserving, Environmentally Sound Agricultural Alternatives. Cambridge, Massachusetts (August).
Buttel, F., M. Kenney, J. Kloppenburg, Jr.
1985 "From Green Revolution to Biorevolution: Some observations on the changing technological bases of economic transformation in the Third World." *Economic Development and Cultural Change* (October).
Butterfield, F.
1982 "2 areas show a path to jobs in technology." *NYT* (8 August): 1, 5.
Bylinsky, G.
1980 "DNA can build companies, too." *Fortune* (16 June): 144–53.

California Biotechnology, Inc.
1983 *Prospectus*. Palo Alto, California: California Biotechnology, Inc.

California Rural Legal Assistance
1981 "Brief submitted to the California Fair Political Practices Commission re: Potential conflicts of interest among University of California academic personnel." *California Rural Legal Assistance* (18 September).

Cambridge BioScience Corporation
1983 *Prospectus.* Framingham, Massachusetts: Cambridge BioScience Corp.

Campbell, J.
1980 "Technology transfer: Did Harvard say no?" *Harvard Independent* (13–19 November): 3.

Cane, A.
1983 "The tumors that save calves' lives." *Financial Times* (10 October): 14.

Canteley, M., and K. Sargeant
1981 "Biotechnology: A challenge to Europe." *Revue d'Economie Industrielle* 18 (4e trimestre): 323–34.

Carey, W. D.
1980 "Don't scare the experts." *Business and Society Review* 37 (Spring): 5–6.

Casey, J. F.
1976 "High fructose corn syrup—a case history of innovation." *Research Management* 19 (5): 27–32.

Cavalieri, L. F.
1981 *The Double-Edged Helix.* New York: Columbia University Press.

Centocor, Inc.
1982 *1982 Annual Report.* Centocor, Inc.: Malvern Hills, Pennsylvania.

Cetus Corporation
1981a *Prospectus.* Berkeley, California: Cetus Corporation.
1981b "Securities and Exchange Commission 10-K Filing." Berkeley, California: Cetus Corporation.

Chandler, A. D.
1962 *Strategy and Structure: Chapters in the History of Industrial Enterprise.* Cambridge, Massachusetts: MIT Press.

Chase, M.
1983 "New growth hormone can benefit children physically and socially." *WSJ* (24 June): 1, 14.

Chemical and Engineering News (CEN)
1982a "Biotechnology firm IPRI in financial trouble." *CEN* (1 November): 6.
1982b "USDA proposes agricultural research changes." *CEN* (8 November): 23.
1983a "DNA technology: Bacterial gene works in plant cell." *CEN* (24 January): 6.
1983b "Genes moved into plant cells, retained in plants." *CEN* (21 February): 6.
1983c "Industry support of academic research growing." *CEN* (21 February): 18.

1983d   "Rohm and Haas' Gregory details blueprint for 1980s." *CEN* (23 May): 13–17.

1984   "Michigan to get molecular genetics lab." *CEN* (23 July): 21.

Chemical Manufacturers Association

1982   *The Chemical Balance: Benefiting People, Minimizing Risks.* Washington: D.C.: Chemical Manufacturers Association.

Chemical Week (CW)

1980   "Biotechnology: Research that could remake industries." *CW* (8 October): 23–36.

1981a   "Will drug firms go after bulk chemicals?" *CW* (7 January): 37.

1981b   "It's hard to find jobs for industrious bugs." *CW* (14 January): 40–41.

1981c   "Wanted: More genetic engineers—and soon." *CW* (25 March): 29.

1982a   "Biotechnology's drive for new products." *CW* (24 February): 47–52.

1982b   "This biotech alliance focuses on processing." *CW* (19 May): 23.

1982c   "The hot market in herbicides." *CW* (7 July): 36–40.

1982d   "Genentech adds top slot." *CW* (6 October): 16.

1982e   "Innovative in their labs and in their financing." *CW* (3 November): 33–34.

1983a   "The reworking of Monsanto." *CW* (12 January): 42–47.

1983b   "A Japanese firm will fund university research here." *CW* (26 January): 39.

1983c   "In biotechnology, cross-country leap." *CW* (26 January): 40–41.

1983d   "Limited partnerships fund biotech research." *CW* (2 February): 55–56.

1983e   "Dexter: New glamour for an old New England firm." *CW* (8 June): 34–36.

1984   " 'Possibly the largest' bioventure." *CW* (20 June).

Chesnais, F.

1981   "Biotechnologies et modification des structures de l'industrie chimique: Quelques points de repere." *Revue d'Economie Industrielle* 18 (4e trimestre): 218–30.

Christensen, K.

1980   "Gene splicers develop a product: New breed of scientists-tycoons." *WSJ* (24 November): 1, 27.

Clark, M., S. Begley, and M. Hager

1980   "The miracles of spliced genes." *Newsweek* (17 March): 62–71.

Cohen, S., A. Chang, H. Boyer, and R. Helling

1973   "Construction of biologically functional bacterial plasmids *in vitro*." *Proceedings of the National Academy of Sciences* 70 (November): 3240–44.

Collaborative Research, Inc.

1982   "Securities and Exchange Commission 10-K Filing." Lexington, Massachusetts: Collaborative Research, Inc.

1984   *1984 Annual Report.* Waltham, Massachusetts: Collaborative Research, Inc.

Comai, L., L. C. Sen, and D. M. Stalker

1983   "An altered aroA gene product confers resistance to the herbicide glyphosate." *Science* 221 (22 July): 370–71.

Conrad, G. W.
1982   "Authorship and responsibility in scientific publications and manuscript reviews." *Trends in Biochemical Sciences* 7 (May): 167–68.
Cooke, R.
1981   "Endless possibilities for ideas—and jobs." *Boston Globe* (16 September): 1, 18.
Cooper, D. S.
1981   "The Whitehead Institute proposed." *GEN* 1 (November/December): 1, 7.
1982   "Biotech center for N.C." *GEN* 2 (January/February): 1, 23.
Cornell Chronicle
1983   "With corporate help, biotech institute launched." *Cornell Chronicle* (7 April): 1, 10.
Cornell Communiqué
1979   "Technology transfer: Income from Cornell inventions." *Cornell Communiqué* (September): 10.
Cornell University
1982   "A proposal for the establishment of a Cornell University Biotech Institute." Copy of a memorandum (2 April).
Cornell University Faculty Council
1982   "Notes taken at May 12 Faculty Council meeting." Cornell University.
Council for Financial Aid to Education
1981   *Voluntary Support of Education, 1979–1980*. New York: Council for Financial Aid to Education.
Crick, F.
1974   "The Double Helix: A personal view." *Nature* 248 (26 April): 768.
Culliton, B. J.
1977   "Harvard and Monsanto: The $23-million alliance." *Science* (25 February): 759–63.
1981   "Biomedical research enters the marketplace." *New England Journal of Medicine* 304 (14 May): 1195–1201.
1982a "The academic-industrial complex." *Science* 216 (28 May): 960–62.
1982b "The Hoechst Department at Mass General." *Science* 216 (11 June): 1200–03.
1983   "Drug firm-UC settle interferon suit." *Science* 219 (28 January): 372.

David, E. E., Jr.
1982   "Striking a bargain between company and campus." *Environment* 24 (July/August): 42–48.
David, P.
1983   "Living with regulation." *Nature* 305 (27 October): 755.
Dawkins, R.
1978   *The Selfish Gene*. New York: Oxford University Press.
Di Iorio, R. C.
1981   "Design course produces items for industry clients." *Tech Talk* (10 June): 3.

Dickson, D.
1978   "Friends of DNA fight back." *Nature* 272 (20 April): 664–65.
1979   "Recombinant DNA research: Private actions raise public eyebrows."
        Nature 278 (5 April): 494–95.
1980a   "Inventorship dispute stalls DNA patent application." *Nature* 284 (3
        April): 388.
1980b   "More commercial genetic manipulation." *Nature* 287 (30 October):
        769.
1981   "US industry moves into biotechnology." *Nature* 292 (30 July): 397.
Ditzel, R. (Patent Administrator, University of California)
1982   Presentation at Cornell University. (September).
1983   Personal communication. (25 August).
Djerassi, C.
1981   "Prepared statement and testimony of Carl Djerassi at a hearing
        before the Subcommittee on Investigations and Oversight and the
        Subcommittee on Science, Research and Technology of the
        Committee on Science and Technology, U.S. House of
        Representatives." June 8–9, 1981. In *Commercialization of Academic
        Biomedical Research*, 146–55. Washington, D.C.: U.S. Government
        Printing Office.
DNA Plant Technology Corporation (DNAPT)
1983   *Prospectus*. Cinnaminson, N.J.: DNA Plant Technology Corporation.
Dolan, C.
1983   "How high-tech ideas often become reality in the Silicon Valley."
        WSJ (2 August): 1, 14.
Dorfman, D.
1981   "Questions about Cetus." *San Francisco Chronicle* (8 February): D1,
        D4.
Dorfman, P. (Editor, *Genetic Engineering News*)
1983   Personal communication. (21 November).
Douglas, J.
1978   "US geneticists look to Europe for research facilities." *Nature* 275 (21
        September): 170.
Downs, C.
1983   "High tech: MSU updates its land-grant mission." *MSU Today* 2
        (February): 2.
Drug and Cosmetic Industry
1982   "Biotechnology forges ahead despite economy, confusion over
        patent." *Drug and Cosmetic Industry* (November): 32–34,
        36.
Dummer, G. H. (Director, Office of Sponsored Programs, MIT)
1982   Personal interview. (15 February).
Dunner, D. R.
1981   "Future impacts of patentability." *Recombinant DNA Technical
        Bulletin* 4 (July): 55–61.
Du Pont Corporation
1983   "Biomedical products department background." Du Pont, xerox
        copy.

Dwyer, P. E.
1983a   "Fildes shifts Cetus policies as new vaccine is launched." *Bio/Technology* 1 (June): 313–15.
1983b   "IPRI struggles to survive, seeks aid." *Bio/Technology* 1 (June): 316–20.
1983c   "Industry scientists' salaries stabilizing in U.S. as competition heats up." *Bio/Technology* 1 (October): 641–44.

Eagle, J., and D. Coyman
1981   "A case study of Biogenetics, Inc." Cambridge, Massachusetts: Harvard Business School.

Edwards, C.
1983   "Patent pooling could dramatically shift corporate–university relations." *Bio/Technology* 1 (May): 217.

Edwards, M. G.
1983   "Business plan for a university licensing association for biotechnology (ULAB)." Stanford University (June).

Eggers, E. R.
1981   "Prepared statement and testimony of E. Russell Eggers at a hearing before the Subcommittee on Investigations and Oversight and the Subcommittee on Science, Research and Technology of the Committee on Science and Technology, U.S. House of Representatives." June 8–9, 1981. In *Commercialization of Academic Biomedical Research*, 105–16, 131–32. Washington, D.C.: U.S. Government Printing Office.

Ellis, P. B. S.
1982   "Biotechnology: Industry Emergence, Development, and Change." M.S. thesis, Massachusetts Institute of Technology (June).

Elman, G. J.
1982   "Breeders question validity of patent on plant hybrids." *GEN* 2 (November/December): 1, 35.
1983   "Bio-Rad Labs sues Cetus, cites trade secret conflicts." *GEN* 3 (January/February): 4.

Essex, M., M. F. McLane, T. H. Lee, L. Falk, C. W. S. Howe, J. I. Mullins, C. Cabradilla, and D. P. Francis
1983a   "Antibodies to cell membrane antigens associated with human T-cell leukemia virus in patients with AIDS." *Science* 220 (20 May): 859–62.

Essex, M., M. F. McLane, T. H. Lee, N. Tachibana, J. I. Mullins, C. K. Kasper, M-C. Poon, A. Landay, S. F. Stein, D. P. Francis, C. Cabradilla, D. N. Lawrence, and B. L. Evatt
1983b   "Antibodies to human T-cell leukemia virus membrane antigens (HTLV-MA) in hemophiliacs." *Science* 221 (9 September): 1061–64.

Evans, D. A., J. E. Bravo, and W. R. Sharp.
1983   "Applications of tissue culture technology to development of improved crop varieties." In *Biotech 83: Proceedings of the International Conference on the Commercial Applications and Implications of Biotechnology*, 419–511. Middlesex, U.K.: Online Conferences, Ltd.

Fabricant, S.
1978   "Prepared statement of Solomon Fabricant in hearings before the Joint Economic Committee, Congress of the United States." June 8–9, 13–14, 1978. In *Special Study on Economic Change*, 494–553. Washington, D.C.: U.S. Government Printing Office.
Farley, P. J.
1980   "Prepared statement and testimony of Peter J. Farley at a hearing before the Subcommittee on Science, Technology, and Space of the Committee on Commerce, Science, and Transportation, U.S. Senate." May 20, 1980. In *Industrial Applications of Recombinant DNA*, 21–27. Washington, D.C.: U.S. Government Printing Office.
Feder, B.
1982   "Biotechnology shakeout is seen in cash squeeze." *NYT* (16 March): D1, D5.
Feinschreiber, R.
1981   "New tax benefits for genetic engineering R and D." *GEN* 1 (November/December): 1, 14–15.
Feldman, M. M., and E. P. O'Malley
1982   *The Biotechnology Industry in California*. Sacramento: California Commission on Industrial Innovation.
Financial Times
1983   "Du Pont drug for asthmatics." *Financial Times* (18 November): 6.
Finn, R.
1982   "Cal biotech, with recombinant DNA stars Baxter and Shine, backed by E. F. Hutton." *GEN* 2 (November/December): 3, 21.
Flexner, A.
1910   "Medical education in the United States and Canada." Carnegie Foundation for the Advancement of Teaching, Bulletin No. 4.
Fong, I., and J-L. Scofield
1981   "Five profs form DNA firm." *The Tech* (10 April): 1.
Food Engineering
1979   "Hydrolyzed lactose: New source of sweeteners." *Food Engineering* (November): 30–31.
1983   "Developments in genetic engineering." *Food Engineering* (November): 18–19, 21.
Foundation News
1980   "Research Corporation: A winning combination." *Foundation News* (June): 25.
Fox, J. L.
1981a   "Can academia adapt to biotechnology's lure?" *CEN* (21 October): 39–44.
1981b   "More nutritious corn aim of genetic engineering." *CEN* (7 December): 31–33.
1982a   "Biotechnology: A high-stakes industry in flux." *CEN* (29 March): 10–15.
1982b   "Armos: Profile of biotechnology firm's failure." *CEN* (13 September): 8–12.

Franklin, D.
1983   "Biotechnologists build a better bug." *BioScience* 33 (11): 678–79.
Fred, E. B.
1973   *The Role of the Wisconsin Alumni Research Foundation in the Support of Research at the University of Wisconsin.* Madison, Wisconsin: Wisconsin Alumni Research Foundation.
Freeman, K.
1983   "Monsanto link lasts well." *Nature* 304 (7 July): 9.
French, A. P.
1981   "Whitehead Institute Proposal: Remarks made at MIT Faculty Meeting, November 18, 1981." Unpublished mimeograph furnished by author.
Frey, N.
1982   "Prepared statement and testimony of Nicholas Frey before the Subcommittee on Investigations and Oversight of the Committee on Science and Technology, U.S. House of Representatives. June 9, July 28, 1982. In *Potential Application of Recombinant DNA and Genetics in Agricultural Sciences*, 92–121. Washington, D.C.: U.S. Government Printing Office.
Friedland, W. H., and A. E. Barton
1976   "Tomato technology." *Society* 13 (September–October).
Froelich, W.
1985   "They're using Moore's cells, but they didn't tell him." *San Diego Union* (4 January): A12.
Frutchy, J. (Contributions Associate, Sohio)
1983   Personal communication. (23 August).

Gaden, E. L., Jr.
1981   "Production methods in industrial microbiology." *Scientific American* 245 (September): 180–97.
Garner, R.
1983   "Strong effort to build up biotechnology." *Financial Times* (19 September): 18–19.
Garrison, S.
1982   " 'Glean' Spearheads Weed War." *Du Pont News* 11 (August): 1, 7.
Gartner, T. C.
1980   "Stock's amazing day." *San Francisco Chronicle* (15 October): 1, 20.
Gebhart, F.
1983   "Quality and consistency improved, the automated gene synthesizer market is on the rebound." *GEN* 3 (September/October): 1, 10.
Gefter, M. L. (Executive Officer, Department of Biology, Massachusetts Institute of Technology)
1981   Letter to colleagues regarding Whitehead Institute. Massachusetts Institute of Technology (11 November).
Genentech, Inc.
1980a   *1980 Annual Report.* South San Francisco: Genentech, Inc.
1980b   "Securities and Exchange Commission 10-K Filing." South San Francisco: Genentech, Inc.

1982   *1982 Annual Report.* South San Francisco: Genentech, Inc.
1983   "First quarter report." South San Francisco: Genentech, Inc.
n.d.   "Letter Agreement/Biological or Other Materials Supply." South San
        Francisco: Genentech, Inc.
General Accounting Office
1981   "Letter to Congressman Albert Gore, Jr. from the Comptroller
        General of the United States regarding the Hoechst–MGH contract."
        (16 October).
Genetic Engineering, Inc.
1982   *1982 Annual Report.* Denver, Colorado: Genetic Engineering, Inc.
Genetic Engineering News (GEN)
1981a   "University Genetics is formed." *GEN* 1 (January/February): 9.
1981b   "Danger in talent raids." *GEN* 1 (March/April): 4.
1982a   "Stanford signs up 71." *GEN* 2 (January/February): 1, 26.
1982b   "BRL obtains $8M refinancing in bond issue: Original investors
        participate." *GEN* 2 (May/June): 4.
1982c   "Monsanto, Rockefeller U. announce basic research accord." *GEN* 2
        (May/June): 29.
1982d   "IPRI founder to form new biotech-computer venture." *GEN* 2 (July/
        August): 3.
1982e   "Schering-Plough acquires DNAX Ltd." *GEN* 2 (July/August):
        3.
1983a   "IPRI, major plant biotech company in cash crunch." *GEN* 3
        (January/February): 3.
1983b   "University, Roche settle cell line rights litigation." *GEN* 3 (March/
        April): 4.
1983c   "Phytogen regenerates cotton plants from tissue culture." *GEN* 3
        (May/June): 3.
1983d   "Settlement reached in UCSD hybridoma dispute." *GEN* 3 (May/
        June): 27.
1983e   "IPRI finds new life in takeover by Bio-Rad." *GEN* 3 (July/August):
        14.
1983f   "Cetus, Nabisco Brands join in food application R and D pact."
        GEN 3 (November/December): 50.
1984a   "Du Pont buys 7 percent of Biotech Research Labs." *GEN* 4
        (September): 7.
1984b   "Third annual *GEN* guide to biotechnology companies." *GEN* 4
        (November/December): 15–37.
Genetic Systems Corporation
1982   *1982 Annual Report.* Seattle, Washington: Genetic Systems
        Corporation.
Genex Corporation
1982a   *1982 Annual Report.* Rockville, Maryland: Genex Corporation.
1982b   "Securities and Exchange Commission 10-K Filing." Rockville,
        Maryland: Genex Corporation.
Germann, P.
1981   "NIH rDNA advisory group moves to drop guidelines." *GEN*
        (September/October): 5–6.

Gershman, A. P., and F. Scafetta, Jr.
1982 "Patents on microorganisms." *IDEA* 21 (1): 1–36.
Giamatti, A. B.
1982 "The university, industry, and cooperative research." *Science* 218 (24 December): 1278–89.
Gibson, P.
1978 "Petrochemicals: Gloom but where's the doom." *Forbes* (2 October): 35–38.
Glick, J. L.
1981 "Prepared statement and testimony of J. Leslie Glick at a hearing before the Subcommittee on Investigations and Oversight and the Subcommittee on Science, Research and Technology of the Committee on Science and Technology, U.S. House of Representatives." June 8–9, 1981. In *Commercialization of Academic Biomedical Research*, 132–46. Washington, D.C.: U.S. Government Printing Office.
Goeddel, D., H. Heyneker, T. Hozumi, R. Arentsen, K. Itakura, D. Yansura, M. Ross, G. Miozzari, R. Crea, and P. Seeburg
1979a "Direct expression in *Escherichia coli* of a DNA sequence coding for human growth hormone." *Nature* 281 (18 October): 544–48.
Goeddel, D., D. Kleid, F. Bolivar, H. Heyneker, D. Yansura, R. Crea, T. Hirose, A. Kraszewski, K. Itakura, and A. Riggs
1979b "Expression in *Escherichia coli* of chemically synthesized genes for human insulin." *Proceedings of the National Academy of Sciences* 76 (January): 106–10.
Goldstein, J. A.
1982 "A footnote to the Cohen–Boyer patent and other musings." *Recombinant DNA Technical Bulletin* 5 (December): 180–88.
Gray, P.
1981 "Prepared statement and testimony of Paul Gray at a hearing before the Subcommittee on Investigations and Oversight and the Subcommittee on Science and Technology, U.S. House of Representatives." June 8–9, 1981. In *Commercialization of Academic Biomedical Research*, 28–60. Washington, D.C.: U.S. Government Printing Office.
Greenberg, D. S.
1967 *The Politics of Pure Science*. New York: New American Library.
Gurin, J., and N. Pfund
1980 "Bonanza in the bio lab." *Nation* (22 November): 543–48.

Halluin, A. P.
1982 "Patenting the results of genetic engineering research: An overview." In *Patenting of Life Forms*, edited by David W. Plant, Niels F. Reimers, and Norton Zindler, 67–91. Cold Spring Harbor, New York: Cold Spring Harbor Laboratory.

Hanson, B.
1983   "The pros and cons of the Whitehead Institute." Manuscript prepared
        for International Student Pugwash Conference in Ann Arbor,
        Michigan. June 20–26, 1983.
Hardy, R.
1980   "Prepared statement and testimony of Ralph Hardy at a hearing
        before the Subcommittee on Science, Technology, and Space of the
        Committee on Commerce, Science, and Transportation, U.S.
        Senate." May 20, 1980. In *Industrial Applications of Recombinant
        DNA*, 21–33. Washington, D.C.: U.S. Government Printing Office.
1982   "Colloquium: Agricultural research—its future funding." Presentation
        sponsored by Plant Pathology Graduate Student Council, Cornell
        University (14 October).
Harsanyi, Z.
1981   "Prepared statement and testimony of Zsolt Harsanyi at a hearing
        before the Subcommittee on Investigations and Oversight and the
        Subcommittee on Science, Research and Technology of the
        Committee on Science and Technology, U.S. House of
        Representatives." June 8–9, 1981. In *Commercialization of Academic
        Biomedical Research*, 117–22. Washington, D.C.: U.S. Government
        Printing Office.
Hart, D.
1983   "Patent policy for industrial genetic engineering." Senior thesis,
        Wesleyan University (June).
Harvard Gazette
1981a   "MGH, Hoechst sign $50 million research agreement." *Harvard
        Gazette* (22 May): 1, 7.
1981b   "Du Pont gives Medical School $6 million research grant." *Harvard
        Gazette* (2 July): 1.
1983   "Company agrees to sponsor research at Harvard." *Harvard Gazette*
        (14 September): 2.
Harvard University
n.d.   "Agreement for use of plasmids." Executing officer, Steve Atkinson,
        Harvard University.
1975   "A statement of policy in regard to patents and copyrights as adopted
        by the President and Fellows on November 3, 1975." Cambridge,
        Massachusetts: Harvard University.
1976   "The Harvard–Monsanto relationship." Unpublished copy, redraft (22
        March).
Harvey, S.
1982   "Rich Richardson bets on Du Pont's strategic advantage."
        Pharmaceutical Executive 2 (10).
Heirich, M.
1979   "Why we avoid the key questions: How shifts in funding of scientific
        inquiry affect decision-making about science." In *Recombinant DNA
        Debate*, edited by D. A. Jackson and S. Stich, 234–60.
Hess, C.
1982   "Prepared statement and testimony of Charles Hess at a hearing
        before the Subcommittee on Investigations and Oversight and the
        Subcommittee on Science, Research and Technology of the

Committee on Science and Technology, U.S. House of Representatives." June 16–17, 1982. In *University/Industry Cooperation in Biotechnology*, 49–88. Washington, D.C.: U.S. Government Printing Office.

Hightower, J.
1973   *Hard Tomatoes, Hard Times.* Cambridge, Massachusetts: Shenkman.

Hilts, P. J.
1982a   *Scientific Temperaments.* New York: Simon and Schuster.
1982b   " 'Rules' drawn for marketing gene research." *Washington Post* (28 March): A1, A6.

Hirshson, P. E.
1980   "Harvard rejects role in DNA business." *Boston Globe* (18 November): 1, 19.

Hoozer, G.
1982   "Genetic engineering: A revolution in livestock health." *Big Farmer Entrepreneur* (June): 14–15.

Hopson, J. L.
1977   "Recombinant lab for DNA and my 95 days in it." *Smithsonian* 8 (June): 54–65.

Hopwood, D. A.
1981   "The genetic programming of industrial microorganisms." *Scientific American* 245 (September): 90–125.

Howard, T.
1979   "Patenting life." *The Progressive* (September): 34–37.

Howard, N.
1982   "Genetic engineering's manpower problem." *Dun's Business Month* (January): 92–94.

Hunkapiller, M., L. Hood, and S. Eletr
1983   "Sequenceurs et microsequenceurs de proteines." *Biofutur* (May): 37–40.

Hybritech, Inc.
1982   *Prospectus.* San Diego, California: Hybritech, Inc.

Inman, V.
1983   "Professors are taking more consulting jobs with college approval." *WSJ* (31 March): 1, 16.

Integrated Genetics Corporation
1983   *Prospectus.* Framingham, Massachusetts: Integrated Genetics Corporation.

International Plant Research Institute
1982   Personal interview, name withheld by request. (6 June).

Interview
1981   Personal interview, name withheld by request. Department of Chemical Engineering, Ivy League University (28 September).

Itakura, K., T. Hirose, R. Crea, A. Riggs, H. Heyneker, F. Bolivar, and H. Boyer
1977   "Expression in *Escherichia coli* of a chemically synthesized gene for the hormone somatostatin." *Science* 198 (9 December): 1057–63.

Jackson, D. A.
  1979   "Principles and applications of recombinant DNA methodology." In
          The Recombinant DNA Debate, edited by D. A. Jackson and S.
          Stich, 39–55. Englewood Cliffs, N.J.: Prentice-Hall.
Jackson, D. A., and S. Stich
  1979   *The Recombinant DNA Debate*. Englewood Cliffs, N.J.: Prentice-
          Hall.
Jacob, F.
  1982   *The Logic of Life*. New York: Pantheon.
Jaschik, S.
  1983   "C.U. to give corporations exclusive patent license." *Cornell Daily
          Sun* (21 June): 1, 3.
Jaschik, S., and C. Kuntz
  1982   "Professors describe reasons for industries to join institute." *Cornell
          Daily Sun* (30 September): 9.
Johnson, C. R.
  1982   "Why the microbe makers got stung." *NYT* (14 March): 2.
Johnson, M.
  1981   "Biotechnology: Ethics and stock prices." *San Francisco Chronicle* (8
          March): D1.
Johnson, R. S.
  1983   "Martin Marietta draws three biotech firms to 'consortium.' " *GEN* 3
          (March/April): 1, 22.
Johnstone, B.
  1983   "Japanese solve riddle of salmon-cloning." *New Scientist* (3
          November): 328.
Journal of Commerce (JOC)
  1982   "Allied Chemical announces acquisition of Nitragin Co." *JOC* (3
          August): 22B.
  1983a   "Schering-Plough to build interferon plant in Ireland." *JOC* (17
          February): 22B.
  1983b   "Biotech firms moving closer to US level." *JOC* (6 June): 4C, 7C.
  1983c   "New industrial department announced by Du Pont." *JOC* (22 June):
          22B.
  1983d   "Ciba-Geigy building research center in NC." *JOC* (18 August):
          22B.
  1983e   "Molecular biology head appointed by Du Pont." *JOC* (22 August):
          22B.
  1983f   "Biotechnica, Monsanto sign research agreement." *JOC* (31
          September): 22B.
  1983g   "Genetics Institute completes offering." *JOC* (13 October): 22B.
  1983h   "Oxford and Monsanto sign research agreement." *JOC* (16
          December): 22B.
  1983i   "Allied to sell assets of liquid fertilizers." *JOC* (22 December): 22B.
Judson, H. F.
  1979   *The Eighth Day of Creation*. New York: Touchstone.

Kahne, S.
  1982   "Cracks in the ivory tower." *IEEE Spectrum* (March): 69–73.

Kalvert Nationwide Services
1983   "Nationwide positions." *Bio/Technology* 1 (April): 209.
Kania, E. M., Jr.
1982   "Case study of Advanced Genetics Sciences, Inc." Cambridge,
        Massachusetts: Harvard Business School.
Katzenstein, P. J., and S. Tanaka
1984   "Biotechnology: Japan's industry in competitive perspective."
        Paper presented at Policy for High Technology in Japan: An
        Example for the United States Conference. New York, New York
        (17–19 March).
Keegan, J.
1979   "Chemicals current analysis." In *Standard and Poors Industry Survey*,
        C1–C31 (27 September).
Kennedy, D. (President, Stanford University)
1981a   "Interview with Donald Kennedy." *SIPIscope* 9 (January–February):
        1–7.
1981b   "Prepared statement and testimony of Donald Kennedy at a hearing
        before the Subcommittee on Investigations and Oversight and the
        Subcommittee on Science, Research and Technology of the
        Committee on Science and Technology, U.S. House of
        Representatives." June 8–9, 1981. In *Commercialization of Academic
        Biomedical Research*, 6–28. Washington, D.C.: U.S. Government
        Printing Office.
1981c   Letter to David Saxon, President of University of California. Stanford
        University (27 July).
1981d   Letter from Donald Kennedy to David Saxon. Stanford University
        (28 August).
1982   "The social sponsorship of innovation." *Technology in Society* 4 (4):
        253–66.
Kenney, M.
1983a   "Is biotechnology a blessing for Less Developed Nations?" *Monthly
        Review* (April): 10–19.
1984   "Schumpeterian entrepreneurs: The case of the biotechnology
        industry." Manuscript.
1985   "Biotechnology and the Information Age: Some observations
        on the commercial competition between the U.S. and Japan."
        Manuscript.
Kenney, M., and F. H. Buttel
1985   "Biotechnology: Prospects and dilemmas for Third World
        development." *Development and Change* (January).
Kenney, M., F. H. Buttel, J. T. Cowan, and J. Kloppenburg, Jr.
1982   "Genetic engineering and agriculture: Exploring the impacts of
        biotechnology on industrial structure, industry–university
        relationships, and the social organization of U.S. agriculture."
        Rural Sociology Bulletin No. 125, Cornell University, July.
Kenney, M., and J. Kloppenburg, Jr.
1983   "The American agricultural research system: An obsolete structure?"
        Agricultural Administration 14 (1): 1–10.

Kenney, M., J. Kloppenburg, Jr., and F. Buttel
 1983   "Genetic engineering and agriculture: Socioeconomic aspects of
        biotechnology R and D in developed and developing countries." In
        *Biotech 83: Proceedings of the International Conference on
        Commercial Applications and Implications of Biotechnology*, 475–90.
        Middlesex, U.K.: Online Conferences, Ltd.
Kilian, M.
 1983   "C.U. seeks funds for biotech building." *Cornell Daily Sun* (3
        March): 1, 16.
King, J.
 1978   "New diseases in new niches." *Nature* 276 (2 November): 4–7.
 1981a "Patenting modified life forms: The case against." *Environment* 24
        (July/August): 38, 40–41, 57.
 1981b "Prepared statement and testimony of Jonathan King at a hearing
        before the Subcommittee on Investigations and Oversight and the
        Subcommittee on Science, Research and Technology of the Committee
        on Science and Technology, U.S. House of Representatives." June 8–9,
        1981. In *Commercialization of Academic Biomedical Research*, 61–76.
        Washington, D.C.: U.S. Government Printing Office.
Kipnis, D. M.
 1982   "Prepared statement and testimony of David M. Kipnis at a hearing
        before the Subcommittee on Investigations and Oversight and the
        Subcommittee on Science, Research and Technology of the
        Committee of Science and Technology, U.S. House of
        Representatives." June 16–17, 1982. In *University/Industry
        Cooperation in Biotechnology*, 8–48. Washington, D.C.: U.S.
        Government Printing Office.
Kleinfeld, N. R.
 1983   "Birth of a health-care concern." *NYT* (11 July): D1, D3.
Kloppenburg, J., Jr., and M. Kenney
 1984   "Biotechnology, seeds, and the restructuring of agriculture."
        Insurgent Sociologist 12 (3): 3–18.
Knox, R. A.
 1981   "German firm, MGH in $50M research pact." *Boston Globe* (20
        May): 1, 22.
Knox, R. A., and R. Cooke
 1981   "$120M biology center planned for MIT." *Boston Globe* (8 July): 1,
        14.
Koeffler, H. P., and D. W. Golde
 1978   "Acute myelogenous leukemia: A human cell line responsive to
        colony-stimulating activity." *Science* 200 (9 June): 1153–54.
Kohler, R. E.
 1975   "The history of biochemistry: A survey." *Journal of the History of
        Biology* 8 (Fall): 275–318.
 1976   "The management of science: The experience of Warren Weaver and
        the Rockefeller Foundation programme." *Minerva* 14 (Autumn): 279–
        306.
 1982   *From Medical Chemistry to Biochemistry: The Making of a
        Biomedical Discipline*. New York: Cambridge University Press.

Kossiakoff, A. (Chief scientist at Johns Hopkins Applied Physics Laboratory)
1980   "Discussion draft—encouraging technology transfer at Johns
        Hopkins." (30 December).
Kramer, N.
1982   "Companies producing interferon: Who's doing what?" *GEN* 2
        (January/February): 17–19.
Krimsky, S.
1981   "Patents for life forms sui generis: Some new questions for science,
        law and society." *Recombinant DNA Technical Bulletin* 4 (April): 11–
        15.
1982a   *Genetic Alchemy: The Social History of the Recombinant DNA
        Controversy.* Boston: MIT Press.
1982b   "Development of recombinant DNA policy and regulations in the
        U.S. 1973–1980." *Telegen Annual Review* (November): 5–13.
1984   "The corporate capture of academic science and its social cost." A
        paper presented at the conference entitled "Genetics and the Law:
        Third National Symposium." (2 April) Boston, Massachusetts.
1985   Personal communication. (12 June).
Krimsky, S., A. Baeck, and J. Balduc
1982   "Municipal and State Recombinant DNA Laws." Report prepared for
        the Boston Neighborhood Network (June).
Kuntz, C., and S. Jaschik
1982   "C.U. solicits $100M from industries." *Cornell Daily Sun* (30
        September): 8.

Lamont-Havers, R.
1981   "Testimony of Ronald Lamont-Havers at a hearing before the
        Subcommittee on Investigations and Oversight and the Subcommittee
        on Science, Research and Technology of the Committee on Science
        and Technology, U.S. House of Representatives." June 8–9, 1981. In
        Commercialization of Academic Biomedical Research, 87–95.
        Washington, D.C.: U.S. Government Printing Office.
Lancaster, H.
1980   "Profits in gene splicing bring the tangled issue of ownership to fore."
        WSJ (3 December): 1, 20.
1981   "Throngs descend on genetic conference, where science confronts the
        profit motive." *WSJ* (4 May): 25.
1982   "Shakeout nears in gene-splicing industry as capital dries up for
        second-tier firms." *WSJ* (12 March): 25, 45.
Latour, B., and S. Woolgar
1979   *Laboratory Life: The Social Construction of Scientific Facts.* Beverly
        Hills, California: Sage Library of Social Research.
Lear, J.
1978   *Recombinant DNA: The Untold Story.* New York: Crown.
Lepkowski, W.
1982   "Shakeup ahead for agricultural research." *CEN* (22 November): 8–
        16.

1983 "Corporate/university ties growing stronger." *CEN* (3 January): 32–33.

Lewin, R.
1978a "Profile of genetic engineer." *New Scientist* (28 September): 924–26.
1978b "Modern biology at the industrial threshold." *New Scientist* (5 October): 18–19.

Lewin, T.
1982 "The patent race in gene-splicing." *NYT* (29 August): 3.

Lewontin, R. C.
1974 "Essay Review." *Journal of the History of Biology* 7 (Spring): 155–61.
1982 "Agricultural research and the penetration of capital." *Science for the People* (January/February): 12–17.
1983 " 'The corpse in the elevator': An exchange." *New York Review of Books* (28 April): 42–43.

Eli Lilly and Company
1977 "Comments on the proposed revision of the *Guidelines for Recombinant DNA Research*." In *Recombinant DNA Research*, Volume 3, *Appendices*, pp. A36–A47, by National Institutes of Health, Public Health Service, U.S. Department of Health, Education, and Welfare.
1978 "Letter from C. W. Pettinga, executive vice president, to Donald Fredrickson." In *Recombinant DNA Research*, Volume 4, *Appendices*, pp. A272–A275, by National Institutes of Health, Public Health Service, U.S. Department of Health, Education, and Welfare.

Love, C.
1981 "Biotech business seminar October 26–27." *GEN* 1 (September/October): 12.

Mandel, E.
1978 *Late Capitalism*. London: Verso.

Manning, J.
1981 "Memorandum to Dr. David Pratt, Chairman of Graduate Group in Microbiology, University of California, Davis, from JaRue Manning, Graduate Advisor, Graduate Group in Microbiology, University of California, Davis." University of California, Davis (24 September).

Marshall, E.
1982 "USDA research under fire." *Science* 217 (2 July): 33.

Marx, J.
1982 "Can crops grow without added fertilizer?" *High Technology* (March/April): 62–67.
1985 "The 23-million dollar quest pays off." *Science* 230: 161.

Massachusetts General Hospital (MGH)
1981 "Contract between MGH and Hoechst AG." Cambridge, Massachusetts (13 May).

Massachusetts Institute of Technology (MIT)
n.d. "Summary of sponsored research agreement between MIT and Exxon Research and Engineering Company." Massachusetts Institute of Technology.

1982   "Revised record of the faculty meeting of November 18, 1981." (11 February).

MIT News Office and Exxon Research and Engineering Company
1980   "MIT and Exxon Research and Engineering Co. enter 10-year research agreement." Joint press release (28 April).

McDonald, K.
1983a   "Amid controversy, U.S. agriculture department seeks improvements in its research system." *Chronicle of Higher Education* (12 January): 1, 12–13.
1983b   "Companies capitalize on new technique in genetic research." *Chronicle of Higher Education* (8 June): 1, 6–7.

Medawar, P. B.
1968   "Lucky Jim." *New York Review of Books* (28 March): 3–5.

Mensch, G.
1979   *Stalemate in Technology: Innovations Overcome the Depression.* Cambridge: Ballinger.

Merchant, M. E.
1980   "Present status and future trends of integrated manufacturing systems in the U.S.A." In *Proceedings of the 4th International Conference on Production Engineering*, 177–84. Tokyo, Japan.

Meyerhoff, A. H.
1982a   "Campus research." *San Francisco Examiner* (26 March): A11.
1982b   "Prepared statement and testimony of Albert H. Meyerhoff at a hearing before the Subcommittee on Investigations and Oversight and the Subcommittee on Science, Research and Technology of the Committee on Science and Technology, U.S. House of Representatives. June 16–17, 1982. In *University/Industry Cooperation in Biotechnology*, 49–88. Washington, D.C.: U.S. Government Printing Office.

Meyerhoff, A. H., R. S. Abascal, T. H. McCarthy, R. Hawk, and P. Barnett
1981   "Potential conflicts of interest among University of California personnel." San Francisco: California Rural Legal Assistance (August).

Michigan State University (MSU)
1983   "MSU receives $695,000 from high tech firm." Michigan State University, Division of Public Relations (11 January).

Michigan State University News-Bulletin
1982   "Research, high tech and MSU." *MSU News-Bulletin* 14 (2 December): 1, 4.

Miller, J. A., and J. C. Amatniek
1984   "Crossroads for gene regulation." *Science News* 125 (11 February): 84.

Miller, L. I.
1985   "Biotechnology mergers signal industry consolidation." *GEN* 5 (2): 26.

Milstein, C.
1983   "Letter stating stipulations for receptors of hybridoma line." (28 November).

Misrock, S. L., and G. D. Stern
1981   "To publish or profit: The current research quandary." *GEN* 1 (March/April): 1, 5–7.
Molecular Genetics, Inc. (MGI)
1982   "Securities and Exchange Commission 10-K Filing." Minnetonka, Minnesota: MGI.
1983   Press release. Minnetonka, Minnesota: MGI (24 May).
Monoclonal Antibodies, Inc.
1982   "Securities and Exchange Commission 10-K Filing." Monoclonal Antibodies, Inc.: Mountain View, California.
Mooney, P. R.
1979   *Seeds of the Earth.* Ottawa: Inter Pares, Canadian Council for International Cooperation and the International Coalition for Development Action.
Monsanto Company
n.d.   "The research center: Our investment in the future." Saint Louis: Monsanto Company.
Monsanto Company Public Relations
1983   "Biotechnology and Monsanto: An overview." Saint Louis: Monsanto Company (April).
Morris, B.
1983   "Some food companies bet on bolder research that goes well beyond tinkering with recipes." *WSJ* (11 August): 44.
Munger, H. M. (Professor Emeritus, Department of Plant Breeding, Cornell University)
1983   Personal communication. Cornell University (3 November).
Murray, J., and L. Teichner
1981   *An Assessment of the Global Potential of Genetic Engineering in the Agribusiness Sector.* Chicago: Policy Research Corporation and Chicago Group, Inc.
Muscoplat, C.
1982   "Prepared statement and testimony of Charles Muscoplat at a hearing before the Subcommittee on Investigations and Oversight and the Subcommittee on Science, Research and Technology of the Committee on Science and Technology, U.S. House of Representatives." June 16–17, 1982. In *University/Industry Cooperation in Biotechnology*, 89–104. Washington, D.C.: U.S. Government Printing Office.

National Academy of Sciences
1972   *Report of the Advisory Committee on Research to the U.S. Department of Agriculture.* Washington, D.C.: National Academy of Sciences.
National Association of State Universities and Land-Grant Colleges (NASULGC)
1982   "Emerging biotechnologies in agriculture: Issues and policies." Committee on Biotechnology, Division of Agriculture, NASULGC (November).

National Council of Churches of Christ (NCCC)
1982   "Study paper on bioethical concerns." Washington, D.C.: NCCC (3 November).
National Institutes of Health (NIH)
1979   "Minutes of RAC meeting of September 6–7, 1979." In *Recombinant DNA Research*, Volume 5, pp. 150–87. NIH, Public Health Service, Department of Health, Education, and Welfare.
1981   *Extramural Trends FY 1972–1981.* Bethesda, Maryland: NIH.
1985   Personal communication with Kathy McCleave, budget analyst, National Cancer Institute. (January).
National Science Foundation
1982   *Development of University–Industry Cooperative Research Centers: Historical Profiles.* Washington, D.C.: National Science Foundation.
1984   *National Patterns of Science and Technology Resources 1984.* Washington, D.C.: U.S. Government Printing Office.
1985a   Personal communication with John Chirichiello, senior staff associate (December).
1985b   Personal communication with Judith Coakley, program analyst (December).
Nature
1982   "Universities, profit and research." *Nature* 296 (4 March): 1.
Neogen Corporation
n.d.   "Brochure describing Neogen." East Lansing, Michigan: Neogen Corporation.
New Scientist
1983   "Decision due in billion-dollar patent row." *New Scientist* (30 June): 923.
New York Times (NYT)
1980a   "Harvard considers commercial role in DNA research." *NYT* (27 October): A1, A17.
1980b   "Profit—and losses—at Harvard." *NYT* (13 November): A34.
1982   "The worm in the bud." *NYT* (21 October): A30.
1983   "Biotechnology retrenchment." *NYT* (19 February): 29, 31.
New York's Food and Life Sciences Quarterly
1983   "Biotechnology at Cornell." *New York's Food and Life Sciences Quarterly* 15 (1): 1–28.
Newsweek
1982   "The big bucks of biology." *Newsweek* (5 April): 9–70.
Noble, D.
1982   "The selling of the university." *The Nation* (6 February): 1, 143–48.
Noble, D., and N. Pfund
1980   "Business goes back to college." *The Nation* (20 September): 246–52.
Norman, C.
1976   "Laying the guidelines bare." *Nature* 263 (9 September): 89.
1981a   "MIT agonizes over links with research unit." *Science* 214 (23 October): 416–17.
1981b   "Whitehead link approved." *Science* 214 (4 December): 1104.

1982   "White House plows into ag research." *Science* 217 (24 September): 1227–28.
Norman, C., and E. Marshall
1982   "Boom and bust in biotechnology." *Science* 216 (4 June): 1076–82.
Nossiter, D. D.
1982   "Designer genes." *Barron's* (22 February): 8–9, 22, 24.

Office of Technology Assessment (OTA)
1981   *Impacts of Applied Genetics*. Washington, D.C.: U.S. Government Printing Office.
1982   *An Assessment of the United States Food and Agricultural Research System*. Washington, D.C.: U.S. Government Printing Office.
1984a   *Commercial Biotechnology: An International Assessment*. Washington, D.C.: U.S. Government Printing Office.
1984b   *Technology, Innovation, and Regional Economic Development*. (July). Washington, D.C.: U.S. Government Printing Office.
Olby, R.
1974   *The Path to the Double Helix*. Seattle: University of Washington.
Omenn, G. S.
1981   "University/industry research linkages: Arrangements between faculty members and their universities." Paper presented at AAAS Symposium on Impacts of Commercial Genetic Engineering on Universities and Non-Profit Institutions. Washington, D.C. (6 January).
Organization for Economic Cooperation and Development (OECD)
1980   *Technical Change and Economic Policy*. Paris: OECD.
Owen, B., and R. Braeutigan
1978   *The Regulation Game*. New York: Ballinger.

Pajaro Dunes Biotechnology Conference Prospectus
1981   "Commercialization of university research." Early draft, xerox copy (27 August).
Pajaro Dunes Biotechnology Conference Statement
1982   "Statement issued after Pajaro Dunes Biotechnology Conference." Reprinted in *Tech Talk* (7 April): 8.
Pake, G. E. (Vice-President for Corporate Research, Xerox)
1981   "Industry–university interactions." *Physics Today* (January): 44–48.
Patterson, W. P.
1983   "Where are the biotech products?" *Industry Week* (7 February): 48–55.
Peat, Marwick, Mitchell and Company (PMM)
1981   "Report to the members of the Corporate Liaison Committee, Cornell University." New York: Peat, Marwick, Mitchell and Company (30 October).
Peel, C., D. Bauman, R. Gorewit, and C. Sniffen
1981   "Effect of exogenous growth hormone on lactational performance in high yielding dairy cows." *Journal of Nutrition* 111 (September): 1662–71.

Pellon, J., and A. Sinskey
n.d.   "Genetic engineering for food and additives." Manuscript, Department of Food Sciences, MIT.

Penman, S. (Professor of Biology, MIT)
1982   Personal interview. (16 February).

Perelman, M.
1977   *Farming for Profit in a Hungry World.* Montclair, N.J.: Allanheld, Osmun and Company.

Perlman, D.
1977   "Scientific announcements." *Science* 198 (25 November): 782.

Petit, C.
1977a   "A 'triumph' in genetic engineering." *San Francisco Chronicle* (2 December): 1, 17.
1977b   "The bold entrepreneurs of genetic engineering." *San Francisco Chronicle* (2 December): 2.

Pfund, N.
1983   "Rx for the future: Biotechnology and public policy in California." Report to the Office of Appropriate Technology of the State of California (March).

Pinkelman, F. (Auditor General, State of Michigan)
1982   *Audit Report: Michigan State University, July 1, 1976 through February 28, 1982.* Office of the Auditor General, State of Michigan.

Pitzer, K. S.
1955   "Role of the university in basic research." *Science* 121 (2 June): 789–92.

Portugal, F. H., and J. S. Cohen
1977   *A Century of DNA.* Cambridge, Massachusetts: MIT.

Potter, R.
1983   "Cetus puts new focus on genetic research." *JOC* (6 July): 7A.

Powledge, T. M.
1983a   "Biogen in transition: From research specialist to manufacturer." *Bio/Technology* 1 (July): 398–405.
1983b   "New trends in financing biotechnology." *Bio/Technology* 1 (September): 545–59.

Prager, D. J., and G. S. Omenn
1980   "Research, innovation, and university–industry linkages." *Science* 207 (25 January): 379–84.

Pramik, M. J.
1982   "Novel approach to research funding." *GEN* 2 (January/February): 22.
1983a   "Genetic Engineering, Inc. capitalizing on innovation in embryo sexing." *GEN* 3 (January/February): 8–9.
1983b   "Sperm selection technology proving lucrative for Sausalito-based firm." *GEN* 3 (January/February): 14–15.
1983c   "Wisconsin Alumni group invests in Cetus." *GEN* 3 (January/February): 20.
1983d   "Biotechnology patent 'pool' proposed at IBA meeting." *GEN* 3 (May/June): 1, 35, 39.

Prescott, L. M.
1981   "Johnson and Johnson backs Scripps Research." *GEN* 1 (September/October): 8–9.
1983a   "Hybritech: Portrait of a monoclonal specialist." *Bio/Technology* 1 (April): 157–61.
1983b   "Three contracts with major drug firms give Techniclone a niche in monoclonals." *GEN* 3 (May/June): 23.
1983c   "Quidel developing monoclonal diagnostics while researching lymphokines as therapeutics." *GEN* 3 (July/August): 28, 32.

Raub, W.
1981   "Prepared statement and testimony of William Raub at a hearing before the Subcommittee on Investigations and Oversight and the Subcommittee on Science, Research and Technology of the Committee on Science and Technology, U.S. House of Representatives." June 8–9, 1981. In *Commercialization of Academic Biomedical Research*, 77–87. Washington, D.C.: U.S. Government Printing Office.
Raugel, P-J.
1983   "Nothing ventured, nothing gained." *Biofutur* 14 (June): 7–13.
Reimers, N. (Director, Office of Technology Licensing, Stanford University)
1983   Personal communication. (5 October).
Research Corporation
1981   *Report of 1981*. New York: Research Corporation.
The Rockefeller Foundation and Office of Science and Technology Policy
1982   *Science for Agriculture*. New York: The Rockefeller Foundation.
Rose, A. H.
1981   "The microbiological production of food and drink." *Scientific American* 245 (September): 126–39.
Rosenberg, R.
1981a   "Patent or perish." *GEN* 1 (January/February): 5.
1981b   "The process of profits in genetics." *Boston Globe* (14 September): 1, 8.
1982   "The learning center at the top end of Silicon Valley." *Boston Globe* (16 November): 1, 56–57.
Rosenzweig, R. (Vice-President for Public Affairs, Stanford University)
1981a   "Letter from Robert Rosenzweig to David Saxon, Chancellor of the University of California System." Stanford University (17 September).
1981b   "Letter to participants in the biotechnology conference." Stanford University (20 October).
1982   "Prepared statement and testimony of Robert Rosenzweig at a hearing before the Subcommittee on Investigations and Oversight and the Subcommittee on Science, Research and Technology of the Committee on Science and Technology, U.S. House of Representatives." June 16–17, 1982. In *University/Industry Cooperation in Biotechnology*, 105–30. Washington, D.C.: U.S. Government Printing Office.

Rowland, B. I.
1982   "Not 'for research use only.' " *GEN* 2 (March/April): 4.

Samejima, H. (Managing Director, Kyowa Hakko Company)
1984   Personal interview. (June).
San Francisco Examiner
1981   "New corporate–university venture." *San Francisco Examiner* (14 September): C1.
Sanford, R.
1983   "Monsanto grows in biotechnology." *St. Louis Post-Dispatch* (14 February): C1–C2.
Sanger, D. E.
1982   "Corporate links worry scholars." *NYT* (17 October): A18.
1983   "U. of California puts limits on private research pacts." *NYT* (21 August): 22.
Scarr, L.
1985   "World hunger targeted." *San Diego Union* (19 January): A1.
Scherer, F. M.
1980   "Useful but abused." *Business and Society Review* 37 (Spring): 6–7.
Schneider, N. M.
1980   "Prepared statement of Nelson Schneider at a hearing before the Subcommittee on Science, Technology, and Space of Committee on Commerce, Science, and Transportation, U.S. Senate." May 20, 1980. In *Industrial Applications of Recombinant DNA Techniques*, 44–49. Washington, D.C.: U.S. Government Printing Office.
1981   "Scrambling on the gene train." *GEN* 1 (January/February): 4.
Schneiderman, H.
1982   "Prepared statement and testimony of Howard Schneiderman at a hearing before the Subcommittee on Investigations and Oversight and the Subcommittee on Science, Research and Technology of the Committee on Science and Technology, U.S. Senate." June 16–17, 1982. In *University/Industry Cooperation in Biotechnology*, 8–48. Washington, D.C.: U.S. Government Printing Office.
Schumpeter, J. A.
1964   *Business Cycles*. New York: McGraw-Hill.
Schwartz, C.
1975   "Academics in government and industry." Manuscript, Department of Physics, University of California, Berkeley (September).
Schwartzkopf, A. (Program Manager, Productivity Improvement Research Section, NSF)
1984   Personal communication. (15 October).
Seidel, G. E., Jr.
1982   "Prepared statement and testimony of George Seidel, Jr. at a hearing before the Subcommittee on Investigations and Oversight of the Committee on Science and Technology, U.S. House of Representatives." June 9, July 28, 1982. In *Potential Applications of Recombinant DNA and Genetics on Agricultural Sciences*, 141–73. Washington, D.C.: U.S. Government Printing Office.

Senich, D.
1982   "Prepared statement and testimony of Donald Senich at a hearing before the Subcommittee on Investigations and Oversight and the Subcommittee on Science, Research and Technology of the Committee on Science and Technology, U.S. House of Representatives." June 16–17, 1982. In *University/Industry Cooperation in Biotechnology*, 105–30. Washington, D.C.: U.S. Government Printing Office.

Shaffer, P.
1983   "The architect's strategic role in planning and designing facilities for biotechnology." *GEN* 3 (March/April): 23, 25.

Shapley, D.
1982   "Human insulin." *Nature* 300 (11 November): 100–01.
1983   "Silver cloud with a leaden lining." *Nature* 302 (10 March): 83.

Siekevitz, P. (Professor of Neurobiology, Rockefeller University)
1980   "Of patents and prizes." *Trends in Biological Sciences* 5 (9): VI–VII.
1984   Personal communication. (31 January).

Simmonds, N. W.
1983   "Conference review: Genetic engineering of plants." *Tropical Agriculture* 60 (January): 66–69.

Slack, C. W.
1981   "Corporate ties: A look back at Monsanto." *Harvard Crimson* (24 July): 3.

Smith, R.
1982   "Interesting possibilities to challenge breeding industry." *Feedstuffs* (29 November): 13–14.

Snider, J. H.
1981   "Harvard's gene-splicing affair: A new relationship between the university and industry." Senior thesis, Harvard University.

Snyder, R. B. (Executive Director, Cornell Biotechnology Program)
1985   Personal communication. (January).

Sohio Company
1983a   Sohio advertisement. *Science* 219 (25 February): 912.
1983b   Sohio advertisement. *Science* 219 (4 March): 1015.

Solbrig, O. T.
1982   "The funding of science and academic freedom." A paper presented at AAAS Symposium on the Impacts of Commercial Genetic Engineering on Universities and Non-Profit Institutions. Washington, D.C. (6 January).

Sonquist, C.
1981   "Designer genes: The emergence of genetic engineering." Senior thesis, University of California, Santa Cruz.

Sprague, G., D. Alexander, and J. Dudley
1980   "Plant breeding and genetic engineering: A perspective." *BioScience* 30 (January): 17–21.

Standard and Poors Company
        Industry Surveys. Various years.

Stanford Graduate Student Association (SGSA)
  1982a   "Symposium on university entrepreneurship and graduate
          student education." Academic Affairs Committee, SGSA (22
          March).
  1982b   "Memorandum to Academic Council Committee on Research."
          Academic Affairs Committee, SGSA (8 April).
Stanford University
  n.d.   Poster reading "Conflicts of Interest." Contact person, John Goheen,
          Stanford University Ombudsman.
Stanford University Committee on Research
  1981   "Report to the Senate of the Academic Council." Stanford University
          (26 May).
Stanford University Patent Licensing Agreement
  1981   "Stanford University patent license agreement." Office of Technology
          Licensing, Stanford University (15 December).
Stark, E.
  1982   "What is medicine?" *Radical Science Journal* (12): 46–89.
Starr, P.
  1983   *The Social Transfer of American Medicine*. New York: Basic
          Books.
Steiner, D.
  1980   "Discussion memorandum—technology transfer at Harvard
          University." Harvard University (9 October).
Stetten, D., Jr.
  1981   "Recombinant molecules: Anxieties and hazards." In *Proceedings of
          the 1981 Battelle International Conference on Genetic Engineering*,
          Volume 1, pp. 54–68, held in Rosslyn, Virginia. June 6–10, 1981.
Steward, F., and G. Wibberley
  1980   "Drug innovation—what's slowing it down?" *Nature* 284 (13 March):
          118–20.
Stockton, W.
  1980   "On the brink of altering life." *New York Times Magazine* (17
          February): 18–19, 62–64, 76–78.
Storck, W. J.
  1983   "Monsanto's Richard Mahoney: Ready to take on the 1980s." *CEN*
          (26 September): 10–13.
Strickland, S. P.
  1972   *Politics, Science, and Dread Disease*. Cambridge: Harvard University
          Press.
Strom, M.
  1983   "Two more corporations to fund biotech institute." *Cornell Daily Sun*
          (20 September): 3.
Sun, M.
  1982   "DNA rules kept to head off new laws." *Science* 215 (26 February):
          1079–80.
  1983a   "A one-stop shop for gene-splicing patents." *Science* 219 (18 March):
          1302–03.
  1983b   "Scientists settle cell line dispute." *Science* 220 (22 April): 393–94.

Sward, S.
  1983   "UC acts on 5 possible faculty conflicts of interest." *San Francisco Chronicle* (23 August): 4.
Sylvester, E. J., and L. C. Klotz
  1983   *The Gene Age.* New York: Scribner's.

Tanaka, M.
  1983   "Biotechnology in Japan." In *Biotech 83: Proceedings of the International Conference on Commercial Applications and Implications of Biotechnology*, 1–12. Middlesex, U.K.: Online Conference, Ltd.
Tanaka, S.
  1984   "Japan Newsletter." *GEN* 4 (January/February): 26.
Tangley, L.
  1983   "Engineered organisms in the environment? Not yet." *BioScience* 33 (11): 681–82.
The Tech
  1982   "Conflicting interests." *The Tech* (14 April): 4.
Tech Talk
  1981   "MIT, Whitehead plan biomedical partnership." *Tech Talk* (8 July): 1, 4.
  1982a   "Pajaro Dunes Biotechnology Statement." *Tech Talk* (7 April): 8.
  1982b   "MIT-industry consortium focuses on fuel research." *Tech Talk* (14 April): 1, 7.
  1982c   "Grace funds microbiology research." *Tech Talk* (11 August): 1, 4.
Thomas, L.
  1981   "Interview with Lewis Thomas." *SIPIscope* (July–August): 1–5.
Tinsely, S. (Director of Corporate Technology, Union Carbide)
  1983   Public lecture at Cornell University. (7 December).
Treble, M. J.
  1982   "Scale-up of hybridoma business ventures: Investment requirements and perspectives." *GEN* 2 (July/August): 5.
Turner, S.
  1980   "Prepared statement and testimony of Stephen Turner at a hearing before the Subcommittee on Science, Technology, and Space of the Committee on Commerce, Science, and Transportation, U.S. Senate." May 20, 1980. In *Industrial Applications of Recombinant DNA*, 46–51. Washington, D.C.: U.S. Government Printing Office.

Ullrich, A., J. Shine, J. Chirgwin, R. Pictet, E. Tischer, W. Rutter, and H. Goodman
  1977   "Rat insulin genes: Construction of plasmids containing coding sequences." *Science* 196 (17 June): 1313–19.
U.S. Congress
  1976   *Oversight Hearing on Implementation of NIH Guidelines Governing Recombinant DNA Research.* (22 September). Washington, D.C.: U.S. Government Printing Office.
  1980   *Industrial Applications of Recombinant DNA.* (20 May). Washington, D.C.: U.S. Government Printing Office.

1981   *Commercialization of Academic Biomedical Research.* (8–9 June). Washington, D.C.: U.S. Government Printing Office.

University Genetics

1981   "Budget and information guidelines." Norwalk, Connecticut: University Genetics (31 December).

n.d.   "Program of contracts for research in genetic engineering." Norwalk, Connecticut: University Genetics.

Upjohn Company

1978   "Letter from Murray D. Welch, Jr., associate general counsel and director, to Donald Fredrickson." In *Recombinant DNA Research*, Volume 4, *Appendices*, pp. A256–60. NIH, Public Health Service, U.S. Department of Health, Education, and Welfare.

VerMeulen, M.

1982   "Harvard passes the buck." *TWA Ambassador* (January): 41–55.

Wade, N.

1975   "Recombinant DNA: NIH group stirs storm by drafting laxer rules." *Science* 190 (21 November): 767–69.

1977a   "Gene-splicing: At grass-roots level a hundred flowers bloom." *Science* 195 (11 February): 558–61.

1977b   "Gene-splicing: Senate bill draws charges of Lysenkoism." *Science* 197 (22 July): 348–49.

1977c   "Recombinant DNA: NIH rules broken in insulin gene project." *Science* 197 (30 September): 1342–46.

1979   "Recombinant DNA: Warming up for the big payoff." *Science* 206 (9 November): 663–65.

1980a   "The company and the laboratory." *Trends in Biological Sciences* 5 (4): IX.

1980b   "Cloning gold rush turns basic biology into big business." *Science* 208 (16 May): 688–92.

1980c   "Hybridoma: A potent new biotechnology." *Science* 208 (16 May): 692–93.

1980d   "University and drug firm battle over billion-dollar gene." *Science* 209 (26 September): 1492–94.

1981   "La Jolla biologists troubled by Midas factor." *Science* 213 (7 August): 623–28.

Waldholz, M.

1983   "Ballyhoo has faded, but interferon still has boosters at high levels." *WSJ* (30 September): 1, 14.

Walgate, R.

1980   "Hormone growth." *Nature* 284 (11 December): 528.

Walker, E. A., and R. G. Hampel

1974   "Improving industrial R and D—university relations." *Research Management* (September): 23–28.

Wall Street Journal (WSJ)

1980a   "Cetus is second firm in genetics field planning to go public." *WSJ* (3 December): 20.

1980b   "Cooper looks for its own niche in brave new world of gene splicing."
        WSJ (15 December): 16.
1982   "Big firms gain profitable foothold in new gene-splicing technologies."
        WSJ (5 November): 23.
1983a   "Hybritech sees profit for '83 for first time after five years of losses."
        WSJ (17 August): 16.
1983b   "Genentech arranges interferon production." *WSJ* (22 August): 36.
1983c   "Merck says vaccine against hepatitis A is in clinical testing." *WSJ*
        (31 October): 17.
1983d   "Genex acquires Kentucky plant." *WSJ* (7 November): 8.
1984a   "Advanced Genetics taps Dyott as President, Chief Operating
        Officer." *WSJ* (30 May): 25.
1984b   "Lubrizol Corp. set to buy firm for $110 million." *WSJ* (27
        September): 8.

Walsh, J.
1969   "Universities: Industry links raise conflict of interest issue." *Science*
        164 (25 April): 411–12.
1982   "Did success spoil ag research?" *Science* 217 (13 August): 615.

Watson, J. D.
1968   *The Double Helix.* New York: New American Library.
1970   *Molecular Biology of the Gene.* Menlo Park, California: Benjamin.

Watson, J. D., and J. Tooze
1981   *The DNA Story.* San Francisco: Freeman.

Weaver, W.
1970   "Molecular biology: The origin of the term." *Science* 170 (6
        November): 581–82.

Weiner, C.
1982   "Science in the marketplace: Historical precedents and problems."
        In *From Genetic Engineering to Biotechnology—The Critical
        Transition*, edited by W. J. Whelan and S. Black, pp. 123–31.
        New York: Wiley.
1984   Personal communication. Boston, Massachusetts (17 October).

Yamamoto, K. R.
1982   "Faculty members as corporate officers: does cost outweigh benefits?"
        In *From Genetic Engineering to Biotechnology—The Critical
        Transition*, edited by W. J. Whelan and S. Black, pp. 195–201. New
        York: Wiley.

Yanchinski, S.
1981   "Bacteria to textiles in U.K. plant." *GEN* 1 (March/April): 1, 3.

Yoxen, E. J.
1981   "Life as a productive force." In *Science, Technology, and the Labour
        Process*, edited by L. Levidow and R. Young, pp. 66–122. Atlantic
        Highland, N.J.: Humanities.
1983   *The Gene Business.* London: Pan Books.
1984   "Assessing progress with biotechnology." In *Science and Tech-
        nology in the 1980s and Beyond*, edited by P. Gummett. London:
        Longmans.

Zamparutti, T.
   1982   "Gray, Low speak on industrial ties." *Tech Talk* (2 April): 1, 3.
Ziff, E.
   1973   "Benefits and hazards of manipulating DNA." *New Scientist* (25 October): 274–75.
Zoler, M.
   1981   "Chakrabarty case still debatable." *GEN* 3 (May/June): 1, 8–9.

Index

The following abbreviations are used in the index:

CEO	Chief Executive Officer
DNAPT	DNA Plant Technology, Inc.
HMS	Harvard Medical School
IPRI	International Plant Research Institute
LGU	Land Grant Universities
MGH	Massachusetts General Hospital
MNCs	Multinational Corporations
NIH	National Institutes of Health
NSF	National Science Foundation
RDLP	Research and Development Limited Partnership
rDNA	Recombinant DNA
SAB	Scientific Advisory Board
UCB	University of California, Berkeley
UCD	University of California, Davis
UCSD	University of California, San Diego
UCSF	University of California, San Francisco
ULAB	University Licensing Pool for Biotechnology
WARF	Wisconsin Alumni Research Foundation
WI	Whitehead Institute